THE OLD FARMER

AND HIS

ALMANACK

THE
OLD FARMER
AND HIS
ALMANACK

Being some OBSERVATIONS on Life and Manners
in New England a *Hundred Years Ago*

Suggested by Reading the Earlier Numbers of
MR. ROBERT B. THOMAS's FARMER'S
ALMANACK

*Together with Extracts Curious, Instructive, and En-
tertaining, as well as a Variety of
Miscellaneous Matter*

BY GEORGE LYMAN KITTREDGE

EMBELLISHED WITH ENGRAVINGS

Cambridge
HARVARD UNIVERSITY PRESS
1 9 2 0

PREFACE

NOTHING is more strictly contemporary than an almanac, except, perhaps, a newspaper. It is issued for the time being, and it becomes obsolete, by a natural and inevitable process, when its successor appears. But this very quality of contemporaneousness which relegates last year's almanac to the dust heap, makes the almanac of a hundred years ago an historical document of some importance. An author who has his eye on posterity may distort his own environment in order to stand well with his future readers; but an almanac-maker is subjected to no such temptation. He appeals to the immediate present, and his records have all the value of incidental testimony.

When Mr. Robert B. Thomas published the first number of his Farmer's Almanack, in 1792, he had no thought of providing material for the student of New England life and manners in the twentieth century. He wished to earn his living and to furnish his fellow-citizens with something better for their sixpence than they were in the habit of receiving from other purveyors of similar intellectual wares. If he had foreseen that his little annual would continue to be issued for more than a century, he would doubtless have been overwhelmed by the responsibilities of his undertaking. He addressed himself to the men of his

own time, whom he thoroughly understood, and thus he has enabled us too to understand them the better.

Few volumes can claim so intimate an association with the people of New England as the Old Farmer. " Books to them," wrote Channing in his Wanderer, speaking of the un-lettered population of a remote corner of the seacoast, —

> " Books to them
> Are the faint dreams of students, save that one, —
> The battered Almanac, — split to the core,
> Fly-blown, and tattered, that above the fire
> Devoted smokes, and furnishes the fates,
> And perigees and apogees of moons."

The library of Thousandacres, in Cooper's Chainbearer, was somewhat more extensive; it consisted of " a fragment of a Bible, Pilgrim's Progress, and an almanac that was four years old." But Mr. Thomas did not speak to the uneducated only. His audience was, in the main, intelli-gent and enlightened. If it is true, as it seems to be, that the progress of our country has been largely determined by the spirit and energy of New England men and women, one may claim, without fear of gainsaying, a position of some dignity for this unpretentious annual, which has, in its successive issues, been their secular manual of faith and practice for so many years. No apology, then, is neces-sary for the volume herewith presented to the friendly reader. It follows in the traces of an accredited guide. It avails itself of what Milton calls " the sure guess of well-practised feet."

Mr. Thomas, of course, had collaborators. His annual acknowledgments to patrons and correspondents give ample credit to those who assisted him. In particular, there is a mystery attaching to the authorship of a portion

of the Farmer's Calendar which has never been completely dissipated, because the ingenious contributor, whoever he was, desired to remain anonymous. For convenience, therefore, the name of the general editor has been freely used in speaking of this part of the Almanac. We are sure, at all events, that the precepts of the Calendar were fully approved by Mr. Thomas, even if he did not write them all with his own hand.

A miscellany like the present is happily exempt from the obligation of drawing up and observing a definite programme. *Quidquid agunt homines —*

> Whate'er men do, or say, or think, or dream,
> Our medley paper seizes for its theme.

Some of our subjects demand serious treatment, for they concern the greater interests of mankind. Others, though beneath the dignity of history, are none the less significant to such as wish to understand what manner of men our forefathers were. Still others are trifles — " the perfume and suppliance of a minute." Yet the minor antiquities of a race are not to be despised. What would scholars give if they could discover an Old Farmer's Almanack for Shakspere's century, or for Rome in the days of Julius Cæsar?

In developing the topics suggested by the Almanac, I have had recourse particularly to our older New England writers and to foreign travellers in America, of whom there were many soon after the War of Independence. At times, however, the temptation to go farther afield has been irresistible, as in dealing with astrology and witchcraft, or in tracing the history of the engravings which adorn the Calendar.

One of the chief pleasures of writing a book consists in exercising an author's privilege of consulting his friends, and the main object of a preface, after all, is to express gratitude for favors received. To Mr. Joseph Willard I am indebted for calling my attention to an important passage in Judge Sewall's Diary which would otherwise have escaped my notice. Mr. Charles Armstrong Snow and Mr. Henry Herbert Edes have been of material assistance in elucidating Mr. Thomas's reference to Lady Hayley's Garden. The chapter on Indian Summer is based on the learned researches of Mr. Albert Matthews, who has allowed me to make free use of his article on the subject, but who must not be held responsible for certain conclusions at which I have tentatively arrived. Mr. Matthews has also given me valuable information with regard to mediæval calendars. The libraries of Harvard College and the American Antiquarian Society have placed their treasures at my disposal. Professor Putnam, of the Peabody Museum of Archæology and Ethnology, has had the great kindness to permit the reproduction of a sketch of a Massachusetts Indian which was prepared, under his direction, by Mr. C. C. Willoughby, and to explain the method of reconstruction of which this interesting figure is the result. Mr. Horace E. Ware has given my pages the benefit of friendly criticism and has made many fruitful suggestions. I have also consulted an article on the Thomas Almanacs by Mr. James H. Fitts, in the twelfth volume of the Essex Institute Historical Collections. And finally, I must express my gratitude to Dr. Nathaniel Ames the Younger, who, in 1758, while a student at Harvard College, wrote down, at the beginning of his Diary, with

noble disregard for pointing, the following sentences, which may serve as a peroration: —

"They who see this in future times may know that it is the covering of an old Almanack 1758. And do not despise old times too much for remember that 2 or 3 centurys from the time of seeing this you will be counted old times folks as much as you count us to be so now, many People in these times think the Consumation very nigh much more may you think so, and do not think yourselves so much wiser than we are as to make yourselves proud for the last day is at hand in which you must give an account of what you have been about in this state of Probation & very likely you are more given to Vice than we are, and we than the last Century folks; if you have more arts than we have that you yourselves have found out impute it not to our inability that we could not find them out for if we had had only those very arts that we have now when we first came to settle in N. America very like we should have found out those very things which you have the honour to be the Inventors of. — Dinner is ready I must leave off."

In this new impression it is my painful duty to retract my ignorant exoneration of the barberry on page 332. Recent investigations have established the fact that the common (not the Japanese) barberry plays an important rôle in the history of Black Stem Rust, a disease which in 1916 caused a loss of about thirty million bushels of wheat in Minnesota alone.

G. L. K.

CAMBRIDGE, February 13th, 1920.

CONTENTS

THE GREAT MOON HOAX 251

ENTERTAINMENT FOR MAN AND BEAST 262

ON THE ROAD 285

HAVE AN EYE TO THE MOON ! 305

WHAT TO READ 315

BARBERRIES AND WHEAT 327

INDIAN TALK 333

MORE INDIAN TALK 367

INDEX 379

LIST OF ILLUSTRATIONS

THE OLD FARMER AND HIS ALMANACK

THE MAN AND HIS BOOK

ROBERT BAILEY THOMAS has been a familiar name to American ears for more than a century, and for a considerable part of that time his venerable features have been equally well known. Doubtless in the minds of many New Englanders he is intimately associated with Benjamin Franklin, whose portrait in miniature has for many years appeared, along with that of Mr. Thomas, in the ornamental border on the cover of the Old Farmer's Almanack. This association, though rather sentimental than historical, — for it does not appear that the two were acquainted in this life, — has reason and justice on its side. For both were typical New Englanders; both achieved success from humble beginnings; both were printers and publishers, and each was the putter-forth of an almanac which has its place in the intellectual history of our nation. Nor is this all. Different as they were in many respects, — in character, endowments, and career, — Dr. Franklin and Mr. Thomas resembled each other in the profession and practice of a certain homely philosophy of life which is not the least marked of their characteristics. Franklin, to be sure, was a genius, and Thomas was simply a man of talent who knew how to make the most of the gifts he had. But they were alike in their remarkable endowment of common sense and in their ability to recognize and grasp an

opportunity.   Finally, they were both genuinely American in the best sense of that much abused and vaguely
applied word.   Franklin's biography is known to everybody.   Thomas, however, is a somewhat shadowy figure
in the minds of most of us.   Yet his life, quiet as it was,
is of some interest to the student of American manners,
and we are fortunate in having authentic materials for its
reconstruction, — nothing less, indeed, than a brief autobiography, published in successive numbers of his own
annual from 1833 to 1839, and introduced by a sprightly
paragraph in the issue for 1832 : — "It is not unfrequently
observed to the Editor, by persons residing in neighbouring States, or remote from his residence, that they supposed him long since numbered with the dead; and that
the Farmer's Almanack was calculated and edited by a
connexion of the former editor.   To satisfy such, and con-
ceiving it may afford amusement to our patrons generally,
I have concluded, if my life and health should be continued,
in our next to give a concise memoir of myself and ancestors."   On the basis of this sketch, with the help of other
trustworthy evidence, the following life of Robert B.
Thomas has been put together.

The earliest ancestor of whom we have any knowledge
was William Thomas, Robert's grandfather, a native of
Wales, who came to America about 1718.   Family tradition, which the author of the Almanac, with characteristic
caution, refuses to vouch for, reported that he settled at
Stonington, Connecticut.   At all events, he was certainly
an inhabitant of Marlborough, Massachusetts, in or about
1720, and he resided there until his death in 1733 (July
25).   William Thomas married Lydia Eager, the daughter
of a respectable farmer of Shrewsbury, and had six children, two sons and four daughters, — all born in Marlborough, the eldest in 1721 and the youngest, who received
the singular name of *Odoardo*, in 1731.   The eldest son

William, born March 10, 1725, was the father of Robert
Bailey Thomas.

William Thomas, the elder, was an educated man, having
been a student at Christ's College, Cambridge. His son
William had no such opportunities, but he seems to have
inherited his father's fondness for books. His mother died
when he was ten years old (Oct. 12, 1735) and he went to
live in Shrewsbury with his maternal grandmother, Lydia
(Woods) Eager, who had lost her husband in the preceding year. Mrs. Eager died in 1739, and William Thomas
then returned to Marlborough, where his great-aunt, Lucy
(Eager) Morse, received him into her family. Here he
remained for some years, attending the town school in the
winter, according to the New England custom. The terms
were short, but the boy made the best use of his opportunities. He was fond of reading, and, in the words of his
son, "he purchased many books and soon became quite a
scholar for those days." At the age of nineteen (1744) he
took charge of a school at Brookfield, and later in the
same year he "commenced in Hardwick, being the first
schoolmaster in that town."

Shortly after William Thomas came of age, he undertook what proved to be an unsuccessful quest for a property
in Wales to which he had some claim as his father's heir.
With this in view, he left America in April, 1747, but was
captured in the next month by a French privateer from
Dunkirk and lost all he had. He was soon ransomed and
arrived in Boston in October. Two years later he sailed
for England again, stayed some time in London, and visited
Wales. His claim was outlawed, however, and he returned
to America no richer than before.

William Thomas apparently had a taste for adventure,
which, as well as his fondness for books, he may have inherited from his father, the emigrant and student of Christ's
College. Possibly he was also desirous of making reprisals

on the French. At all events, he received a lieutenant's commission in Capt. Samuel How's Marlborough Company, and took part in the expedition to Crown Point in 1756, serving for six weeks and two days. In 1757 he again volunteered. This time he served for only nineteen days, but it was active service. He was a lieutenant in Capt. John Phelps's Company, which formed a part of the Worcester County Regiment commanded by Col. Ruggles. The regiment went to the relief of Fort William Henry, leaving Rutland in August, 1757, and marching two hundred and fifty miles.

His subsequent career is summed up by his son, who says that it would be difficult if not impossible to follow it step by step. He still kept school at intervals, became "assistant in a store," and afterwards "went into a small way of trade himself." In 1764 he bought a farm in the North Parish of Shrewsbury, now West Boylston, and in the next year he married, — late in life, for those days, for he was nearly forty years old. His wife was Azubah, daughter of Joseph Goodale, a farmer of Grafton, at whose house Robert Bailey Thomas was born, April 24, 1766.

Two years later, William Thomas removed to his farm in the North Parish of Shrewsbury, and there Robert was brought up. He records with amusement that "he resided in four incorporated towns, and two distinct parishes, and one precinct" without leaving this same farm. The explanation of this paradox illustrates the rapid and perplexing changes in early New England topography. "Shrewsbury leg," as the strip of land where the farm was situated was called, was united to the Second or West Parish of Lancaster in 1768. In 1781 this parish was incorporated as the town of Sterling. In 1796 certain parts of Boylston, Sterling, and Holden were set off as a precinct, by the name of the Second Parish of the towns of Boylston, Sterling, and Holden, and in 1808 this became the town of

West Boylston. The paradox in question was a matter of local remark, as appears from the words of the Rev. C. C. P. Crosby, minister of West Boylston, in his history of that town, in The Worcester Magazine and Historical Journal for August, 1826:— "Among other strange things, there is a singular fraternity of men, who have lived in five incorporated towns, and two parishes, and yet, have never resided off the farms where they were born. This is explained by the tract called the leg being so often transfer[r]ed to other towns."

The education of Robert Bailey Thomas is an interesting example of the training of a studious New England boy. His grandfather, we should remember, was a Cambridge University man, and his father offered to give Robert a liberal education,— that is, probably, to send him to Harvard College in the new Cambridge, founded by an Emmanuel College man. Robert declined, — for his tastes, as he tells us, were mechanical rather than literary, — but he seems to have grasped every other means of improving his mind. He read his father's books assiduously, — and he says there were a good many of them. He went to school in the winter and received much instruction from his father, for whose learning he evinces considerable respect, and who "wished to make him a scholar." Superior penmanship was then regarded as a very valuable accomplishment, and writing schools were much resorted to. Dr. T. Allen had the reputation of "writing the most beautiful copy hand of any person in the country" (that is, in that region), and William Thomas sent his son to Spencer in the winter of 1783–84 to have the benefit of his instruction. How much stress was laid upon the art is shown by the fact that Robert followed his teacher to Sterling when the winter term was over and continued his lessons until the following April.

It is curious to note that until he was twenty years old

Robert Thomas had made no progress in mathematics. In the winter of 1785–86, he records, "I was agreeably and closely occupied in the study of arithmetic, under my father's inspection, who was well versed in this science, but had never before allowed me to pay it any attention, saying, he could learn me figures at any time." [1]

The introduction to arithmetic, late as it was, seems to have had a determining effect on the career of Robert Thomas. Perhaps he was all the more attached to the beauties of the science from not having its difficulties presented to him when he was too young to grapple with them. His father's library contained a good many scientific books, among them Ferguson's Astronomy, which the young man read with great satisfaction, and from which, he says, "he first imbibed the idea of calculating an almanack." This plan he never relinquished. It became, to use his own words, "his hobby." He made many astronomical computations, but found himself unable to carry them far enough for the purpose without further instruction.

Meantime he had temporarily adopted the family profession of schoolmastering. He began in 1786, in his native town, and succeeded so well that the term was lengthened by subscription after he had, in the phrase of the time, "kept out the town's money," that is, kept school until the money appropriated by the town for that purpose was exhausted. He was obliged to "board round," and, like most country schoolmasters in their first term, found many of his pupils older than himself. For the next six years Thomas kept school every winter. The terms were short, and he had the spring, summer, and early fall to himself. He worked on his father's farm and continued the study of astronomy, but he still found it impossible to make all the

---

[1] The reader will remember that *learn* in the sense of "teach" was formerly in good use. It is improper nowadays, not because of anything essentially wrong about it, but because it is an archaism that has lost caste.

computations necessary for an almanac. It was in 1792,
near the end of his career as a pedagogue, that he made
the acquaintance of Miss Hannah Beaman, of Princeton,
who afterwards became his wife (November 17, 1803).
The mechanical turn of mind which, as already mentioned,

BOOKS BOUND and
Sold, Gilt or plain, by
Andrew Barclay,
Next Door but one to the sign of the Three KINGS
Three KINGS in Cornhill
BOSTON

AN EIGHTEENTH-CENTURY BOOKBINDER

had manifested itself in early life, found employment in
bookbinding, — a business which had long attracted him.
He bound up manuscripts and account-books and repaired
old books for the neighbors.   From this to bookselling
was but a step. In 1790 he employed N. Coverly, the
Boston printer, to print for him a thousand copies of
Perry's Spelling Book.   These, and other school-books, he

bound up himself, and " commenced bookseller." In April, 1792, he formed a partnership with his younger brother Aaron, and they carried on the binding business, at first in a room in their father's house, afterwards in a bindery built for the purpose near by. The firm seems to have had no lack of work, some of which came from publishers in Boston.

The fact that he was now an established dealer in books, and had turned his back on the profession of teaching, gave Thomas renewed hopes of publishing an almanac of his own. Accordingly in June or July, 1792, he went to Boston and entered the mathematical school kept by Osgood Carleton " in an unfinished building in Merchant's Row." Here he worked until the latter part of August, and made all the calculations for the first number of the Farmer's Almanack, that for 1793. Carleton was a man of some ability and himself the author of an almanac. Mr. Thomas refers to him with gratitude in one of his early numbers (1802): — "The Editor would be very happy to recognize, among his correspondents, his much respected patron and friend O. C. who, not long since, quitted a confined employment in town, for a rural one in the country." Carleton seems to have been noted for the purity of his English accent, — an accomplishment which, shortly after the Revolution, caused him more embarrassment than satisfaction. In 1790, at all events, he published a remarkable advertisement in one of the Boston newspapers, the Herald of Freedom : [1] —

Osgood Carleton,

HAVING been frequently applied to for a decision of disputes, and sometimes wagers,* respecting the place of his nativity, and finding they sometimes operate to his disadvantage : Begs leave to give this public information — that he was born in Nottingham-west, in the State of New-Hampshire — in which

[1] H. M. Brooks, The Olden Time Series, Boston, 1886, IV, 55.

An ASTRONOMICAL DIARY

OR, AN

ALMANACK,

For the Year of our LORD

1792,

Being BISSEKTILE, or LEAP YEAR, and the Sixteenth
of the INDEPENDENCE of the *United States of America,*
which commenced the 4th of July.

Calculated for the Meridian of BOSTON, in Latitude 42 Degrees
and 25 Minutes North, and Longitude 71 Degrees West of Greenwich
Observatory; but will serve, without any essential Error, for all the
New-England States.

CONTAINING,

Lunations; Eclipses; Aspects; Judgment of the Weather; Times of Rising, Setting, &c. of the Sun, Moon,
and of several Stars and Planets; High-Water at Boston, and a Table, shewing the Time of High-Water
at the other most noted Ports in America; List of
Roads; Federal and State Courts; Duties on Spirits
imported, and on those distilled within the United
States; with many other interesting Matters.

By OSGOOD CARLETON,

Teacher of Mathematicks, in BOSTON.

HOW wonderous this Starry Frame!
No Bounds or Limits can we name;
Could we these Stars fly Ages through,
We more new Objects still might view.
Sceptic! 'tis not th' Effect of Chance;
A GOD did spread the vast EXPANSE.

BOSTON:

Printed and sold by SAMUEL HALL, No. 53, Cornhill:
Also, by THOMAS C. CUSHING, at his Printing-Office,
in SALEM

state he resided until sixteen years old; after which time, he traveled by sea and land to various parts, and being (while young) mostly conversant with the English, he lost some of the country dialect, which gives rise to the above disputes.

    * *Several Englishmen have disputed his being born in America.*

BOSTON, AUGUST 20, 1790.

Mr. Thomas's account of his sojourn in Boston is worth reproducing for its topographical interest, if for no other reason.

" While at Mr. Carlton's school," he writes, " I boarded in Milk Street, with J. Allen, a Scotchman. His wife was a young Englishwoman, with whom I enjoyed many a social hour; Mr. Allen was bred a gardener in Scotland, and at this time had the sole care of the then noted Lady Hayley's garden, situated on Pemberton Hill, late the estate of G. Green, but now entirely eradicated."

In the garden and mansion-house I spent many pleasant hours in the company of the female members of the family. I was invited to take a ride to Cambridge at Commencement with my young associates, and enjoyed a pleasant time. In the course of the summer I made an excursion with a party to the fashionable resort *Fresh Pond*, in Watertown, where we passed the day in different amusements, and spent our money freely. I boarded in Milk Street, in the same house that Mr. D. Hill since owned, and where he kept a grocery store adjoining. Mr. Hill was noted for selling the best *dry fish*, or, at least, he possessed the faculty of making his customers believe it.

Mr. Thomas's mention of Lady Hayley's garden, in which, as well as in the mansion house, he says he spent many pleasant hours, recalls not only a notable Boston estate, but a singular romance of provincial days. The fullest account of Madam Hayley (the title of Lady did not properly belong to her) is to be found in William Beloe's

eccentric work, The Sexagenarian; or the Recollections of a Literary Life, 1817, in which she appears as "Mrs. H——." Beloe was a Londoner, who is described by Southey, in one of his letters, as "an odd man who talks in a dialect of his own, which puzzled me confoundedly." [1] He seems to have been well acquainted with the subject of his sketch, which may be accepted as correct in the main, though some of the details appear to be erroneous. Mrs. Hayley, he says, "was the sister of John Wilkes, of the famous memory, had a large portion of his intellectual endowments, and was very little his inferior in vivacity, humour, and wit. She was married first to an opulent merchant, who was succeeded in his business by his head clerk, Mr. Hayley, whose fortunes were made by his obtaining the hand of the widow. He was afterwards Alderman Hayley, and was a near relation of Hayley, the poet. He was a plain, sensible, good sort of man, wholly absorbed in commercial pursuits, and soon found it expedient, for the sake of a quiet life, to suffer his *cara sposo* to do as she liked. She was exceedingly well informed, had read a great deal, possessed a fine taste, and, with respect to literary merit, considerable judgment. She accordingly sought with much avidity, the society of those who were distinguished in the world by their talents and their writings. When the expression of *those* is used, it must be understood to apply to men only, for on all occasions she was at no pains to conceal her contemptuous opinion of her own sex; and it was no uncommon thing to see her at table, surrounded with ten or twelve eminent men, without a single female.

"She had great conversation talents, and unfortunately, like her brother, she seldom permitted any ideas of religion, or even of delicacy, to impose a restraint upon her observations.

[1] To Grosvenor Bedford, Jan. 28, 1800, Selections from Letters, ed. Warter, I, 91.

" Her disregard of propriety was also and conspicuously
manifested on other occasions.   She invariably attended
all the more remarkable trials at the Old Bailey, where she
regularly had a certain place reserved for her.   When the
discussion or trial was of such a nature, that decorum, and
indeed the Judges themselves, desired women to withdraw,
she never stirred from her place, but persisted in remaining
to hear the whole, with the most unmoved and unblushing
earnestness of attention." [1]

After the death of her husband, Madam Hayley came
to America to attend to his affairs in New England, where
large sums were due him.   Here we may abandon Beloe
and pass over to the Recollections of Samuel Breck, who
was born in Boston in 1771 and passed his youth there,
so that he is a good authority for Madam Hayley's American experiences.   She was pleased with Boston, he says,
and " purchased a beautiful house in Tremont Street, formerly the residence of the Varsall [i. e. Vassall] refugee
family. . . . Thus splendidly lodged, she formed her whole
establishment in a style suitable to the mansion.   The
gayest liveries and equipage, the richest furniture, the
most hospitable and best-served table — all these were displayed to the greatest advantage by the widow Hayley.
She had certainly passed her grand climacteric, and in her
mouth was a single tooth of an ebon color.   Her favorite
dress was a red cloth riding-habit and black beaver hat.
In these she looked very like an old man.   Thus attired
on some gala day, she was paying a visit to Mrs. Hancock,
when Van Berkle, the Dutch envoy, happened to be in
Boston.   He came, of course, to salute the Governor, with
whom, however, he was not personally acquainted.   On
entering the room, he saw a venerable head, decorated
with a hat and plumes, belonging to a person robed in
scarlet and seated in an arm-chair in a conspicuous part of

[1] Beloe, The Sexagenarian, 2d ed., 1818, I, 324–5.

the room, and knowing that Governor Hancock was too gouty to walk, he very naturally concluded that the person before him was the master of the house. He accordingly approached, and, bowing, said he hoped his Excellency was better; that being on a visit to Boston, he had ventured to introduce himself, for the purpose of testifying in person his high admiration, etc., etc. Before his compliment was finished, the lady undeceived him, but in such a manner as put the minister perfectly at his ease."

According to Mr. Breck, she was " the principal star " of Boston society. "Nothing," he declares, " could more exactly resemble her brother than she did, except in the double squint, which she had not; and as he was the ugliest man in England, the family likeness so strongly stamped on the face of the sister left her without any claim to beauty. Yet her highly gifted mind and elegant manners much more than balanced that deficiency."

"This most excellent woman," continues Mr. Breck, " had surrounded herself with a menagerie, so that the court-yard was filled with cockatoos, poll parrots, and monkeys; yet she felt herself lonely, and set her cap for a husband. There was a young Scotsman then in Boston who was agent for a British mercantile house. His name was Jeffrey — a man well educated and of gentlemanly address. To him Mrs. Hayley gave her hand and fortune. Out of sixty or seventy thousand pounds sterling, she did not reserve a shilling for herself; but, in a fit of girlish love, poured the whole into the pocket of this young stranger, whose age could not have been one-half her own. Of this act of egregious folly she lived long enough to repent." [1] The marriage of Patrick Jeffrey, Esq., and Mary Hayley took place at Trinity Church, Boston, February 13, 1786. She had not been in Boston more than five years, for her former husband, Alderman Hayley, died in

[1] Harper's Magazine, LIV, 827–8.

1781.[1] Neither Beloe nor Breck gives any dates, so that it is necessary to supply them from other sources. We may now return to Beloe, who fully justifies Southey's opinion of his style : —

The hours of rapture, even with younger subjects, (votaries at the Hymeneal shrine) do not always extend beyond the honeymoon. When a female, approaching to seventy, leads to the altar a bridegroom who has not seen thirty, these hours of Elysium seldom continue quite so long. In a very short interval, a separation was mutually thought expedient. The lady . . . had confided everything to the generosity of her husband, and, with such an allowance as he thought proper to make her, she took a very early opportunity of re-crossing the Atlantic ; and after a short residence in London, fixed herself at Bath, where she passed

"An old age of cards." [2]

Beloe's account of the disparity of age is partly borne out by the records. Jeffrey died in 1812, aged sixty-four,[3] so that he must have been about thirty-eight years old when he married Madam Hayley. There is no evidence that he was illiberal to his wife when they parted. After they separated he removed to Milton, where he bought the Governor Hutchinson house and lived in considerable state.[4]

Mrs. Jeffrey's death is thus recorded in the Gentleman's Magazine, under date of May 9, 1808 : — " In Gay-street, Bath, Mrs. Jeffrey, relict of Alderman Hayley, and sister to the long-celebrated John Wilkes, esq., whose wit and abilities she in great measure possessed, added to a most benevolent heart." [5]

The Vassall house, which Breck says was purchased by

[1] Nichols, Literary Anecdotes, IX, 453. Her first husband was Samuel Storke, who died about 1753.

[2] Beloe, The Sexagenarian, 2d ed., 1818, I, 332.

[3] Boston Town Records ; Milton Town Records, p. 231 ; Columbian Centinel for May 13, 1812.

[4] E. J. Baker, in History of Milton, ed. by Teele, p. 138.

[5] LXXVIII, 469; cf. p. 555.

the Widow Hayley, is the mansion to which Mr. Thomas refers. Breck's account of the matter is not quite accurate. The purchase was made by Jeffrey, in 1790, four years after his marriage to the widow. This was one of the most famous estates in Boston. It included what is now Pemberton Square and had a frontage of 163 feet on Tremont Street. Vassall bought it in 1758 of the heirs of Judith Cooper, who was Judge Sewall's daughter and had inherited the property from him. The previous owners had been successively the Rev. John Cotton, his son, Seaborn Cotton, and John Hull, the famous mint-master, whose daughter Hannah was Sewall's first wife. Sir Henry Vane had lived there when he was in Boston. Vassall paid £1,250 for the property, — a sum which brings home to one the advance in the price of real estate in this vicinity!

Jeffrey sold a part of the property to Jonathan Mason in 1802, and this Mason transferred to Gardiner Greene in the next year. Greene's lot included considerably more than the present Pemberton Square, for it ran back to Somerset Street and came down to Tremont Street. He afterwards added an adjacent estate, so that his Tremont Street frontage was three hundred feet.[1] When Mr. Thomas was in Boston, in 1792, preparing the first number of his Almanac, the property had been in the hands of Jeffrey and his wife for a couple of years. Naturally enough, the beautiful terraced garden, which was one of the sights of the town, was called Lady Hayley's, rather than Mrs. Jeffrey's. That lady had become so famous under her former designation that she continued to be known by it even after her marriage to Patrick Jeffrey.

In August, 1792, the smallpox became so prevalent in Boston that Mr. Thomas left town. After a few weeks,

---

[1] For the history of the estate, see the long editorial note in the Diary of Samuel Sewall, Coll. Mass. Hist. Soc., 5th series, V, 59 ff.

he submitted himself to inoculation in "the hospital in Worcester, situated on the hill a mile north of the street." His account of this experience, though brief, is not without interest, for it gives one an inkling of his philosophy of life. " I flattered myself," he writes, " and was flattered by the doctor, of being a good subject, and would have the disease light, *having never exposed myself to heat and cold nor excessive labor, and had ever been temperate;* but it turned out quite otherwise. I had the disease very severely. For many days my life was despaired of; and, in fact, it was, I afterwards learned, currently reported in the neighboring towns that I was dead." He was five weeks at the hospital, and he speaks in the warmest terms of the kind attention he received. The autobiography concludes with these words: — " After I returned home I was weak and feeble for some months; after which I enjoyed good health, and, in general, have to this day, though advanced in life."

Mr. Thomas lived several years after the publication of his autobiography. He died at his home in West Boylston, May 19, 1846, " leaving a large estate to his widow, and the two children of his deceased brother." [1] The Almanac for 1847 begins with these words, which are his most fitting obituary: —

In presenting to our friends the *Fifty-fifth Number of the Almanac,* our pleasure is saddened by deep and heartfelt regret, at having to announce the death of the senior editor of the work, whose name it bears. He died May 19th, 1846, aged 80, after a long and useful life, beloved and respected by all who knew him, in deed and in truth, " that noblest work of God, an honest man." We feel that it is due to him, that this testimony to the purity of his character should be recorded here. He was a man of strong practical good sense, " kind of heart and open of hand," virtuous, upright, and scrupulously honorable in all his dealings.

[1] Dr. Samuel A. Green, in the Almanac for 1892, the hundredth number.

The house in which Mr. Thomas lived for many years has lately been removed in clearing the ground for the great Reservoir of the Metropolitan System of water-works.[1]

A small portrait of Mr. Thomas — a woodcut — appeared in the Almanac for 1837, with a characteristic

ROBERT BAILEY THOMAS
(From the Farmer's Almanack for 1838)

note : — " In justice to myself, I ought to state that my likeness is inserted . . . at the special desire of my publishers." The cut is repeated in 1838. There is a full-length portrait, painted by an unknown artist,[2] in the hall of the American Antiquarian Society at Worcester, and this is reproduced in the hundredth number of the Almanac (1892),

---

[1] See New York Observer, May 11, 1899; Worcester Evening Gazette, May 23, 1899.
[2] Sometimes ascribed to one Talcott : see Proc. Amer. Antiq. Soc., New Series, VII, 357.

to accompany a brief biography by Dr. Samuel Abbott Green. Both likenesses are given in the present volume.[1]

The first number of the Farmer's Almanack, that for 1793, was issued in the latter part of 1792. It was a significant moment in American history. National consciousness was in the full tide of development. Washington's first administration was drawing to a close. Five years before, the Constitution had been framed, and four years before it had been ratified by the requisite number of States, and had gone into effect as the highest law of the land. There was reasonable assurance that the United States government would succeed. The strong men of the Revolutionary period were in the vigor of mature manhood. It was a time of energetic and intelligent effort in all directions. "It has been a question," said President Stiles of Yale, in his sermon on The United States Elevated to Glory and Honour, delivered in 1783, " whether *Agriculture* or *Commerce*, needs most encouragement in these states? But the motives for both seem abundantly sufficient. Never did they operate more strongly than at present. The whole continent is activity, and in the lively vigorous exertion of industry."[2] Men's hopes were high; nothing seemed too great for the future to bring forth. " All the arts," said the same eloquent preacher, " may be transplanted from *Europe* and *Asia*, and flourish in *America* with an augmented lustre."[3] He even ventured to predict that " the rough sonorous diction of the English language may here take its Athenian polish, and receive its Attick urbanity; as it will probably become the vernacular tongue of more numerous millions, than ever spake one language on earth."[4] The latter part of this prediction has been fulfilled.

Mr. Thomas addressed a prosperous, intelligent, and

[1] See p. 16, and Frontispiece.
[2] P. 50.   [3] P. 86.   [4] P. 87.

2

aspiring community. He got the ear of his audience at the outset and has never lost their attention. The one hundred and thirteen successive issues of his Almanac cover almost exactly the same period as the history of the United States under the Constitution. The changes and the development of more than a century may be followed step by step in its pages. It need not surprise us, therefore, that a file of these old almanacs affords an abundance of curious information and not a little entertainment.

The first number was presented to the public with a prefatory address which must be copied in full: —

PREFACE.

FRIENDLY READER,

H AD it not been the prevailing custom to usher these periodical pieces into the world by a preface, I would have excused myself the trouble of writing, and you of reading one to this: for if it be well executed, a preface will add nothing to its merit; if otherwise, it will be far from supplying its defects.

Having, for several years past, paid some attention to that divine science, *Astronomy*, the study of which must afford infinite pleasure and satisfaction to every contemplative mind, it is this, with the repeated solicitations of my friends, that have induced me to present you with these Astronomical Calculations for the year 1793; which I have thought proper to entitle the *Farmer's Almanac*, as I have made it my principal aim to make it as useful as possible to that class of people: Therefore, should there be any thing in it that may appear of small moment, it is hoped the *Literati* will excuse it.

The arrangement of this Almanac is novel, though I have the vanity to believe it will be found to be as useful and convenient as any other almanac either of a double or single calendar. I have taken peculiar care to make the calculations accurate in every respect; and beside the more than usual astronomical calculations, I have added the rising, setting, or southing of the

[Nᵒ· I.]

THE
FARMER's ALMANAC,

CALCULATED ON A NEW AND IMPROVED PLAN,

FOR THE YEAR OF OUR LORD
1793:

Being the first after Leap Year, and seventeenth of the
Independence *of* America.

Fitted to the town of BOSTON, but will serve for any of
the adjoining States.

Containing, besides the large number of ASTRO-
NOMICAL CALCULATIONS and FARMER'S CA-
LENDAR for every month in the year, as great a vari-
ety as are to be found in any other Almanac,
Of NEW, USEFUL, *and* ENTERTAINING MATTER.

BY ROBERT B. THOMAS.

"While the bright radient sun in centre glows,
The earth, in annual motion round it goes;
At the same time on its own axis reels,
And gives us change of seasons as it wheels."

Published according to Act of Congress.

PRINTED AT THE Apollo Press, IN BOSTON,
BY BELKNAP AND HALL,
Sold at their Office, State Street; also, by the *Author*
and M. Smith, Sterling.
[*Sixpence single,* 4*s. per dozen,* 40*s. per groce.*]

seven stars, for every evening through the year. As to my judgment of the weather, I need say but little ; for you will in one
year's time, without any assistance of mine, very easily discover
how near I have come to the truth. And now, friendly reader,
this being only an essay, which, should it meet with the Public's
unprejudiced approbation, you may expect to hear again from
your's, and the Public's

Most obedient humble servant,

ROBERT B. THOMAS.

Sterling, Sept. 15.

Fifty years later, in the Almanac for 1842, the venerable author looks back over the past with modest pride.
His annual had become a recognized New England institution, and his feeling that his yearly admonitions were
now read by the grandsons of his first patrons and correspondents lends additional interest to his reminiscences.
They are not the random jottings of a casual recollection,
but rather the systematic memories of a chronicler who has
habituated himself to sum up each year as it passed.

FIFTY YEARS AGO !

It is just fifty years, Friends and Patrons, old and new — we
know not which are the most numerous, or the most kind, you
who have gone hand in hand with us for half a century, or you
who have known us but a few short summers — it is just fifty years
since we started our unpretending, but, as we trust, useful annual !
Fifty years ! It is a life by itself ! — In that time how many millions, who were, half a century ago, living, breathing and moving,
full of hope, of young life, of energy and of vigor, have gone down
to the silent grave ! In that time what countless millions of the
human race have been called "to sleep the sleep that knows no
waking ! " It is now but a little over fifty years since the immortal
Franklin, author of that quaint, but time-honored work, " Poor
Richard's Almanac," died ; he who " wrested the lightning from
the heavens, and the sceptre from the tyrant." Fifty years since,

and the high and pure-souled Washington, one of the noblest
characters that our country, ay! or any country has produced,
was alive, directing with his wisdom, and giving, by his presence
and counsels, new vigor to those energies which the people of
these United States hardly dared to hope that they possessed !

Within fifty years, while we have gone on, in the even tenor of
our way, our blessed country has stretched upward, from the lithe
and pliant sapling, to the strong and mighty tree, spreading abroad
her majestic branches, giving shade and protection to all who have
sought her shelter, and firmly establishing herself among the other
nations of the earth, with a population increased, during that time,
from hardly four millions to seventeen millions.

Fifty years ago, and cities, now full of thousands of souls, were
the hunting-ground of the Indian, and covered only by the forest
or the swamp. Fifty years ago, and the city of New York contained but about 33,000 inhabitants; it has now 312,000. Boston then about 18,000, now 93,000. Philadelphia then about
40,000, now 260,000. Baltimore, which then had but about
13,000, has now 100,000.

Fifty years ago, and we had nothing of the gigantic wonders of
steam; we had no boiling cauldrons traversing the land and
water, puffing and groaning, and pulling or pushing enormous
masses with fury along, now here, now there, as the master spirit
which controlled them might dictate. Fifty years ago, the worthy
fathers and mothers of the present generation were willing to
dress in their own homespun; the busy wheel was whirring by
the kitchen fireside, the knitting-needles were plied, and the wool
woven in the house, and the finer fabrics dressed at the fulling-
mill, which has given away to the spacious factory. The water-
fall and steam engine, the improved spindles and other machines,
manufacture now millions of yards, where fifty years since only
hundreds were made, and that by the industrious and thrifty
hands of the mothers and daughters of the hardy farmers of those
days.

With all the changes that have been going on in the great world,
the course of our America has been " onward and upward." We

have had as presidents, our Washington, Jefferson, Madison, Monroe, Adams, father and son, Jackson, Van Buren, Harrison, and now Tyler. England has had her Georges III. and IV., her William IV., and now has her Victoria. France has had more changes, has been the scene of more violence and more exciting and terrible commotions, than almost any other part of the civilized world, and from which, thanks to a kind Providence, we have been measurably exempt. Within fifty years Russia and all the countries of the old world have had their changes, some natural, others startling and impressive. The South Sea Islander has become converted to the gospel — the whole continent of New Holland, fifty years since a barren wilderness, has been partly peopled. The Turk has recognized the Jew as a human being and a brother; he has exchanged dress with the Christian.

Within the past fifty years science has done wonders for the human race; she has by her discoveries, the facilities she has created, the powers she has developed, added to the wealth and happiness of almost every class in our land. The farmer, among others, is indebted to her for his well constructed ploughs, his improved breeds of cattle and swine, new varieties of seeds and grain, as well as trees, shrubs, and vines, and his improved implements of every kind, from the simple apple-peeler to the steam threshing machine. Domestic economy too has been indebted to science for implements to add to our convenience and comfort. Within the past fifty years, commerce has made brethren and friends of the remote inhabitants of the earth, the cause of Peace has, as we trust, been progressing, that of Philanthropy and Temperance is rapidly advancing, and we trust as nations grow wiser, better acquainted, more civilized, that vice and ignorance will give place to virtue and knowledge, and the horrors of war to the quiet blessings of peace and good fellowship.

Though we have now accomplished what has seldom been done in this or any other country, as we believe, the getting up and publication for half a century of a manual, edited by the same person, even as unpretending as our modest and homely annual, we do not mean to rest here; should we be spared, we shall go

on, as we trust, to "a good old age," and though we may not reach the 100th number of the "OLD FARMER'S ALMANAC," yet we shall endeavor to improve as we progress, and continue to unfold our yearly budget to our patrons as long as Providence permits, hoping always to meet them with a smiling face, and that they will not be disposed to cut our acquaintance, as a modern dandy would a rusty cousin from the backwoods, because we look, as we pride ourselves in looking, a little old-fashioned, a little too independent to change our dress for each "new-fangled notion" — a little "t'other side of fifty."

Friends and Patrons! The form of the editor who has jogged along side by side with the older ones of you for fifty years, will, with many other forms now full of life and vigor, before another half century, be crumbling in the dust! The world that now seems so joyous will ere that time have passed away from many millions now alive, it may be from the reader as well as from us ; and if so, may we receive the reward of the pure in heart, may our sins be forgiven us, and may our virtues be held in fond remembrance by those who have best known us on earth, and may we pass to our final account as those

> " . . . who wrap the drapery of their couch
> About them, and lie down to pleasant dreams!"

The facsimile of Mr. Thomas's signature occurs at the end of the preface for the first time in this fiftieth number.

In the Almanac for 1847, after announcing the death of Mr. Thomas, the editor goes on to say : —

Previous to Mr. T.'s death, arrangements were made with the Publishers of the Almanac, for its continuance, and matter for succeeding numbers having been furnished us, it will be issued

annually as heretofore, and we hope, with the assistance and encouragement of the friends of the work, numerous and kind as they have ever been, to continue the Almanac, (the oldest one in the country,) through the present century, at least.   Under these circumstances, and from respect to the memory of Mr. T. who first planned the Almanac, and has edited it so long, and whose name is associated with it in the minds of the friends of the work, that name will always be connected with it in future as in past time.

Accordingly, the words

ESTABLISHED IN 1793,
BY ROBERT B. THOMAS.

have appeared on every title-page since the death of the founder, and for many years the successive prefaces have closed with a quotation from Mr. Thomas and a facsimile of his signature.   The preface for the first number of the twentieth century sums up, briefly and forcibly, the long career of the Almanac, and suggests its intimate connection with the life of our country.   It illustrates, also, the unity of purpose which has governed the book through more than a hundred years and which may be ascribed, in no small degree, to the individuality of the only author whose name the title-page has ever borne: —

TO PATRONS AND CORRESPONDENTS

First issued for the year 1793, The Old Farmer's Almanac has come down through the remaining years of the *Eighteenth Century*, and the entire *Nineteenth Century*.   We now give hearty greetings to our readers at the opening of the *Twentieth Century*.

During the space of time above indicated, a period unprecedented in human progress, whether in science, in exploration and discovery, in invention, in the growth of popular government, in the spread of civilization, or in the divers other directions of physical and mental energy and effort, we have kept on our quiet

way, grateful for the words of commendation and encouragement we have ever and anon received from among the successive generations of men and women of New England who have read and studied our publication.   And it is with additional pride and gratification that we reflect how prominent has been the part taken by these same men and women of New England, and the descendants of many of them living in other regions, in the stupendous measure of human achievement referred to.

Such having been our course, we are led to believe that the results of our efforts have not been without merit.   And it is from what we have done in the past, and because of the character of the number of the Almanac we now present, rather than from any promises we might make, that we hope for your continued confidence and support, for

"It is by our works and not by our words we would be judged : these we hope will sustain us in the humble though proud station we have so long held.[1] . . .

Robt. B. Thomas."

[1] The sentence quoted from Mr. Thomas first appears in the Almanac for 1836, where it is preceded by the quietly humorous phrase, "Notwithstanding our customary professions."

[No. III.]

THE
FARMER's ALMANACK.

Calculated on a new and improved Plan.

FOR THE YEAR OF OUR LORD.

1795.

Being the third after Leap Year, and Nineteenth of the Independence of America.

Fitted to the town of Boston, but will serve for any of the adjoining States.

Containing, besides the large number of Astronomical Calculations, and Farmer's Callendar for every month in the year, as great a variety as any other Almanack, of

New, Useful, and Entertaining Matter.

By ROBERT B. THOMAS.

"Hail, Nature! fountain inexhaustible ;
Thy rising and decaying scenes ; as heaven,
With hand unerring, turns the silent spheres,
And in rotation brings the seasons round.

PRINTED IN BOSTON,
FOR JOSEPH BELKNAP, No. 8 *Dock-Square*,
and THOMAS HALL, in *State-Street*. Sold by them, by
the Author and M. Smith, *Sterling*, and by the Booksellers.
Price 40s. a Grose,—4s. a Dozen—6p Single.

THE OLD FARMER AND HIS COR-
RESPONDENTS

M R. THOMAS is never more entertaining than in
his replies to his numerous correspondents. His
Almanac became popular so rapidly that, al-
most from the outset, he received all sorts of material from
interested readers, — poems, anecdotes, and puzzles, observations on agriculture, jests, riddles, mathematical
problems. Agricultural observations were particularly
welcome. In the preface to the second number (1794),
the author, in stately, old-fashioned phrase, invites contributions of this kind : —

My precepts and observations on agriculture, I have the vanity
to believe, have been approved of by farmers in general. Agriculture affords an ample field in this country for the ingenious to
expaciate upon, in which improvements are making every day ;
and as my greatest ambition is to make myself useful to the community in this way, 'tis my sincere wish that men of experience
and observation in agriculture, would be kind enough to forward
me such hints towards improvement, as are capable of being rendered serviceable and of general utility to the public.

And again, in 1795 : —

Experiments in Agriculture ever afford me the greatest degree
of pleasure and satisfaction ; wherefore, I earnestly repeat my
solicitations, that gentlemen farmers, who have leisure and genius
for making experiments in husbandry, would be kind enough to
communicate their improvements which may be made useful to

the husbandman ; in doing which, they will not only receive the grateful acknowledgements, but, confer the greatest favours on the Author of the following sheets.

In 1796 Mr. Thomas met with a disagreeable experience, as may be seen from a passage in his preface for the next year: " It is with much regret, that the Author is under the necessity to apologize for the admission of some pieces of entertainment in his last year's Almanack, which was owing to his indulging the printer in that peculiar province, who took the liberty to retrench several useful matters to make room for a ' Sermon in favour of thieving,' and several ludicrous anecdotes, which were highly disgusting to many of the friends of the *Farmer's Almanack*, and for which he humbly asks forgiveness, acquainting them at the same time, that those pieces were unknown to him. In future, he is determined to make all the arrangements himself." From this time he scrutinized the lighter pages of his annual with the same care which he bestowed on the astronomical computations.

In 1801 begins the series of " acknowledgments to correspondents," which continued without a break for many years. The author is brief and pointed, — sometimes his frankness must have been rather startling ; but men were much in the habit of speaking their minds in those days, and Mr. Thomas had a touch of humor which deprived his sharp speech of much of its wounding potentiality. The closing words of the preface for 1801 embody in a summary form much that was to come in detail, addressed to various persons in subsequent years : " Several favours received are deferred, for want of room ; some, it is necessary to say, for want of merit."

In 1807 there is a very outspoken remark: " J. P. is thanked for his good-will, but his *Anecdote* is too obscene for admission." In 1808 " S. D. is thanked for his kind

intentions; but his riddle is not sufficiently enigmatical: besides, it has been often published." Another correspondent in the same year appears to have been *too* enigmatical: " Margaret Snufftaker's hints, are unintelligible and futile." Originality was ever a desideratum, and S. B., in 1809, seems therefore to have been treated with much consideration on the whole; his " communications," he is told, " were very acceptable, though," adds Mr. Thomas, " we should have been better pleased if they had not been quite so stale, — have published the most interesting." T. K., who is noticed in 1813, must have been what we should now call a stimulating or suggestive writer; his " favours," we are told, " though crude, are always acceptable, as they are generally capable of producing much sagacity." This is assuredly high praise!

When contributors expostulated Mr. Thomas took high ground: " J. H. seems to think himself unfortunate — we feel to commiserate him, but we must claim the right to judge the palm " (1822). He is not to be dictated to, even by the ladies: " Mrs. H. wishes us to give her communication ' at full length ' — we really think a *miniature* would be quite as creditable to her, and we are certain it would be to us " (1827). In 1830 " our friend A. B. is thanked for his contribution, but at this time we have a superabundance of this kind of ware."

Very rarely the full names of correspondents are given, as in 1837, when there had been some discussion about the correct answer to a problem: " Our friend Jerh. Hallet of *Yarmouth*, contends that Mr. O. Norcross, of *Belchertown*, is under a mistake respecting his question, as in our Almanack for 1835, and wishes us to insert his demonstration. Not having room, we rather prefer the gentlemen would settle it between themselves." This shows how carefully the Almanac was read and how entertaining its patrons found it. The old numbers were preserved, and

the correspondents, as in the present instance, kept run of each other from year to year. The whole history of the Hallet-Norcross imbroglio covers the period from 1835 to 1838, when the controversy is judicially summed up by Mr. Thomas: "Messrs. Norcross and Hallet's misunderstanding seems to be in Mr. N.'s misconception of the question."

"G. H.," writes the editor in 1837, "may know how to manufacture salt — but we perceive he is no *astronomer*, or he would know the *moon* is not the only agent that governs the *tides*." In 1843, "W.'s puzzle might be called a jumble — we confess we see no propriety in calling it a puzzle." In the same number there are certain "Home Questions for the New Year," which, though not a part of the Answers to Correspondents, stand so near that department that they may come in here, especially as they are worth saving, not only for their common sense, but because they show the complete identity of spirit and method between this, the fifty-first number of the Almanac, and its earliest issues: —

Are your accounts all balanced up to Jan. 1, 1843? "Short settlements make long friends." Are you insured against fire? Did you look to the cellar, the roofs of your house and barn, and the wood-pile, and to putting away your ploughs and other utensils before winter set in? Your children, of course, go to meeting and to school regularly! Do you take a well-conducted newspaper? Have you made your will? settled all misunderstandings with neighbors? and do you avoid endorsing? The Scriptures, you know, say "Leave off contention before it be meddled with," and also, "He that hateth suretyship is sure!"

The volunteer poets gave Mr. Thomas a good deal of bother, and when to the offence of doggerel, anonymity was added, the long-suffering editor felt under no obligation to be mealy-mouthed. Thus in 1810 he relieved his mind in the following epigram: "Lines on inebriety, have

not sufficient spirit to preserve them even one year, nor correctness to entitle them to more than one perusal — the
author has credit for one thing only, they are without a
name." Toward juvenile talent Mr. Thomas is more tender-
hearted : " T. L.," we learn in 1811, " displays some genius
at poetry, but if we are not much mistaken, they are youthful effusions, which riper years might bring to maturity."
Incorrectness and lack of polish are frequent subjects of
complaint.   Thus, in 1812, " A Riddle by J. D. wants many
corrections ; the author might be better employed behind
the counter, than making riddles," — a critical snub which
reminds one of Lockhart's sending Keats "back to the
shop."   In the same year we hear of one " C. C." apparently a local Dr. Johnson : " *The Midnight Ghost,* is too
incorrect to appear in print.   We advise the author to
hand it to his townsman C. C. after which it will *appear.*"
Another rebuke to youthful bumptiousness is tempered
with Olympian praise : " Our young friend, who conceives
himself ' behind the curtain,' has given himself abundance
of airs, which, in some instances, partake of impertinence
and vanity — however, as they are conceived to be the
effusions of a juvenile fancy, they are easily pardoned.
His poetry is far above mediocrity for one of his years —
his prose is wrote with care, and he displays no small degree of mathematical knowledge.   We think, however, his
riddle is not entirely original " (1813).   One would like
to see the packet which this Gifted Hopkins had sent to
the philosopher of West Boylston.   Anyhow he was not
satisfied, and returned to the charge the next year ; but
Mr. Thomas is placid : " Our young correspondent X Y
and Z seems to indulge a propensity for which he had our
pardon last year. — Does he think we shall put up with
insolence without notice ?   We confess, there are instances
where it is the greatest wisdom.   We are ever desirous to
encourage the efforts of youthful genius, as far as our limits

will admit — his poetry to head the Calendar pages is decent, and would have been inserted this year if we had not been under prior claims."

It is good to know that the object of these strictures was not beyond repentance.   In 1819 Mr. Thomas receives him into favor with frank cordiality: "We were much pleased at hearing again from our young friend X. Y. Z. and especially to experience his reformation of manners, if we may so express it — he has our well wishes and hearty forgiveness — With his other favours, we have to acknowledge the receipt of a Bank-bill, of which, sixty-two cents is placed to his credit in advance. — His future Correspondence is respectfully solicited."   It is impossible not to recognize the quiet humor of the last sentence.   It is like the waggish variation on the editorial formula: "All communications must be accompanied by *a five-dollar bill*, not necessarily for publication, but as a guaranty of good faith."   Sometimes, indeed, a wrong-headed or sensitive contributor got the notion that money would secure the admission of poems or riddles to the columns of the Almanac.   One of these, a lady, is gently set right in 1835:   "Our friend Adelaide is mistaken in supposing, 'a necessary accompaniment,' was a pecuniary requisition — it had reference to a solution of a query, which is always requisite to secure an insertion. — If any innovations, in her last, she will be pleased to point them out, — we confess we have not discovered them."

Mr. Seaman, the satirist, in addressing the present poet-laureate, remarks, speaking of a poem which Mr. Austin had recently published, —

> The editor avers it is a sonnet:
> I wish to make a few remarks upon it.

Similarly affected was Mr. Thomas by a communication which he acknowledges in 1815:   "C. E. has favoured

us with some lines which he is pleased to call ' a Riddle,' we confess they are neat and pretty; but we think an epitaph would be equally as appropriate."

In 1817 Mr. Thomas's memory saved him from becoming the victim of a mortifying imposition. His rebuke to the plagiarist is gentle enough, when the circumstances are considered, particularly since the "Thomas' Almanack" to which reference is made was that of Isaiah Thomas, to which the Old Farmer had been for years a successful rival: " S. F's Riddle will not answer our purpose for several reasons, one is, its *obviousness*, others we forbear to give, as they might wound his feelings. — We are sorry our friend should have such an itching for writing Riddles. — We should be culpable in publishing many poetical communications, which could only be interesting to their writers — ' Stanzas, to head the Calendar Pages,' he might have saved himself the trouble of transcribing, by referring us to *Thomas' Almanack* for 1789. — The anecdote not original, nor even new."

" *Hydrometrynarean's* Poetry, is too much allied to his name, to be useful to us," is a comment of 1818. Another, in the same year, is still more crushing, but it was apparently addressed to an anonymous offender: " We have received a large packet with Northfield post mark, purporting to be poetry, &c. The author may have it again by sending to the Editors." Praise and censure are judiciously commingled in 1821: " P. N. R's Picture, though of the doggerel species, is not a bad likeness. — If he will take the trouble to point his lines and correct the orthography, and favour us with a copy, it shall embellish our next No." The poet was complaisant, and filed his verses. They appear, according to promise, in " our next No.," and here they are. for the edification of his grandchildren : —

PICTURE OF A DRUNKARD.

(Communicated.)

His eyes are red, a confus'd head,
  And face of crimson die ;
His coat in slits, and patch'd with writs,
  The execution nigh.

His hat much worn, his jacket torn,
  And pantaloons the same;
An empty purse, and what is worse,
  That rum is all his game.

His limbs are lame, tottering with pain,
  His vital power decay,
His body thin, immers'd in sin,
  While rum bears all the sway.

His note alas, goes for the glass,
  And everything he's got ;
But the last cent, will soon be spent,
  And he a drunken sot.

His house once good, tho' made with wood,
  Does now begin to go ;
His barn all rack'd — while boards it lacks,
  Amidst the drifting snow.

His wife once bright, his heart's delight,
  Is faded and forlorn ;
His farming lot, is quite forgot,
  And he a nuisance grown.

                                    P. N. R.

N. H. Feb. 1821.

Now and then Mr. Thomas suggests that verses of a certain length are best suited to the width of his columns, though he does not insist that the poet shall always do homage to the typographer. In 1831 " O. C. is sincerely thanked for his ingenious *Enigma* : we should have been better pleased if the lines had contained less syllables,

eight is the utmost we are able to get into a line — have reserved it for our next."

In 1837 S. H. C. is informed that his "Riddle appears rather lame — in fact, it is any thing but poetry." A similar criticism is passed in 1838: "Mrs. S. B.'s *Riddle* is any thing but poetry — abounding in unhappy metaphors. — Hope she will excuse us — though not possessed of youthful gallantry, we should be very sorry to be thought wanting in politeness to the ladies!" To appreciate this, we must know that it appears on the same page with a woodcut of the author, then seventy-two years of age, with his hair tied in a queue, — the same portrait that is reproduced on page 16 of this book. No doubt Mrs. S. B. forgave him.

A charmingly courteous remark, which must have gratified the person to whom it was addressed, unless he was fully acquainted with Mr. Thomas's humorous wrinkles, appears in 1840: "J. W. D. is pleased to favor us with his poetical effusions, for which he is entitled to the editor's grateful acknowledgements." The recipients of donative volumes of minor poetry might do worse than to have these golden words engraved in facsimile of their handwriting; editors, too, might copy them, and give up the familiar "declined with thanks." For anything more delightfully restrained we must go to Artemus Ward, who, when a stranger remarked that it was a fine day, replied "Middling," not wishing to commit himself.

Postage was always a sore point in the old days. It might be either prepaid or collected on delivery, and unlucky recipients of long-winded epistles or other useless matter often had a substantial grievance. Mr. Thomas's first allusion to the subject (in 1806) is appended to a compliment which he pays to a highly respected Quaker correspondent: — "*Friend* R. D. is tendered the Editor's best thanks, for his several valuable communications, at the

3

same time, solicits a continuance of his correspondence.
The postage the Editor will ever be happy in paying,
though in some is a great looser." One of the *losing* cases
appears in 1809: "A. R. Q. is thanked for his seasonable
information. — Though we would remind him that his communications came so *coated up* that we are obliged to pay
double postage on them, we would advise him in future
to leave off the *wrapper* or pay the *postage.*" Again, in
1810: "E. W. and others will be kind enough to pay
postage on answers to Riddles in future, or they will not
be noticed." In 1811: "G. S. our Boston querist — have
no objection to his asking questions every day in the year,
provided he pays the *postage* — he will find an answer to
his queries, without a fee, at No. 75, Cornhill," the book-
shop of John West, who published the Almanac from
1797 to 1820. E. F., in 1812, appears as a sinner against
several principles: his "*anecdote* is of the coarser kind,
and not capable of being polished without injuring the
pith. His Meteorological observations, if correctly taken,
would be useful. He will do well to remember the postage
in future." By 1814 the postage nuisance seems to have
become intolerable. Not only is "J. H. jr." informed that
"we conceive his Questions to be unimportant, and not
worth the money we paid for them," but there is an emphatic pronunciamento to the world at large: —

 ☞ No notice will in future be taken of any answer to queries,
unless *post paid*.

Even this was ineffectual, for, in 1824, "B. B's Riddle
we think is rather a dear one, containing only eight short
lines, and to be taxed eighteen cents and a quarter —— We
will repeat what we have said once and again, that no
question will be noticed unless accompanied with a complete answer, or demonstration, *post paid.*" Finally, in 1832,
Mr. Thomas is able to reply to a contributor who "is

at a loss why his 'communications are not noticed'" that " this is rather unaccountable, when we have given notice, not less than ten different times, 'that no notice will be taken of any Query, &c., unless a solution accompany it, *Post Paid*.'"

Nobody worries about postage to-day, and, though we all know that it cost more to send letters in old times, few of us have the details in mind.   They were complicated and must have been pretty vexatious.   The Almanac furnishes all necessary information on the subject.   Thus in 1798 we have this table : —

Rate of POSTAGE of every single Letter by land.

	MILES.	CENTS.
	30	6
	60	8
	100	10
	150	$12\frac{1}{2}$
For every single letter	200	15
	250	17
	350	20
	450	22
For more than	450	25

No allowance is to be made for intermediate miles.   Every double letter is to pay double the said rates ; every triple letter, triple ; every packet weighing one ounce, at the rate of four single letters for each ounce.

In 1800 there is a different table, and the postage on short distances is increased : —

RATES OF LETTER POSTAGE.

EVERY Letter composed of a piece of paper, conveyed not exceeding   40 miles,   8 cents.

Over 40 miles, and not exceeding	90	10
Over 90 do.	150	$12\frac{1}{2}$
Over 150 do.	300	17
Over 300 do.	500	20
Over 500 do.		25

Every Letter composed of two pieces of paper, double those rates.

Every Letter composed of three pieces of paper, triple those rates.

Every Letter composed of four pieces of paper, and weighing one ounce, quadruple those rates; and at the rate of four single letters for each ounce any letter or packet may weigh.

Until 1816, this table, with a few changes, is printed nearly every year; in 1816, however, the rates take a considerable jump: —

RATE OF POSTAGE OF EVERY SINGLE LETTER BY LAND.

Miles.	Cents.	Miles.	Cents.
40	12	300	25½
90	15	500	30
150	18¾	For more than 500	37½

No allowance is to be made for intermediate miles. Every double letter is to pay double the said rates; every triple letter, triple; every packet weighing one ounce, at the rate of four single letters for each ounce.— Every ship letter originally received at an office for delivery 9 cents. Magazines and pamphlets, not over 50 miles 1 1–2 ct. per sheet.— Over 50 miles, and not exceeding 100 do. 2 1–4 cts. — Over 100 do. 3 cts.

In 1817 the minimum rate settles back to six cents for thirty miles, which continued till July 1, 1845, when a new law went into effect, fixing the rate at five cents for three hundred miles, the weight not to exceed half an ounce. Single postage was added for each additional half ounce or fraction thereof. The other provisions of the new law need not detain us. An abstract was furnished by the Almanac for 1846. The three-cent rate was adopted in 1851 for any distance under three thousand miles, — for more than that distance six cents was charged. In 1863 three cents became the rate without regard to distance, and in 1883 two cents. The maximum weight for a single

postage was increased to one ounce in 1885. The history
of American postage from 1793 may be followed in the
successive issues of the Almanac.

Here, as well as anywhere, may be appended a table
which contains many novelties for the schoolboy of to-
day, but which all New Englanders of forty will recognize
as embodying much information once vitally necessary
in making change. It is taken from the Almanac for
1797: —

The Value of the several Pieces of Silver Coin now in Circulation
in the United States, in Federal Currency.

	Cents.	Mills.
One fourth of a Pistareen or half Dime .	5	0
Four pence halfpenny	6	2½
Half Pistareen, or Dime	10	0
Nine pence piece, or ⅛ of a Dollar . . .	12	5
Pistareen or two Dimes	20	0
Quarter of a Dollar	25	0
Half a Dollar	50	0
Dollar	100	0
Half a Crown, French	55	0
Half a Crown, English	55	5
Crown, French	110	0
Crown, English	111	0

10 MILLS *are*   1 CENT.
10 CENTS —   1 DIME, or DISME.
10 DIMES —   1 DOLLAR.
10 DOLLARS — 1 EAGLE.

Similar tables, and others more complicated, appear
in the Almanac for many years. In particular there is the
regular schedule of the values of the shilling in various
parts of the country. Instead of reprinting it, we may
quote a passage from the autobiography of Lieutenant
John Harriott, an English half-pay officer, who knew
America well: —

The various currencies of money, in the different states, are troublesome and harassing even to the natives of the United States, and still more so to strangers. A dollar, in sterling money, is four shillings and six pence; but, in the New-England states, the currency is six shillings to a dollar; in New-York, eight shillings; in New-Jersey, Pennsylvania, and Maryland, seven shillings and six pence; in Virginia, six shillings; in North Carolina, eight shillings; and, in South Carolina and Georgia, four shillings and eight pence. All agree that the evil is great and wants to be remedied; but they say, such is the prejudice of the country-people in the different states in favour of the currency they have always been accustomed to, that it is feared, were an act of congress passed to enforce a general uniform currency, the country-people would consider it as bad as they formerly did the stamp-act. To this, I have frequently taken the liberty of observing, to several members of congress and others, that, if an act were passed for no book-debt, bond, note, bill, &c. to be admitted as evidence in their courts of law, except such as were kept or made in dollars and cents, (which all the public offices and banks already do,) the evil would soon be removed without other coercion than that of self-interest.[1]

Most of us can remember when the shilling of $16\frac{2}{3}$ cents, the ninepence, two and thrippence, fo'pence ha'penny, and two shillings were terms constantly used in making small trades. To the rising generation these terms have merely an historical significance.

[1] Struggles through Life, London, 1807, II, 29-30.

ASTROLOGY

FROM the outset Mr. Thomas kept his Almanac free from astrology. This was not so hard to do in 1793 as it would have been seventy-five years earlier, but it was nevertheless a sufficiently creditable feat. The false science of the stars is so nearly obsolete nowadays among intelligent people that one finds it hard to realize what a hold it had upon the popular mind in the eighteenth century and even later. But an example or two will conduct us back to an age when the stars in their courses were regarded as potent in all human affairs, and we may well be surprised to see how short, both in time and in space, is the journey that we have to go.

About the middle of the eighteenth century, it was customary, in some parts of New England, to employ an astrologer to cast a horoscope in order to determine the exact day and hour at which a vessel should weigh anchor for an important voyage. This seems to have been particularly common in the case of slavers, perhaps on account of the great possibilities of profit and the peculiar risks which their traffic involved. Mr. George C. Mason, of Newport, whose extremely interesting account of the colonial slave-trade [1] gives a multitude of details drawn from original business papers, had " seen hundreds of these horoscopes " and prints a facsimile of one dated August 22, 1752, and prepared for a voyage to the Guinea coast.

[1] The African Slave Trade in Colonial Times, in The American Historical Record, 1872, I, 311–19, 338–45.

He appends an extract from an astrologer's letter to a Newport merchant referring to a more rigorous computation of the moon's place than was to be found in the current almanacs, for which the cunning man professes a dignified contempt. A marginal note, doubtless from the hand of the shipmaster, on one of these horoscopes, remarks that " 6 D. & h [i. e. the sixth day and hour] always wins the profits," which seems to point to some personal superstition on the captain's part, derived perhaps from his experience in lucky and unlucky seafaring. Sailors are proverbially superstitious (and no wonder), but without much evidence one would scarcely have believed that our hard-headed New England forefathers on the coast were at all addicted to the elaborate trifling which the practice of so abstruse a science as astrology involves.

There is a casual reference to the same subject in the Diary of President Stiles, of Yale College, where, under date of June 13, 1773, he mentions, as lately dead, " Mr. Stafford of Tiverton," who " was wont to tell where lost things might be found, and what day, hour and minute was fortunate for vessels to sail." [1]

Poor Robin's Almanack for 1690 contained a burlesque horoscope, which the author called " the ass-trological scheme." A comparison with that drawn up for the Newport shipmaster will show that it was not a bad parody. " By this Scheme," adds the jocose author, " a man may foretel things that never will be, as well as those that never were ; and is as proper for an Almanack as a Nose for a mans Face : for as a Face looks ill favouredly without a Nose, so doth an Almanack without a Scheme."

Astrology turns up now and then in the theses discussed by candidates for the degree of Master of Arts at Harvard College, and that too at a comparatively late date. Thus in 1762 it was decided that " the heavenly bodies produce

---

[1] Literary Diary of Ezra Stiles, ed. Dexter, I, 386.

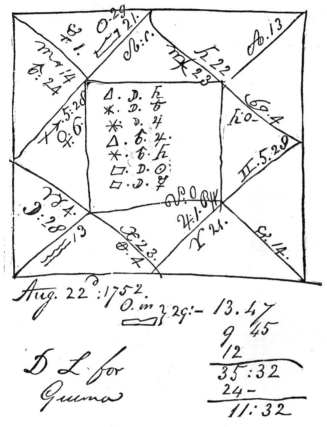

SHIP'S HOROSCOPE FOR A GUINEA VOYAGE

changes in the bodies of animals." Perhaps this may not
be regarded as genuine astrology, but no one can doubt
the nature of the following question, which was negatived
in 1728: — "Do medicinal herbs operate by planetary
power?" In 1694 it was decided that "divinations by the

MOCK HOROSCOPE

(From Poor Robin's Almanack for 1690)

planets are not justifiable." Two questions must not be
mistaken as astrological: "Will a comet be the cause of
the world's final conflagration?" (settled affirmatively in
1759) and "Is a comet which only appears after many years
more a foreshadowing of divine wrath than a planet which
rises daily?" (negatived in 1770).[1]

[1] Proc. Mass. Hist. Soc., XVIII, 123 ff.

An irrefutable proof that the whimsicalities of astrology, palmistry, and physiognomy were not unknown among the country people in New England at the beginning of the nineteenth century is found in the circulation of the so-called Book of Knowledge. This curious manual purported to be written by "Erra Pater, a Jew Doctor in Astronomy and Physic, born in Bethany, near Mount Olivet in Judea," and to have been "made English" by W. Lilly, the famous astrologer. I have examined an undated edition with the imprint "Worcester, Printed by Isaiah Thomas, Jun.," and another printed at Suffield by Edward Gray, in 1799. The title-page, after the old fashion, furnishes one with a pretty complete table of contents. The little book, which was meant to be hawked about the country by book-peddlers, is said to treat of "the Wisdom of the Ancients" in four parts. The first part shows "the various and wonderful Opperations of the Signs and Planets, and other celestial Constellations, on the Bodies of Men, &c." The second gives "Prognostications for ever necessary to keep the Body in Health; with several choice Receipts in Physic and Surgery." The third is an "Abstract of the Art of Physiognomy and Palmistry, together with the Signification of Moles, and the Interpretation of Dreams, &c." The fourth is "The Farmer's Calendar, containing, 1st. Perpetual Prognostications for Weather. 2d. The whole Mystery of Husbandry. 3d. The complete and experienced Farrier and Cowleech, &c." Among the miscellaneous matter are a number of forms for bills, bonds, indentures, deeds, bills of exchange, and the like — as in the "Every Man his own Lawyer" of our own day. All this in a little book of less than a hundred and twenty pages. Truly the buyer got a good deal for his shilling!

The astrology is of the simplest and most popular kind. The main definitions are given, and the familiar elementary

principles of nativities. Thus we learn that "the sun being in *Virgo*, makes the men [born at that time] fortunate and successful in household affairs, wise and fruitful, stout and ambitious: his wife shall die suddenly in his absence; he shall have many things stolen from him, but shall be revenged on his enemies. He shall be so much given to talk, that he cannot keep his own secrets. — It also shews one fair-faced, of a genteel behaviour, a lover of women, and delightful to be in the courts of princes and noblemen," and so on. "If the native be a maiden, she will be witty, honest, and modest; of a willing mind, diligent and circumspect; and shall be married about the age of fifteen years." This last remark comes in with unconscious humor in close connection with the "willing mind" just referred to.

The precepts of physiognomy are amusing, and some of them are still familiar in folk-lore or proverbial saying. "A large head shows a person stupid and of a dull apprehension, also a very small head signifies the same." This reminds one of the nursery rhyme: —

> Great head, little wit;
> Small head, not a bit.

Outworn wisdom frequently takes refuge in the adages of the nursery. More startling are the remarks that "a fat face shews a man to be a liar, and foolish," "a long slender neck shews a man to be a coward," and "slender legs denote ignorance."

Almanacs were of course astrological from the beginning. They existed largely for the purpose of designating the days and hours upon which the particular influence of this or that planet would be operative. Let us take an instance from the "Monthly Observations," for March, 1700, in Partridge's almanac for that year.[1]

[1] Merlinus Liberatus, published by the Company of Stationers.

1   Last Quarter, the first day, at noon.

2

3   The General Affairs of *Europe* begin
4 to move and look with an angry face;
5 yet I do not think things are yet ripe
6 for Action, or fit for what they are
7 design'd. Yet a little while and you'll
8 see.
9 New ☽ 9 day, 3 ho. 53 min. afternoon.
10 If his Majesty of *Poland* was born,
11 as some say, *Apr.* 27. or, as others, *May*
12 the 2d. 1670; he is like to have a very
13 troublesome year of this, and that from
14 the lay Transit of *Mars* through *Scor-*
15 *pio* all this Summer, and some other
16 First Q. 16 day, 49 min. past 11 at night.
17 things. There is a Fire kindling in
18 those Northern parts, I hope to a good
19 purpose.
20 *Mars* hath lately been in Trine to
21 the Sun, and now running Retrograde
22 in a fixed Sign. The Souldiery of Na-
23 Full ● 23 day, 20 min. past 5 at night.
24 tions may sleep a while, but I think
25 not long, perhaps this Century may
26 end first; and perhaps not, if *Nostra-*
27 *dame* says true.
28

29

30 Last Q 31 day, 35 min. past 6 morning.
31

Partridge and Gadbury were the best known almanac-makers of their day. They were equally popular in their lifetime, but in posthumous reputation Partridge has distanced his rival. He owes his immortality not so much to his own performances as to the satire of Swift. The

affair is one of the most celebrated episodes in Queen Anne literature, but, familiar as it is, it can hardly be passed by without a word. In 1707 Swift published, under the name of Isaac Bickerstaff, Esq., " Predictions for the Year 1708, Wherein the Month and the Day of the Month are set down, the Persons named, and the great Actions and Events of next Year particularly related, as they will come to pass. Written to prevent the People of England from being further imposed on by vulgar Almanack Makers." The writer professed to be a scientific astrologer and ridiculed Partridge and his fellows as ignorant pretenders to the art. The first of his predictions is the most famous, and, indeed, it is the gist of the whole satire. With splendid audacity he actually specified the day and the hour when, as he foretold, Partridge was to die : —

My first Prediction is but a trifle ; yet I will mention it, to show how ignorant those sottish pretenders to Astrology are in their own concerns : it relates to PARTRIDGE the *Almanack* maker ; I have consulted the star of his nativity by my own rules ; and find he will infallibly die upon the 29th of March next, about eleven at night, of a raging fever ; therefore I advise him to consider of it, and settle his affairs in time.

This prediction Swift followed up in a second paper, purporting to be a letter to a lord from a revenue officer and to describe the accomplishment of Bickerstaff's prediction. Here an account was given of Partridge's last moments and of his repentance for the injuries he had done and the frauds he had perpetrated. " I am a poor ignorant fellow," he exclaims to the person who makes the report, " bred to a mean trade ; yet I have sense enough to know that all pretences of foretelling by Astrology are deceits." And he adds, sighing, " I wish I may not have done more mischief by my physic, than by astrology ! although I had some good receipts from

my grandmother, and my own compositions were such as I thought could, at least, do no hurt."

Partridge of course protested furiously in his almanac for 1709. But Swift took advantage of his anger to write still another paper, in which he proved that Partridge must undoubtedly be dead, as he had predicted.

Literary historians have probably exaggerated the effect of Swift's satires. They may have had some influence with educated people, who were only too much given to relying on astrological predictions, but they did not change the character of the popular almanacs in England. Throughout the eighteenth century and well into the nineteenth these continued to go on in their old course, though, as we have seen, the principal almanac of New England contemned such fooleries.

Partridge's and Gadbury's almanacs continued to be published, with no essential change in their character, long after the death of their founders. The Company of Stationers, who owned the copyrights, were unwilling to suppress them or to modify their contents, for the sales were enormous and the populace was wedded to its idols. In 1827 the Society for the Diffusion of Christian Knowledge took a hand in the matter by publishing the first number of the British Almanac (for 1828). This was a direct challenge to the Stationers. In a preface the editors attack the two most popular almanacs of the day, Moore's and Partridge's, for their charlatanry. The object of the new publication was to educate the public taste and intelligence. The British Almanac was successful at the very outset, and it is still issued. At first the price was two shillings and threepence, for there was a stamp duty of fifteen pence on every almanac — a tax which brought in more than thirty thousand pounds a year. In 1835, when the duty had been abolished, the size of the book was increased and the price was put down

to a shilling. The effect of respectable competition was marked. The Stationers changed the character of their almanacs, and Moore's, which is still published, is no longer a monument to ancient delusions. With the issue of 1870 the British Almanac itself passed into the hands of the Stationers' Company.

It must not be inferred that astrological almanacs no longer circulate in England. There are two rival publications which are as absurd as anything that the dark ages could produce, — Zadkiel's and Raphael's.

Both Zadkiel and Raphael take pride, from year to year, in pointing out what they call the fulfilment of their predictions. Since these works are not much known in this country, the reader may be diverted by an extract from Zadkiel's Almanac for 1903, designated as the " seventy-third yearly edition." It will be observed that there is much vagueness in the predictions and considerable license of interpretation in the fulfilment.

FULFILLED PREDICTIONS.

END OF THE WAR IN SOUTH AFRICA.

Predictions.	Fulfilment.
" The SUN shines once again on Old England after the storms and tempests of the last two years."	In the spring quarter of 1902, the negotiations for peace were begun in April, and the submission of the Boers was made on
" ☉ in ♈. — We shall secure peace by showing our enemies that we are prepared for war."	the 31st of May, when the Treaty was signed by the five Boer leaders at 10.30 p. m., at Pretoria ; just before Jupiter became stationary in *Aquarius*
" Should peace be preserved, as it should be if only our Government be resolute as well as clever in diplomacy, our foreign trade will increase." — *Almanac*, 1902, pp. 5, 11, 56.	17° 15' in the mid-heaven of the horoscope of London.

THE CORONATION.

Predictions.	Fulfilment.
"SUN enters *Cancer*, June 22nd. — At London, Venus is culminating. The elevation of Venus is of happy omen for the Monarch, and promises a splendid Coronation attended with great martial pomp, and public rejoicing in earnest." — *Almanac,* 1902, p. 59.	The Coronation took place in the summer quarter, as foretold, viz., on the 9th of August, having been postponed from the 26th of June, owing to the alarming illness of the King. In the Abbey the splendour of the scene was magnificent. The public rejoicing at His Majesty's recovery was indeed earnest and heartfelt.
" The 23rd of June brings a crisis." — *Ibid.*, p. 21.	
" Mars in the ascendant of London, in opposition to Uranus. I trust that no serious accident will mar the public festivities at the opening of this month " (July). — *Ibid.* p. 23.	On the 23rd of June the King became seriously ill, and the operation was performed on the following day — when it was announced that the Coronation was postponed, to the consternation of the people of the empire. This most unfortunate accident marred the brilliant festivities planned and begun for the end of June and the beginning of July.

There was of course much ridicule of astrological and other prophecies. Thus Rabelais, in his Pantagrueline Prognostication : —

No matter what these crazy astrologers of Louvain and Nuremberg and Tübingen and Lyons tell you, do not believe that in this year there will be any other governor of the universe than God the creator.

.   .   .   .

This year the blind will see only a very little ; the deaf will not hear very well ; the dumb will not have much to say ; the rich

will fare rather better than the poor and the well than the sick;
several sheep, oxen, pigs, birds, chickens, and geese will die.[1]

In 1697, Poor Robin's Almanack, in deliberate burlesque
and with an express reference to Rabelais, makes certain
salutary suggestions for January: —

This Month is the best of all the twelve (saith the ingenious
Rabelais) to pick the lock of a Cup-board, to steal a bottle of
wine out of it.   But yet Reader, if thou hast money, let me advise thee rather to go to the Tavern, call for a quart of Canary,
and wish *Poor Robin* some part of it, to heat hi[m] within this cold
Weather; but above all, let Scholars have a great care of drinking the best Wine, for of good Wine they cannot make bad Latin.
The Weather being so cold, hot broths in a morning are very comfortable: Pope *Alexander* by the advice of a Jew his Physician
did so, and lived till his dying day, in despight of all his enemies.

In the same year Poor Robin characterizes December,
with a hit at the decline of old-fashioned hospitality: —

This Month will be more Employment for Cooks and Fiddlers,
than for Reapers and Haymakers; but how if there should be
more Cooks than there will be Employment for 'em; truly, as
the Stars seem posited, it is a thing very much to be fear'd: And
the Phisicians do assure us that very few poor Men this *Chrismas*
will get Surfeits by over-eating 'emselves at rich Mens Tables, and
the reason thereof is, because my Lady *Pride* hath turn'd good
Houskeeping out of doors; instead of a Cook, a Butler, a Groom,
a Huntsman; and a 2 or 3 brace of neat-handed serving-Men,
maintaining a Butterfly Page, a stiff swearing Coach-man, and a
tawdry Skip-kennel, pulling down the Larder, locking the Buttry
door, and reducing the Kitchin to the bigness of a Cobler's Stall.
A blessed Reformation.

A middle ground is occupied by Woodward's almanac
for 1690, which, though it cannot deny the influence of the

---

[1] Chaps. 1 and 3.

4

stars in their courses, is inclined to think that free-born Englishmen are less subjected to them than foreigners: —

SAPIENS DOMINABITUR ASTRIS.

Altho the Stars have an Influence on all Persons and things sublunary, yet as we are Englishmen and Christians, let us live so after the Dictates of the Divine Will, that the Stars may have no Power over us, as to Evil; for they only incline, not compel. Besides, we inhabit a Land that flows with Milk and Honey, are govern'd by a glorious Monarch and his Consort of our own Religion, have the blessed Gospel florishing more than in any Kingdom of *Europe*, just Laws to punish Offenders; wherefore if we live not in Tranquillity or Union one with another, can we expect anything but the great Indignation of Heaven, by provoking God's severe Displeasure against us for our Treachery and backsliding —? But Thanks be to God we have a prospect of so well-settled a Government, that Popish Contrivers shall not have Power to alter for the future.[1]

Mr. Thomas, as we have seen, was no astrologer. But he was a humorist, and now and then he uses the formulas of the star-gazing prophets to good purpose, as in the following note from the Calendar for October, 1803: —

Now is an excellent time for old bachelors to visit old maids, as the sun is in Libra, which promises a balance of affection to the wedded pair.

February, being a short month, afforded room for such jocose remarks at the foot of the column of days, particularly when leap-year came round. Thus, in 1804, we read: —

It is hoped that old maids and bachelors will enjoy much satisfaction this year.

[1] Daniel Woodward, Ephemeris Absoluta, London, 1690.

In 1808 the same hope is expressed, but with a good deal more confidence : —

It is expected that the hearts of bachelors and old maids will beat in unison this year.

More satirical are the verses appended to the same month in 1809 : —

> Thy changing weather like a modish wife,
> Thy winds and rains forever at a strife ;
> So Termagant, awhile her thunder tries,
> And when she can no longer scold — she cries.

In 1810 we are brought back to the domain of sentiment in a reminiscence of a pretty passage in Virgil's eclogue : —

> The bashful lover sues in vain
> The favours of the fair to gain ;
> She flies, yet flying hopes the swain
> Quickly her footsteps will detain.

In 1812, which is leap-year, we have another jest about those who have postponed marriage beyond their first youth : —

There will be this year many *conjunctions* and fewer *oppositions* than usual, between bachelors and old maids.

This pleasant method of filling up the February column was followed for a good many years. A few more specimens may be given : —

> Ye lasses be prudent and wise,
>   Nor listen to Neddy's false voice ;
> A happiness pure if ye prize,
>   Let merit alone claim your choice.   (1821.)

TO MARRIED LADIES.

Whatever is your lot in life,
Be still the good and loving wife ;
Content with little, meek with riches,
But let the *Husband* wear the *breeches*.   (1823.)

A SENTIMENT. — " The married and single.   Wives, as they are — maids, as they would be — bachelors, as they should be." (1828.)

PREDICTIONS.

He who marries this year will run a great risk — that is, if he does it in a hurry — of finding the angel of light to be one of darkness.   (1832.)

LEAP-YEAR.

Tradition this year doth report,
That maidens are allowed to court.   (1836.)

A PREDICTION.

Much this year will be done
That many will wish undone.   (1840.)

Bachelors and maids, don't despair,
Time has brought about leap year.   (1844.)

This is truly a rough-hewn couplet and it comes near marking the close of an epoch, for in 1846 the practice in question was abandoned and the column was filled by lengthening the last few lines of the Farmer's Calendar.

THE MAN OF THE SIGNS

ONE of the notable things about the Farmer's Almanack is that, from the very beginning, it has excluded from its pages the picturesque image known as the Man of the Signs, or the Moon's Man.

The figure of a man, surrounded by the twelve Signs of the Zodiac, each referred to some part of his body by means of a connecting line or a pointing dagger, is still seen in some almanacs and was once regarded as indispensable. The Anatomy, as it was often called, was a graphic representation, intelligible alike to the educated and to those who could not read, of a vitally important principle in medicine and surgery. Each sign of the zodiac " governed " an organ or part of the body, and, in selecting a day to treat any ailment, or to let blood, it was necessary to know whether the moon was or was not in that sign. In the language of the Kalender of Shepherdes, as published by Pynson in 1506, " a man ought not to make incysyon ne touche with yren ye membre gouerned of any sygne the day that the mone is in it for fere of to grete effusyon of blode that myght happen, ne in lykewyse also when the sonne is in it, for the daunger & peryll that myght ensue." Pynson's Kalender of Shepherdes is something more than its name implies. It is a rather large compendium, affording not only all manner of astronomical and astrological lore, but information on health, religion, physiognomy, and pastoral life. It was originally written in French, and the oldest known edition (though not, apparently, the first) appeared at Paris in 1493. It was im-

mensely popular.   There were no less than twenty other
editions in French before 1600, not to speak of those
printed in the seventeenth and eighteenth centuries.
There were two distinct translations into English, and
numerous editions.[1] The work, then, was authoritative,
and we may accept its precepts without hesitation as
giving a correct idea of what men believed.

The Kalender of Shepherdes is not content with one
illustration of the dominion of the planets.   Besides that
just mentioned there are two more, — another body and a
skeleton.   The body is intended to exhibit the position
of the veins, and is accompanied by directions for bleeding.   The skeleton is encircled by the planets, each with a
label and a line or ribbon attaching it to the central figure.
Thus over the man's head is the Sun, with a label " Sol
the heart" and a ribbon attaching the sun to that place in
the skeleton where the heart would be.   The sun, we are
to understand, " hath myght and domynacyon " over the
heart.

Most almanacs, however, are satisfied with a single
figure — that of the man surrounded by the zodiacal beasts
— the *Homo Signorum* or " Man of the Signs."   Who
invented the figure is a question.   The conjecture of
Halliwell [2] that it originated with Petrus de Dacia, a Danish
astronomer and mathematician who was Rector of the
University of Paris in 1326, is apparently without foundation; [3] Peter compiled tables for determining the moon's
place, but there is no evidence that he was an artist.   The
Moon's Man is common in manuscript calendars of the
fourteenth century, and may be considerably older.   There

---

[1] See the edition by H. Oskar Sommer, London, 1892, Critical Introduction.

[2] Essay on Early Almanacs, in Companion to the British Almanac
for 1839, p. 56.

[3] See G. Eneström, Swedish Academy, Stockholm, Öfversigt af Förhand-
lingar, 1885, No. 3, pp. 15 ff., No. 8, pp. 65 ff; 1886, No. 5, pp. 57 ff.

is a succinct statement of the doctrine of which the *Homo Signorum* is merely a pictorial representation in the famous astronomical poem of Manilius, which dates from the beginning of the Christian era, and the Roman poet was of course merely borrowing from earlier Greek sources.

> Accipe divisas hominis per sidera partes,
> Singulaque in propriis parentia membra figuris,
> In quis praecipuas toto de corpore vires
> Exercent. Aries caput est ante omnia princeps
> Sortitus, censusque sui pulcherrima colla
> Taurus, et in Geminis aequali brachia sorte
> Scribuntur connexa humeris, pectusque locatum
> Sub Cancro est, laterum regnum scapulaeque Leonis ;
> Virginis in propriam descendunt ilia sortem ;
> Libra regit clunes, et Scorpios inguine gaudet ;
> Centauro femina accedunt, Capricornus utrisque
> Imperat et genibus, crurum fundentis Aquari
> Arbitrium est, Piscesque pedum sibi iura reposcunt.[1]

These verses are translated in hexameters which have escaped the notice of all students of English metre, in " A New Almanacke and Prognostication, for the yeare of our Lord God 1628. By Daniel Browne, willer[2] to the Mathematickes, and teacher of Arithmeticke, and Geometry: "

> Head and face Aries, necke and throate Taurus vpholdeth,
> To Gemini th' armes, to Cancer brest stomacke and lunges:
> As Leo rules the backe and heart, so Virgo delighteth
> In guts and belly : reignes and loynes Libra retaineth.
> Scorpio the secrets and bladder challengeth : of thighes
> Only Sagitarius the gouernour is : Capricornus
> The knees as subiects doth guid, but Aquarius holdeth
> The legs : and Pisces maintaine the feet to be their right.

Through Ptolemy, the Alexandrian astronomer of the second century after Christ, the doctrine came down to the middle ages and so to modern times. Thus we find

---

[1] Marcus Manilius, Astronomica, ii, 453 ff.
[2] Misprint for *well-willer*.

it in Chaucer's treatise on the Astrolabe, which he wrote
as an elementary text-book of astronomy for his little son
Lowys (or Lewis): " Everich of thise twelve signes hath
respect to a certein parcelle of the body of a man, and
hath it in governance; as Aries hath thyn heved, and
Taurus thy nekke and thy throte, Gemini thyn armholes
and thyn armes, and so forth." [1]   Chaucer says nothing
of the Anatomy, the Man of the Signs, but it was well
known in his day, and it is not unlikely that he would have
described it fully if he had not left his book unfinished.

As time went on, the theory of a close relation between
man's body and the signs of the zodiac fell into disrepute,
and the Anatomy became a laughing stock.   In 1609
Thomas Dekker, the dramatist and pamphleteer, published a burlesque called The Ravens Almanacke, to
which, according to custom, he prefixed the figure of the
Homo Signorum, with the usual title " The Dominion of
the Moone in Mans body."   This is his humorous comment: " At the beginning of euerie Almanacke, it is the
fashion to haue the body of a man drawne as you see,
and not onely baited, but bitten and shot at by wilde
beasts and monsters."   The image, he says, is called " the
Man of the Moone, or the Moones Man, or the Man to
whom the Moone is mistris." [2]   Dekker's jest, oddly enough,
was revived by Josh Billings, who can hardly have been
aware of its previous vogue, in his comic publication the
Old Farmer's Allminax, which appeared for the first
time in 1870: —

SIGHNS OV THE ZODIAK.

The undersighned iz an Amerikan brave, in hiz grate tragick
akt ov being attaked bi the twelve constellashuns. — (*May the
best man win.*)

[1] Part i, § 21 ; Skeat's Oxford Edition, III, 187.
[2] The Non-Dramatic Works of Thomas Dekker, ed. Grosart, IV, 179–80.

Then follows the figure, with an indescribably droll parody on the regular directions for its use: —

KEY TEW THE ABUV PERFORMANCE.

Tew kno exakly whare the sighn iz, multiply the day ov the month bi the sighn, then find a dividend that will go into a divider four times without enny remains, subtrakt this from the sighn, add the fust quoshunt tew the last divider, then multiply the whole ov the man's boddy bi all the sighns, and the result will be jist what yu are looking after.

In 1657 Bishop Bramhall makes an ingenious application of the Anatomy in his controversy with Hobbes the philosopher. He is arguing for free will and objects to Hobbes's theory of necessity on the ground that it lowers the dignity of human nature: —

T. H. maketh him [man] to be in the disposition of the second causes: sometimes as a sword in a man's hand, a mere passive instrument; sometimes like "a top, that is lashed" hither and thither "by boys"; sometimes like "a football," which is kicked hither and thither by every one that comes nigh it. . . . Surely this is not that man that was created by God after His own image, to be the governor of the world, and lord and master of the creatures. This is some man that he hath borrowed out of the beginning of an almanac, who is placed immovable in the midst of the twelve signs, as so many second causes. If he offer to stir, Aries is over his head ready to push him, and Taurus to gore him in the neck, and Leo to tear out his heart, and Sagittarius to shoot an arrow in his thighs.[1]

The almanac-makers of the seventeenth century were sorely perplexed about the "misshaped anatomy," as the

[1] Castigations of Mr. Hobbes his last Animadversions, Works, Oxford, 1844, IV, 417.

poet Cleveland called it.[1]   None of them put any confidence in it, but all of them wanted to sell their books, and the people clamored for the time-honored monstrosity. Now and then we find a versified apology.   Thus Edward Pond, in 1633, admitted that he had inserted the caricature for business purposes only : —

THE ANATOMIE.

Should I but dare t' omit the *Anatomie*,
Which long enough hath gul'd my country friend,
He with contempt would straight refuse to buy
This book, and 't is no *Almanack* contend.
Ask him its use, he 'le say he cannot tell;
No more can I : yet since he loves 't so well,
I 'le let it stand, because my Book should sell.[2]

Poor Robin's Almanack for 1697 is equally frank and more humorous : —

Here is presented to your Eye
The Figure of th' Anatomy,
For where that this Gue-Gaw doth lack,
Some will not buy that Almanack :
Then stand here that my Book may sell,
Though for what Use we cannot tell.

The same embarrassment was felt by astronomers in America.   Samuel Clough, in the New England Almanack for 1703, expressed himself with more vigor than metrical correctness : —

The *Anotomy* must still be in
Else th' *Almanack*'s not worth a pin :
For Country-men regard the Sign
As though 'T were Oracle Divine.
But do not mind *that* altogether,
Have some respect to Wind and Weather.

[1] "All other forms seem in respect to thee
The almanack's misshaped anatomy."
(The Hetacomb, verses 89–90.)
[2] See S. Briggs, The Essays, Humor and Poems of Nathaniel Ames, Cleveland, 1891, p. 61.

Here the reader is warned not to trust the oracle too much. So in Poor Will's Almanack for 1797,[1] we have "The Anatomy of Man's Body, as said to be governed by the Twelve Constellations," with the conventional rule for its interpretation and use; but there follows immediately a caveat in solemn prose against taking it too seriously.

Dr. Nathaniel Ames, of Dedham, ignored the Anatomy in the first two numbers of his Almanac (1726–28), and this is the more noteworthy since he was, at the outset, avowedly astrologistic. In his first issue he speaks of an eclipse of the moon in terms that remind us of Edmund in King Lear: "This Eclipse of the Moon happens so near the Great Benevolent *Jupiter*, the Effects 't is hop'd will not be ill." And in that for 1728 he is still more outspoken: —

OF THE ECLIPSES THIS YEAR, 1728.

The first of these Eclipses (moon) is Celebrated in 6 degrees of Virgo, the second Sign of the earthy Triplicity, which (authors say) portends the Scarcity of Fruit and Corn.

The second of these Eclipses, viz: That of the Sun on the 28th of February happens in 20 degrees of Pisces, the House of Jupiter, and Exaltation of Venus: learned Authors affirm, when Jupiter bears Rule, and is Lord of an Eclipse (as in this he is) he signifies Glory, Fertility, Tranquillity, Peace and Plenty; and such as are signified by Jupiter, especially Ecclesiastical Persons do flourish and live in great Estimation. The Laws are well Executed, and many Upright and Just Judges are very Active for the Publick Good; new Customs or Privileges, new Corporations, new Honours, &c., are now most happily conferr'd upon People in general; And these are the Natural Portends of Jupiter when he bears Rule in an Eclipse.

Astrologer though he was, Ames hoped to avoid the absurdity of perpetuating the Homo Signorum. But in

---

[1] Philadelphia : Printed for and Sold by Joseph Crukshank.

1729 he yielded, rather reluctantly, to the pressure of public opinion, and inserted the image. His reluctance — his feeling that this was a superstitious ornament, unworthy of the serious attention of a "student in physick and astronomy," — is evinced by the roughhewn verses that accompany the picture: —

> The Blackmoor may as eas'ly change his Skin,
> As Men forsake the ways they 'r brought up in;
> Therefore I 've set the Old Anatomy,
> Hoping to please my Country men thereby,
> But where 's the Man that 's born & lives among,
> . . . . . Can please a Fickle throng? [1]

Ames's figure is excessively ugly, but not original. He had it from his predecessor, the almanac "printed and sold by B. Green and J. Allen in Boston," appearing as Clough's New-England Almanack in 1703, afterwards edited by Thomas Robie, Daniel Travis, and others.

The hithering and thithering of New England almanacs with regard to the Man of the Signs is excessively curious. In Isaiah Thomas's Massachusetts, Connecticut, Rhode-Island, New-Hampshire and Vermont Almanack for 1782, there is an elaborate Anatomy. Yet this is a somewhat rationalistic number after all. It contains a skeptical Essay on Conjuration and Witchcraft, in which, after speaking of various wonders of the invisible world, the author remarks: "We are not to believe such reports, unless the evidence of the truth of the fact be equal to the strangeness of the thing." In 1783 the Anatomy appears again, but in 1784 it is omitted, with the note " *The Anatomy of Man's body, &c.* inserted last year." In 1785 we find the figure; but not in 1786 or 1788. In 1789, 1790, and 1791 it reappears in much handsomer form. In 1792 it is omitted. And so on. After 1800 there seems to have been a reac-

[1] See Briggs, as above, pp. 47, 57, 60.

tion in favor of the Anatomy.   It appears, with only one
break, from 1801 to 1807.   About this time some almanacs
actually gave the mystic figure a place of honor on the
combined cover and title-page; so Smith and Forman's
New-York and New-Jersey Almanac for 1809 and 1810.

No wonder the people were attached to the Anatomy.
It was not merely a fetich, though there was a touch of
fetichism in the reverence paid it.   It was a graphic sum-
ming up of the whole doctrine of astrological medicine.
And medicine, for many centuries, had been permeated
with astrology, both in theory and practice.   Chaucer's
physician in the Canterbury Tales always selected a "fortunate ascendant" in treating his patients, — that is, he
observed the condition of the heavens, constructed a
horoscope, and acted accordingly.   Otherwise his ministra-
tions might do more harm than good.   Paracelsus declared,
we are told, that no physician ought to write a prescription
without consulting the stars.   The science of one age
becomes the superstition of the next, but what the Anatomy
typified remained the doctrine of the learned for centuries, and when at last it sank to the position of a " vulgar
error " it retained its hold with a tenacity proportionate
not only to its antiquity but to the high authority which
it had so long enjoyed.   It is much to Mr. Thomas's
credit that he steadfastly refused to countenance a prevalent superstition by admitting this time-honored effigy
into his Almanac.

ARTISTIC EMBELLISHMENT

IN an editorial greeting to the Old Farmer's Almanack for 1903, the New York Sun comments appreciatively on the pictures which typify the different months. "Each month," says the Sun, " has its lines of poetry and its lifelike portrait of a sign of the zodiac. The Crab looks good enough to eat, and the tail on the horse of the Archer has a sweep, range and boldness that must recommend it to all farriers, blacksmiths and hostlers." [1]

The figures of the signs which are thus deservedly commended, — as well as the portrait of Father Time, with his scythe and water-jar, which embellishes the title-page, — go back to 1853. In the preface to the Almanac for 1852, the editor announces a change in the artistic adornment of his venerable annual. " For about forty years past," he writes, " we have used, upon our Title-page and Calendar-pages, wood-cuts or engravings done when the art of engraving was not as advanced as now; but as time, the press, and constant use have worn down the surface of the cuts, we intend, in our next number, to insert new and better engravings of the same subjects, which we hope will please all." And in 1853 the pledge is redeemed : — " Agreeably to promise," says the editor, " we have somewhat changed our appearance by the engravings, which we insert in this number, but though ' Father Time' may be burnished up, and improved in his outward adornings, his heart is in the right place, and we trust that we shall never forget the good old times of ' Lang Syne,' that we have had together; and though the signs of the constellations may

[1] New York Sun, Nov. 1, 1902.

THE
FARMER'S ALMANACK,

CALCULATED ON A NEW AND IMPROVED PLAN,

FOR THE YEAR OF OUR LORD,

1810.

Being the Second after BISSEXTILE or LEAP-YEAR, and Thir-
ty-fourth of the *INDEPENDENCE* of *AMERICA.*

Fitted to the Town of BOSTON, but will serve for any of the adjoining States.

Containing, besides the large number of Astronomical Calculations, and the Farmer's Calendar for every month in the year,
as great a variety as any other Almanack, of

New, Useful, and Entertaining Matter.

BY ROBERT B. THOMAS.

THOU great first cause, thy hand divine did raise
This solid Earth, and spread the flowing seas;
Did make the Sun in central glory shine,
And every planet round his orb incline;

BOSTON:—Printed for JOHN WEST & Co.
Proprietors of the Copy-Right;

And for sale at their Bookstore, No. 75, *Cornhill,* and by most other Booksellers in *Boston, Salem, Newburyport,* &c. by the AUTHOR in *West Boylston,* and by other Booksellers and Traders in *New-England.*
Price 9 *dollars* per gross, 87½ *cents* per dozen, and 12½ *cents* single.

E. G. HOUSE, *Printer, No. 5, Court Street.*

be a little more artistic, too, in their appearance, they are the same *signs* of pleasant months, and joyous hours, spent together in many a happy home, and by many a cheerful fireside." The new cuts are believed to be the work of Hammatt Billings, and were originally engraved by Nichols. They have indeed " pleased all," as the editor ventured to hope, and there seems to be no reason why they should ever be changed so long as the seasons continue the same and the zodiac remains in fashion with the astronomers.

The set of figures that preceded the woodcuts ascribed to Billings began to appear in 1809, and were not materially altered until 1853, though they were occasionally rein-graved, as small variations, particularly in the length of Father Time's beard, make manifest. They were pretty grotesque, though not without life, as may be seen from the facsimiles.

From 1800 to 1808 the artistic department of the Alma-nac was in a state of experimental ferment. Before 1800 there were no cuts at the heads of the calendar pages, each month being characterized in a short piece of verse. In 1793 there was no illustration on the title-page; but a figure of a man in knee-breeches ploughing, with a rural scene in the background, appeared the next year, and was retained until 1797 (see p. 25), when it was replaced by a woman seated, with emblems of agriculture at her feet and a ploughing scene in the distance. This continued to be the adornment of the title-page, though with some vari-ation in detail, until Father Time ousted it in 1809. Mean-time, in 1800, cuts had been introduced to reinforce the verses at the head of each month. These were, until 1804, not the Signs of the Zodiac, but little scenes illustrative of the changing seasons or of the occupations appropriate to the month in question. Thus for January, we have two men, or a man and a boy, on the ice, one skating, the other whipping a top; for February, cattle looking at the bleak

landscape; for March, two boys, in high hats (one of which
has blown off), on their way to school; for April, a sower;
for May, an angler; for June, a shepherd in the shade; for
July, a load of hay; for August, a foot-passenger, with a
pack on his back and a dog at his heels, striding along to
gain the timely inn; in September, a reaping scene; in
October, two hunters, resting in the wood;[1] in November,
a man driving a herd of cattle; in December, a man

JANUARY, 1800

AUGUST, 1800

carrying home a great load of fagots. This method of
representing the months belongs to a very old artistic tradition, as we shall see in a moment. Meantime we may
complete our account of the cuts for the calendar by re-
marking that from 1804 to 1808 there is, instead of the
scenes just described, a series representing the signs of the
zodiac in a rather peculiar way, — not as independent sym-
bols, but as realistic figures with an environment of land-

[1] See also the facsimile of the Farmer's Calendar for October, 1800, p. 81,
below.

scape. Aquarius (for January) is an actual man pouring water into a stream; the Fishes (for February) have been caught and laid on the bank with their tails neatly tied together; the Ram (for March) lies under a tree, with no suspicion that he is a zodiacal beast; the Twins (for May) are taking a walk in a field, with an altar on one side and a small New England house on the other, and one of them has a star on his cap to indicate that they are Castor and Pollux; the Archer (for November) is plainly at home in

MAY, 1801–1803

DECEMBER, 1804–1808

the midst of rugged scenery and defending himself against an invisible enemy.

The method of designating the several months by pictures, whether of the zodiacal signs or of the occupations or labors of the year, is a very ancient and curious matter, which will repay a little consideration. As for the signs of the zodiac, we need not linger over them. Their origin is lost in antiquity, and it is enough for us to trace them back to the Greeks and Romans. The reader will find on page 79 a picture of an Italian altar inscribed with a Farmer's Calendar in columns, each column headed by a figure of

5

the sign.   An Athenian sacred calendar has also been preserved, in which the months are separated by similar figures. On the page opposite is a more complicated illustration, which includes both the signs and the labors of the months. It is taken from the Kalender of Shepherdes, as published in 1503.[1]

This figure is a compendious pictorial calendar. The central circle contains two figures, a woman with a nosegay, who represents warm weather, and a man sitting out-of-doors by a fire, who represents cold weather.   In the second circle are the months, each typified by an appropriate scene: January, by a man slaughtering a boar; February, by a man sitting at a table with a tankard before him; March, by a woman warming her hands and feet at a fire; April, by a pruner at work; May, by a lover and his lass out a-Maying; June, by a plowman; July, by a mower; August, by a reaper; September, by a man with a mattock; October, by a man driving a horse; November, by a vintager; December, by a shepherd. If these occupations do not suit our climate, we must remember that they were not designed for it, but rather for the south of Europe, for we are dealing with a very old set of conventional figures.   In the outermost circle are the signs of the zodiac, each divided between two months.

Illuminated calendars dating from Anglo-Saxon times preserve an interesting series of the labors of the months which continued, with some variations, through the middle ages " and even appears in the printed calendars and almanacs of the sixteenth century in England, Germany, and the Low Countries." [2]   The killing of swine, which is in the Kalender of Shepherdes, was a favorite subject for November or December.   It is found, for instance, on an old Norman font at Brookland, in Kent, on the archivolt of

1 On this work see page 53, above.
2 Thomas Wright, Archæological Album, London, 1845, p. 64.

THE CIRCLE OF THE MONTHS
(From the Kalender of Shepherdes, 1503)

the great west doorway of St. Mark's Cathedral at Venice,
at the side of the central doorway of the façade of the
cathedral at Lucca, on the tympanum of the doorway of
the monastery of St. Ursin, in France, on a capital in the
Doge's palace at Venice, in a mosaic pavement at Piacenza
and again at Aosta, in the famous paintings by Giotto in
the great hall at Padua. A very vigorous example occurs
in a fourteenth-century medallion of painted glass in Dews-

JANUARY, 1809–1852

NOVEMBER, SINCE 1852

bury Church, Yorkshire, which may have been meant as a
type of the whole season of winter. The edge of the axe
is turned backward, and the boar is tied by the snout to
the stump of a tree.[1]

Such figurative representations of the months and
seasons turn up everywhere, as the examples already
given have doubtless suggested, from one end of Europe
to the other. In introducing them into his Almanac Mr.
Thomas was simply following the fashion of his time,

[1] Archæologia, XLIV, plate V, opposite p. 178.

but he was unconsciously attaching his little annual to a very venerable tradition. We must refrain from pursuing the subject, attractive as it is. The reader who wishes to know more will be able to satisfy his curiosity by consulting a learned article by Mr. James Fowler in the forty-fourth volume of the Archæologia, the official publication of the London Society of Antiquaries.

Except for symbolical illustrations such as we have just considered, Mr. Thomas did not yield to the temptation to embellish his Almanac with engravings, for the occasional diagrams to elucidate eclipses and other astronomical matters and the map of New England are not for show but for use. The first departure from this rule was when, in 1835, he yielded to the solicitations of his publishers and consented to let his portrait appear.

Some of the early New England astronomers had less self-restraint, and tricked out their books with all manner of eccentric novelties. Ames does so with peculiar zest in his issue for 1772, which is advertised on the cover as "containing, besides what is usual in Almanacks, a Description of the Dwarf that lately made her Appearance in this Town; as also a curious Method of taking Wax and Honey without destroying the Bees." The dwarf was Miss Emma Leach, born in Beverly, "about 20 Miles distant from this town," in 1719. The description is reinforced by a very disagreeable cut on the cover. Besides this monstrosity, we have a large portrait of "J-n D-k-ns-n, Esq; Barrister at Law," that is John Dickinson (1732–1808) of the Continental Congress, who is described in the title as "The Patriotic American Farmer" and as one "who with Attic Eloquence, and Roman Spirit, hath asserted the Liberties of the British Colonies in America." Dickinson is resting his elbow on Magna Charta and holds in his hand a scroll inscribed "Farmer's Letters," — his well-known book in defence of freedom. The same num-

ber also exhibits a ridiculous full-length portrait of " Mrs. Catharine M'Caulay," the admired authoress, who is standing in a constrained attitude, holding a little bird (probably a canary) on her extended hand.

Bickerstaff's Boston Almanack was also a sinner in this direction. It showed a penchant for savages — men and beasts. Thus in 1768 the cover exhibits a terrific picture of a family of Patagonian giants. Other numbers have figures of New Zealanders (1775), "the Orang Outang" (1769), and "an exact and elegant representation of that *Furious* WILD BEAST" which ravaged the South of France in 1764 and 1765.[1]

The Wild Beast of the Gévaudan, as the creature was called from the district where its depredations were most extensive, appears to have been a hyena escaped from a travelling show. The contemporary accounts are obviously exaggerated, for there was a veritable reign of terror in Languedoc. Still, if only half of what was reported is true, the situation was bad enough. The most sensational narrative, but one of the best authenticated, comes from Montpellier, Feb. 8, 1765 : —

On the 12th ultimo the wild beast attacked seven children, five boys and two girls, none of whom exceeded eleven years of age. The beast flew at one of the boys; but the three eldest of them by beating him with stakes, the ends of which were iron, obliged him to retire, after having bitten off a part of the boy's cheek, which he ate before them. He then seized another of the children; but they pursued him into a marsh which was close by, where he sunk in up to his belly. By continually beating him, they rescued their companion; who, though he was under his paw for some time, received only a wound in his arm, and a scratch in the face. A man at last coming up, the creature was put to flight. He afterwards devoured a boy at Mazel, and, on the 21st, flew on a girl, who, however, escaped

[1] Bickerstaff for 1773.

with some dangerous wounds. The next day he attacked a woman, and bit off her head. Captain Duhamel, of the dragoons, is in pursuit of him, and has caused several of his men to dress themselves in women's apparel, and to accompany the children that keep cattle.

The bravery of the children was recognized by King Louis XV, who awarded four hundred livres to the eldest of the boys, who had particularly distinguished himself, and ordered three hundred to be distributed among his companions. The description of the beast printed in the St. James's Chronicle for June 6, 1765, along with a wood-cut, from which that in Bickerstaff's Boston Almanack was doubtless taken, is disquieting enough: —

It is larger than a Calf of a year old, strongly made before, and turned like a Grayhound behind. His Nose is long and pointed, his Ears upright and smaller than a Wolf's, his Mouth of a most enormous size, and always wide open; a Streak of Black runs from his Shoulders to the Beginning of his Tail. His Paws are very large and strong; the Hair on his Back and Mane thick, bristly, and erect; his Tail long and terminating in a Bush, like that of a Lion; his Eyes small, fierce, and fiery. From this description it appears that he is neither a Wolf, Tiger, nor Hyena, but probably a Mongrel, generated between the two last, and forming, as it were, a new Species.

The animal was killed in September, 1765, but not, we are gravely assured, until it had destroyed more than seventy persons.[1]

[1] Mason Jackson, The Pictorial Press, its Origin and Progress, London, 1885, pp. 206–13.

MURDER WILL OUT

AN almanac as conceived by Mr. Thomas should be an annual compendium of human interests. Now nothing is more interesting than Murder. Murder is the material of great literature, — the *raw* material, if you will, but is not raw material essential to production, as well in art as in manufactures? What distinguishes De Quincey's famous Postscript on certain memorable murders from the grewsome scareheaded "stories" of the purveyor for the daily press? Surely not the matter! The bare plot of the sublimest of Greek tragedies, the Agamemnon of Æschylus, finds its closest parallel in a horrible butchery in low life that occurred in New York a few years ago. Conventional phrases are always tiresome enough, but none is more so than that of "morbid curiosity" as applied to the desire to know the circumstances of a great crime. The phrase is like a proverb: it is only half true, though it masquerades as one of the eternal verities. Curiosity is natural; without it a man is a mere block, incapable of intellectual advancement. And curiosity about crime and criminals is no less natural, no further morbid — that is, diseased or abnormal — than that which attaches to any other startling event or remarkable personage. Like all other forms of curiosity, it may *become* morbid, and perhaps it is well to restrain it, — but that is not the question.

On one point, at all events, all reasonable men will agree: The detection of murder is laudable and necessary. Nobody can be blamed for what everybody must feel, — an interest in the thousand ways in which murders come

to light.   The old theory was that this crime was so abominable in God's sight that he would not suffer it to be concealed.   As Chaucer says, in a deservedly famous passage : —

> O blisful God, that art so iust and trewe!
> Lo how that thou biwreyest mordre alway !
> *Mordre wol out !* that se we day by day.
> Mordre is so wlatsom [1] and abhominable
> To God, that is so iust and resonable,
> That he ne wol nat suffre it heled [2] be ;
> Though it abyde a yeer, or two, or three,
> Mordre wol out, this my conclusioun.

God's Revenge against Murder was a famous seventeenth-century book.   It was even held that the ordinary laws of nature were sometimes suspended or supplemented by miraculous intervention, if the guilty man could be revealed in no other way.

With all this in view, we may fairly hold that Mr. Thomas would not have done his duty by his time if he had not given his readers a specimen of the countless anecdotes that illustrate our theme.   Accordingly, it is with no small satisfaction that the philosophic observer of life and letters notes the following article in the Farmer's Almanack for 1796 : —

MURDERS STRANGELY DISCOVERED.

IN the second year of the reign of King James I, one Anne Waters settling an unlawful love, or rather lust, on a young man in the neighbourhood ; and finding their frequent meetings were interrupted by her husband, they agreed to strangle him : which being done, they buried him under a dunghill, in the cow-house. The man being missed by his neighbours, and the woman artificially dissembling her grief, and admiring what was become of him, all were at liberty to make their own conjectures ; but none

[1] That is, " loathsome."   [2] That is, " hidden."

suspected the wife of contributing to his absence, but assisted her inquiries after him.   In this time one of the inhabitants of the village dreamed, " That his neighbour Waters was strangled, and buried under a dunghill in the cow-house ; " and, telling his dream to others, it was resolved the place should be searched by a constable ; which being done, Waters's corps was found ; and some other concurring suspicions appearing, the wife was apprehended ; and, confessing the truth, was burnt, according to law in that case provided.

PARTHENIUS, treasurer to Theodobert, King of France, having killed his dear friend, Ausanius, and his wife ; when no man accused, much less suspected him guilty of such a crime, Providence so ordered the affair, that he discovered it himself after this strange manner.   As he was taking his repose in bed, he suddenly cried out, "Help, help, or I am ruined to eternity ; " and being demanded what made him in such a terrible fright, he, between sleeping and waking, answered, " That his friend Ausanius, and his wife, whom he had murdered long ago, summoned him to answer before the tribunal of God Almighty."   Upon which words he was apprehended, and, upon conviction, stoned to death.

A close parallel to the first of these stories is an item in the New England Journal for December 1, 1729 :[1]—

Last week, one belonging to Ipswich came to Boston and related, that, some time since, he was at Canso, in Nova Scotia ; and that on a certain day there appeared to him an apparition in blood and wounds, and told him, that at such a time and place, mentioning both, he was murdered by one, who was at Rhode Island, and desired him to go to the said person, and charge him with the said murder, and prosecute him therefor, naming several circumstances relating to the murder; and that since his arrival from Canso to Ipswich, the said apparition had appeared to him again,

[1] As quoted by J. B. Felt, History of Ipswich, Essex, and Hamilton, Cambridge, 1834, pp. 208–9.

and urged him immediately to prosecute the said affair. The abovesaid person, having related the matter, was advised and encouraged to go to Rhode Island, and engage therein, and he accordingly set out for that place on Thursday last.

While we are on this subject, it will not be improper to instance an article of New England belief which, if not actually credited when the Farmer's Almanack began to appear, in 1792, was in full force, and apparently recognized in legal procedure, as late as 1769. This was the superstition that the corpse of the victim would bleed when touched by the murderer, or even, it might be, on his mere approach. The ordeal by touch was once practised, it is safe to say, in every nation of Europe, and our forefathers of course brought the custom with them when they came to New England.

In 1769 the young wife of Jonathan Ames, in the West Parish of Boxford, Massachusetts, died suddenly. The circumstances were suspicious. The body was disinterred, and the physicians who examined it found abundant evidence of poison. The marriage had not been happy. Ames's mother, who lived with him, had shown violent enmity towards her daughter-in-law, and had predicted her death in terms which, when recollected, seemed darkly significant. Both Mrs. Ames and her son were bidden to touch the body, but, guilty or not, they refused to submit to the ordeal. The examination, according to the record, " gave great occasion to conclude that they were concerned in the poisoning," and they were committed to jail at Salem. There was no conclusive proof, however, and both were acquitted. Shortly after, they left the village and were lost sight of. The mystery of the Ames Murder was never cleared up.[1]

The antiquary who gives an account of this celebrated

[1] Sidney Perley, The Essex Antiquarian, 1898, II, 1 ff.

case is of opinion that he is recording the only instance of the ordeal by touch in New England history. But he is mistaken. Two striking examples of the ordeal may be found in Winthrop's Journal. The first occurred in 1644, and is graphically narrated by the colonial governor. One Cornish, living at Agamenticus, "was taken up in the river, his head bruised, and a pole sticking in his side, and his canoe laden with clay found sunk. His wife (being a lewd woman, and suspected to have fellowship with one Footman) coming to her husband, he bled abundantly, and so did he also, when Footman was brought to him; but no evidence could be found against him." [1] Footman was discharged, but the woman was convicted, though not, it seems, on the testimony of the ordeal of blood. In the second case, which came two years later, in 1646, confession followed the ceremony, as must often have happened. A poor creature had killed her child, and " when she was brought before the jury, they caused her to touch the face of it, whereupon the blood came fresh into it," and she confessed the truth.[2] This remarkable providence could not escape the all-recording Cotton Mather. He narrates it in his Magnalia, deriving his information from Winthrop's Journal. Characteristically enough, he improves the narrative. According to him the blood actually flowed anew, and did not merely " come fresh into the face," as Winthrop declares.[3]

Another instance from the same century is related by Cotton Mather in a passage which may serve as a specimen of his best style : —

Several Indians were made horribly drunk by the drink which the English had sold unto them. Returning home over a little

---

[1] Winthrop, ed. Savage, 1853, II, 258.
[2] The same, II, 369.
[3] Book vi, chap. 5, ed. 1853, II, 398.

ferry, eight of them were drown'd (from December to March) one of their dead bodies came ashore very near the place where they had been supplied with their drink; and lying on the shore, it bled so plentifully, as to *discolour* the water and sand about it. Upon which the considerate spectators thought of that scripture, " the stone shall cry out of the wall " against him that " gives his neighbour drink." They thought there was a loud cry of " Blood ! blood! " against some wicked English in this matter.[1]

The murder of Sassamon, one of the most celebrated cases in the annals of Plymouth Colony, affords us another opportunity to observe the " ordeal of the bier." John Sassamon, who is said to have studied in the Indian School at Cambridge, was at one time King Philip's secretary. But he returned to his English allegiance and was appointed preacher to the Indians of Middleborough. In 1674, learning of Philip's hostile preparations, Sassamon gave warning to the governor at Plymouth, though he was well aware that he did so at the risk of his life. Soon after his body was found in Assawomset Pond with the neck broken and other marks of violence upon it. Beyond question he had been put to death as a traitor by Philip's orders. Three Indians were convicted of the murder, and executed at Plymouth in June, 1675. The jury, according to custom, consisted of both white men and Indians, and there can be little doubt that the evidence was satisfactory. Increase Mather thinks it worth noting that when Tobias, who seems to have been the chief culprit, " came near the dead body, it fell a bleeding as fresh as if it had been newly slain, albeit it was buried a considerable time before that." [2] If we may believe Cotton Mather's account of the trial, the experiment was tried more than once, and always with the same result.[3]

[1] Magnalia, book vi, chap. 5, ed. 1853, II, 402.
[2] A Relation of the Troubles which have hapned in New-England, by reason of the Indians there, Boston, 1677, p. 75; Drake's ed. p. 236.
[3] Magnalia, book vii, chap. 6, § 5.

There is a large collection of similar cases in Pitcairn's Criminal Trials in Scotland.[1] The most extraordinary is that of Johan Norkott in England (1628), as reported by an eminent lawyer. On this occasion the minister of the parish, " a very reverend person," testified (and his evidence was corroborated) that when the body was touched by the defendants thirty days after death, " the brow of the dead, which before was of a livid and carrion colour, begun to have a dew or gentle sweat arise on it, which increased by degrees, till the sweat ran down in drops on the face. The brow turned to a lively and fresh colour, and the deceased opened one of her eyes and shut it again: And this opening the eye was done three several times. She likewise thrust out the ring or marriage finger three times, and pulled it in again; and the finger dropped blood from it on the grass."

[1] Edinburgh, 1833, III, 191 ff.

WIT AND WISDOM OF THE FARMER'S CALENDAR

F ARMER'S Calendars are of respectable antiquity. A typical example from ancient Rome is preserved in the Naples Museum. It is inscribed on a block of marble about two feet and a half in height, and a foot and a half in length and breadth. Each face includes three months, and each month stands in a column by itself. The language is of course Latin, and the contents are very simple, as may be seen by the following translation of the calendar for May and September: —

Month
May.
Days, 31.
Nones on the 7th.
Day, 14 hours.
Night, 9 hours.
Sun in Taurus.
Under the protection
  of Apollo.
Crops are hoed;
Sheep are sheared;
Wool is washed;
Bullocks are tamed;
Vetch for fodder
  is cut;
Crops
  are purified by lustrations.
Sacrifices to Mercury
  and to Flora.

Month
September.
Days, 30.
Nones on the 5th.
Day, 12 hours.
Night, 12 hours.
Equinox
8th day before the Ka-
  lends of October.
Sun in Virgo.
Under the protection
  of Vulcan.
Wine jars
  are sealed with pitch;
Apples are gathered;
Trees
  are dug round.
Feast
  to Minerva.

Another copy, on a three-sided block, with four months on each face, was also found at Rome.[1]

It will be noted that we have here a combination of an ordinary calendar with memoranda for farmers. There are a few simple astronomical facts of general importance, the appropriate occupations of the season are set forth, and the chief festival of the month closes the account.

ROMAN FARMER'S CALENDAR

The resemblance to the modern almanac needs no emphasizing.

The miscellaneous precepts of the Almanac are likewise modern representatives of an ancient line. Many passages in Cato's treatise on Agriculture might be inserted in the Farmer's Calendar without our knowing the difference, except for a phrase or two that show some incompatibility of climate or custom. Here, for instance, are two extracts

[1] See Mommsen, Corpus Inscriptionum Latinarum, I, 358–9 ; Römische Chronologie, 2d ed., 1859, p. 68; Real Museo Borbonico, II, ta. xliv.

from Cato, closely translated. They are almost startling in their resemblance to our Almanac. Yet Mr. Thomas is no more likely to have consulted Cato's Latin treatise than Cato is to have imitated the Old Farmer. The connection is one of subject and temper, of obscure but immemorial tradition, not of literary imitation.

Your oxen should be scrupulously looked after. Humor your ploughmen in some respects, so that they may be more willing to take care of the oxen. Have good ploughs and ploughshares. Don't plough rotten soil or drive a wagon or cattle over it. If you are not careful where you drive, you will lose three years' profit. Bed your sheep and oxen carefully, and let their hoofs be attended to. Protect sheep and cattle from the scab: this usually comes from insufficient feed or from exposure to the rain. Finish every job promptly; for, in farming, if you are late about one thing, everything will be behindhand. If straw is scarce, gather oak-leaves and use them as bedding for your sheep and oxen.[1] Have a good large compost heap. Save manure carefully; when you carry it out [to the compost heap] cleanse it and pulverize it. Cart it out [on the land] in the fall. Loosen the soil round olive-trees in the fall and manure them. Cut the leaves of poplars, elms, and oaks in the season: store them up before they get too dry as fodder for sheep. After the fall rains sow turnips, fodder, and lupines. — Cato, *De Agri Cultura*, cap. 5, § 6.

In rainy weather find something to do indoors. Don't be idle, but clean up about the buildings. Remember that expenses go on even if work stops. — Cap. 39, § 5.

In Mr. Thomas's earlier numbers the Farmer's Calendar is almost exclusively given to short directions for work appropriate to the successive days of the month: that is,

---

[1] Compare the Farmer's Calendar for October, 1834: — "[Leaves] are collected and laid in stables instead of straw, and thus make a very good litter for cattle."

OCTOBER, Tenth Month. 1800.

Pomona joyous fpreads her copious ftores,
And with her bleffings glads the fertile fhores ;
The fky ferene affumes a deep'ning blue,
And ev'ry grove puts on a motley hue.

M. D.	W. D.	Courts, Aspects, Holidays, Weather, &c. &c.	Farmer's Calendar.
1	4	Cool breezes.	Winter apples fhould now
2	5	Midd. tides. ☽ eclip. vifible.	be gathered in, as hard frofts
3	6	Day breaks 4h. 30m. ♂ ftat.	hurt them much ; remove thofe
4	7	Yard L rifes 10h. 40m. Cold	underneth the tree, and pick off
5	E	17th Sun. paft Trin. ftorm.	with the hand all you can con-
6	2	☌ ☽ 7*'s or together.	veniently before you fhake the tree.
7	3	S. J. C. Len. C. P. Boft. Mach.	Harveft your Indian corn
8	4	☽ Apo. Pleaf. [Nant. Newbp.	without delay—the birds and
9	5	St. Dennis. ant for the	fquirrels I am confident will.
10	6	Very low tides. feafou.	Potatoes not dug this week will be regretted next.
11	7	Clouds	Flax that was put a rotting
12	E	18th Sun. paft Trin. up.	laft month, look to often the
13	2	More falling	heavy dews at this feafon will
14	3	weather.	rot it very faft.
15	4	7*'s fou. 2h. 6m.	Indulge not your children in
16	5	Q. of Fr. behead. 1793. ☌ ☽ H	eating too much fruit, and ef-
17	6	Burgoyne fur. 1777. Pleafant.	pecially that which is hard and unmellow, if you would fave
18	7	St. Luke. ☉ eclip. invifi.	the doctor a vifit.
19	E	19th Sun. paft. Trin.	Let not Indian corn lie long
20	2	High tides. Rain.	in a heap before it be hufked.
21	3	S. J. C. Taun. C P Portl ☽ Per	Cyder finifh making as foon
22	4	♀ sets 6h. 10m. High, rough	as poffible ; to have it fine and clear, grind the apples the eve-
23	5	winds.	ning previous to laying it up,
24	6	Yard L. rifes 9h. 30m. More	lay it up early in the morning
25	7	Crifp. moderate,	and prefs it out moderately.
26	E	20th Sun. paft Trin. with	Plough for summer fallows
27	2	□ ☉ ♃ [Sts. Sim. & Jude.	at every opportunity that lei- fure will admit.
28	3	S. J. C. Camb. C. P. Tifb. wind	Roots in general may now
29	4	and rain.	be gathered in, and the land
30	5	Pref. ADAMS born. 1735.	manured and hove up in ridges
31	6	Warm again.	for the next year's crop.

It is a calendar in the strictest sense, as may be seen in the facsimile on the opposite page. Only in the winter season, particularly in December, the farmer's holiday time, is a tendency visible toward longer and more general observations, and even here these are pretty carefully kept within the limits of the calendar form. The farmer is bidden to square his accounts; he is encouraged to read aloud in the long evenings; he is exhorted to remember the poor. Here, for instance, is the complete Farmer's Calendar for December, 1796.

Very little can be done on a farm, this month to much profit.

Lay in dry fuel, while the snow keeps off.

Prepare and put in order, your sleds and sleighs as they will come in use very soon.

Look well to your barns, and fatting heards. — " Live temperately, and spend frugally."

The cultivation of the earth, ought ever to be esteemed, as the most useful and necessary employment in life. The food, and raiment, by which all other orders of men are supported, are derived from the earth. Agriculture is of consequence ; the art which supports, supplies, and maintains all the rest.

" Remember, ye wealthy and affluent, the sons and daughters of affliction and distress ! Think of those, into whose shattered dwellings poverty enters to increase the inclemency and the horrours of the present season. Distribute bread to the hungry, and clothes to the naked." Discharge all the debts you have contracted the last year, with mechanics, shopkeepers, labourers, &c. before a new year commences.

The advice to square accounts in December is often repeated, and the author shows a good deal of ingenuity in varying the form of his precepts. In the first number of the Almanac (that for 1793), the admonition is short and sharp: "Adjust your accounts; see that your expenditures do not exceed your incomes." Next year there

is a humane suggestion with respect to the distress that may result from neglecting to pay trifling debts: — "Settle with, and pay off your mechanics, labourers, and servants; for, though the sum[s] due to them be but small, they may be of more consequence to them than you may imagine."

But Mr. Thomas was never inclined to give impracticable advice. Before long he began to feel that he had perhaps been rather uncompromising. It is all very well to say "Pay your bills and collect your debts," but both of these things may be difficult to accomplish at a given time. Hence, in 1798, he somewhat modifies the rigor of his doctrine, but without abandoning the excellent principle which he wishes to enforce: —

Now to preserve a good understanding and continue in friendship with friends and neighbours, call upon all those you have had any dealing with the preceding year, and make a complete settlement; pay them off, if convenient, if the balance be in their favour — if in yours and they find it not convenient to pay, put it to the new account and pass receipts. By practising this method you will not only be able to ascertain your neat income, but prevent those disagreeable altercations and petty law-suits which take place too often between man and man from a delay of settlement.

"Scoring charges up" comes in for a touch of good-natured satire in the Almanac for 1806 (December): —

There is little to be done this month except to enjoy the fruit of your past labour; but in the first place make a settlement of accounts with all. I trust you have continually kept an account book; if not, obtain one immediately, and depend no longer on your memory, nor on promiscuous chalks, marks and scratches about the walls of your house.

Before long Mr. Thomas discovered that by a rigid adherence to his first scheme in the arrangement of the

Farmer's Calendar, this column, which was one of the most original features of his annual, and which had much to do with its great and immediate popularity, would become intolerably monotonous. With his usual frank and humorous good-nature he at once took his readers into his confidence and explained his dilemma. Thus in January, 1799, he began as follows: —

Ever desirous that the FARMER'S CALENDAR might be useful to those for whom it is designed, induces the Editor to be attentive in making experiments, and collecting observations from men eminent for improvements in Agriculture. Notwithstanding which, there will appear a sameness in pursuing each month, which is unavoidable while the seasons continue the same.

Accordingly he soon ceased to limit himself to directions about what to plant and when, or to cataloguing the " works and days." Though such matters are not neg-lected, we find little moral and prudential observations interspersed. Here is one from the Calendar for May, 1811. The text of the brief sermon is a proverb which still has a certain appropriateness: —

Boston folks, they say, *are full of notions* — and so are country folks. By this time perhaps you think that I am a silly, notional creature. No matter for that. Perhaps it is but a notion, but I think it will be for our interest to gratify these Boston people in their notions, by raising peas, beans, beets, carrots, cabbage, squashes, turnips and potatoes &c. for their market. If you would know how this is to be done, go and look in your old almanacks.

The " notions " of Boston folks included, in 1817, a fine discrimination in cider, as appears from an item under September: —

'There are a power of things,' said uncle Zachariah, 'to be attended to this month; and what is of much consequence, is

our cider; my neighbour Dupy has got a nack of making his cider so good and nice, that he gets about double price for all of it. The Boston folks have got a taste of it, and they are full of notions, as the saying is, you know, and they love good things and will give a good price for them too. Now no sooner is my neighbour Dupy's cider ready for market, than they grab it as quick as a hound will a wood-chuck, and pay him his price down upon the nail. Zuckers, John, let's try what we can do!'

Here is Mr. Thomas's opinion of dogs, which is not favorable. Incidentally we get a rather drastic picture of low life in the country. The exclamation points are Mr. Thomas's own: —

Now I know of no use for a great lazy dog in a family, yet there are many poor people who keep them, and seem to be more fond of Jowler than of their children. It is not more than a year since I sent my black man on an errand into a neighbour-hood of people, who were generally all poor. When he returned, he said he had been treated with a good meal of boiled pork and potatoes, but he sat down with a large family of ragged hungry children and three large fat dogs, without either knife, fork or spoon upon the table. The woman pulled the pork apart with her fingers for her family, and Sip made use of his jacknife for himself!!! (May, 1813.)

Frugality was so essential on the New England farm that it is not surprising that Mr. Thomas lays frequent emphasis on this virtue. But he was a liberal man himself, and he knew the difference between saving and scraping. He believed in a good table and thought it stupid for a farmer to neglect his opportunities. His catalogue of "garden sauce" is appetizing enough: —

Beans, peas, young potatoes, carrots, beets, squashes, cabbage, turnips, onions, green corn, apples, pears, plumbs, cucumbers, water and musk melons; every variety of vegetables are to be

found in Boston market — and they are all very nice, comfortable
and convenient to the inhabitants; but I never yet ate any of
them there that so well suited my palate, as those taken immediately from my own garden.   Here we have the advantage of our
friends in town.   They have them not till after they have become
more or less wilted, dead and tasteless; but we use them fresh
from the ground, which makes them much more palatable and
wholesome.   My neighbour, Oldfield, however never cares for
these, if he can get a plenty of salt beef, turnip and stewed
pumpkin.   He is for no extravagances at his table; though it
has been reported that he once went so far as to suffer his wife
to make a mince pye out of liver and turnip; but it was on an
important occasion, when the parson and his lady made them a
visit.   Economy is to be recommended, but I hate a niggard.
(July, 1813.)

Another reason for cultivating the kitchen garden is
given in the Calendar for May, 1807, — two reasons,
indeed; but how seriously the second of them was meant
to be taken is problematical.   At all events, Mr. Thomas
was not a bigoted vegetarian.

Plant garden seeds, such as beans, peas, squashes, melons, &c.
Farmers in general too much neglect their gardens.   The more
sauce we eat, the less meat we want, and that the latter costs
much more than the former, I need not tell you.   Animal food
has a tendency, it is said, to make man ferocious like dogs, wolves
and tigers, whereas vegetables incline them to docility and
kindness.

Here is a paragraph relating to fretfulness, economy,
and that old New England institution the " hired man,"
— three subjects which the author shows some skill in
bringing together under one head: —

You have now probably hired a man for a few months, to help
along with your work — If you have a good faithful one, then

set store by him and treat him well, and, mind me now, don't
you fret. — *Steady, boys, steady*, is the song for a farmer — If
you get yourself into a habit of continually fretting, as some do,
then it is ten to one if you can get good men to work for you.
But some prefer a dull, lazy lubber, because he is cheap! but
these *cheap* fellows I never want on my farm.   (May, 1815.)

As time went on, and his literary courage developed,
Mr. Thomas found a complete remedy for the sameness
which at first seemed inseparable from his plan. He
gradually fell more and more into the attitude of a general
mentor, not confining himself to purely agricultural or
even prudential counsels, and he gave freer play to his
natural *bonhomie* and homely sense of humor. Popular
proverbs were interspersed. Little character sketches, under whimsical names indicative of the person described,
began to make their appearance in the Farmer's Calendar
column, and these sometimes took shape in brief apologues
or anecdotes which are still good reading and which must
have been peculiarly welcome to his agricultural patrons.

So clear cut are some of the little sketches that they were
now and again given a personal application by the readers
of the time, who took keen delight in recognizing various
local celebrities, of good or evil repute, in the *genre* pictures
so cleverly sketched by the philosopher of Sterling. Mr.
Thomas even found it necessary to warn his readers that
the portraits were typical, not individual, and that he was
not ambitious to be regarded as a personal satirist: —

"What a strange mass of nonsense this almanack-maker sends
out every year," cried an old codger the other day. "And now
I affairm, I believe our *Suzy* could write as nice as he does; and,
now you, I thought he was rather too tight upon Mr. Captain
Bluster." I told the good old man that, in the Farmer's Calendar no particular person was ever meant to be satirized by any
thing there written. He appeared to be satisfied and went off to

taking in his cabbages; housing his tools, and preparing for winter as all of us should now be doing. (November, 1810.)

This caveat is itself a racy little bit of portraiture, and the ingenious transition to the duties of the season is delightful. The passage which the "old codger" thought a little too severe may be found under July of the year before (1809): —

Steady is the word with good farmers. You may begin to hoe your corn for the last time; but 't is said that Captain Bluster in the heat of his passion to finish haying before any other in town, has forgotten to hoe his corn but once! The proverb says, *he who fixeth his soul on show, loseth reality.* Keep your earliest cucumbers for seed.

Mr. Thomas's disclaimer was undoubtedly sincere. Yet his characters are too lifelike to be regarded as mere typical abstractions or composite photographs. He was a shrewd observer, with a keen eye for points, and he knew the country. Hence his sketches form a valuable, as well as an extremely diverting, series of documents for the student of manners and morals in New England. Their snatches of colloquial dialogue lend them also some significance as examples of the Yankee dialect. No apology is needed, then, for the reproduction, without further preamble, of several choice specimens of Mr. Thomas's humorous portraiture.

[OLD HUNKS.]

Hunks possesses a large interest, yet is afraid of coming to want. He has also a monstrous appetite for news; wants to read all the newspapers, yet will take none himself. What an excellent member of society such a man makes! How favoured is that town which can have the supreme honour of boasting of his citizenship! In the society of such men, publick spirit would thrive like a clover field, and its sweet fragrance be scented from afar. (December, 1808.)

[GOING TO MEETING.]

Good morning, Squire Thimbleberry! So then you are carrying out your whole family to meeting this morning to hear the new-year's sermon? "O yes, Mr. Weatherwise, I always intend that my family shall attend meeting at all times of the year, and on every Sunday unless they have special reason for staying at home. There are a few fashionable bucks in the neighborhood who would persuade my boys to go to the tavern rather than the church; but, by my troth, sir, may I see my sons borne to their graves sooner than follow the practices of these swelling, swearing, swaggering, smoking, soaking, fopish, fuddling fools! Zounds, sir, I have no patience, when I think on the folly of the times." (January, 1815.)

[HASTE MAKES WASTE.]

Do not get in your hay half made, merely to get done haying before your neighbour. This kind of sport will do for boys — but sober, rational and prudent farmers will be guilty of no such follies — you might as well, for the sake of dispatch, tumble your beef half bred and without salt into your meat tub. 'I well remember,' said neighbor Simpkins, 'when I was a boy, old capt. Swash declared he would be done haying one year before any body. So he hired Tom, Dick and Harry, and at it they all went — half cut their grass and half made their hay, and to be sure got done about the time that others began. Next morning he put on his great coat and walked up and down the street, complaining of cold weather, &c. My father understood the intended joke, but only said, *haste makes waste;* and this maxim was verified in the foolish conduct of capt. Swash, for before spring his mow smoked like a dung heap, and his cattle could not eat his hay, which being scarce he had to pay a high price for, to keep his cattle alive.' (July, 1815.)

[THE FARMER'S CONCERT.]

"Music, there, music!" Aye, boy, the music of the flail and cider-mill, you mean. Well, John, let's put things in order, that we may give them the farmer's concert. Let the cider-mill scream the treble — Caleb and Jo. shall slambang the tenor with their flails; neighbour Flatstall's bull will keep up the fundamental bass; while Ben Bluster will hollow the counter, with *Kid up, old Dobbin! Whoe, gee, Spark! Come in there, Berry! All together now, I say!* (September, 1816.)

[OLD BETTY BLAB.]

"Rumour is a pipe blown by surmises, jealousies, conjectures; and of so easy and so plain a stop, that the blunt monster with uncounted heads, the still discordant wavering multitude, can play upon it." Old Betty Blab is a dabster on this instrument; she knows exactly how to time and to key her tune to give the proper effect; she can perform in diatonic, cromatic, or enharmonic with vast variety and astonishing modulation. Sometimes you will hear her whizzing and twittering aloft, like a swallow or curlew; then in a moment she will drop into the croaking of a cormorant; then, by a sort of *twisty-cum-quirk*, she passes into the *bob-a-lincorn*, and here she excells all description. Next succeeds a touch of the affectuoso, and then this delightful solo ends in a sort of whisper, like the notes of an humble bee in a pumpkin blossom. It is impossible for me to do justice in describing her powers. In all her compositions she is a master hand in *thorough base*. Your garden must be attended to; a plenty of sauce greatly diminishes the butcher's bill. (April, 1817.)

[PUTTING ON AIRS.]

Now, if you want time to pass away, go, buy an old horse or watch, give your note for 60 days and you will be gratified. Where is the benefit in allowing young Ebenezer to swagger around with a paltry old watch in his pocket and a seal as big as

a kitten's head, puffing his segar like a wind broken horse? O, it is passing strange that we should let the wholesome habits of good old times pass away and be forgotten. Send your boys to school and see that they are also learnt something at home. The barn-floor, — the linter — the flail & the curry-comb are not to be neglected. To be sure it is well enough, and indeed it is very proper to have recreation; but to have nothing else doing will ultimately bring ruin. Either the body or mind must be engaged in honest industry; for idleness is like grog — take nothing else and — "you 're gone, man." (February, 1819.)

[THE LOTTERY.]

I wish you a happy new year, Mr. Reader, but I fear you will not find it. I have seen forty years, no one of which has been free from care and anxiety. To be sure I have often imagined that I had lit upon the path where happiness had passed along, and fancied I should very soon be saluted with the brightness of her countenance. *Here — here !* cried I to neighbor Simpkins, *here is the way.* See — every guide board *points in this direction.* 'Ah, zuckins,' cries neighbor Simpkins, 'you will soon find yourself mistaken. Your path leads down to the gloomy pits of ruin. Your charming enticer is in reality a haggard hobgoblin — look out, neighbor, look out.' I was putting my hand in my pocket book to take out a bill to purchase a ticket in the lottery, but my neighbor's caution prevented my throwing away my money in this manner. ' Here,' said I to my boy, ' here, Tom, take this *five dollar bill* to the widow Lonesome ; tell her, it is at her disposal; then hasten back to your school. I will to my team and my wood-lot.' (January, 1813.)

[THE IDES OF MARCH.]

" Pray, Uncle Jacob," cried old Goody Dowdy to one of my neighbours, who is said to know a great deal about the weather and the stars, and the planets, and all the signs and wonders in the heavens, "what do they mean by the Ides of March?"

" Tut," says Uncle Jacob, " easy enough answered — why, madam, the Ides were eight old women, the Nones nine, and Calind another, making eighteen in the whole. Their breath was poison as the effluvia of asps. In the month of March, particularly when other folks kept in, by reason of bad going, these old hags were sure to be abroad, blurting and puffing their venom against every good reputation, to which they were mortal enemies. Old mother Calind took the lead, next went the Nones, and last the Ides followed as gleaners. To whatsoever was true, honest, just, pure, lovely, or of good report, their breath was as blasting and mildew. These monsters are now no more ; but they so leavened the world with their abominable practices that their influence will never be eradicated." (March, 1816.)

[MARGARET AND THE MARE.]

" My dear Margaret, heaven gave you not that sweet voice to be employed in scolding ; nor those delicate features to be disfigured with anger. Softly, my dear, softly. You see I am about to go, head and ears, right into the swamp to get muck for manure. The mare cannot go by any means, as we shall want her in the team. The ladies must put by their ride, otherwise I shall lose this opportunity of carting my compost ; and you must know, my dear, that mud is money to a farmer." " By jinks," retorts madam, " the mare shan't go ? my word for 't but she shall ! yes, here's a husband for a horse ! The mare shall go in spite of men, money, or mud." (November, 1816.)

[TRADITION AND PARSNIPS.]

" A happy new year to you, Mr. Comfortable ; will you lend me a mess of parsneps for dinner ? " " Parsneps ! what, lend parsneps ? No, I will give you some ; but have you raised none ? " " Why, yes ; but I never dig mine till spring. I think they are a great deal better for it. This used to be my father's and grandfather's practice, and I approve of it as the best plan." " Poh, nonsense ! The best plan to keep yours in the ground, and so

beg parsneps all winter, rather than vary from a superstitious and foolish notion of your grandmother ! " " Ichabod, my son," said goody Slipshod, " never dig your parsneps in the fall. Depend upon it, you 'll never prosper, Ichabod, if you vary from the good old rules of your grandfather, Catnip. You can borrow once in a while from Squire D. and so pay in the spring. That is the safest, my son." Fudge, fudge ! Let fools enjoy their folly, and we 'll enjoy our parsneps and pot luck. Dig them about the last of November. Keep them in a cool cellar or out house, covered with dry sand or sods. They will be sweet and excellent food for man or beast. They require a deep, rich, mellow, and rather a sandy soil to be sweetest. (January, 1830.)

[TAXES ARE HIGH.]

My old friends and worthy patrons, it is pleasant once more to come among you, and to salute you with the cordiality of long-established friendship. Toil and care, and occasional perplexities, may wrinkle our brows and grizzle our locks, but our employment never tends to sour our tempers or cause any uncouth greetings. We drive our teams with merry hearts, and every thing pertaining to our occupation inculcates a spirit of gratitude and thanksgiving. In the sweat of the brow, to be sure, we toil for the pittance which Providence awards to industry ; but this labour and exercise also bring health of both body and mind. When winter, with its iron jaws, clinches upon the face of nature, shuts every pore, and arrests the process of vegetation, we are not without our innocent employments and rational enjoyments. We sit not in moping melancholy, growling and snarling, like angry mastiffs, at the prosperity of industrious neighbours ; neither do we churlishly retort to a goodnatured and gentle salute of " How fare ye, Mr. Ploughbeam ? " We indeed would use the whole passing world, as well as ourselves, without abuse ; knowing that in a little while we must depart. Why then should we not try to be happy? " Ah, well," says old Pinchback, " you preach curiously, but taxes are darn'd high." (January, 1832.)

[THE CATTLE SHOW.]

This is the month for cattle shows, and other agricultural exhibitions — Premiums are offered by various societies for the greatest crops; the best stock, and the best domestic manufactures, and thousands are pulling away for the prize, with all their might.

The great Bull of Farmer Lumpkins is a nosuch !

Peter Nibble has raised a monstrous field of white beans !

Jo Lucky's acre of corn has seven stout ears to the stalk !

Dolly Dilligence has outstript all in the bonnet line !

Tabitha Twistem's hearth rug is up to all Market-street !

The Linsey-Woolsey Manufacturing Company have made the finest piece of satinet that ever mortals set eyes on !

There is the widow Clacket's heifer, she is to be driven !

And, O, if you could only see 'Squire Trulliber's great boar ! They say it is as big as a full grown rhinoceros !

Huzza, huzza for the premiums ! Here's to the girl that can best darn a stocking, and to the lad that shall raise the biggest pumpkin ! (October, 1824.)

[THE BAKER.]

Hark ! 't is the jingle of the baker's bells. Hot bread, who buys? Have a care now, Mr. Sweetmouth, how you let this bill run up. Wheat loaves, gingerbread, hot buns and seed-cakes — these are all very clever. But there is my aunt Sarah's brown bread, sweet, pleasant and wholesome ; don't give it up for a cartload of muffins and jumbles. There is no discount on my aunt Sarah's cooking ; she is the personification of neatness and nicety. Give me a plate of her nutcakes in preference to all the sweetmeats of the city. It has become somewhat fashionable to cast off old *Rye-and-Indian* for *Genesee, Howard-street,* &c. — also to give up heating the oven. I imagine that this change is vastly convenient for the shoe-peggers. "Tell the baker he may leave us half a dozen of his three cent biscuit," said Mrs. Crispin. Now

three times six are eighteen, and eighteen times 365 are $65.70 —
whew! This will never do. In our haste to get rich, we must
look at both ends of the railcut. Bread is denominated the *staff*
of life, the main supporting food; but this so important article
may, as well as a whistle, come too dear. Let your good wife,
then, have her own hands in the kneading trough, nor heed too
much the morning music of the baker's boy. (May, 1837.)

In 1813 the whole of the Farmer's Calendar for three
months (October to December) is occupied by a continuous narrative sketch: —

My neighbor Freeport had a knack at telling a story, cracking
a joke and singing a song, and these talents made him a favourite
of his townsmen. Every town meeting and training was sure
to gather round him a crowd of jovial fellows, and my neighbour
pretty soon added to his other acquisitions that of handsomely
swigging a glass of grog. The demands for stories, jokes and
songs encreased with the reward he received for them; and
Freeport had not a heart to refuse either, till the tavern became
his common resort. But while Freeport was so musical at the
tavern his affairs got out of tune at home. His wife took a high
pitch, and often gave him an unwelcome solo. Her stories had
much of pith, and her sarcasms were of the keenest sort. She
insisted that their affairs were going to rack and ruin. Sometimes the neighbour's cattle had broken into the corn — the
rye had been ruined by laying out in the storm — the hogs had
broken in and rooted up the garden — the hay was half lost for
want of attention — the fences were broken down, &c. &c. And
then the children — (October.)

Alas! the poor children were shoeless, coatless and heartless;
for they had become the scoff and sport of their little companions
by reason of their father's neglect to provide them with decent
and comfortable apparel. They were unable to read, for they
had no books. The sheep — here the poor woman sorely wept
— were sold by the collector to pay taxes. So there was no
chance for any wool to knit the children's stockings. No flax

had been raised, and of course they could have no shirts. To hear all this and ten times more was not very welcome to the ears of Freeport, whose heart was naturally tender and humane, so to get rid of it, he used to return to the tavern like a sow to her wallowing. His shop bills run up fast, while his character was running down. In this way he went on about two years, till old Scrapewell and Screwpenny got his farm; for all this time these usurers had been lending him money, and thus encouraging him to pursue this dreadful course. (November.)

Old Capt. Gripe also came in for a share of poor Freeport's estate; and there was Plunket, the cobler, he had lent him nine pence several times and now had cobbled it up to a court demand. Bob Raikins had swapped watches with him, and came in for the boot. The widow Nippet had lent him her mare twice to mill and once to a funeral, and had sold the boys an old tow jacket for a peck of whortleberries, and also given them a mess of turnips, and so she made out her account and got a writ. Tom Teazer, well known at the grog shops for a dabster at shoemaker loo, old Jeremiah Jenkins, the Jew, Stephen Staball, the butcher, and all the village moon-cursers came in for their portion of the wreck. So poor Freeport gave up vessel and cargo to these land pirates, sent his disconsolate wife again to her father with one of their babes, the rest were provided for by the town; and as for himself, miserable wretch, he became an outcast, a vagabond, and died drunk in the highway! (December.)

There is undeniable merit in this unpretentious narrative. It is somewhat crude, to be sure, but any attempt at polish would have defeated the author's purpose. The tragedy is humble, and even sordid, but it is complete and unsparing; it moves forward pitilessly to the bitter end with the steadiness of fate. Some of the details are hardly susceptible of improvement. The matter-of-fact brutality of poor Freeport's petty creditors is a fine piece of vigorous realism. What could be better in its way than the single brief sentence which pillories the village sharper: " Bob

Raikins had swapped watches with him, and came in for the boot"! It is a masterpiece of suggestive reticence.

The secret of Mr. Thomas's success in this little story is easy to discover: he was not trying to be " literary "; he was writing of what he had seen and known. The contrast is striking between the Tragedy of Neighbor Freeport, hidden away in the Farmer's Calendar, and the attempts at formal story-writing familiar to the student of American letters in the columns of the literary journals of the time.

One or two points in the sketch may require a word of comment. " Shoemaker loo " was a round game at cards. How it differed from ordinary loo does not appear. " Moon-curser " is not in the dictionaries, but it ought to be, for it is a highly picturesque and imaginative word. A moon-curser is a wrecker. Of that there is no doubt, for the term is still in use on Cape Cod, and probably elsewhere. Its origin is conjectural, but admits of little doubt. The old-time wrecker was not an angel of mercy. To him, as to the witches in Macbeth, fair was foul and foul was fair. Darkness and storm were his opportunities, and he *cursed the moon*, whose light deprived him of his chance for plunder. Another application of the term may be seen in Richard Head's Canting Academy, 1673 : —

The Moon Curser is generally taken for any *Link-Boy;* but particularly he is one that waits at some Corner of Lincolns-Inn-Fields with a Link in his hand, who under the pretence of Lighting you over the Fields, being late and few stiring, shall light you into a Pack of Rogues that wait for the comming of this Setter, and so they will all joyne in the Robbery.

Some of these were found to be Labourers so called, such who wrought all day in the Ruins of the City and were paid by their Master Workmen, and at night found an easier way to pay themselves by lying in the Ruins, and as they saw occasion would drag in people into Vaults and Cellars and there rob them.[1]

[1] P. 101.

One is tempted to go on indefinitely with the Old Farmer's sketches of life and manners, and the stock is by no means exhausted, but enough has been quoted to show not only their literary interest but their significance for the student of social conditions in New England.

7

LAWYERS AND QUACKS

"THE best houses in Connecticut are inhabited by lawyers," wrote Henry Wansey in 1794.[1] Here was a great change from the state of things when Thomas Lechford found it so hard to practise his profession in Boston that he was constrained to warn the colonists not to " despise learning, nor the worthy lawyers of either gown (civil or ecclesiastical), lest you repent too late." [2] But there were corners of New England in which the old order long maintained itself, and one of these was West Boylston, the home of Mr. Thomas. When, in 1826, the local minister, the Rev. Mr. Crosby, wrote his brief history of the town for the Worcester Magazine, he remarked that there were three justices of the peace, one of them being Mr. Thomas himself, but that they had little to do and that there was no resident man of law.[3]

It was natural, then, as well as sensible, for the Almanac to bid its readers beware of litigation. " I would not run to 'Squire Fraylove," says Mr. Thomas in the Farmer's Calendar for April, 1815, " at every petty dispute with a troublesome neighbour. You will be sure to be advised to a suit, and then comes business enough." And still earlier, in December, 1810, after a hearty commendation

---

[1] Journal of an Excursion to the United States of North America in the Summer of 1794, Salisbury, 1796, p. 70.

[2] Plaine Dealing, 1642, p. 28; ed. Trumbull, p. 68.

[3] Worcester Magazine and Historical Journal, August, 1826, II, 201. West Boylston was set off from Sterling and Boylston in 1808 (cf. pp. 4–5, above).

of married life, the farmer's counsellor has a sly fling at
the legal profession: —

Now having been industrious in the summer, you will have the
felicity of retiring from the turbulence of the storm to the bosom
of your family. Here is divine employment. Surely if happiness
can any where be found on earth, 't is in the sweet enjoyment of
the fireside, surrounded by a domestic throng — a lovely wife and
prattling babes. Ye cold and barren fens of celibacy, behold
the delightful regions of matrimony! Leave your frigid abodes,
and come and dwell in society, and taste the rational pleasures of
a connubial state. *Lawyers gowns are lined with the wilfulness
of their clients.* Then let us be accommodating and not run to
the lawyer at every little offence. An honest and upright attorney
is an advantage to a town; but one that is ready to set his neighbors at variance to govern a few thereby is a pest to society.
'T is not likely that we have many of the last description in New
England as we have so very *small a number* in the whole.

The distinction between honest attorneys and pettifoggers is clearly made, but the closing sentence ingeni-
ously takes back a large portion of the compliment that
precedes it. Yet it is clear that Mr. Thomas made a sharp
distinction between reputable men of law and pretenders.
Of the latter there seem to have been a good many in
the country districts. John Adams, in 1760, speaks of
"the multiplicity of pettifoggers" in Braintree, which had
become proverbial for litigation, and specifies one " Captain H.," who, he says, "has given out that he is a sworn
attorney till nine tenths of this town really believe it." [1]

In December, 1818, Mr. Thomas varies his usual advice
to settle up the year's accounts by introducing some
reflections on going to law: —

Now prepare your papers and make it a business to go round
and settle with all your neighbours with whom you have accounts

[1] Works, ed. C. F. Adams, Boston, 1850, II, 90–91.

open. Avoid wrangling and law fighting. It is never worth your while to go to law at the expense of $500 about nine pence ; but should you ever be forced into a law suit, take the advice of respectable counsel and then keep your tongue within your teeth. If you foolishly blab your case to your neighbours they will all, men, women and children, become prodigiously wise and know-ing. They will talk law at a great rate, and distress you with their wisdom.

Five kinds of pestilence are associated in a single prayer for immunity in August, 1813 : —

From quack lawyers, quack doctors, quack preachers, mad dogs and yellow fever, good Lord, deliver us! This is my sincere prayer, let others do and say as they will. A respectable attorney is an advantage to a town and ought to have the esteem of his fellow citizens ; but a meddlesome pettifogger deserves the treatment of any other sneaking puppy that runs his nose into your closet. As for strolling preachers, 'O ye generation of vipers'! I would hear any evil far better than the gabble of one of these intruding boobies. Yet how many forsake all business and pleasure that they may enjoy the ecstatic bliss of listening to their empty disgusting and blasphemous nonsense! It is a serious misfortune to have a woman, a head of a family, yet be-witched by one of these fellows. Whenever this happens, farewell to all business, to all comfort! No more dairy, no more spinning or weaving or knitting or sewing. Forenoon, afternoon and evening nothing but attending lectures to hear the charming, the pious, the godly Mr. Bitemslily — totally regardless of that text of the sacred volume which says 'six days *shalt thou labour* and do all thy work.'

For physicians and ministers, as well as for upright attorneys, Mr. Thomas had plenty of respect, but he could not abide a charlatan. Quack doctors come in elsewhere for some rather slashing satire. Thus in September, 1806, we read : — " *There are a great many asses without long ears.*

Quack, Quack, went the ducks, as doctor Motherwort rode by with his saddle-bags stuffed with maiden-hair, and golden-rod. Don't let your wife send Tommy to the academy six weeks, and make a novice of him."

And in September, 1813, there is a drastic description of "the famous Dr. Dolt": "A larnt man is the doctor. Once he was a simple knight of the lapstone and pegging awl; but now he is blazoned in the first orders of quack heraldry. The mighty cures of the doctor are known far round. He is always sure to kill the disorder, although in effecting this he sometimes kills the patient."

An agreeable and ingenuous letter addressed to Mr. Thomas in 1801, by an esteemed correspondent in Franklin, Massachusetts, called out a comparison not very flattering to the legal profession. The writer is worried by the apparent neglect to answer certain questions proposed in the Almanac five years before. He expostulates with the editor in a strain of dignified forbearance, and improves the occasion to commend the work highly. His letter was printed in the Almanac for 1802, with a full reply to each of the problems. The reader will remember that both millers and tailors had, in old times, a reputation for pilfering.

MR. THOMAS,

In looking over the Farmer's Almanack for the year 1796, I there found four *Miscellaneous Questions*, viz. 1st. Whether the Sun goes round the earth and the earth stands still? &c. 2dly. Which is counted the most honest employment of the three folowing, viz. a Tailor, a Lawyer, or a Miller? 3dly. Whether the Shrub commonly called Fern, bears or produces any seed? &c. 4thly. How long it is since smoking tobacco, and taking of snuff, has been in use in England; the time when? &c.

Now, SIR, I have been a constant patron of your Almanack, and have waited in anxious expectations these four years last past, of seeing answers to the above questions, but have ever been disappointed; I would not be misunderstood, SIR, that you

intended to deceive your patrons, or to cast any reflections on your ability to answer them, for the precepts and observations you have given in your preceding numbers thoroughly demonstrate your knowledge of natural philosophy; but rather to some accident they have slipped your memory.

I must say I have been highly pleased with your Almanack, and posterity anticipate your further usefulness as a man of reading and observation. I doubt not but that your Almanack will very soon exceed in circulation any other published in the United States, and I may venture to say, without *flattery*, it now is equal to any in estimation. Therefore, SIR, I humbly hope, that in your next number (viz. X.) I shall see your answers to the above questions.

I am, Sir, with sincere Esteem,

Your must humble Servant,

Franklin, March 10, 1801.   S. H.

ANSWERS.

To the MISCELLANEOUS QUESTIONS in the FARMER'S ALMANACK for the Year 1796.

Answer to Question 1st. — I AGREE with the best modern astronomers, that the Sun is an immoveable centre, round which the planets (of which the earth is one) move by different revolutions. But the figure, which the earth annually describes, is not circular, but elliptical or oval; which is the reason why it does not continue equidistant from the Sun. But as once a year it travels round the Sun, so in the compass of 24 hours it moves round its own axis; whence arises the alternate succession of day and night.

2d. — Fie! join a lawyer with such company; they hold no comparison with each other! I know what you'll say, that the miller's clacks, and the lawyer's clacks are in perpetual motion, with the like sound and sense; and that as the first grinds down your corn, the other grinds down the land it grows upon. But then the lawyer is in a fair way to break the miller. You may urge too, that the tailor and lawyer equally ruin you with their

long bills; but then, consider, the tailor's bill is full of fustian-
nonsense, scrolls, blots, and repetitions of the same things, differ-
ently placed, and, by consequence, not worthy your understanding;
whilst your lawyer, in his cramp law terms, is as much above your
understanding, and therefore preferable : and tho' you know not
what you give your money for to either, yet, certainly, any would
give more for a parcel of fine significant words, than for so many
false spelt blunders. 'T is true, they both furnish you with suits;
but which is the best workman, the tailor, who must have matter
to work upon, or the lawyer, who can make a long suit out of
nothing? Your tailor's suit is gone in half a year, but the lawyer's
will last often to your posterity; suppose he hurries you out of
breath upon a wrong scent, yet then he will give you time by a
writ of error or demurrer, to recover yourself, and keep in fast
friendship to you whilst you have the strength of one fee left.
And though he runs some out of their estates, he often gives to
others other people's estates, which is yet some compensation.
Say, he then manages the cause accordingly, which is something
analogical to equity; nay, put the worst, that you are quite ruined;
he tells you it comes from your own mis-informing of him, which,
whether you apprehend or not, you ought to believe, as supposing
he best understands what belongs to his own business. Now
your miller and tailor are by no means capacitated for such fine
qualifications as these.

The replies to the third and fourth questions need not
be reprinted, since they are less interesting nowadays than
they were in 1802.

We may close this brief chapter with a quotation from
the diary of Dr. Nathaniel Ames the younger, himself a
composer of almanacs, which belongs to this same year: —

A Lawyer in every man's mess here, nothing will go with Fools
without a Lawyer, but from good company they are excluded!
or if they get in, they spoil it.[1]

[1] April 3, 1802, Dedham Historical Register, XI, 103.

THE TOAD AND THE SPIDER

HERE is an item of natural history from Rhode Island. It is extracted from the Almanac for 1798: —

A TOAD was seen fighting with a spider in Rhode-Island; and when the former was bit, it hopped to a plantain leaf, bit off a piece, and then engaged with the spider again. After this had been repeated sundry times, a spectator pulled up the plantain, and put it out of the way. The toad, on being bit again, jumped to where the plantain had stood; and as it was not to be found, she hopped round several times, turned over on her back, swelled up, and died immediately. This is an evident demonstration that the juice of the plantain is an antidote against the bites of those venomous insects.[1]

Nothing could be simpler or more straightforward than this anecdote. It bears every appearance of being a mere bit of local observation. Yet there is a good deal to be learned about the story, for it turns out, on examination, to be a variant of a widespread piece of legendary lore. Van Helmont, the great Flemish chemist and medical reformer, who died in 1644, may be summoned as the first witness. In his treatise on the Plague he tells almost exactly the same tale, on the authority of a noble lady of his acquaintance: —

[1] Plantain, by the way, is said by Josselyn, in his New England's Rarities Discovered, 1672, to be one of the herbs that "have sprung up since the English planted and kept cattle in New England." The Indians, he tells us, call it "Englishman's foot, as though produced by their treading" (ed. Tuckerman, p. 217).

And indeed the Lady of *Rommerswal* Toparchesse in *Ecchove,*
a noble, affined, and honest Matron, related to me in candour of
spirit, that she once beheld a duel between a Spider, and a Toad,
for a whole afternoon : For this, when he felt himself to be stricken
by the Spider descending from above, and that he was presently
swollen in his head, he runs to an herb which he licked, and
being most speedily cured, his swelling asswaged ; from whence he
setting upon a repeated fight, was again also smitten in his head,
and hastened unto the same herb ; And when as the thing had now
the third time happened, the Spectatresse being tired, cut off the
Plant with her knife (but it was the Plantain with a narrow leaf)
and when as the Toad returned thither the fourth time, and found
not the herb, he most speedily swelled all over, and being sore
smitten with terrour, presently died : But he betook not himself
unto the neighboring plants of the same Plantain, and those
frequently growing (for the image of the conception of fear, and
sorrow, produceth a speedy death, the hope of a most speedy
remedy perisheth in a most furious disease) for when he found
not his own Plantain, he who before encountred from a hope of
presently recovering, forthwith despairing through fear and an
idea of terrour, died.[1]

Van Helmont explains the remissness of the toad in
accordance with his peculiar system of medical philosophy,
but his narrative coincides in almost every particular with
the report from Rhode Island.

From Flanders we may pass to England.   There the duel
between the Toad and the Spider received poetical treatment at the hands of Richard Lovelace, whose studies
were not of a kind to acquaint him with Van Helmont's
dissertation.   The piece in question was first published in
1659, but was written some time before.[2]   It begins with
all the pomp and circumstance of an epic.

[1] Tumulus Pestis, or the Plague-Grave, chap. 17, in Physick Refined, translated by John Chandler, London, 1662, p. 1151.
[2] Posthume Poems, 1659; see Lovelace's Poems, ed. Hazlitt, pp. 199 ff.

Upon a day when the Dog-star
Unto the world proclaim'd a war,
And poyson bark'd from his black throat,
And from his jaws infection shot,
Under a deadly hen-bane shade
With slime infernal mists are made,
Met the two dreaded enemies,
Having their weapons in their eyes.

After some skirmishing the Toad is bitten by the Spider:

And wounded now, apace crawls on
To his next plantane surgeon;
With whose rich balm no sooner drest,
But purged is his sick swoln breast;
And as a glorious combatant,
That only rests awhile to pant,
Then with repeated strength, and scars,
That smarting, fire him to new wars,
Deals blows that thick themselves prevent,
As they would gain the time he spent:
So the disdaining angry toad,
That calls but a thin useless load
His fatal feared self, comes back,
With unknown venome fill'd to crack.

Thus the combat is renewed. Bitten again, the Toad
returns to seek his antidote. But his opponent has a
divine ally, — no less a personage than the goddess Pallas,
whose interest in the struggle will not seem unnatural if
we remember the myth of Arachne, charmingly told by
Ovid in the sixth book of his Metamorphoses. The
Lydian maiden Arachne, proud of her skill in weaving,
had presumed to challenge Pallas herself to a match and
had produced a web which even the goddess could not
surpass. Pallas tore the fabric to pieces and smote her
audacious rival on the forehead. Arachne hanged herself,
but the goddess pitied her and forbade her dying. She
transformed Arachne into a spider, and in that shape the

Lydian damsel still practises her art. No wonder, then, that Pallas intervened in this duel as she did on a memorable occasion in the Trojan War. She summoned the Spider's protecting genius, and sent him to the plantain: —

> He learned was in Nature's laws,
> Of all her foliage knew the cause,
> And 'mongst the rest in his choice want
> Unplanted had this plantane plant.

So the Toad died, " with a dismal horrid yell."

From literature we may turn to science, and call in the evidence of an expert who had not only considered the question seriously, but had put its truth to a test that seems practically decisive. This investigator is Sir Thomas Browne, the learned physician of Norwich (1605–1682). In his Vulgar Errors, Sir Thomas devotes a whole chapter[1] to the Toad, discussing not only its venomous quality, but also the precious jewel which, according to Shakspere, it bears in its head. In another passage of the same work[2] he treats of the common belief in " the antipathy between a toad and a spider " and of the assertion " that they poisonously destroy each other." He could be well content to know the facts about these duels, since such knowledge might provide us with valuable antidotes. " But," he adds regretfully, " what we have observed herein, we cannot in reason conceal; who having in a glass included a toad with several spiders, we beheld the spiders, without resistance to sit upon his head and pass over all his body; which at last upon advantage he swallowed down, and that in few hours, unto the matter of seven."

As we bid farewell to the famous Duel of the Toad and the Spider, we may pause to note another New England combat, less widely notorious, but perhaps more strictly historical. It is recorded as occurring in Massachusetts

---

[1] Book iii, chap. 13. [2] Book iii, chap. 27, § 6.

in 1632, only two years after the settlement of Boston.
As we read the account of it which Governor Winthrop
gives in his Journal, we shall doubtless wonder what deep
significance the divines of the early colonial period would
have discovered in the Rhode Island marvel if it had
happened in their time: —

At Watertown there was (in the view of divers witnesses) a
great combat between a mouse and a snake; and, after a long
fight, the mouse prevailed and killed the snake. The pastor of
Boston, Mr. Wilson, a very sincere, holy man, hearing of it, gave
this interpretation : That the snake was the devil; the mouse was
a poor contemptible people, which God had brought hither, which
should overcome Satan here, and dispossess him of his kingdom.[1]

To appreciate the Rev. Mr. Wilson's interpretation one
must remember that nobody doubted in the seventeenth
century that the Indians worshipped the Devil.   Cotton
Mather, who in such matters was but the child of his
time, held that the American continent was populated by
the special exertions of the foul fiend.   Satan, he con-
tended, " seduced the first inhabitants into it " in order to
keep them and their posterity " out of the sound of the
silver trumpets of the Gospel." [2]   And he quotes a converted sachem as declaring that he had " often employ'd
his god, which appear'd to him in form of a snake, to kill,
wound, and lame such whom he intended mischief to." [3]
As late as 1773, so enlightened a thinker as President
Stiles of Yale College had no doubt that " the Powaws of
the American Indians are a Relict of [the] antient System
of seeking to an evil invisible Power."   " Something of it,"
he adds, " subsists among some Almanack Makers [Note
that this was before the time of Mr. Thomas!] and Fortune

---

[1] Winthrop's History, ed. Savage, 1853, I, 97.
[2] Magnalia, book i, chap. i, § 2, ed. 1853, I, 42.
[3] Magnalia, book vi, chap. vi, § 3, ed. 1853.

Tellers . . . But in general the System is broken up, the Vessel of Sorcery shipwreckt, and only some shattered planks and pieces disjoyned floating and scattered on the Ocean of the human Activity and Bustle. When the System was intire, it was a direct seeking to Satan." [1]

There was nothing peculiar in the mental attitude of the New England divines toward the beliefs of the American Indians. It had always been the theory of the church that the heathen everywhere were devil-worshippers, and that sorcery and pagan sacrifices were but different varieties of Satanic ritual. Every reader will remember that the fallen angels are described by Milton as masquerading in the guise of the pagan divinities of old time, and in this idea the poet is in complete accord with the Greek and Latin fathers. It would be superfluous to multiply seventeenth-century evidence, but it may not be amiss to call in the testimony of the Jesuit missionaries in Canada. Father Lejeune, in 1635, after giving an account of a Huron medicine-woman, remarks: " Thus the devil beguiles this unfortunate people, substituting his impieties and superstitions for the conformity that they ought to have with the providence of God and the worship that they ought to render him." [2] And again, the medicine-men " are, in my opinion, genuine wizards, having access to the devil." [3] Father Jouvency identified the Manitou of the Acadian aborigines " beyond a doubt with the enemy of the human race." [4] And Father Biard, writing from Port Royal, declares that " though they have a kind of slender knowledge of the one most high God, yet they are so depraved in sentiments and practice that they also worship the devil." [5]

To Cotton Mather a Jesuit was scarcely less an object of

---

[1] Diary, June 13, 1773, ed. Dexter, I, 385–6.
[2] Jesuit Relations, ed. Thwaites, VIII, 126.
[3] The same, VIII, 124.
[4] The same, I, 286.
[5] The same, II, 76.

horror than an Indian powwow, and Father Lejeune would doubtless have reciprocated this feeling fully. Yet on the point of belief in the Satanic character of the Indian worship neither the Boston minister nor the French priest could have found anything objectionable in the teachings of the other.

It was this idea that the Indians were sorcerers and devil-worshippers that had no small part in the outbreak of superstition known as the Salem Witchcraft Delusion, though the causes of this particular tragedy were complex enough. The Indian woman Tituba was one of the three persons first accused of the crime, and her admissions were of great importance to the prosecutors. By 1793, however, when Mr. Thomas published his first Almanac, a far more rational temper prevailed among the clergy. In 1789 Dr. Jeremy Belknap, of honored memory, who had been reading Mather's Magnalia, wrote to his friend Hazard in terms of humorous good sense : —

Were I to preach on the subject of *witchcraft*, I would have this for my text : " O foolish Galatians ! who hath bewitched you ? " I would first endeavour to show that people may be *bewitched;* secondly, that they are great *fools* for being bewitched ; and, thirdly, that it concerns them to enquire *who* has bewitched them ; and my inference should be, if there were *no fools*, there would be *no witchcraft;* or rather I would transpose the second and third heads. The same inference would come out better.[1]

It should. not be forgotten that, even in the eighteenth century, few persons were absolutely convinced that witchcraft was an impossible crime. Enlightened opinion hardly went farther, in general, than to ridicule the absurdity of most witchcraft stories, to emphasize the ignorance of those who held to the old popular creed in this regard,

[1] Belknap Papers, Coll. Mass. Hist. Soc., 5th Series, III, 205.

and to refuse belief to this or that specific case of diabolical possession.   An out-and-out denial of the theoretical
possibility of witchcraft was quite a different matter.   Most
people were inclined to think that there had been witches
" in old times," — at all events, " in *Bible* times " ;   and nobody felt quite sure when compacts with the devil had
become obsolete.   Rationalism itself often turned pale at
specific phenomena, as indeed it sometimes does to-day.

Reckless denouncers of New England for the witchcraft
delusion of the seventeenth century forget many things — or
never knew them.   The wonder is, not that such an outbreak should have taken place, but that it should have
come to an end so soon.   The attack was as short as it
was sharp ;   and its sharpness was by no means extraordinary when compared with the violence with which the
disorder raged in other parts of the world.   Few persons
have the time or the inclination to explore the gloomy
literature of demonology ;   but it is not too much to ask of
the historical student, or even of the general reader, that
before he passes judgment on his ancestors in so weighty a
matter, he should make an attempt to put himself in contact with the history of European thought and with the
general state of opinion in the seventeenth and the early
eighteenth century.   One can at least read the witch stories
in the supplement to the Antidote against Atheism of Dr.
Henry More, the famous Cambridge Platonist, and in the
Triumph over the Sadducees [1] of Dr. Joseph Glanvil, who
was chaplain in ordinary to King Charles II, a Fellow of
the Royal Society, and the author of a celebrated treatise
on the Vanity of Dogmatizing.   Glanvil's witch-book appeared in a fourth edition as late as 1726, and was thought
to have demolished the arguments of the doubters.

A little reading of this kind is a good corrective spice,

---

[1] *Sadducismus Triumphatus* is the title, but the book is in English.   It
was first published in 1681.

as Lord Bacon would have called it.   Our whole difficulty
in estimating the significance of the troubles at Salem
comes from lack of perspective.   They make a great noise
in the annals of New England, and we find it hard not to
think of them as something monstrous or abnormal.   But
they were neither.   Deplorable as the witchcraft persecution was, it should not be treated hysterically or as if it
were an isolated phenomenon.   Here were the New Englanders settled on the edge of the wilderness and in daily
contact with a savage race whom all the world believed to
be worshippers of Satan.   They had brought from England the same beliefs in the intervention of the devil in
human affairs that everybody held, and they had seen no
occasion to modify them.   Nor had their countrymen who
remained at home in England suffered any change of
heart.   Is it reasonable to demand from the New Englanders, lay or clerical, exposed as they were to peculiar
terrors in a wild country, a degree of calm rationality
which was not found among their contemporaries in England "who sat at home at ease"?

There is nothing strange, then, in the outbreak of witchcraft persecution in Massachusetts.   It was inconceivable
that the Colony should pass through its first century without such a calamity.   The wonderful thing is that it did not
come sooner and last longer.   From the first pranks of Mr.
Parris's unhappy children (in February, 1692) to the col-
lapse of the prosecution in January, 1693, was less than a
year.   During the interval twenty persons had suffered
death, and two are known to have died in jail.[1]   If to
these we add a few sporadic cases, there is a total of between twenty-five and thirty victims; but this is the whole
reckoning, not merely for a year or two but for a complete century.   The concentration of the troubles in Massa-

[1] C. W. Upham, Salem Witchcraft, Boston, 1867, II, 351.

chusetts within the limits of a single year has given a wrong turn to the thoughts of many writers. This concentration makes the case more conspicuous, but it does not make it worse. On the contrary, it makes it better. It is astonishing that there should have been less than half a dozen executions for witchcraft in Massachusetts before 1692, and equally astonishing that the delusion, when it became acute, should have raged for but a year, and that but twenty persons should have been executed. The facts are distinctly creditable to our ancestors, — to their moderation and to the rapidity with which their good sense could reassert itself after a brief eclipse.

No one has ever made an accurate count of the executions for witchcraft in England in the seventeenth century, but they must have mounted into the hundreds.[1] Matthew Hopkins, the infamous "witch-finder general," is thought to have brought sixty persons to the gallows in Suffolk in 1645 and 1646; by his efforts fifteen were hanged in Essex in 1645 and sixteen at Yarmouth the year before. His confederate Stern puts the sum total of Hopkins's victims at two hundred.[2] In Scotland, where there was no Hopkins, the number was much greater than in England. On the continent of Europe many thousands suffered death in the sixteenth and seventeenth centuries. Nicholas Remy (Remigius) of Lorraine gathered the materials for his work on the "Worship of Demons," published in 1595,[3] from the trials of some nine hundred persons whom he had sentenced to death in the fifteen years preceding. The efforts of the Bishop of Bamberg from 1622 to 1633 resulted in six hundred executions, the Bishop of Würzburg, in about the same period, is said to have put nine hundred persons

[1] See Hutchinson, Historical Essay concerning Witchcraft, 2d ed., London, 1720, pp. 45 ff.
[2] Lives of Twelve Bad Men, edited by Thomas Seccombe, London, 1894, p. 64.
[3] Dæmonolatreia, Lugduni, 1595.

to death.[1]   These figures, which might be multiplied almost
indefinitely,[2] help us to regard the Salem Witchcraft in its
true proportions, — as a very small incident in the history
of a terrible superstition.

The last execution for witchcraft in Massachusetts took
place in 1693, as we have seen; indeed, twenty of the total
of about twenty-five cases fall within that and the preceding
year.   There were no witch trials in New England in the
eighteenth century.   The annals of Europe are not so clear.
In England Jane Wenham was condemned to death for this
imaginary crime in 1712, but she was pardoned.[3]   The act
against witchcraft was repealed in 1736, but in 1751 Ruth
Osborne, a reputed witch, was killed by a mob in Hertford-
shire.[4]   The last execution for witchcraft in Germany took
place in 1775.   In Spain the last witch was burned to death
in 1781.   In Switzerland Anna Göldi was beheaded in 1782
for bewitching the child of her master, a physician.   In
Poland two women were burned as late as 1793.[5]   Just
before the arrest of Jane Wenham, Addison, in the Spectator for July 11, 1711, had expressed the creed of a
well-bred and sensible man of the world: "I believe in
general that there is, and has been such a thing as Witchcraft; but at the same time can give no Credit to any
particular Instance of it."   And with this significant utterance we may close our brief discussion of a subject that
has been much misunderstood and return to our toads.

The toad is a distinguished figure both in literature and
in popular superstition or folk-lore, and he owes his fame

[1] Soldan, Geschichte der Hexenprozesse, ed. Heppe, Stuttgart, 1880, II,
38 ff.
[2] See the extraordinary enumeration in Roskoff, Geschichte des Teufels,
Leipzig, 1869, II, 293 ff.
[3] Thomas Wright, Narratives of Sorcery and Magic, London, 1851, II,
319 ff.
[4] The same, II, 326 ff.
[5] Soldan, II, 314, 322, 327.

to his supposed venomous qualities quite as much as to his ugliness. The Roman ladies, if we may believe Juvenal, poisoned their husbands with a preparation of the *rubeta*, a small toad,[1] — a more delicate instrument of murder, he suggests, than Clytemnestra's axe. "To give one frogs instead of fish" is an old proverbial variation of the Biblical "If he ask for a fish, will he give him a serpent?" An ingredient of the witches' caldron in Macbeth was a

> Toad, that under cold stone
> Days and nights has thirty-one
> Swelter'd venom sleeping got,

and one of the commentators who will not allow Shakspere to make a mistake refers to a learned disquisition in the "Transactions of the Royal Society for 1826," in which a certain Dr. Davy proves "that the toad *is* venomous, and moreover that 'swelter'd venom' is peculiarly proper, the poison being diffused over the body immediately under the skin." According to Milton, when Satan wished to suggest wickedness to the sleeping Eve he "squat like a toad" at her ear and whispered temptation to her. Even in our own time it is impossible to convince people that to handle toads does not induce warts.

The alleged venom of the toad has likewise made him a considerable figure in medical science. In the seventeenth century he was regarded as a protection against the plague. There is a good passage to this effect in one of the oddest pieces of strange learning ever produced by mortal man, Sir Kenelm Digby's Discourse touching the Cure of Wounds by the Powder of Sympathy, originally delivered in 1657 before a learned assembly at Montpellier. Digby believed that he could heal a wound by treating, not the patient, but some article that was stained with the patient's blood, — the knife, for instance, that had done the injury.

---

[1] Satires, i, 70; vi, 659.

He had obtained the secret from a Carmelite friar, who had learned it in the East. He put it in practice on James Howell, whose hand was badly cut in an affray and was in danger of gangrene. In this case it was Howell's garter, which had been used as a bandage, that Digby treated, with the happiest results, and to the delight and amazement of King James I. There can be no doubt about the cure, though we should now be inclined to ascribe it, not to Digby's honest hocus-pocus, but to his advice to Howell to throw away the plasters and medicaments which the doctors had applied and to keep the wound clean. We are at present concerned, however, not so much with the facts as with the theory on which they were accounted for. This is set forth with much skill and eloquence in Digby's Discourse. There is, he believes, a subtle relation, or sympathy, between anything that has at any time been a part of one, like a severed limb or shed blood, and the person himself, and this relation persists even at considerable distances. It operates by a constant stream of emanations, so to speak, which are merely one form of a system of sympathies which bind like things together in the order of nature. The same theory underlies the belief (still more or less prevalent) that a man feels pain when an amputated leg or arm is maltreated or not comfortably disposed of.[1]

The interest which Sir Kenelm Digby's sympathetic powder roused throughout the civilized world finds its reflection in the Harvard Theses for A. M. In 1693 these seem to assume complete belief in the reality of the cure, but evince some scruples as to its propriety: " Is the cure of wounds by sympathetic powder lawful? " The same question was debated in 1708. Of course, the doubt was whether sorcery entered into the method used by Sir

---

[1] A case of this kind is described in a letter written by John Winthrop, F.R.S., to Cotton Mather in 1716 (Coll. Mass. Hist. Soc., 6th Series, V, 333–4).

Kenelm. The decision in both years favored the legality
of sympathetic cures, and indeed it is difficult to see how
their perfect innocence can have been doubted by anyone
who had read the discourse in which Digby, rejecting
all mystery, endeavored to explain in the most rigidly
scientific fashion the whys and wherefores of what so
many persons regarded as the greatest wonder of the age.
The question " Is there a magnetic method of curing
wounds? " was discussed in 1698 and settled affirmatively,
and in 1703, 1708, 1710, " Is there a sympathetic powder? "
was similarly answered.[1]

Closely associated with sympathetic powder is the
general doctrine of magnetic treatment, concerning which
we have Digby's remarkable letter to John Winthrop the
Younger, describing the curing of ague by hanging the
parings of the patient's nails round the neck of an eel.[2]

Digby illustrates his sympathetic philosophy by many
curious examples, and thus he comes to speak of toads
as an antidote to the pestilence: " In time of common
Contagion," he says, " they use to carry about them the
powder of a Toad, and sometimes a living Toad or Spider
shut up in a box; or else they carry Arsenick, or some
other venomous substance, which draws unto it the contagious air, which otherwise would infect the party: and
the same powder of a Toad draws unto it the poison of a
Plague-soar. The Farcey is a venemous and contagious
humour within the body of an Horse; hang a Toad about
the neck of the Horse in a little bag, and he will be cured
infallibly; the Toad, which is the stronger poison, drawing
to it the venom which was within the Horse."[3]

Van Helmont also believed in the efficacy of the toad

[1] Proc. Mass. Hist. Soc., XVIII, 132.
[2] Coll. Mass. Hist. Soc., 3d Series, X, 17.
[3] A Late Discourse, etc., rendered faithfully out of French into English
by R. White, 4th ed., London, 1664, pp. 76–77.

as a remedy or prophylactic, though his theory of its operation was somewhat different from Digby's. A disciple of Helmont's once put the prescription to the test, and has left an account of the result in a very rare book called The Pest Anatomized, which appeared in 1666. This was George Thomson, one of the leaders in the revolt against the Galenical or "regular" physicians which made so much noise in England in the seventeenth century, and, in spite of the vagaries of the innovators, accomplished a great reform in medical practice. In 1665, when the plague was raging in London, Thomson had the courage to dissect a "pestilential body" in the hope of making some discovery that might be of advantage to mankind. He took the infection, and since the two best physicians of his own school were suffering from the disease and he would trust no Galenist, he was obliged to treat himself. His principal effort was to support nature, instead of weakening it by the bleedings and heroic purges then most in favor, and to induce perspiration. But he also had recourse to the batrachian cure. He hung a large dried toad about his neck, and he assures us solemnly that the creature "became so tumefied, distended, (as it were blown up)" with the venom which it attracted from the patient's body into its own "that it was an object of wonder to those that beheld it."[1] Thomson adds a queer bit of experimental philosophy regarding the toad: "It is observed," he says, "that the *Bufo* is a Creature so extreamly fearful, that if you take the advantage to look upon it with a firmly fixed intentive eye for a quarter of an hour, there being no avoidance of your countenance, it will shortly dye with very terrour, as I have tryed."[2]

Thomson got well and lived to write his book. We need not suspect him of lying, but we shall do well to

[1] ΛΟΙΜΟΤΟΜΙΑ: or the Pest Anatomized, London, 1666, p. 86.
[2] The same, p. 170.

remember that one effect of the plague, as he says himself, was to disorder the intellect of the sufferer for the time being.

So much for the venom of the toad. As to spiders, it is well known that some of them are dangerous, and popular credulity is prone to generalize. The testimony of the Rev. John Beal, a friend of Boyle the physicist, will suffice. "I think," he writes in 1663, "this land and climate does not breed stronger or quicker poison in any vegetable, animal, serpent, or insectile, than in the spider, though I have heard of some men, that can eat and digest spiders; and I have seen young turkeys eat them for an antidote, and particularly when strawberries, (either in kind, or in quantity, as causing a surfeit) was their poison, and had killed many, that had not eaten spiders." [1]

Spiders, like toads, were hung about the patient's neck, as a remedy for divers diseases. Ashmole, the antiquary, when suffering from ague, resorted to this specific. In his diary we read, on May 11, 1681: "I took, early in the morning, a good dose of elixir, and hung three spiders about my neck, and they drove my ague away. *Deo Gratias!*" [2]

What Mr. Thomas thought of spiders we do not know; but he had enlightened views on the subject of toads and snakes. In his Farmer's Calendar for May, 1813, we find: — "I never suffer any of my family to kill those little innocent animals called striped snakes, for they do me much service in destroying grasshoppers, and other troublesome insects. Toads are of essential service, especially in a garden, to eat up cabbage-worms, catter-pillars, &c."

The essential element in the story of the duel between the Toad and the Spider lies in the doctrine that animals know what is good for them, and in particular that they

---

[1] Letter to Robert Boyle, Boyle's Works, ed. Birch, 1744, V, 455.
[2] W. G. Black, Folk-Medicine, London, 1883, p. 60.

instinctively seek curative herbs when they have suffered an injury. This doctrine is universal. It finds poetical expression in Alphonsus, a tragedy by Shakspere's unfortunate contemporary Robert Greene : —

> The silly serpent, found by country swain,
> And cut in pieces by his furious blows,
> Yet if his head do 'scape away untouch'd,
> As many write, it very strangely goes
> To fetch an herb, with which in little time
> Her batter'd corpse again she doth conjoin :
> But if by chance the ploughman's sturdy staff
> Do hap to hit upon the serpent's head,
> And bruise the same, though all the rest be sound,
> Yet doth the silly serpent lie for dead,
> Nor can the rest of all her body serve
> To find a salve which may her life preserve.[1]

One of the most curious accounts of this instinctive recognition of remedies by the lower animals is that given by Giraldus Cambrensis in his Irish Topography.[2] According to the not altogether trustworthy evidence of this imaginative twelfth-century writer, the weasels in Ireland, when their young have been killed by an injury, restore them to life by means of a certain yellow flower. Giraldus declares that he is following the testimony of eye-witnesses who have killed young weasels for the sake of experiment. The creature, we are told, first blows in the wound and in the mouth and nostrils of the dead animal, and then applies the flower in question, with the happiest effect. There is a similar incident in the Old French lay of Eliduc, written by Marie de France about 1180, in which a human being is brought to life by a friend who notices the actions of the weasels and applies his observation. Examples might be multiplied indefinitely, but perhaps we have had enough of Toads and Spiders.

[1] Works, ed. Dyce, London, 1831, II, 14.
[2] Topographia Hibernica, i, 27, Opera, ed. Dimock, V, 60–61.

SUGAR AND SALT

IN his generous enthusiasm for America and American products, the author of the Farmer's Almanack does not forget Maple Sugar. He regards it as preferable in every way to the sugar imported from the West Indies, and believes that every humane and patriotic citizen should use it exclusively. Here are some of his precepts, all under March, the proper month for "sugaring off": —

1794. Attend to making maple sugar.

1798. Those who have trees will not neglect the making of maple sugar, which is not only the most wholesome and pleasant sweetening, but being the product of our own country, will ever have the preference by every true American.

1800. As soon as the frost begins to quit its hold of the sugar maple, be prepared to take its luxuriant juice, as the first taken is much the richest.

1801. "*A penny saved is as good as two-pence earned ;* " that is, if you have maple trees, and have to buy sugar in the summer, you *pay too dear for your rattle.*

1804. "He that has money," says cousin Simpkins, "may eat honey. And so my home-made maple sweetening, must answer my purpose. Yet," continues he, "it affords me much consolation to reflect that my poor maple stuff, as they call it, possesses no mingled tears of misery; no desponding slave ever groaned over my cauldrons or fanned them with his sighs : No ; this little lump in my hand is the reward of my own labour on my own farm."

1805. Make your own sugar, and send not to the Indies for it. Feast not on the toil, pain and misery of the wretched.

1807. Economy now calls your attention to your maple trees. Make all the sugar you can, for you know not what may happen to prevent its importation. Besides, there is a great satisfaction derived from living as much as possible upon the produce of one's own farm; where no poor slave has toiled in sorrow and pain; where no scoundrel has lorded over your fields; but where honest industry walks peaceful amidst the smiling fruits of his labour.

1808. Pies, puddings, and pancakes are best with sweetening, and as sugar is as cheap and agreeable an article as we can find for this use, we had better be attending to our cauldrons. Heaven has been extremely propitious to our country, in causing the growth of this valuable tree; the maple. *He who lives well, sees afar off.*

1818. As for myself I have done using sugar, and feel much better for it. But those who will still use this luxury, as I shall call it, had better be attending to their maple trees.

When Mr. Thomas began to issue his Almanac, in 1792, and for years thereafter, many inland families used no sugar but that which they made themselves from the sap of the maple. Every farmer in the districts where these trees flourish wished to have his " sugar orchard," and "sugaring off" was as much a part of the agricultural year as plowing or haymaking. On the coast, cane sugar imported from the West Indies was in use, but this was of course more expensive to the farmer than that which he could extract from his own trees. In 1784 President Stiles of Yale noted in his Diary: — "Sixteen Thous^d pounds of Maple Sugar made at Norfolk in one year about 1774. This year 1784 about one Third more. Sell at 6^d ℞ lb. or 50/ ℞ cw^t made by 180 families. Now 230 families in Norfolk. About one hundred fam^{ys} made the sugar. Two pail fulls of sap make one pound — one Tree gives a pound a day. Mr. Robbins 2 little sons made two hundred weight of Sugar from one hundred Trees this year. Sugar Works

in Goshen have lasted above fourty years & still good." [1]
" The sugar," wrote Jeremy Belknap about 1792, " is clear
gain to the industrious husbandman." The sap was collected and boiled down at a time of year when there was
little or nothing to do on the farm, and the yield was generous, with small labor, — labor, too, which partook of the
nature of frolic and therefore was scarcely felt as work at
all. Belknap remarks that " one man and a boy have collected a sufficiency of sap for five hundred pounds of sugar,
and a man, with two boys, for seven hundred. The boiling is often performed by women." [2] The syrup, or that
portion of the sap which would not granulate, was a
substitute for molasses. The Duc de la Rochefoucault-
Liancourt, driven from his native country by the French
Revolution, spent some three years (1795–1797) in the
United States and Canada. He was a philosophical traveller of the school of Arthur Young, and was sufficiently
interested in maple sugar to set down what he could learn
about it under no less than twelve heads. In general he
testifies to the fact that he found no scarcity of excellent
sugar.[3]

In 1794 the English clothier, Henry Wansey, in com-
menting on the " excellent provisions " served at Frederick
Bull's tavern in Hartford, remarks that there were " three
sorts of sugar brought always to the table ; — the musco-
vado,[4] the fine lump sugar, and the maple." " From the
novelty of it," he adds, " I preferred the last, though I could
not find much difference in the taste of it." [5] This is curious, since maple sugar certainly has a flavor of its own.
Bull's lump sugar was a rarity, not to be expected in any

[1] Literary Diary of Ezra Stiles, May 19, 1784, ed. Dexter, III, 121.
[2] History of New Hampshire, 1792, III, 116.
[3] Travels, English translation, 1799, I, 125–6.
[4] I. e., raw sugar.
[5] Journal of an Excursion to the United States of America in the Summer
of 1794, Salisbury, 1796, pp. 60–61.

but first-class inns. At Durham, in the same State, the traveller was not so well satisfied. The tavern was "a very mean house, the worst he had seen." The bread was " cake made of rye, and only half baked "; the beefsteaks for breakfast were fried in lard; the tea and coffee were smoky. Here, of course, only maple sugar was provided. Apparently Wansey spoke of it with appreciation, for one of his fellow-passengers — a Yankee with an eye to business — offered him five hundred weight of it for fourpence halfpenny sterling a pound; "but," adds Wansey regretfully, " it is contrary to the laws of England to import it." [1]

The art of making maple sugar was learned by the settlers from the Indians, who had practised it from time immemorial. A brief description of the art as practised by the savages of Canada "longer then any now living among them can remember," was published by the Royal Society in 1685.[2] In 1720 Paul Dudley communicated to the same learned body another account of the process, which was duly printed in the Philosophical Transactions; [3] but he does not mention the Indians. " Our physicians," he avers, " look upon it not only to be as good for common use as the West India sugar, but to exceed all other for its medicinal virtue." We have seen that toward the end of the eighteenth century this sugar was in common use in New England. The farmer who was fortunate enough to have a sugar orchard valued it highly, and counted upon its product as a regular part of his supplies for the year. It appears, however, that although the white people had early observed the practice of the Indians in this respect, they were rather slow in imitating them to any extent. Thus, in the highly interesting volume entitled Historical Memoirs Relating to the Housatunnuk Indians, by the Rev.

[1] Journal, as above, p. 64.
[2] Philosophical Transactions, XV, 988.
[3] Philosophical Transactions, XXXI, 27–28.

Samuel Hopkins of Springfield, published in 1753, there is
a long note on the subject, which concludes with the suggestion that it would be prudent for farmers to spare their
maple trees, and to utilize them from year to year in supplying themselves with sugar and molasses. Mr. Hopkins
also suggests that rum, which we must remember was regarded as a necessity by our ancestors, might perhaps be
made of the sap, though he says that the experiment has
not been tried so far as he knows. If the sap is fermented,
he remarks, after three or four barrels have been reduced
to one by boiling, it " makes a very pleasant drink which
is sufficiently spirituous." His account of Indian sugar-
making is worth transcribing for its antiquarian significance, and his economic speculations are curious : —

The *Indians* make their *Sugar* of the Sap of *Maple Trees*.
They extract the Sap by cutting the tree on one Side, in such a
Form as that the Sap will naturally gather into a small Channel
at the Bottom of the Hole cut ; where they fix into the Tree a
small Chip, of 6 or 8 Inches long, which carries the Sap off from
the Tree, into a Vessel set to receive it. Thus they tap a Number
of Trees ; and, when the Vessels are full, they gather the Sap, and
boil it to such a Degree of Consistence, as to make *Sugar*. After
it is boil'd, they take it off the Fire, and stir it till it is cold, which
is their Way of *graining* it. The *Sugar* is very good, of a very
agreable Taste, and esteemed the most wholesome of any. It
might doubtless be made in great Plenty ; and, I cannot but
think, to the great Profit of the Undertakers. If some Man would
build him a *Sugar-House*, and provide a set of *Boilers*, and other
Utensils as they have in the *West-Indies*, I am persuaded he would
find his Account in it, beyond what those in the *West-Indies* can
do. For the Gentleman, who hath a Plantation in the *West-
Indies*, is at great Expence in preparing his Ground ; planting
his *Cane*, and cultivating it for more than a Year, before it is fit
for Use : in cutting, triming, and toping it ; for Mills to grind it ;
and not till all this be done is the Sap of the *Cane* ready for boil-

ing.   All this Charge might be substracted from the Gentleman's
Account, who uses *Maple Trees* instead of *Cane*, except the Expence of taping the Trees, and gathering the Sap, which is as
nothing compar'd with the other.

It is true indeed, that the Sap of *Maple Trees* is not so rich as
that of the Sugar *Cane ;* but I suppose the Disproportion is not
by far so great as that of the Expence.   For, I have been inform'd
that two Men, under the Disadvantage of boiling it in two Kettles,
and in the open Air, have, in a good Season, made a Barrel in a
Week.   What then would a Number of Hands do, with a Sett of
West-India Boilers, Coolers, and other Advantages of Dispatch,
which they are furnish'd with?   Trees fit for this Business are
very plenty, in the vast uncultivated Wilderness between *Connecticut* and *Hudson's* Rivers, as also in all the Northern Borders
of this Province.   And, could the one Half of them be us'd, I
suppose they would more than furnish all the *British* Colonies
upon the *Continent* with *Sugar*.[1]

The scarcity of all imported articles during the Revolutionary War, which led to so many eccentric substitutions,
could not fail to turn speculative minds towards the possibilities of native sugar-making.   Dr. Benjamin Rush, the
celebrated Pennsylvania surgeon, and a signer of the
Declaration of Independence, conducted an experiment,
at which Alexander Hamilton was present, to prove that
maple sugar is not inferior in strength to that from the
West Indies.   In 1791 he sent a paper on the subject to
the American Philosophical Society, in which he displayed
much freedom of scientific fancy.   His mere facts, to be
sure, are sober enough.   " For a great number of years
many hundred private families in New-York and Pennsylvania have supplied themselves plentifully with this sugar
during the whole year."   He has heard of " many families
who have made from two to four hundred pounds in a

[1] Historical Memoirs, Boston, 1753, p. 26.

year; and of one man who sold six hundred pounds, all
made with his own hands in one season." But his hopes
are extravagant and go far beyond the speculations of
Mr. Hopkins. He thought that we might develop this
industry so far as not only to supply the domestic market,
but to export enough to destroy the sugar plantations in
the West Indies, which from the settlement of this country
had been the chief source of our supply. This hope gave
him pleasure not only on economic grounds, but for
humane reasons as well. He actually imagined that maple
sugar might enfranchise the West Indian slaves. We
might export enough, perhaps, " to render the commerce
and slavery of our African brethren in the sugar islands
as unnecessary, as it has always been inhuman and unjust." [1]
The sanguine character of this prophecy may be understood when we remember that in the preceding year
(1790) the United States had imported more than seventeen and a half million pounds of brown sugar from the
West Indies, and more than two hundred thousand pounds
of loaf sugar and other varieties. In 1798, the total
importation of brown sugar amounted to nearly sixty-seven
million pounds, and that of loaf sugar etc. to more than
twenty and a half million pounds. Of the former more
than five-sevenths came from the West Indies, and the
rest from the East Indies chiefly, that trade having
developed in the meantime; of the loaf sugar practically
the whole amount was West Indian.[2] Maple sugar is a
palatable and wholesome luxury — " an agreeable sweet,"
as Dr. Belknap calls it, — but it was not destined to eman-
cipate the slaves of the sugar islands. That did not come

[1] Essays, Literary, Moral and Philosophical, Philadelphia, 1798, pp.
284, 285-6, 294.
[2] The World's Sugar Production and Consumption, 1800-1900, Monthly
Summary of Commerce and Finance of the United States, Jan., 1902,
pp. 2683-4.

till 1834, and it required an Act of Parliament and a *douceur* of £16,500,000.

Dr. Rush's forecast seems absurd enough nowadays, and we may accuse him of being more of a humanitarian than an economist.   One thing, however, he could not predict, — the sugar industry of our own South.   At the very time when Rush was reading his essay, Antonio Mendez, of New Orleans, was making the first sugar ever produced in that State, and in the following year (1792) Rendon, the Spanish intendant, used as a curiosity a small quantity of his loaf sugar at a banquet.   A few years later, Étienne de Bore produced sugar in Louisiana in paying quantities, and in or about 1820, the introduction of the purple or red ribbon canes, native to Java, settled the main business of that State for good and all.[1]   All this Dr. Rush could not foresee, any more than he could predict the Louisiana Purchase of 1803, or the enormous development of the beet-sugar industry in our own day.

Philadelphia was fertile in projects.   A few years after Dr. Rush read his paper on the maple, experiments were tried in that city with a view to procuring a supply of sugar from watermelons.   Half a pint of syrup was obtained " by gradually boiling the strained pulp and juice of a melon that weighed 14 lb."   Bordley, the writer of an esteemed work on husbandry, who had tasted a sample, computes that at this rate an acre of land would produce a hundred and forty-three dollars' worth of syrup.   " Here," he adds, " are flattering circumstances to induce experiments that may prove how easily the country family may become independent of foreign countries for sweets of the class of sugars, and at a very cheap rate."[2]   There was also an idea, — though not, perhaps, in Philadelphia, —

[1] W. C. Stubbs, Sugar Cane, [1898?], pp. 6–10.
[2] J. B. Bordley, Essays and Notes on Husbandry and Rural Affairs, 2d ed., Philadelphia, 1801, pp. 530, 531.

that molasses might be made from sweet apples. This project was mentioned by Timothy Pickering in an address before the Essex (Massachusetts) Agricultural Society in 1820. Mr. Pickering admitted that he " had never tasted any sweet apple molasses " and that it probably had not " the rich sweet of molasses from the sugar cane," but he thought it might do well enough " for family uses in general." He knew a gentleman of first-rate practical judgment who maintained " that it would not be difficult, by forming orchards of sweet apples, to supply molasses for the general consumption of the United States." [1] We hear also of molasses from cornstalks as manufactured in considerable quantities, about 1792, by Captain Jonathan Devoll, one of the New England settlers at Farmers' Castle (Belpré) on the Ohio.[2]

Dr. Rush and his fellow-experimenters were not the only prophetic dreamers on this continent whose economic visions were never to be realized. *Sugar* suggests *salt*, and at about the time when the learned Philadelphian was conducting his experiments with maple syrup, another industry was establishing itself in Eastern Massachusetts with far better prospect of profit and permanence. In 1800 the Rev. Dr. Timothy Dwight, then in the sixth year of his presidency of Yale College, made a never-to-be-forgotten journey to the extremity of Cape Cod. At Yarmouth his eyes were greeted with a novel spectacle, the salt-works. In the next town, Dennis, he studied this interesting enterprise with pleased amazement. Always on the alert for anything that promised a combination of material prosperity with moral and religious advancement, this learned theologian and entertaining writer deliberately spread the wings of his imagination for a dignified flight: —

[1] Discourse read before the Essex Agricultural Society, in Massachusetts, Feb. 21, 1820, Salem, 1820, p. 26.
[2] S. P. Hildreth, Pioneer History, Cincinnati, 1848, p. 393.

The sight of these works excited in my mind a train of thought, which others, perhaps, will pronounce romantic. I could not easily avoid thinking, however, that this business might one day prove the source of a mighty change in the face of this country. The American coast, as you know, is chiefly barren, and of course thinly inhabited. It is also almost everywhere low and level; and therefore, while it is unsuited to most other employments, is remarkably fitted to this. Why, then, may it not be believed, that many thousands of persons may, one day, be profitably employed in making salt along the immense extent of our shore? Why may not comfort, and even wealth be easily, as well as usefully, obtained here by great multitudes, who otherwise might hardly earn a subsistence? For ought that appears, this business may be followed with success and profit, to an extent, which it would be very difficult to define. A small capital is sufficient to begin the employment with advantage. The demand for salt is at present very great, and is every year increasing. There are (1811) seven millions of inhabitants within the United States: within a moderate period there will be seventy. The West-Indian sources, from which we principally derive this necessary article of life, are now more than sufficient. The time is near, in which the demand will exceed the supplies from that quarter. To what means can the inhabitants of this country so naturally betake themselves, as to those which I have specified? Will they not of course erect works of this nature, in succession, from St. Mary's to Machias? Will not comfort, therefore, and even affluence, spring up on sands and wastes, which now seem doomed to everlasting desolation? Will not towns and villages smile in tracts, which are now condemned to gloom and solitude? May not multitudes, who habitually spend life in casual and parsimonious efforts to acquire a bare subsistence, interluded with long periods of sloth and drunkenness, become sober, diligent, and even virtuous, and be formed for usefulness and immortality?[1]

[1] Timothy Dwight, Travels in New-England and New-York, New Haven, 1822, III, 81–82.

The object of Dr. Dwight's poetic fancy was worthy of his best efforts, and we may well pause a moment to contemplate the rise and fall of an almost forgotten industry.

"Can that which is unsavory be eaten without salt?" asks the protesting Job. With the ocean at their very doors, no wonder the colonists of New England early turned their attention to the manufacture of salt by evaporation. In 1624 a salt-maker was sent from England to instruct the Plymouth settlers in the art. The experiment failed dismally. Its ill success is graphically described by Governor Bradford,[1] whose disgust at the empty boasting of the pretender to special knowledge is a matter of record: —

He whom they sent to make salte was an ignorante, foolish, self-willd fellow; he bore them in hand he could doe great matters in making salt-works, so he was sente to seeke out fitte ground for his purpose; and after some serch he tould y⁰ Gov'ʳ that he had found a sufficente place, with a good botome to hold water, and otherwise very conveniente, which he doubted not but in a short time to bring to good perfection, and to yeeld them great profite; but he must have 8. or ten men to be constantly imployed. He was wisht to be sure that y⁰ ground was good, and other things answerable, and y' he could bring it to perfection; otherwise he would bring upon them a great charge by imploying him selfe and so many men. But he was, after some triall, so confidente, as he caused them to send carpenters to rear a great frame for a large house, to receive y⁰ salte & such other uses. But in y⁰ end all proved vaine. Then he layed fault of y⁰ ground, in which he was deceived; but if he might have the lighter to cary clay, he was sure that he could doe it. Now though y⁰ Gov'ʳ & some other foresaw that this would come to litle, yet they had so many malignant spirits amongst them, that would have laid it upon them, in their letters of complainte to y⁰ adventurers, as to be their falte y' would not suffer him to goe on to

[1] Bradford, History of Plimouth Plantation, Boston, 1898, pp. 203-4.

bring his work to perfection; for as he by his bould confidence
& large promises deceived them in England that sente him, so he
had wound him selfe in to these mens high esteeme hear, so as
they were faine to let him goe on till all men saw his vanity. For
he could not doe any thing but boyle salt in pans, & yet would
make them y^t were joynd with him beleeve ther was so grat a
misterie in it as was not easie to be attained, and made them doe
many unnecessary things to blind their eys, till they discerned
his sutltie. The next yere he was sente to Cap-Anne, and ye pans
were set up ther wher the fishing was; but before so͞mer was out,
he bur̃te the house, and the fire was so vehemente as it spoyld the
pans, at least some of them, and this was the end of that charg-
able bussines.

Salt was one of the main sources of income on which the
investors in the Massachusetts Bay Company relied for
their profits. In the preliminary financiering which came
before the emigration, we find salt-making mentioned
among the four great monopolies which the adventurers
felt authorized to dispose of.[1] Experiments began early.
That inventive genius, John Winthrop the Younger, had
a process of his own devising, — "a compendious and
cheap way," as it is called by the Secretary of the Royal
Society in a letter in which he begs Winthrop to communicate it to the *savants* of the mother country.[2] In 1638
Winthrop was authorized to build salt-works at "Ryall-
Side," now a part of Beverly, and it is probable that he
got to work as early as the spring of 1639.[3] Subsequently
he received further privileges of the same nature, and the
General Court made an agreement with him for the price of
" good white salt at Boston, Charlestown, Salem, Ipswich,

---

[1] Mass. Colony Records, I, 64.

[2] Henry Oldenburg to John Winthrop, Jr., Aug. 3, 1664, Coll. Mass.
Hist. Soc., 3d Series, X, 48; cf. X, 49 ff. Winthrop's process required fire.

[3] T. F. Waters, Sketch of the Life of John Winthrop the Younger,
Ipswich Hist. Soc. Publ., VII (1899), 25.

and Salisbury." There are many other entries of a similar
character scattered through the colonial records of our
Commonwealth. All who are familiar with Judge Sewall's
Diary will remember the salt-works on Boston Neck in
which he was financially interested. " Salt was the will-o'-
wisp of seventeenth century manufacture." [1] Efforts were
repeatedly made to extract this essential commodity from
the sea. It seemed wasteful to import it from the West
Indies, or from Spain and Portugal, when the ocean came
up to one's very doors. It was needed in large quantities
for curing fish and other purposes, and its scarcity, in
Mr. Weeden's words, "limited enterprise." Some of the
West India salt was of inferior quality. That from the
Tortugas discolored the fish. Projectors were often
encouraged by special grants and privileges, but with
slight results. None of the early experiments turned
out well.

Evaporation was effected by means of artificial heat.
But, cheap as wood was in those days, this process was
wasteful and laborious, and much of the profit went up in
smoke. In 1776 the Continental Congress procured the
circulation of a pamphlet on the " Art of Making Common
Salt, particularly adapted to the use of the American Colonies," being an essay which appeared in the Pennsylvania
Magazine for March of that year. The pamphlet was published at Philadelphia by order of the General Assembly
of Pennsylvania, and was immediately reprinted at Boston.
It calls attention to the manufacture of the so-called " bay-
salt" by evaporation, as practised in the French marshes,
and urges the Colonies to institute it, since boiling is more
expensive and produces an inferior article. Little came
of this, however, for, as in the colonial days, it was impossible to find natural soil suitable for retaining the brine

[1] Weeden, Economic and Social History of New England, Boston, 1890,
I, 169.

during evaporation. In the same year, however, Capt. John Sears, of Dennis, devised a new method of evaporating salt-water by means of the sun's rays. Of course he was laughed at, but he persevered, and after several failures he succeeded in getting salt in paying quantities.[1] The Revolution was very favorable to the industry. The chief source of foreign supply had been the West Indies, and scarcity began to be felt as soon as the war broke out. In July, 1775, the Provincial Congress of Massachusetts restricted the ration of each soldier to a gill a week. Premiums were offered by several colonies for the establishment of salt-works, bounties on salt were voted now and again, and the matter attracted the serious attention of the Continental Congress,[2] as we have seen.

A particular account of the process of salt-making on Cape Cod, — a method which produced both the common article and the medicinal substances known as Epsom and Glauber's salts, — was contributed in 1802, by Dr. James Thacher, of Plymouth, to the Memoirs of the American Academy of Arts and Sciences.[3] At this time the business was flourishing. There was a considerable duty on imported salt, and the domestic manufacturer counted upon a yearly profit of from twenty-five to thirty-five per cent. Dr. Thacher is almost as enthusiastic about the future of the industry as Dr. Dwight. In due time, he thinks, " we may exhibit upon our shores a source of wealth little inferior to the celebrated salt mine of Cracow."

Fifteen years later the traveller Kendall was entertained by Richard Sears, one of the principal salt manufacturers of Chatham, and collected much information on the subject. He learned that some four hundred thousand dollars was

[1] For a full account of his process see Coll. Mass. Hist. Soc., 1802, VIII, 135 ff.

[2] See Smith, On the Scarcity of Salt in the Revolutionary War, Proc. Mass. Hist. Soc., XV, 221 ff.

[3] Vol. II, Part II, pp. 107 ff.

invested in salt-works in Barnstable County, and that the
annual production amounted to a hundred thousand bushels,
besides a considerable quantity of Glauber's salts. In Dennis, the original home of the process then in use, the vats
covered an area of more than 650,000 square feet. The
product was of excellent quality, superior in strength, it
was said, to the best imported salt by one-fifth.[1]

Thoreau found the salt-works a picturesque feature of
the landscape when he made his tour of the Cape in 1849.
" The wind-mills on the hills, — large weather-stained oc-
tagonal structures, — and the salt-works scattered all along
the shore, with their long rows of vats resting on poles
driven into the marsh, their low, turtle-like roofs, and their
slighter wind-mills, were novel and interesting objects to
an inlander." [2]   All this has vanished. The salt springs of
Onondaga proved a formidable rival.[3] The removal of the
duty on foreign salt, with the increase in the cost of lumber
and the rise in wages, made the business unprofitable, and
the mills and vats were suffered to go to wreck, or removed and their materials utilized for the cheaper kinds
of building.

Many will remember the large boards, fantastically
marked with the stains of spreading rust and marine chem-
icals, but rendered almost proof against decay by their long
contact with " lingering pickle," which twenty-five years
ago were so plentifully worked up into sheds and barns,
and even houses, in all parts of Cape Cod. President
Dwight's prophetic vision of an Atlantic coast lined with
salt-works was not destined to be fulfilled. In Barnstable,
for instance, where in 1808 there were half-a-million square

[1] E. A. Kendall, Travels through the Northern Parts of the United States,
New York, 1809, II, 131 ff.
[2] Cape Cod, Stage-Coach Views, ed. 1877, pp. 19–20.
[3] See Benj. De Witt, Memoir on the Onondaga Salt Springs, Albany,
1798; cf. S. P. Hildreth, Pioneer History, Cincinnati, 1848, pp. 409, 475-7.

feet of vats, there is nothing to mark the site of the manufacture but a few indentations in the marsh, once reser-
voirs, and a single gallows-like structure, fallen into ruin,
and scarcely recognizable as the timber frame of an old
windmill.

THE FLYING STATIONER

THE last page of the Almanac for 1797, in the course of a long advertisement of Mr. Thomas's book and stationery business at Sterling,[1] makes particular mention of "Small Histories, Chapmen's Book[s], &c." and goes on to enumerate "Female Policy Detected, French Convert, Royal do., History of the Holy Bible, Seven Wise Masters, Robinson Crusoe, Tom Thumb's Exhibition, New Year's Gift, Little King Pippin, Mountain Piper — *with a great number of other small, entertaining histories.*" This entry is of some importance to the bibliographer, who finds in such "small entertaining histories" at once his delight and his despair. The chapmen in question were, of course, book-peddlers, or what used to be called in Scotland "flying stationers." They are best known to literary historians and collectors of rare volumes, as well as to students of folk-lore, by the cheap little pamphlets of a popular character called "chapbooks," that is, books designed to be sold by chapmen or travelling traders. These were of every sort, as Mr. Thomas's advertisement indicates. Some were moral or prudential, but many aimed simply at entertainment. Jest books and garlands (or song-books) abounded. Many an old romance — like Guy of Warwick or Bevis of Hampton — found its last redaction in a condensed prose version meant to be hawked about the country. One of the most singular transformations of this kind is seen in the fate of the old tale of Barlaam and Joasaph. This was originally a col-

1 See pp. 318 ff., below.

lection of Buddhistic parables, but it gradually came to be understood as a Christian legend, and its popularity in this guise led to the admission of a supposed St. Josaphat into the Calendar of the Greek Church, — a saint in whom modern investigators have somewhat gleefully recognized the Buddha himself, the founder of the rival religion which has of late sent various learned and picturesque missionaries to our shores.   Finally the tale of Barlaam and Joasaph turns up in chapbook form as the History of King *Jehoshaphat!*

The Seven Wise Masters, which appears in Mr. Thomas's list, is also of Oriental origin and has an equally long and complicated history.   It gets its name from the Seven Sages to whom the education of the hero, a very accomplished prince, has been entrusted.   The prince is falsely accused by his stepmother and condemned to death.   He cannot defend himself, for he has learned by inspecting the stars that he must speak no word for a week on pain of instant destruction.   As he is being led to the scaffold, the first of his tutors stops the king and warns him that in putting his son to death he is acting as foolishly as the knight did when he killed his hound.   Of course the king asks for the story, and the Sage agrees to tell it if he will give the prince a respite for one day.   That night the queen convinces her husband, by a counter-story, that he is being tricked by his advisers, and he resolves to have his son executed next morning.   This time the second Sage intervenes, and secures a postponement for another day.   Thus the narrative proceeds, until the week is past and the prince is at liberty to speak.   The queen is punished and the Seven Sages meet with well-merited honor.   The reader will recognize the same kind of device for stringing stories together that is familiar to all in the Arabian Nights.   The Seven Sages was vastly popular throughout Europe from the middle ages to

modern times and it deserved its popularity. It warms
one's heart to meet with this old favorite, in its abbreviated
chapbook form, on the shelves of the early New England
booksellers. Michael Perry, of Boston, had three copies
in stock when his inventory was taken in 1700, and they
were valued in the lump at two shillings. The same
document shows five copies of the History of Fortunatus,
valued at three shillings and fourpence, and one copy of
Godfrey of Bulloigne, valued at sixpence. Perry had also
nine packs of playing cards on hand, as well as a good
supply of sermons and theological works.[1]

A good many chapbooks were reprinted in this country
in the eighteenth and the early nineteenth century, and
there were also not a few of American origin. Mr. Thomas
was no doubt well furnished with both kinds.

The Almanac itself was largely circulated by the itinerant
booksellers, and in the Farmer's Calendar for January,
1821, there is a lively sketch of the arrival of such a
chapman at a farmer's house and of the conversation
between him and the daughter of an old customer. "Tim
Twilight" is the felicitous name assigned to the merry
itinerant: —

"Bless my heart, mother, here comes old Tim Twilight the
pedler again to wish us happy new year. Well, uncle Tim, it is
just a year to a day since you was here before and sold me *The
life and adventures of Betty Buttermilk, dairywoman to the
Duchess of Dumhiedikes*. Come, let's see, what have ye now,
old daddy?" "Why, my pretty damsel, here's the works of
Sir John Sinclair, the great Scotch farmer. Here's another book
called *The Guide to Health*. Shewing how a diligent hand
maketh rich. Here's another, called *The Great Quiltrey at
farmer Cleverly's*. Hah! what say ye to reading the life of
My Lady Lummucks? But here's the best of all, my *Farmer's*

[1] See the inventory as printed by Whitmore in his edition of John
Dunton's Letters from New England, pp. 315, 316, 317.

Almanack. . . . So my good friends, I must bid you good bye.
If Providence gives me leave, I 'll call again in '22 — you may
read over what is here in haste penn'd down; it will serve to
pass a winter evening or so. — Good bye."

Tim Twilight sometimes greeted his friends and customers in rhyme.   So in January, 1822: —

> "IN *eighteen hundred twenty-two,*
> I wish my friends a *happy new-*
> *Year!*   You see, I 've got more Al-
> Manacks; so thought I would just call
> And say, good morning to ye, honies!
> 'T is for no favour — save your monies."

"Poh, uncle Tim," methinks you say, "give us no more
paltry doggrel."   Well, in plain prose, gentlemen and ladies,
you see here! come again, pop, at the hour!   I 'm come to tell
many things good, and many things not so very good; but the
good and the bad in everything are all packed up together now-
a-days.   So here 's my almanacks; they 've cost no little labour,
I 'll assure ye.   "Bless me," cried old Betty Winkle, "a man
must have a monstrous long head, to make all these 'ere calculations."   Ah, good woman, indeed he must.   The head of an
almanack-maker is nothing more nor less than a telescope, reach-
ing from pole to pole, and of sufficient diameter to embrace the
whole face of the heavens above, and the earth beneath!   The
firmament to him is a sort of checker-board, and the earth a bowl-
ing-green!   Come, who buys my wares?   Here 's the Sun, Moon
and Stars all for sale!

And again in 1824: —

> Through drifting snow and cutting sleet
> I 've truged and toiled my friends to greet;
> And tug'd beneath my lumb'ring gear
> To wish you all a *happy year.*
> Ye, gentle folks, shall I unpack,
> The precious store upon my back

My wallet, crowded to the brim,
And all the wealth of *Pedlar Tim?*
I 've books of various sorts and sizes;
Come, buy, just as your fancy prizes.

Walk up, gemmen! Now's your time to make a fortune!
Come, who takes this? Here is a Thacher's Orchardist; a
book that ought to be in the possession of every farmer. The
price one dollar, and Capt. Thrifty says he would give five
dollars rather than be without one. Here's another excellent
work, a Treatise on Gardening, by William Cobbett, the great
Porcupine! Be not afraid of his quills. The tiger is softened
to the lamb. He was once as fierce as a bull; but now he is as
calm as a sheep. His arrows were as sharp as a pitchfork; but,
now they are as blunt as a beetle! Now, my friends, is the
time to read books, crack nuts and tell stories — so here's
another of my Almanacks, which contains as much as the former
ones, and, I hope, as entertaining.

In 1825 the genial itinerant called when a wedding was
in progress and made himself quite at home: —

Say, would you hear what fun and cheer
We had at Simon's wedding, O?
'T was New-Year's day, we pack'd away
And thought no more of sledding, O —

We had all got cleverly together, and the Parson had commenced operations. The bow was already fixed around cousin
Simon's neck and well pinned and the Parson was about fetching
the bride under the yoke, when, who, the deuce should interrupt
us but old *Tim Twilight*, the peddler! "Apropos," said he, as
he burst in upon the ceremony, "I shall now find a market for
my Treatise on Good-Housewifery." "Hush!" cried aunt
Molly. "Mum!" said uncle Tim, and so hush it was to the end
of the service. Amen! said the parson, "amen," cried uncle
Tim. "And now, my good friends, will you suffer me to
introduce the contents of a poor peddler's pack; and give me

leave to say, Sir Simon, that the next thing, after a wife, is an *almanack*. This, Sir, is the chart book of the whole voyage. — Here is another little work upon butter and cheese making. — Here 's the *Farmer's Guide* and here 's the *Orchardist* again — and here comes the very tiptop of the climax, Dr. Dean's *Georgical Dictionary*. Hah, a glass of wine — long life to matrimony."

Tim's wares were not all chapbooks. Dr. Dean's Georgical Dictionary, for instance, is a substantial volume, to which we shall return on another occasion,[1] and the book-peddler in Theodore Sedgwick's Hints to my Countrymen, a rambling work published at Boston in 1826, had a good deal of solid literature in his pack.

Ballads have formed a part of the peddler's stock in trade from time immemorial, and we may be sure Tim Twilight did not neglect them. There is a good scene in John Davis's Travels in the United States which illustrates this point. Davis, who was touring on foot in 1801, spent the night at a log-cabin in the woods of Virginia : —

We had breakfasted next morning, and the old man was gone to cultivate his tobacco, when a pedlar came to the door. The appearance of *Sam Lace* lighted up joy in the eyes of *Mary* and *Eliza*.

The pedlar first exhibited his ballads. " Here," said he, " is the whole trial, examination, and condemnation of *Jason Fairbanks*, who was executed at *Philadelphia* for cutting off *Peggy Placket's* head under a hedge on the road to *Frankfort*."

Lord ! said *Eliza*, what a wicked fellow. I would not live in one of those great big towns for all the world ! But I wonder whether it is true ?

True ! replied *Mary*, certainly it is. Don't you see it is in print.

" And here,' cried the pedlar, " is the account of a whale, that

---

[1] See p. 309, below.

was left ashore by the tide in the bay of *Chesapeak,* with a ship of
five thousand tons in his belly, called the Merry Dane of *Dover.*
She was the largest ship ever known."

And is that true too? said *Eliza.*

True! cried *Mary.* How can you ask such a question? Do
you think they would put it in print if it were not true?[1]

Unfortunately this sketch cannot be accepted as a literal
transcript from observation, since Davis, who was an ardent
student of Shakspere, has copied it pretty closely from a
well-known passage in The Winter's Tale. Autolycus, dis-
guised as a peddler, is trafficking with the shepherd's son at
the shearer's feast, and Mopsa begs the clown to buy some
ballads. "I love a ballad in print a-life," says Mopsa,
"for then we are sure they are true." One of the pieces
offered by Autolycus is described as a "ballad of a fish
that appeared upon the coast, on Wednesday the four-
score of April, forty thousand fathom above water, and
sung this ballad against the hard hearts of maids: it was
thought she was a woman and was turned into a cold
fish." There are further resemblances between Shakspere and our jocose traveller, but what has been quoted
will suffice to show Davis's literary method.

Yet Davis is not inventing; he is merely exercising the
traveller's long-recognized right to embellish facts a little.
Jason Fairbanks, to be sure, was not "executed at Philadelphia for cutting off Peggy Placket's head under a hedge
on the road to Frankfort"; but he *was* executed at Dedham, Massachusetts, in 1801, for killing Betsy Fales with
a penknife in a field near her father's house. This case,
which presented some almost inexplicable features, attracted much attention and may well have been worked
up by some balladist, according to a custom not yet quite

[1] Travels in the United States of America, 1798–1802, London, 1803,
pp. 351–2.

obsolete. It certainly gave rise to a very curious chap-book, published at Dedham in 1801, — "The Solemn Declaration of the late Unfortunate Jason Fairbanks, from the Original Manuscript, composed and signed by himself, a very short time before his Death. To which is added, Some Account of his Life and Character. . . . The whole collected and published by Ebenezer Fair-banks, Jun., a Farmer of Dedham."[1] A Report of the Trial[2] was published in the same year and was widely circulated.

There are many ballads extant from the early New Eng-land press. An odd detail with regard to them, as well as to chapbooks, is preserved by the late Joseph T. Buck-ingham, and his reminiscence has to do with the decade in which the Farmer's Almanack began to appear. Mr. Buckingham was in 1796 an apprentice in the office of Thomas Dickman, proprietor of the Greenfield (Massachu-setts) Gazette. "The apprentices (there were two beside me) had the privilege," he says, "of printing such small jobs as they might obtain, without interfering with the regular business of the office, — and, as we clubbed our labors, we not unfrequently gathered a few shillings by printing ballads and small pamphlets for peddlers, who, at that time, were tolerably good customers to country printers."[3]

President Dwight, who was a stern moralist, and whose experience with the peddlers of Connecticut must have been extensive, is rather severe on old Tim Twilight's brethren, though he does not specify the trade in books. In speaking of Suffield, he expostulates with fortune in his inimitably dignified manner: —

[1] Dedham: from the Minerva Press of H. Mann, and sold at his Office, and by E. Fairbanks, Jun., 1801.

[2] Boston, Printed by Russell and Cutler, 1801.

[3] Buckingham, Personal Memoirs and Recollections of Editorial Life, Boston, 1852, I, 26.

A considerable number of the inhabitants of this part of the State have for many years employed themselves in peddling several kinds of articles, of small value, in many parts of this country. The proprietor loads with these one or more horses; and either travels himself, or sends an agent, from place to place, until he has bartered or sold them. In expeditions of this nature considerable numbers have spent no small part of their lives.

The consequences of this employment, and of all others like it, are generally malignant. Men, who begin life with bargaining for small wares, will almost invariably become sharpers. The commanding aim of every such man will soon be to make a good bargain : and he will speedily consider every gainful bargain as a good one. The tricks of fraud will assume, in his mind, the same place, which commercial skill and an honourable system of dealing hold in the mind of a merchant. Often employed in disputes, he becomes noisy, pertinacious, and impudent. A great body of the inhabitants in this part of the country are exempted from any share in these remarks; and sustain the same respectable character, which is common throughout New-England. Still, I believe this unfortunate employment to have had an unhappy influence on both the morals, and manners, of the people, so far as it has extended. [1]

We may be sure that Tim Twilight was a different kind of person. Mr. Thomas certainly believed in him, and that too in spite of the misfortunes of " my neighbour Spinage," who, according to the Farmer's Calendar for October, 1830, " last season, purchased of an honest pedlar a pound of wooden cucumber seeds ! "

[1] Travels in New-England and New-York, New Haven, 1821, I, 306.

FIRE!

IN 1799 the Almanac contained a series of observations on the prevention and extinction of Fire. They are thought to be the work of Benjamin Dearborn (1745–1838), and are particularly amusing from their anecdotical character.

[*The following is inserted at the request of the Massachusetts Charitable Fire Society.*]

DIRECTIONS for *preventing* CALAMITIES by FIRE.

1. KEEP your chimnies and stove-pipes clean, by sweeping them at least once every month.

2. Never remove hot ashes in a wooden vessel of any kind, and look well to your ash-hole.

3. After sweeping a hearth, see that the brush does not retain any particles of fire, before you hang it up in its usual place.

4. Oblige all your servants to go to bed before you, every night, and inspect all your fire-places, before you retire to rest. — For fear of accidents, let a bucket of water be left in your kitchen every night. The writer of these directions once saved his house from being consumed by fire by this precaution.

5. Do not permit a servant to carry a candle to his bed-room, if he sleeps in an unplastered garret.

6. Cover up your fire carefully every night in ashes. Let the unburnt parts of the billets or chunks of wood, be placed next the hearth, but not set upright in the corners, by which means no sparks will be emitted from the wood. Pour a little water upon the burning ends of the wood which are not completely covered by the ashes. Place before the fire a fender made of sheet iron.

FIRE-ENGINE AT WORK

(From a Broadside of 1760)

This contrivance was well known in England many years ago, by
the name of *Coverfeu.* It has lately received (from a top being
added to it) the name of *Hood.*

7. Remove papers and linen from near the fire to a remote
part of the room.

8. Shut the doors of all the rooms in which you leave fire at
night. By thus excluding the supply of fresh air, you will prevent
a flame being kindled, should a coal or spark fall upon the floor,
or upon any of the combustible matter in the room. The smoke
which issues from this smothered fire, will find its way into every
part of the house, and by waking the family, may save it from
destruction.

9. If sickness or any other cause should oblige you to leave a
candle burning all night, place it in such a situation as to be out
of the way of rats. A house was once destroyed by a rat running
away with a lighted candle for the sake of the tallow, and conveying it into a hole filled with rags, and inflammable matter.

10. Never read in bed by candle light, especially if your bed
be surrounded by curtains.

11. Strictly forbid the use of segars in your family at all times,
but especially after night. May not the greater frequency of fires
in the United States than in former years, be ascribed in part to
the more general use of segars by careless servants and children?
—There is a good reason to believe a house was lately set on fire
by a half consumed segar, which a woman suddenly threw away
to prevent being detected in the unhealthy and offensive practice
of smoaking.

*In case of fire attend to the following directions, to prevent or
restrain its terrible consequences.*

1. Do not open the room or closet door where you suspect
the fire to be, until you have secured your family, and your most
valuable effects, nor until you have collected a quantity of water
to throw on the fire, the moment a fresh supply of air excites it
to a flame. Where water cannot conveniently be had, try to
smother the fire by throwing two or three blankets over it. A

British sea captain once saved a king's ship by throwing himself with a spread blanket in his arms, upon a fire which had broke out near the powder room. He was pensioned for life, for this wise and meritorious act.

2. In case it be impossible to escape by a stair-case from a house on fire, shut the door of your bed-chamber, and wait until help can be brought to secure your escape from a window.

3. If safety does not appear probable in this way, wrap yourselves up in a blanket, hold your breath, and rush through the flames. If water be at hand, first wet the blanket.

4. To prevent fire descending from the roof, or ascending from the first story, form by means of blankets or carpets, a kind of dam on each of the intermediate stories, near their stair-case, that shall confine the water that is thrown upon the roof, or into the windows. It will effectually check the progress of the fire downwards or upwards in brick or stone houses.

5. To prevent fire spreading to adjoining houses, cover them with wet blankets or carpets, or old sails.

6. To extinguish fire in a chimney, shut the door and windows of the room. Throwing a quart or more of common salt into the fire. Hold, or nail a wet blanket before the fire-place. If these means fail, throw a wet blanket down the chimney from the roof of the house.

There is a method used in some countries of glazing chimnies when they are built, by burning common salt in them, which renders them so smooth that no soot can adhere to them. Chimnies so constructed can never take fire.

Ladders are commonly used as the means of conveying persons from the windows of houses on fire. Would not a long and stiff pole, with a rope fixed on its upper end, be more portable, and convenient for this purpose?

The famous Mr. John Wesley when a child, was taken out of a window in his father's house whilst in flames, by one man standing upon the shoulders of another. This practice may be used to rescue persons from the first story of a house on fire,

when other means cannot be had with sufficient convenience or
expedition.

. . . .

The Massachusetts Charitable Fire Society, which circulated the Directions just given, was organized in 1792, incorporated in 1794, and still exists. Its object was to
relieve sufferers by fire, and to promote discussion and
invention of the means by which fires may be prevented
or extinguished. For a good many years it held anniversary exercises, consisting of an oration and an ode, but
these were discontinued in 1818. Several of the odes were
written by Robert Treat Paine, Jr., who changed his name
from Thomas Paine on account of his dislike for the author
of the Age of Reason. The celebrated patriotic songs,
" Rise, Columbia" and " Adams and Liberty," were originally written by Mr. Paine for the anniversary celebration
of the Fire Society. The latter was set to the tune called
" To Anacreon in Heaven," but now best known as " The
Star Spangled Banner." A single stanza will recall this
almost forgotten ode to the memory of some readers.

Ye Sons of Columbia, who bravely have fought,
    For those rights, which unstain'd from your sires had descended,
May you long taste the blessings your valor has bought,
    And your sons reap the soil which their fathers defended!
            Mid the reign of mild peace,
            May your nation increase,
    With the glory of Rome, and the wisdom of Greece.
        And no Son of COLUMBIA *shall e'er be a slave,*
        While the earth bears a plant, or the sea rolls a wave.[1]

Benjamin Dearborn, the probable author of the Directions,
was an early member of the society, and served on the
Committee on Machines almost continuously from 1794
to 1818.[2]

[1] H. H. Sprague, An Old Boston Institution. A Brief History of the
Massachusetts Charitable Fire Society. Boston, 1893, pp. 17, 18, 56, 57, 95.
[2] Sprague, p. 33.

It should be remembered that the danger of fire, always sufficiently terrible, was peculiarly distressing at this time, because of the prevalence of frame buildings, and also because of the lack of insurance companies.   An attempt was made to found a fire insurance business in Boston, in 1728, but it was unsuccessful.   There is no evidence that any building in Boston was insured against fire before 1795, when the Massachusetts Fire Insurance Company, afterwards the Massachusetts Fire and Marine Insurance Company, was incorporated.   In 1798 the Massachusetts Mutual Fire Insurance Company was formed.   Rates, however, in the shape of premiums and deposits, were so high that insurance was far from popular.   We learn that the Mutual Company issued " seven-year policies at fifty-five cents per hundred on single wooden buildings, and seventy cents per hundred on wooden buildings in blocks, while thirty-five and forty-five cents per hundred were charged respectively on single and double buildings of brick and stone covered with slate or tile, while in addition deposits of several times the amount charged were required." [1]   It was customary to raise money by subscription for the partial relief of sufferers.

A graphic picture of a fire in Boston not far from the time when Mr. Dearborn's Directions were published in the Almanac, is given in a letter written December 27, 1796, by William Priest, an English musician who was employed in various theatres in Philadelphia, Baltimore, and Boston, from 1793 to 1797 : —

There is no calamity the bostonians so much, and justly dread, as fire.   Almost every part of the town exhibits melancholy proofs of the devastation of that destructive element.   This you will not wonder at, when I inform you that three fourths of the houses are built with *wood*, and covered with *shingles*, thin peices of cedar,

[1] Sprague, pp. 16–17.

nearly in the shape, and answering the end of tiles. We have
no regular fire-men, or rather mercenaries, as every master of a
family belongs to a fire-company : there are several in town, composed of every class of citizens, who have entered into a contract
to turn out with two buckets at the first fire alarm, and assist to
the utmost of their power in extinguishing the flames, without fee
or reward.

I awoke this morning about two o'clock by the cry of fire, and
the jingling of all the church bells, which, with the rattling of the
engines, call for water, and other *et cætera* of a bostonian fire-
alarm, form a concert truly horrible.

As sleep was impossible under such circumstances, I immediately rose, and found the town illuminated. When the alarm is
given at night, the female part of the family immediately place
candles in the windows. This is of great service in a town where
there are few lamps.

I found the fire had broken out in one of the narrow streets,
and was spreading fast on all sides. I was much pleased with the
regularity observed by these *amateur* fire-men. Each engine had
a double row, extending to the nearest water ; one row passed
the full, and the other the empty buckets. The citizens not employed at the engines were pulling down the adjacent buildings,
or endeavouring to save the furniture ; their behaviour was bold
and intrepid. The wind blew fresh at N. W. ; and nothing but
such uncommon exertions could possibly have saved the town,
composed, as it is, of such *combustible* materials. You will naturally inquire, whether they have no other. Yes, brick and stone
in great plenty ; but the cheapness of a frame, or wooden building, is a great inducement for the continuance of this dangerous
practice : but there is one still greater, viz. a strange idea, universal in America, that wooden houses are more healthy, and less
liable to generate or retain contagious infection than those of
brick or stone. This notion has been ably controverted by one
of their best *writers*, but with little effect; and, like all other
deep-rooted prejudices, will not easily be eradicated.[1]

[1] Travels in the United States of America, London, 1802, pp. 168–71.

The Directions make special mention of fire-engines. There were in 1799 thirteen of these machines, new and old, in Boston, the thirteenth going into commission on July 24th of that year.[1] They were, of course, hand-engines. Mr. Dearborn himself, being of an inventive turn of mind, was much interested in such things. In 1781 he communicated to the American Academy of Arts and Sciences a model of what he called a pump-engine, together with a full description, which was published in the Memoirs of the Academy in 1785.[2] A plate accompanies Mr. Dearborn's article and enables us to get a clear notion of his curious contrivance. It consisted of a long vertical tube, which could be attached to the top of an ordinary pump, and at the upper end of which there was a swinging conductor, managed by means of a couple of ropes. " I have," writes Mr. Dearborn, " raised a tube of 30 feet on my pump, but the severity of the season prevents my compleating it; having so far executed it only, as for one person to work at the brake; I can myself throw water on the top of a neighbouring building, the nearest part of which is 37 feet from the pump, and between 30 and 40 feet high." It was thought that this stationary machine might be of use in private families, something like a fire-extinguisher nowadays, but it does not seem to have been extensively adopted. In the next year Mr. Dearborn applied the same principles of construction to a portable engine, which is figured in the same volume. The advantages which he claimed for his invention were cheapness, ease of manufacture, and economy of labor in operation. Apparently, however, it never got beyond the model stage. Mr. Dearborn also devised a

[1] A. W. Brayley, Complete History of the Boston Fire Department, Boston, 1889, p. 105; cf. Belknap's letter, Coll. Mass. Hist. Soc., 1st Series, IV, 188.
[2] I, 520.

FLAMMARUN

IN PAVIDI

Sir, Boston 9 7br 27 1799

The UNITED FIRE SOCIETY

is to meet at Concert Hall on Friday
Evening next at 7 oClock when you are desir'd to
give your punctual Attendance.

Ebenezer Allen Secy

"ladder and receiver" and a "leveller." The former was
a primitive kind of fire-escape, consisting of a ladder
"long enough to reach from the ground to the chamber
windows" and of a sliding box attached to the ladder
and operated by ropes. In the accompanying description
he emphasizes "the expedition and security with which
persons and articles may be transported to the ground
from the chamber windows of a house on fire or in
danger." The leveller was an implement for destroying
buildings by tearing out the posts, sills, and beams.
Models of both inventions were deposited with the Massachusetts Historical Society, but it does not appear that
the contrivances were ever put to a practical use.[1]

One of the most surprising of the anecdotes in Mr.
Dearborn's Directions is that in the ninth section : — "A
house was once destroyed by a rat running away with a
lighted candle for the sake of the tallow, and conveying it
into a hole filled with rags, and inflammable matter." No
one can fail to admire the address and agility of the rat
and to wonder who was present to observe his feat. Mr.
Joseph Willard refers with much pertinency to the peril
of Judge Sewall's household, as set forth in his Diary for
"Midweek," July 13, 1709, where a similar exploit is
conjecturally ascribed to a mouse : —

Midweek, July, 13. 1709. N. B. Last night, between 2 or 3
hours after midnight, my wife complain'd of Smoak ; I presently
went out of Bed, and saw and felt the Chamber very full of Smoak
to my great Consternation. I slipt on my Cloaths except Stockings, and run out of one Room into another above, and below
Stairs, and still found all well but my own Bed-chamber. I went
into Garret and rouz'd up David, who fetch'd me a Candle. My
wife fear'd the Brick side was a-fire, and the children endangered.
She fled thither, and call'd all up there. While she was doing
this, I felt the partition of my Bed-chamber Closet warm ; which

[1] Sprague, pp. 45-46.

made me with fear to unlock it, and going in I found the Deal-Box of Wafers all afire, burning livelily; yet not blazing. I drew away the papers nearest to it, and call'd for a Bucket of Water. By that time it came, I had much adoe to recover the Closet agen: But I did, and threw my Water on it, and so more, and quench'd it thorowly. Thus with great Indulgence GOD saved our House and Substance, and the Company's[1] Paper. This night, as I lay down in my Bed, I said to my Wife, that the Goodness of God appeared, in that we had a Chamber, a Bed, and Company. If my Wife had not waked me, we might have been consumed. And it seems admirable, that the opening the Closet-Door did not cause the Fire to burst forth into an Unquenchable Flame. The Box was 18 inches over, Closet full of loose papers, boxes, Cases, some Powder. The Window-Curtain was of Stubborn Woolen and refus'd to burn though the Iron-Bars were hot with the fire. Had that burnt it would have fired the pine-shelves and files of Papers and Flask and Bandaliers of powder. The Pine-Floor on which the Box stood, was burnt deep, but being well plaister'd between the Joysts, it was not burnt through. The Closet under it had Hundreds of Reams of the Company's Paper in it. The plaistered Wall is mark'd by the Fire so as to resemble a Chimney back. Although I forbad mine to cry Fire; yet quickly after I had quench'd it; the Chamber was full of Neighbours and Water. The smell of Fire pass'd on me very much; which lasted some days. We imagine a Mouse might take our lighted Candle out of the Candle-stick on the hearth and dragg it under my closet-door behind the Box of Wafers. The good Lord sanctify this Threatening; and his Parental Pity in improving our selves for the Discovery of the Fire, and Quenching it. The Lord teach me what I know not; and wherein I have done amiss help me to doe so no more![2]

Mr. Dearborn shared the prejudice of his age against "segars." He enquires whether "the greater frequency

[1] Probably the Society for Propagating the Gospel.
[2] Coll. Mass. Hist. Soc., 5th Series, VI, 257-9.

of fires in the United States than in former years, may not be ascribed in part to the more general use of segars by careless servants and children?" and adds "There is good reason to believe a house was lately set on fire by a half-consumed segar, which a woman suddenly threw away to prevent being detected in the unhealthy and offensive practice of smoaking." It was no new thing for women to smoke. Mrs. Rowlandson's interview with King Philip, when he politely offered her a pipe, will be described in a later chapter, and we shall see that she declined his courtesy because she had overcome her former appetite for tobacco.[1] But the cigar, being still something of a novelty, was regarded with peculiar disapproval by the more staid and conservative members of the community. At almost the very moment when Mr. Dearborn was penning his cautionary Directions, the General Court of Massachusetts was busy with an Act to Secure the Town of Boston from Damage by Fire (1798).[2] This act forbade carrying fire through the streets, except in a covered vessel, as well as smoking, or having in one's possession "any lighted pipe or segar" in the streets or on the wharves. The penalty was fixed at two dollars, or, if the offense was committed in any ropewalk, at from five to one hundred dollars. These provisions were really but a modification of a much older law. In 1638 the General Court ordered "that no man shall take any Tobacco within twenty Poles of any House, or so near as may endanger the same."[3] To "fetch fire" from a neighbor's when one's own hearth was cold was a regular thing in the days of the troublesome flint and steel. It even passed into a proverb. One who made a hasty visit was said to be "in as great a hurry as if he had come to fetch fire." So in Chaucer, when Troilus

[1] See p. 370, below.
[2] Acts of 1798, chap. 27, sects. 6, 7.
[3] Laws, edition of 1672, p. 146.

proposes to cut short his visit to Sarpedon, Pandarus asks
reproachfully —

> " Be we comen hider
> To fecchen fyr and rennen hom ayeyn? "[1]

The danger of this custom is plain enough and was soon
felt by the inhabitants of Boston.   In 1658 an order was
passed to restrain it: —

> Whereas many careless persons carry fire from one house unto
> another in open fire pans or brands ends, by reason of which
> greatt damage may accrew to the towne ; It is therefore ordered
> that no person shall have liberty to carry fire from one house to
> another, without a safe vessell to secure itt from the wind, upon
> the pœnalty of ten shillings to bee paid by every party so fetching,
> and halfe so much by those that permitt them so to take
> fire.[2]

To smoke in the streets was simply a special variety of
" carrying fire."   The peril of the lighted cigar has long
ceased to agitate the fathers of the Commonwealth.   The
prohibition remained in the statutes till 1880, when it was
repealed.[3]   It had long been a dead letter, and the Fire
Commissioners of Boston, who were consulted by the legis-
lators before they decided to annul it, declared that they
were quite willing to have it disappear.

A racy portrait of a rural cigar-smoker, from the
Farmer's Calendar for August, 1836, may serve as an
epilogue.   The compound noun with which it concludes
is worthy of Aristophanes.

> See, what a puffing-pig Bob Linchpin has got to be !   It was
> about a year and a half ago, when he had not yet become

---

[1] Troilus, book v, stanza 70.

[2] Boston Town Records, in Second Report of Record Commissioners,
2d ed., 1881, p. 147.

[3] See Acts of 1818, chap. 171, sect. 10, and, for the repeal, Acts of 1880,
chap. 38.

acquainted with the ton of the city, that Robert went there to market, and to see a cousin or two. He carried down butter and eggs, and a few other articles of the produce of his father's farm. Poor soul! He will rue the day that he ever fell among dandies. But so it was, for his cousins were altogether for being *bursters;* and Bob was initiated into a clan of these mutton-faced non-essentials. So, our friend's name was changed from clever Robert to flashy Bob; and, among other things of fashionable consequence, he learned to wield a *real Spanish.* Whif! see the columns, as they roll away and bring to view his bumps of self-esteem! Poor Bobby, how changed from a right-down, plain, honest plough-jogger to a tippy-dazzlem-fogo-combustibus!

"DROWNED! DROWNED!"

SOMETIME in the Spring of 1787, or '88, a young gentleman at Georgetown, who could not swim, accompanied by one or more of his companions, went into the river to bathe; he unfortunately stepped from a bank of sand, beyond his depth, and was drowned. Attempts were immediately made in various ways to obtain the body, by diving after it, searching with boat-hooks, poles, etc. and by a dragging seine; but all of them proved ineffectual. Similar exertions were made next day without success.

A gentleman mentioned, that he had read of the bodies of drowned persons being discovered by means of quicksilver, placed in a quill, and attached to a loaf of warm bread. — This appeared so chimerical a project, that the bystanders ridiculed the idea. He observed that the experiment might easily be made, and could do no injury. A quill was prepared, filled with quicksilver, and inserted in a loaf of warm bread.

Some persons then got into a boat, and placed the bread on the water so as to be carried with the current in a direction towards the body; when it had floated 10 or 15 yards, it became stationary, and in a short time the body ascended and floated on the top of the water, to the great astonishment of the multitude of spectators. The body had laid under water about 16 or 18 hours.

The experiment above recorded deserves a trial on similar occasions, and might even be the means of restoring life, by discovering drowned bodies soon after they have disappeared.

May not this singular phenomenon be accounted for in this simple manner? The bread is carried down by the current till it comes within the sphere of attraction between the body and the quicksilver: it is then brought by the same attraction over the body; and the specific gravity of the body being but little greater

than that of the water, by the attraction of the quicksilver, a substance of very great specific gravity and proportionate attraction,
the body rises to the surface of the water.

The method of discovering the situation of a drowned
man described in the article just quoted from the Almanac
for 1796 seems to have been rather common in different
countries, and, in one form or another, must be pretty old.
In the Upper Palatinate the peasantry believe that if the
person's name is written on a piece of bread, this will float
to the place where the body lies and then remain stationary. In Bohemia the name is omitted; a consecrated
candle is lighted and stuck into a hole in the bread, which,
as in the Georgetown anecdote, must be fresh.[1] Here, as in
the example from the Palatinate, the process is manifestly
of an occult character. In the one case, the success of the
experiment depends on the mysterious efficacy of the con-
secration. In the other, we may discern the widespread
belief in the sympathetic and essential connection between
the name and the person who bears it. This is a belief
which underlies an almost countless number of superstitions. The berserk Klaufi, in an Icelandic saga, is deprived of his demonic strength when, in the course of a
fierce struggle, some one calls him by name: "Klaufi!
Klaufi! govern your rage!" A werewolf is instantly restored to his proper human shape if his right name is
mentioned in his hearing. The most powerful spirits are
controllable by the magician who knows their names. The
true name of Rome was said to be kept a secret, lest the
enemy, learning it, might employ it in spells to call away
the deities that protected the Eternal City.

In the Almanac, it will be noted, an attempt is made to
account for the phenomena on scientific principles, and
perhaps, as in so many cases, there is in the customs de-

---

[1] Wuttke, Der deutsche Volksaberglaube, 2d ed., Berlin, 1869, § 371, p. 239.

scribed a union of observation and experience with magical principles of long standing. In the Gentleman's Magazine for April, 1767,[1] not very long before the date of the Almanac, is recorded an occurrence which closely resembles that which is said to have taken place at Georgetown. It is worth quoting for its picturesqueness, even if it slightly exceeds the limits of probability:—

An inquisition was taken at *Newbery, Berks*, on the body of a child near 2 years old, who fell into the river *Kennet*, and was drowned. The jury brought in their verdict *Accidental Death.*— The body was discovered by a very singular experiment, which was as follows: After diligent search had been made in the river for the child, to no purpose, a two-penny loaf, with a quantity of quicksilver put into it, was set floating from the place where the child, it was supposed, had fallen in, which steered its course down the river upwards of half a mile, before a great number of spectators, when the body happening to lay on the contrary side of the river, the loaf suddenly tacked about, and swam across the river, and gradually sunk near the child, when both the child and loaf were immediately brought up, with grablers ready for that purpose.

The Indians of Canada, according to Sir James Alexander, use a chip of cedar, which, they suppose, "will stop and turn round over the exact spot" where the body lies. Sir James adds that he has known of an instance in which this was tried with complete success. Similarly a cricket bat, we are told, was thrown into the Thames near the place at which an Eton scholar had been seen to go down. "It floated to a spot where it turned round in an eddy, and from a deep hole underneath the body was quickly drawn." Here natural causes may well be appealed to, as is done by a sensible commentator in Notes and Queries:—"As there

[1] XXXVII, 189. This and other instances may be found in Choice Notes from Notes and Queries, London, 1859, pp. 40–42.

are in all running streams deep pools formed by eddies, in which drowned bodies would be likely to be caught and retained, any light substance thrown into the current would consequently be drawn to that part of the surface over the centre of the eddy hole." [1]

In the fine old ballad of Young Hunting [2] the slain knight is cast into the deepest pot in Clyde Water, " with a green turf upon his breast, to hold that good lord down." The murderess is so confident in the efficacy of this weight upon his breast that she does not hesitate to express a fear that he is drowned in Clyde. The king sends for his " duckers," but they dive for the body in vain. At last a bonny bird that is flying above their heads speaks and discloses the secret : —

"O he 's na drownd in Clyde Water,
　　He is slain and put therein;
The lady that lives in yon castil
　　Slew him and put him in.

" Leave aff your ducking on the day,
　　And duck upon the night ;
Whear ever that sakeless knight lys slain,
　　The candels will shine bright."

Thay left off their ducking o the day,
　　And ducked upon the night,
And where that sakeless knight lay slain,
　　The candles shone full bright.

The deepest pot intill it a'
　　Thay got Young Hunting in;
A green turff upon his brest,
　　To hold that good lord down.

Here the candles may have been real candles inserted in loaves of bread and balanced with quicksilver, as already

[1] See Choice Notes, p. 43.
[2] Child, English and Scottish Popular Ballads, No. 68 A, II, 145.
11

described, or the reference may be to the " corpse lights"
which were believed to hover over the resting place of the
unquiet dead.   The ballad is not explicit.

In 1795 the Almanac prints certain recommendations of
the Massachusetts Humane Society to be followed in cases
of apparent death from drowning: —

As accidents of drowning frequently occur, and as it is very
necessary that every family should be acquainted with the best
method of proceeding in such cases, we have inserted the following

DIRECTIONS

For recovering persons apparently dead from drowning :
as recommended by the HUMANE SOCIETY.

Convey the person to the nearest convenient house, with his
head raised ; strip and dry him as quick as possible ; clean the
mouth and nostrils from froth and mud ; if it is a child, let him
be placed between two persons naked, in a hot bed ; but if an
adult, lay him on a hot blanket or bed, and in cold weather near
a fire — in warm weather, the air should be freely admitted into
the room.   The body is next to be gently rubbed with warm
woollen cloths sprinkled with spirits, if at hand, otherwise dry ; a
heated warming pan may be lightly moved over the back properly
covered with a blanket ; and the body, if of a child, to be gently
shook every few minutes.

Then follow directions for the injection of tobacco smoke.
There is no suggestion of the means employed nowadays
for producing artificial respiration.

Bathe the breast with hot rum, and persist in the use of these
means for several hours.   If no signs of life should then appear,
let the body be kept warm for several hours longer, with hot
bricks, or vessels of hot water applied to the palms of the hands,
and soles of the feet, and this for a longer or shorter time, as
the circumstances of the case may dictate.

The Massachusetts Humane Society (like the Charitable Fire Society, whose recommendations were printed in the Almanac for 1799) [1] was one of the earliest charitable associations founded in this part of the world. It was instituted in 1785, definitely organized in the next year, at the Bunch of Grapes Tavern in State Street, and incorporated in 1791. Its prime object was, and is, to save life, especially in cases of shipwreck or drowning. It erected huts or shelters at exposed places on the coast, gave rewards for rescues, and encouraged the invention of lifeboats and life-saving apparatus. In 1792 it began an agitation for the building of a lighthouse at some point on Cape Cod. It is hard to realize that this dangerous coast was so little protected in those days. From the outset, however, the Society was particularly interested in the means of restoring suspended animation. We shall not be far wrong if we ascribe its foundation to the intense interest felt toward the close of the eighteenth century in the obscure question of the boundary between life and death. This matter had been much canvassed by the English Humane Society, which was founded in 1774, and a large number of cases had been collected and printed in which drowned persons had been brought to life when all traces of animation had vanished. A similar association at Amsterdam had done good work in the same direction, and the proceedings of this body had been published in an English translation by Dr. Thomas Cogan (1773). The period immediately following the Revolution was fertile in projects. It was an era of intellectual activity in America, and the foundation of the Humane Society was a gratifying testimony to the readiness of New England to act on the impulse of a good idea.

The Directions for resuscitation published in the Almanac for 1795 remained for some time the code of the Society. They will be seen to differ in essential points from

[1] See pp. 146 ff., above.

those now issued by the same organization. The use of tobacco smoke, strange as it seems to us, was regarded as of prime importance in the eighteenth century. It is dwelt on in the elaborate and highly interesing treatise on Drowning by Dr. Rowland Jackson (London, 1746),[1] and the Amsterdam Society endorsed it heartily. The opinion in its favor was confirmed by the testimony of Dr. Bulfinch, in a letter addressed to the Massachusetts Society in 1792, to the effect that the American Indians used it to revive the drowned. Gradually, however, doubts arose as to its efficacy. In 1794 the medical committee of the Society reported in its favor,[2] but the very fact that the question had been referred to them indicates that scruples were making themselves felt. In 1805 tobacco smoke is dropped from the official recommendations, and two years later the Rev. William Emerson, in his address to the Society, denounces its employment as absurd and harmful. As early as 1801, the necessity of inducing respiration by artificial means is recognized, and the directions to this end gradually became more elaborate, until they reached the form in which they are now familiar to everyone. In the same year, 1801, electricity is recommended.

In 1805 the Almanac contains a report of an interesting case of resuscitation : —

On restoring life to DROWNED PEOPLE *by means of warm ashes, as related by Mr. Solomon Rockwell, of Winchester, in a letter to the Editors of the Connecticut Courant.*

On Monday, the 9th day of July, 1804, a child of Mr. Caleb Munson, about fifteen months old, was taken out of the water apparently dead. From the place where it fell in it had floated down the stream about sixty feet in a swift current through a gate hole in the bottom of the mill trough, where the water falls six

---

[1] Physical Dissertation upon Drowning, pp. 44–47.
[2] Statement of Premiums, etc., 1829, pp. 48, 49.

feet, and was found lodged in trash under water. It must have been in the water at least fifteen minutes, and it was the universal opinion of those present, that any attempt to restore it to life would be totally unavailing. I however determined to try the experiment of ashes; accordingly I had its clothes taken off, spread some warm ashes taken from the fire-place, on flannel, and wrapped the child in the flannel, with the ashes next its skin; ordered tobacco smoke to be injected into its body, and soon applied an addition of hot ashes directly to its bowels. After operating in this way about eight or ten minutes, together with blowing into its mouth, to the astonishment of all present, signs of life began to appear, and water in large quantities issued from his mouth. A potion of physic was given him in about two hours, and in about twenty-four hours he was able to walk, and is now entirely recovered : (four days after.) This successful experiment ought to operate as a caution to all who read the account not to abandon too hastily to their fate those who are so unfortunate as to be drowned ; but to make trial of the most approved means in circumstances where there is the least possibility of success.

The Physical Dissertation upon Drowning, by Dr. Rowland Jackson, deserves another word. Its collection of cases is vastly curious. Many are quite credible, but a number of them show that scientific investigation was still a desideratum in 1746. Dr. Jackson entertained extravagant notions of the length of time after which one might bring a drowned man to life. He tells of a fisherman who " by means of the ice " was kept under water for three days, and yet came to life. The man remembered that " a large Bladder had been form'd about his Head for his Preservation." This sounds like miracle. At all events the learned doctor does not try to account for the bladder. A similar formation protected the mouth of a Swedish gardener who had a like incredible adventure. Then there was a Swedish woman who lived to the age of seventy-four, though she had been " thrice drowned," — remaining three

days under water on the first occasion. But these examples fade into insignificance before the strange case of Laurence Jones, whose funeral sermon the learned Burmann had listened to.   According to the preacher, Jones, when sixteen years old, fell into the water and remained there for *seven weeks*, but recovered, and lived to be seventy. Even Dr. Jackson is a little doubtful of the accuracy of these figures, though why, he asks, should the learned Burmann misrepresent the words of the preacher, and why should the preacher tell a lie? [1]

It is easy to laugh at such stories, but after all their moral was a good one.   The hasty inference that a man is dead because he has stopped breathing had cost the world a countless number of valuable lives, and needed drastic correction.   A little hyperbole could do no harm.

It may be added that for a long time the true cause of death by drowning was not understood.   A venerable instance of this misapprehension occurs in the Anglo-Saxon epic of Béowulf.   There the hero takes a long dive to the bottom of a haunted pool and enters a subaqueous hall, where he performs a very valorous exploit.   As soon as he enters the hall, he is quite at his ease.   The water, we are told, could not get in to injure him.   Here is the gist of the whole matter.   The theory was that a man was drowned because the water did him some harm rather than because he had nothing to breathe.   Hence the efficacy of the "bladder" that formed before the mouth of the fisherman whom Dr. Jackson tells of.   Even the eminent physicist Boyle was in doubt "whether an animal in an exhausted receiver dies for want of air, or because of the compression of the lungs" and in 1665 suggested an experiment to discover the facts.[2]   And the Royal Society entertained the idea that "a kind of new air" made by the "operation of

[1] Jackson, pp. 7, 10, 11, 15–16.
[2] Birch, History of the Royal Society, II, 31.

distilled vinegar upon the powder of oister-shells" might be "convenient for respiration" and afford a means of breathing under water.[1]

In 1794 the Massachusetts Magazine printed a letter, dated January, 1789, from a member of the Humane Society which suggested an extension of the method of resuscitation then practised to cases of apparent death by cold. The writer had found that apples might be preserved by frost and had seen potatoes ploughed up in the spring " which had lain all winter in the ground, and were as sound and good, though frequently frozen, as those that were dug in the fall of the year." A snake too, he said, might " freeze so hard and stiff that it will break like a pipe-stem " and yet would come to life again. He likewise appealed to the hibernation of swallows, which were believed to spend the winter at the bottom of ponds, either frozen or buried in the mud, and to emerge in the spring.[2] Some days before, the writer had seen the bodies of " eight or ten stout men, frozen hard as rocks," and the melancholy spectacle set him thinking. He ventured to suggest that it might not be amiss to disinter one of the bodies and endeavor to resuscitate it.[3] His proposals came to nothing, but they remain as a record of the speculative activity of men's minds at the end of the eighteenth century, — a disposition to which the world owes much.

[1] Birch, History of the Royal Society, II, 25, 26.
[2] See a paper on this phenomenon in the Memoirs of the American Academy, 1785, I, 494.
[3] Massachusetts Magazine for January, 1794, VI, 23–25.

HUSKINGS AND OTHER AMUSEMENTS

ADMIRAL BARTHOLOMEW JAMES of the Royal Navy, during his excursion on the Kennebec River, in 1791, when he was a captain in the merchant service, had the good fortune to be present at a husking at Vassalborough, which he briefly but appreciatively describes in his entertaining journal: — " During our stay at this place we saw and partook of the ceremony of husking corn, a kind of 'harvest home' in England, with the additional amusement of kissing the girls whenever they met with a red corn-cob, and to which is added dancing, singing, and moderate drinking." [1]

The admiral was fond of diversion and had a penchant for eccentric merrymaking. After he had retired from active service, and when he was enjoying his leisure as a country gentleman, he is said to have entertained the poor of the vicinity with a feast at which the chief dish was a sea-pie of Gargantuan proportions. Mr. Thomas, however, was a practical farmer. He was not averse to seasonable amusement, but he detested waste, and he was always suspicious of any combination of work and play. Here are some of the precepts in his Farmer's Calendar: —

Harvest your Indian corn, unless you intend it for the squirrels. If you make a husking, keep an old man between every two boys, else your *husking* will turn out a *losing*. (October, 1805.)

[1] Journal of Rear-Admiral Bartholomew James, Navy Records Society, 1896, p. 193.

Come, Dolly, my dear, spur up; prepare something good
and cheering, for we will have a husking to-night.   (November,
1806.)

In a husking there is some fun and frolick, but on the whole,
it hardly pays the way; for they will not husk clean, since many
go more for the sport than to do any real good.   (October,
1808.)

Husking is now a business for us all.   If you make what some
call a *Bee*, it will be necessary to keep an eye on the boys, or you
may have to husk over again the whole heap.   (October, 1816.)

Some years later, in 1828, when the brief agricultural
maxims of the Farmer's Calendar had expanded into character sketches and little didactic essays, we find a more
elaborate confession of faith on the subject of the New
England harvest-home: —

" Come, wife, let us make a husking," said Uncle Pettyworth.
" No, no," replied the prudent woman, " you and the boys will
be able to husk out our little heap without the trouble, the waste
and expense of a husking frolick.   The girls and I will lend a
hand, and all together will make it but a short job."   Now, had
the foolish man took the advice of his provident wife, how much
better would it have turned out for him?   But the boys sat in,
and the girls sat in, and his own inclinations sat in, and all be-
setting him at once he was persuaded into the unnecessary
measure, and a *husking* was determined upon.   Then one of the
boys was soon mounted upon the colt with a jug on each side,
pacing off to 'Squire Hookem's store for four gallons of whiskey.
The others were sent to give the invitations.   The mother being
obliged to yield, with her daughters went about preparing the
supper.   Great was the gathering at night round the little corn
stack.   Capt. Husky, old Busky, Tom Bluenose and about
twenty good-for-nothing boys began the operations.   Red ears
and smutty, new rum and slack-jaw was the business of the
evening.   (October, 1828.)

" Red ears and smutty " are fully treated in Joel Barlow's
Hasty Pudding, which was written in the winter of 1792–93
and contains the classic passage on husking parties : —

> The days grow short ; but though the falling sun
> To the glad swain proclaims his day's work done,
> Night's pleasing shades his various tasks prolong,
> And yield new subjects to my various song.
> For now, the corn-house fill'd, the harvest home,
> The invited neighbors to the *husking* come ;
> A frolic scene, where work, and mirth, and play,
> Unite their charms, to chase the hours away.
> Where the huge heap lies centred in the hall,
> The lamp suspended from the cheerful wall,
> Brown corn-fed nymphs, and strong hard-handed beaux,
> Alternate ranged, extend in circling rows,
> Assume their seats, the solid mass attack ;
> The dry husks rustle, and the corn-cobs crack ;
> The song, the laugh, alternate notes resound,
> And the sweet cider trips in silence round.
> The laws of husking every wight can tell —
> And sure no laws he ever keeps so well :
> For each red ear a general kiss he gains,
> With each smut ear he smuts the luckless swains ;
> But when to some sweet maid a prize is cast,
> Red as her lips, and taper as her waist,
> She walks the round, and culls one favored beau,
> Who leaps, the luscious tribute to bestow.
> Various the sport, as are the wits and brains
> Of well-pleased lasses and contending swains ;
> Till the vast mound of corn is swept away,
> And he that gets the last ear wins the day.

This is one of the few passages of eighteenth-century
American verse still remembered. Barlow's ambitious
and unreadable epic, the Columbiad, is as dead as Black-
more's Prince Arthur or Southey's Madoc ; but the mock-
heroic Hasty Pudding, which he must have regarded as
merely an elegant trifle, " the perfume and suppliance of
a minute," is often quoted and even finds a reader now and

then. The circumstances of the poem may account for its superiority to the author's more labored performances. Barlow had gone to Europe in 1788 as agent of the Scioto Company, which dealt speculatively in Western lands. After the failure of this enterprise he had remained in Europe, residing alternately in England and on the Continent, and occupying himself with politics and literature. In the winter of 1792–93 he was at Chambéry, immersed in French political business — he expected to be returned as deputy to the National Convention from the Department of Savoy. His wife was in London, and they were both rather homesick, though Barlow's head was too full of projects to allow him much leisure for reminiscence. One night he was surprised to find on the supper table at the inn a dish which he instantly recognized as the hasty pudding of his native Connecticut:[1] —

> Dear Hasty Pudding, what unpromised joy
> Expands my heart to meet thee in Savoy !
> Doom'd o'er the world through devious paths to roam,
> Each clime my country, and each house my home,
> My soul is soothed, my cares have found an end,
> I greet my long lost, unforgotten friend.

The origin of the pleasant custom attaching to the red ear is lost in obscurity. A curious passage from Colonel James Smith's narrative is here offered for what it may be worth. There is no doubt of Smith's good faith. He was a captive among the Caughnawaga Indians from 1755 to 1759, was adopted into their nation, and spoke three Indian languages, so that he had good opportunities to inform himself. He says: — "Before I was taken by the Indians, I had often heard that in the ceremony of marriage, the man gave the woman a deer's leg, and she gave him a

---

[1] See C. B. Todd, Life and Letters of Joel Barlow, N. Y., 1886, pp. 97–99.

red ear of corn, signifying that she was to keep him in bread, and he was to keep her in meat. I inquired of them concerning the truth of this, and they said they knew nothing of it, further than that they had heard it was the ancient custom among some nations." [1]

Barlow's husking scene limits the drinks to sweet cider; but this is certainly poetic license. We may compare a humorous passage in the Diary of Dr. Nathaniel Ames of Dedham, October 14, 1767: [2] —

Made an husking Entertainm't. Possibly this leafe may last a Century & fall into the hands of some inquisitive Person for whose Entertainm't I will inform him that now there is a Custom amongst us of making an Entertainment at husking of Indian Corn whereto all the neighboring Swains are invited and after the Corn is finished they like the Hottentots give three Cheers or huzza's but cannot carry in the husks without a Rhum bottle they feign great Exertion but do nothing till Rhum enlivens them, when all is done in a trice, then after a hearty Meal about 10 at Night they go to their pastimes.

Mr. Thomas's satire on the husking was written when the agitation for total abstinence was at its height. It was not merely the waste that troubled him, but the new rum and the four gallons of whiskey; for, as we shall see on other occasions, the Old Farmer was an earnest and consistent advocate of moderation in all things. The serious-minded in New England had long been dismayed at the hilarity that sometimes attended the harvest festival. In 1713 Cotton Mather remarks that "the *Riots* that have too often accustomed our *Huskings*, have carried in them, fearful Ingratitude and Provocation unto the Glorious

---

[1] Account of the Remarkable Occurrences in the Life and Travels of Col. James Smith, in Loudon's Selection of Indian Narratives, Carlisle, 1808, reprint of 1888, I, 240.

[2] The Ames Diary, Dedham Historical Register, II, 98, quoted by C. F. Adams, Three Episodes in Massachusetts History, II, 791.

God." He has heard that these riots " are abated," and exclaims " May the *Joy of Harvest* no longer be prostituted unto vicious purposes. *Husbandmen and Householders:* Let the *Night of your Pleasure* be turned into *Fear;* a Jealous *Fear*, Least your Children take their Leave of God, and of Piety." [1]

This outburst of Mather's is associated with a similar denunciation of " Christmas revels" and " Shroves-Tuesday vanities." Our forefathers are known to have been much averse to the celebration of Christmas. They regarded any kind of observance of that festival as papistical and idolatrous. So strong, indeed, was this feeling that many persons now living can remember when " the season wherein our Saviour's birth is celebrated " passed, in the country, without any notice at all, whereas Thanksgiving was honored with both religious and social rites.

On Christmas day, 1621, Governor Bradford had an amusing encounter with some of his raw recruits, who had arrived on the ship Fortune the month before. There were thirty-five of these newcomers, and, to use the Governor's own words, " most of them were lusty yonge men, and many of them wild enough. . . The plantation was glad of this addition of strength, but could have wished that many of them had been of better condition, and all of them beter furnished with provisions ; but y^t," he adds philosophically, " could not now be helpte." [2] Then comes the little clash of conscience: —

One ye day called Chrismas-day, ye Govr caled them out to worke, (as was used,) but ye most of this new-company excused themselves and said it went against their consciences to work on y^t day. So ye Govr tould them that if they made it mater of conscience, he would spare them till they were better informed.

[1] Advice from the Watch Tower, Boston, 1713, p. 35.
[2] History of Plimouth Plantation, ed. 1898, pp. 128–9.

So he led-away yᵉ rest and left them; but when they came home at noone from their worke, he found them in yᵉ streete at play, openly; some pitching yᵉ barr, & some at stoole-ball, and shuch like sports. So he went to them, and tooke away their implements, and tould them that was against his conscience, that they should play & others worke. If they made yᵉ keeping of it mater of devotion, let them kepe their houses, but ther should be no gameing or revelling in yᵉ streets. Since which time nothing hath been atempted that way, at least openly.[1]

Mr. George William Curtis, who has written of the Pilgrim and Puritan Christmas with more toleration for the scruples of the Fathers than some of their descendants show nowadays, takes this bit of humor with undue seriousness. " It was against the Governor's conscience," he says, " that the ' lusty yonge men ' should follow their consciences, and the last sentence of the historian is as significant as Sebastiani's famous words, the modern echo of the *Solitudinem faciunt* of Tacitus — ' Order reigns in Warsaw.' " [2] This is pretty grim, and hardly fair to the excellent Bradford, who might assuredly be suffered to have his little joke, — all the more when logic was so clearly on his side. The young men may have had conscientious scruples against working, but they were under no religious obligation to play stool-ball!

In 1659 the keeping of " any such day as Christmas or the like, either by forbearing of labour, feasting, or any other way " was forbidden by the General Court of Massachusetts, under a penalty of five shillings for each offense. Towards the end of the century, when the population of the towns had become less homogeneous, and the number of Church of England men had greatly increased, the law grew difficult to enforce, and in 1681 it was repealed.[3]

---

[1] History of Plimouth Plantation, pp. 134-5.
[2] Harper's Magazine, for December, 1883.
[3] Mass. Colony Records, IV, i, 366; V, 322.

From this time Christmas began to reassert itself. The discomfort of Samuel Sewall as he contemplated this corruption of manners is pictured in several passages in his Diary, which have been well summed up by Mr. Curtis: —

Four years later Judge Sewall records, with satisfaction, that carts come to town on Christmas-day, and shops are open as usual. "Some, somehow, observe the day, but are vexed, I believe, that the Body of the People profane it; and, blessed be God! no Authority yet to compell them to keep it." The next year the shops and the carts give him great pleasure again, although Governor Andros does go to the Episcopal service with a redcoat on his right and a captain on his left. Eleven years later, in 1697, on the same day: "Joseph tells me that though most of the Boys went to the Church, yet he went not." In 1705 and 1706, to the judge's continued comfort, the carts still came and the shops were open. But in 1714 Christmas fell on Saturday, and because of its observance at the church the unbending judge goes to keep the Sabbath and sit down at the Lord's table with Mr. John Webb, that he may "put respect upon that affronted, despised Lord's day. For the Church of England had the Lord's supper yesterday, the last day of the week, but will not have it to-day, the day that the Lord has made."

The passage in Cotton Mather to which reference has just been made gives a succinct statement of the grounds on which the Puritans objected to Christmas celebration in any form: —

Christmas-Revels begin to be taken up, among some vainer Young People here and there in some of our Towns.

R[emark]. It were to be desired, That Christians *abounding in Wisdom and Prudence,* would Weigh in Equal Ballances, what is to be said, against their keeping any *Stated Holidays*, which our Glorious Lord himself has not instituted; and what more is to be said, about assigning a *Wrong-Day*, to Commemorate a great Work of God, as *thereon* accomplished; and most of all,

how offensive it cannot but be unto the *Holy Son of God*, for Men to pretend his Honour in Committing Impieties, which the Conscience of every Man cannot but assure him, that they are Abominable Things, and hateful to the God, who has not pleasure in Wickedness.[1]

Such arguments did not go unchallenged. Some ten years later there was a little tempest at Marblehead. Mr. John Barnard, the local minister, and one of the ablest of his generation, in a lecture held on Christmas day, 1729, set forth the Puritan view with a good deal of vigor. The Church of England minister, Mr. George Pigot, was much disturbed at this discourse, and at its results. Some of Mr. Barnard's admirers, writes Mr. Pigot, " did frequently and loudly upbraid the Members of my Church, even in the very Streets, with such Tauntings as these: — *What is become of your Christmas-Day now ; for Mr.* B——d *has proved it to be Nothing else but an Heathenish Rioting ? — Will you never have done with your Popish Ceremonies, that you must have Four or Five Days running, to observe, what Mr.* B——d *has made out to be no such Thing as You pretend ?* — These and other unseemly *Scoffings* made the Generality of my Hearers uneasy, and brought divers and hourly Complaints to my Ears." All this was of course extremely unpleasant, and called for reprisals.

At length, in January, 1730, Mr. Pigot replied in a sermon which was afterwards published, " at the desire of the church-wardens and vestry," under the formidable title " A Vindication of the Practice of the Antient Christian, as well as the Church of England, and other Reformed Churches, in the Observation of Christmas-day; in answer to the Uncharitable Reflections of Thomas de Laune, Mr. Whiston, and Mr. John Barnard of Marblehead." There is no occasion to enter into a discussion as to the merits

---

[1] Advice from the Watch Tower, pp. 34-35.

of this controversy. It has lost all interest except as an index to the temper of the times, which permitted Mr. Pigot to speak of Mr. Barnard's parishioners as "his credulous fishermen," and to include their pastor with others under the designation of "some sour spirits." It is almost a pity that Barnard did not allude to this passage at arms in his vastly entertaining Autobiography. He does, however, give us his opinion of his antagonist, in plain terms, as one who " had pretty good school learning, having been usher in his father's grammar school, but never educated at the Universities, nor knew anything of arts and sciences beyond the school; and was a worthless man, with whom we had customary correspondence, but no intimacy." [1] We must at all events exonerate Mr. Barnard from any charge of bigoted opposition to the Church of England. He speaks with great respect of Mr. Pigot's successor, Mr. Malcolm, and he was one of the pall-bearers at the funeral of *his* successor, Mr. Bours. Indeed, he was consulted by the Episcopalians as to the best way to fill Mr. Bours's place, and his advice was followed.[2] And so we may leave this queer little chapter of ecclesiastical history.

Mather's words about Shrovetide are too curious to omit, though it cannot be supposed that the ceremonies that he mentions ever became at all prevalent in this part of the world : —

It is to be hoped, The *Shroves-Tuesday Vanities*, of making *Cakes to the Queen of Heaven*, and Sacrificing of *Cocks* to the Pagan Idol *Tuisco ;* and other Superstitions Condemned in the *Reformed Churches ;* will find very few Abetters, in a Countrey declaring for our Degree of *Reformation.*

Should such things become usual among us, the great God

[1] Barnard's Autobiography, Coll. Mass. Hist. Soc., 3d Series, V, 234.
[2] The same, p. 235.

12

would soon say with Indignation, *How art thou turned Unto the Degenerate Plant of a Strange Vine unto me!*[1]

The last day before Lent is called Shrove Tuesday because it was formerly the custom to go to confession — to *shrive* oneself — on that day. After shrift, all sorts of merriment began. Thus Shrovetide in England corresponded to the Italian carnival season. The Reformation of course put an end to the confessional, but the habit of festivity persisted. Mather is particularly vexed by the eating of cakes and the sacrifice of cocks. The first of these ceremonies he regards as a relic of Mariolatry; the second is, in his eyes, rank paganism. Cakes or doughnuts were a regular English dish on Shrove Tuesday, which was therefore known also as Pancake Tuesday. The sacrifice to which Mather refers is the old sport of " throwing at the cock." The creature was tied to a stake and small cudgels were hurled at him by the contestants from a distance of about twenty-five yards. The winner got the bird.[2] The brutality of the custom should have been enough to condemn it, but Mather thinks less of that than of its impiety. Singularly enough he imagines that it is a sacrifice to " the idol Tuisco." This is a strange piece of learned fancy. Tuisco, or Tuisto, is known to us from a famous passage in the Germania of Tacitus, where we are told that the Germans sing of him as a god born from the earth, and of Mannus, that is " man," as his son. There is no evidence that they ever made images of him. Indeed, Tacitus says expressly that they think it wrong to represent any of the deities under human form. Of course there is no connection whatever between the unfortunate cocks that were battered on Shrove Tuesday and the ancient Germanic divinity. But Mather supposed, it would seem,

[1] Advice from the Watch Tower, p. 35.
[2] Brand, Popular Antiquities, ed. Hazlitt, I, 41 ff.

that Tuisco was identical with Tiw, the deity after whom
Tuesday (the Anglo-Saxon *Tiwes-dæg*) was named. This
specious though mistaken etymology, and the writer's
horror at idolatrous sacrifices to a pagan Germanic god,
show at least the scope of curious learning in old New
England and the complexity of the problem that con-
fronts the student who wishes to comprehend the Puritan
spirit in all its manifestations.

The same regard for efficiency in labor which Mr.
Thomas evinces in his distrust of huskings — the persua-
sion that work and play cannot be profitably combined,
though amusement is well enough in its place — comes
out in a little sermon on the text " Many hands make
light work " in the Farmer's Calendar for June, 1821 : —

" Many hands make light work."

Now, if you have a heavy job to do, call all hands and despatch
it ; but stop ! too many cooks always spoil the broth. There are
some who cannot bear to work alone. If they have a yard of
cabbages to hoe, they must call in a neighbour to change work.
Now this is very pleasant, but it tends to lounging and idleness,
and neglect of business ; for we cannot always have our neighbours
at work with us. We shall reluct at working alone, and if we
can get no one to come to us, we shall be away, leaving our corn,
potatoes, peas and beans to take care of themselves. — " Bugs,
bugs, bugs ! O, the bugs will eat up all the cucumbers ! " No,
they will not, cousin Betty, if we attend to them. We must be up
in the morning, aye in the *morning*, I say ; and not lie in bed
until nigh twelve, like Capt. Dashup's girls, who are thrumming
and drumming and humming all night long with their *penny-forts*
and jews-harps. — I say we must be up before the sun kisses the
pine tops, and see to these bugs and pinch their necks for them.

Several details are worthy of notice in this lively moral
and economic lesson, apart from the instruction itself.
The farmer's custom of " changing works " is humorously

hit off; or, to speak more accurately, the abuses to which it may lead are pleasantly satirized. As for the custom itself, when properly regulated, it was a necessity; some kind of coöperation could not well be dispensed with in the days when small proprietors were many and professional hired laborers were scarce. Barn raisings, spinning bees, and huskings all come under the same category as "changing works," and depend upon the same principle of barter, — for labor was, in simple communities, often a more practicable medium of exchange than money, because there was more of it.

"So vast is the Territory of *North-America*," wrote Benjamin Franklin in 1751, "that it will require many Ages to settle it fully; and till it is fully settled, Labour will never be cheap here, where no Man continues long a Labourer for others, but gets a Plantation of his own, no Man continues long a Journeyman to a Trade, but goes among those new Settlers, and sets up for himself, &c. Hence Labour is no cheaper now, in *Pennsylvania*, than it was 30 Years ago, tho' so many Thousand labouring People have been imported."[1] Yet wages were not high in those days according to the present standard of value. In 1800, Isaac Waldron of Newbury, Vermont, "hired out to Col. Frye Bayley for one year for eighty dollars." Eight dollars a month, with board, was the regular pay of a farm laborer, or "hired man," as late as the third decade of the last century. But there were few temptations to spend money, and ready cash was scarce, so that, even with these wages, the farm hand might easily become a proprietor if he was economical.[2]

Mr. Thomas was of course not an opponent of the harm-

[1] Observations concerning the Increase of Mankind, Peopling of Countries, &c., p. 4, appended to W. Clarke's Observations on the Late and Present Conduct of the French, Boston, 1755.

[2] F. P. Wells, History of Newbury, Vermont, St. Johnsbury, 1902, p. 153.

less, necessary custom of " changing works." It was only when serious application to the task in hand degenerated into frolic that our agricultural mentor felt called upon to protest and admonish.

Another point in the extract just given from the Almanac is the plague of destructive insects — *bugs* as they were, and still are, indiscriminately called in the country. The plan of breeding parasites to destroy these pestilent creatures had not yet been thought of, nor had the simpler method of applying Paris green made every potato patch a terror to people with weak nerves. In another place, however, will be found a suggestion that the bugs may be turned to good account as a substitute for Spanish flies in medicine.[1]

The husking inevitably suggests the spinning bee, descriptions of which are plenty as blackberries. Here is one which coincides almost exactly in date with the first appearance of the Farmer's Almanac. It relates to a spinning party which took place at Falmouth (now Portland), Maine, on May Day, 1788, and comes from the local newspaper. The tone and temper of the item suggest that it was written by the reverend gentleman at whose house the assembly was held.

On the 1st instant, assembled at the house of the Rev. Samuel Deane, of this town, more than one hundred of the fair sex, married and single ladies, most of whom were skilled in the important art of spinning. An emulous industry was never more apparent than in this beautiful assembly. The majority of fair hands gave motion to not less than sixty wheels. Many were occupied in preparing the materials, besides those who attended to the entertainment of the rest — provision for which was mostly presented by the guests themselves, or sent in by other generous promoters of the exhibition, as were also the materials for the

[1] See p. 186, below.

work. Near the close of the day, Mrs. Deane was presented by
the company with two hundred and thirty-six seven knotted
skeins of excellent cotton and linen yarn, the work of the day,
excepting about a dozen skeins which some of the company
brought in ready spun. Some had spun six, and many not less
than five skeins apiece. She takes this opportunity of returning
thanks to each, which the hurry of the day rendered impracticable
at the time. To conclude, and crown the day, a numerous band
of the best singers attended in the evening, and performed an
agreeable variety of excellent pieces in psalmody.

The price of a virtuous woman is far above rubies. . . . She
layeth her hands to the spindle, and her hands hold the distaff.[1]

Mr. Thomas usually takes spinning for granted, and
does not feel that his readers need to be instructed about
so obvious a duty, but now and then there is a bit of
advice on the subject, as in February, 1811 : — " You will
see that your daughters do not want flax, &c. to keep
them industrious. I fear the old fashion of spinning and
weaving are going out of date. Remember to bring up
your children in the way they should go, and then their
good habits will accompany them through life." Most of
his advice to women concerns the dairy, and shows an
anxious care for neatness which seems prophetic of modern
qualms.

When the Old Farmer began his career as mentor
of rural New England, it was an occasional practice for
women to bear a hand in the outdoor work of the farm,
especially in the haying season. This practice seemed
objectionable to Mr. Thomas. He regarded it as one of
those crudities of which a civilized community should
be ashamed, and he inveighed against it with unusual
warmth : —

---

[1] Cumberland Gazette, May 8, 1788, as quoted by William Willis, Journals
of Smith and Deane, Portland, 1849, p. 362, note.

All things must give way to necessity; yet what need is there for a woman to leave her domestic concerns, go into the field, and like an Amazon wield the pitchfork and the rake? 'T is abominable! Is this the duty of a wife? Is such the tenderness of a husband? *Remember she is the mistress of thy house; treat her therefore with respect, that thy children may, also. Consider the tenderness of her sex, and the delicacy of her frame.* (August, 1809.)

SMALL ECONOMIES

FEW miscellaneous scraps are more amusing to run over in an idle hour than those receipts for utilizing the useless or making something out of nothing in which thrifty people have always delighted. The older numbers of the Farmer's Almanack are not deficient in lore of this sort, derived from various sources — the editor's experience, the gossiping pen of the " constant reader," or even the newspapers. A few of the choicest among them are here brought together, without any attempt at classification, and with little or no comment; since for the most part they speak for themselves. A number of them are manifestly of more or less value, but the present writer cannot attach his *probatum est* to any, and therefore prefers to make no attempt at discriminating.

Persons who are fond of potatoes and afraid of coffee, may get comfort from the following extract from the Almanac for 1815. It is a little essay on —

POTATOE COFFEE. — *From a Philadelphia Paper.*

Frugality in domestic expenses, is a virtue, which ought to be practised by the manager of every family ; but more particularly, at a time when commerce stagnates in our ports, the mechanick is thrown out of employment, and the necessaries of life at so high a price as to be obtained only with the greatest difficulty, and when the poor are precluded altogether from many of them. Every discovery therefore, that has a tendency to ameliorate the condition of the poor and the labourer, and add to their comfort, is of great value, and ought to obtain public sanction.

The article *coffee*, a few years back, was looked upon as unnecessary, but is now considered, from the great use made of it, as one of the necessaries of life. The price is now nearly double to what it was in the year 1811, and continues to rise; a substitute for coffee would, therefore, be a great object to society in general — many articles have been tried, but, not answering the purpose, have been relinquished.

The *potatoe* is found to resemble coffee in *taste, smell and colour*, more than any substitute that has been tried; *few persons can distinguish one from the other;* besides which, it possesses other properties and circumstances which ought to recommend it to general use. It is one of our cheapest and most plentiful vegetables; besides its cheapness, it may be obtained in all places and in any quantity, nor are we dependent on foreign commerce for it — This substitute for coffee sits light on the stomach, is nourishing and easy of digestion, and does not irritate the nerves of weak persons or cause watchfulness.

The following is the mode of preparing. — Wash raw potatoes clean, cut them into small square pieces, of about the size of an hazle nut; put them into a broad dish or pan, set them in a temperate stove, or in an oven after the bread is taken out, stir them frequently, to prevent them from sticking together, in order that they may dry regularly; when they are perfectly dry, put them into a dry bag or box secure, and they will keep for any length of time.

When they are to be used, they must be roasted or burnt in the same manner as coffee, and ground in a mill or reduced to powder in a mortar. Small potatoes are as good as large ones — the potatoes generally considered of the meaner kind are better than the mealy, and the skins and parings are best of all. It is hoped none will be so prejudiced against this recommendation as not to try it — a *trial* will confirm what may appear to some to be doubtful.

A laudable attempt to convert tribulations into blessings appears in a communication from Mr. Thomas's own town, which found a place in the Almanac for 1807 : —

To the EDITOR of the FARMER's ALMANACK.

IMPORTANT DISCOVERY.

IT has been discovered that the Flies, which, in this section of the state, have been very plenty on potatoe-vines, are a substitute for the *Cantharides,* (or Spanish Flies,) and are much more active for blistering, when properly prepared.   The fly seems to have a near approach to the beetle kind, has four legs, two pointers at the fore part of the head, a hard case over the wings like the Spanish flies, and is of the size of the fire bug, or fly, which appears here in April, and is of a light slate colour.

The best method to take them is to put a small quantity of vinegar in a tin milk-pan and brush them from the tops of the potatoes with the hand, which immediately kills them ; afterwards they must be dried in the sun.   These animals are the only thing which draw a real blister, except the Spanish flies.   The fly, if not destroyed, eats all the leaves, but the fibrous part, and greatly injures the root ; but by beating them off once or twice, very little damage is sustained.

If they should appear the ensuing year it is to be hoped that farmers will let their boys collect them.   Two reasons will induce them to it.   The first is to prevent the insect from destroying, in some measure, that very valuable and useful vegetable ; and in the next, to preserve a most useful article in medicine.   For Cantharides, our physicians have paid for several years past, from five to sixteen dollars per pound, as I have been informed.   The potatoe fly, or bug, appears about the first of July, and continues until the middle of August — but generally becomes scarce in about four weeks after its appearance.   It has been found on some other vines, particularly on cucumbers.

Sterling, September 1, 1806.

It is safe to assume that the " potato-flies " mentioned by this sanguine correspondent were not quadrupeds, as he asserts, but had six legs, like other insects.   We may even identify them, without much risk, with the " native

cantharides or blister bugs " discussed by Dr. T. W. Harris,
as quoted in the Almanac for 1834. These creatures,
says the distinguished entomologist, " are successfully employed in medicine instead of the Spanish flies, and were
not the price of labor among us so high, might be procured in sufficient quantity to supply the demand in the
markets for this important medicinal agent." The letter
from Sterling calls to mind the heroic counter-irritants of
old-time medical practice. An insect " much more active
for blistering " than the Spanish fly must have been almost
as satisfactory an instrument of torture as the East Indian
moxa described by Sir William Temple in his famous
Essay upon the Cure of the Gout. Temple's informant was
Monsieur Zulichem, a person who " never came into company without saying something that was new." " He said
it was a certain kind of moss that grew in the East Indies;
that their way was, whenever any body fell into a fit of the
gout, to take a small quantity of it, and form it into a figure
broad at bottom as a twopence, and pointed at top, to set
the bottom exactly upon the place where the violence of
the pain was fixed; then with a small round perfumed
match (made likewise in the Indies) to give fire to the top
of the moss; which burning down by degrees, came at
length to the skin, and burnt it till the moss was consumed
to ashes: that many times the first burning would remove
the pain; if not, it was to be renewed a second, third, and
fourth time, till it went away, and till the person found he
could set his foot boldly to the ground and walk." [1]

Here is a suggestion from 1801 which has proved to
be of greater practical value than the receipt for Spanish
flies:—

HOGS' BRISTLES.

EVERY species of information that will be advantageous either
to the land or purse of the FARMER, we esteem it our duty to

[1] Works of Sir William Temple, 1757, III, 246–7.

make public through the medium of the Farmer's Almanack. The Brush Manufactory is a late establishment in this part of the country, and is now carried on to a considerable extent, insomuch that large quantities of Bristles are *imported from Europe*. The price which they command we conceive must operate as an inducement to Farmers to be careful in saving their Bristles for market. The price of Hogs' Bristles, in many parts of the country, particularly in Boston and Medfield, is, we understand, 33 Cents, *in cash*, per pound.

Bristles were sometimes regarded as the perquisites of the boys on the farm. The late Joseph T. Buckingham tells us that when he was fourteen years old he was allowed to sell to a brush-maker "the bristles that came from the swine as they were slaughtered." The first piece of silver that he ever possessed was a ninepence which he earned in this way. This was at Windham, Connecticut, in 1793.[1]

Weeds may be utilized, it seems, as well as "bugs." So, at least, says the Almanac for 1803: —

HORSES.

M R. Cartwright has recently discovered, that the common groundsil, given plentifully to horses in the stable, will effectually cure greasy heels. It is always of importance to know the uses to which weeds may be applied.

Soap and candles may go together, as they do in the Almanac for 1818: —

SOAP MADE OF SNOW.
[From the Baltimore Federal Gazette]

Soap made of snow in the following manner: — Take and cut into very small pieces one pound of good hard soap; dissolve it

---

[1] Personal Memoirs and Recollections of Literary Life, Boston, 1852, I, 23-24.

with a slow fire ; when dissolved, put six or eight pounds of clean snow with it ; and after having boiled them together well for three hours, (or until it shews a lather on its surface,) add a wine glass of fine salt, and let it get cold ; when it will be found the finest soap, and to weigh as much as the snow did originally.

AN IMPROVEMENT IN CANDLES.

A plan for improving mould Candles and the quantity of their light is introduced by a writer in Spofford's American Magazine, for October, 1815, viz : " Place a small straw of rye or oats in the centre of the wick, the ends of which may be stopped by being dipped in some bees wax or bayberry tallow, to prevent the cavity being filled with tallow in the mould or in dipping. Clipping the lower end opens the straw which is easily opened at the upper end by clipping off a little piece ; and on being lighted, the extra labour is not to be regretted."

The following receipt is inserted at this point because it is too good to be lost, rather than because it comes strictly under the head of Small Economies. Yet "old shoes that are *worn out*" are so carefully specified that perhaps our classification is justified after all. It is found in the Almanac for 1804 : —

To prevent Crows pulling up Indian Corn.

A farmer has communicated to the Editor a sure method to prevent Crows visiting corn fields, which he has practised for some years, and has ever been attended with the desired effect. As those mischievous birds have been very troublesome for some years past to many farmers, the following method is thought worthy the public attention.

Take three or four old shoes, that are worn out, and fill the toes of them with sulphur, or the roll of brimstone broken small, make a fire with chips, or any small dry wood in or near the middle of your corn field on a flat rock, or on the bare mould, (a

rock being preferable) after planting your corn field, then lay the toes of the shoes on the fire and let them continue until the leather be burnt through, and the brimstone has taken fire; then after sticking down poles of ten or twelve feet in length at each corner of your field, and inclining them towards the centre, make a string fast to the heal quarters of each shoe, and tie it fast to the top ends of the poles, letting the strings extend half way down, and when swinging, not to interfere with the poles; and no crows will alight on your field that season.

If anything will keep crows out of a cornfield, surely it must be this combination of brimstone, charred leather, and gibbeted shoes!

INDIAN SUMMER AND THE COMET

THE Farmer's Calendar for May, 1818, affords an exhilarating item: —

Planting time is close by and we begin to think of Indian dumplings and puddings. Be not discouraged about raising corn. Uncle Jethro says that the good old *Indian summers* will return again. He is a great philosopher and astronomer, and ascribes our frosty seasons, which have been so troublesome of late, to the spots in the sun, which however he says, will soon be entirely obliterated. The tail of the comet is shortly to pass over the sun's disk, like a dusting brush, and they will be seen no more.

Indian summer is as familiar a phrase as can well be imagined, and the thing itself is confidently expected by all of us when late autumn comes round. The history of the term, however, is obscure enough; but much light is thrown upon it by Mr. Albert Matthews in a learned paper published by the United States Weather Bureau.[1]

The earliest example of the term which Mr. Matthews has discovered occurs in Major Ebenezer Denny's Journal under the date of October 13, 1794: "Pleasant weather. The Indian summer here. Frosty nights."[2] The diarist must surely have used a phrase that was perfectly familiar to him, and of course he adds no explanation, his entry being intended for his own eye alone. Four years later, in June, 1798, Dr. Mason F. Cogswell, describing the pre-

[1] The Term Indian Summer, Monthly Weather Review for January and February, 1902.
[2] Military Journal, Memoirs Hist. Soc. of Penn., VII, 402.

ceding winter at Hartford, Connecticut, remarks: "About the beginning of January the weather softened considerably, and continued mild for several days. Most people supposed the *Indian summer* was approaching (a week or fortnight of warm weather, which generally takes place about the middle of January), but, instead of this, there succeeded to these pleasant days a delightful fall of snow, about a foot in depth, which was bound down by an incrustation of hail, and prevented from blowing in heaps by the winds which followed." [1] In 1803 the French traveller Volney, who visited America between 1795 and 1798, mentioned the Indian summer as occurring towards November and equated it with the "St. Martin's summer" of the French. [2]

These are the only writers of the eighteenth century, so far as we know, who employ the term Indian summer at all. They are, however, quite independent of each other, and their testimony establishes one fact beyond peradventure: the phrase was common among the people in the last decade of that century. The presumption is that it had been in use a good while, and we are not surprised therefore to learn that in 1809 Dr. Shadrach Ricketson, of New York, wrote of the name as "long known in this country." [3] Five more examples have been discovered by Mr. Matthews before 1820, to which that from the Almanac for 1818 may now be added as a sixth. From this time the term becomes frequent. Its picturesqueness and agreeable associations commended it to writers of every grade and it was soon established in literature on both sides of the Atlantic. It lent itself readily to figurative applications. As early as 1830 De Quincey wrote of the great Bentley: "An Indian summer crept stealthily over his closing days; a summer

---

[1] Medical Repository, II, 282.
[2] Tableau du Climat et du Sol des États-Unis d'Amérique, Paris, 1803, I, 283.
[3] Medical Repository, Second Hexade, VI, 187.

JOHANNIS HEVELII
COMETOGRAPHIA.

less gaudy than the mighty summer of the solstice, but
sweet, golden, silent; happy, though sad; and to Bentley
. . . it was never known that this sweet mimicry of summer — a spiritual or fairy echo of a mighty music that has
departed — is as frail and transitory as it is solemn, quiet,
and lovely." [1]   So thoroughly has the term become a part
of the English language, that the Poet Laureate, in addressing Queen Victoria on her birthday in 1899, could find no
more appropriate designation for her gracious old age than
"the Indian Summer of your days."   Few Americanisms
have had so triumphant a progress.

The origin of the term Indian summer is a mystery.
There is no evidence that it was employed in the early days
of American colonization or that it was derived by the
white man from the aborigines.   Nobody has left it on
record, as we have seen, before 1794.   Nor are there any
comments on the phenomenon itself in older writers on
America.   Yet there were several English names for this
charming and elusive season, and some or all of them our
forefathers must have brought to this country with them.
"All-hallown summer," i. e. the summer of All Hallows or
All Saints, is one.   It is jestingly applied to Falstaff by
Prince Hal in the First Part of King Henry IV: — "Farewell, thou latter spring! farewell, All-hallown summer!"
(act i, scene 2.)   Both epithets characterize Falstaff as an
old youth.   Another English name, adapted from the
French, is "St. Martin's summer," which occurs in the
First Part of Henry VI (act i, scene 2): —

> This night the siege assuredly I'll raise:
> Expect Saint Martin's summer, halcyon days,
> Since I have entered into these wars.

All Hallows is November 1 and St. Martin's day is
November 14, so that these designations agree well enough
with the current expectation in America, where we look for

[1] Works, Edinburgh, 1862–63, VI, 180.

13

our Indian summer in the late fall and feel defrauded if we do not get it. "St. Luke's Summer" is also heard in England, but its antiquity is not certain. St. Luke's Day falls on October 18th. Whatever designations for this season the colonists may have brought with them died out and left no trace, and "Indian summer" has been substituted for them, not only in America, but, as we have seen, in England as well, where, however, some of the other names have survived in the dialects.

Naturally enough there is, and always has been, considerable latitude in the date of Indian summer. Thoreau, in his Autumn, notes Indian summer weather, from 1851 to 1860, on September 27th, October 7th, 13th, 14th, 31st, November 1st, 7th, 8th, 17th, 23d, 25th, December 7th, 10th, and 13th, and there are other examples of similar laxity. But that does not really make against the prevailing tendency, which is strongly in favor of late autumn, and this appears to be the time of the German "Old women's summer" (*Altweibersommer*) or "After-summer" (*Nachsommer*) as well.

It is rather idle to speculate as to the original significance of *Indian* in the phrase we are considering, since we are ignorant of the history of the expression before 1794. Many guesses have been made. Charles Brockden Brown, the first American novelist, thought that the season owed its name "to its being predicted by the natives to the first emigrants, who took the early frosts as the signal for winter." [1] This is altogether improbable. The first emigrants needed no aboriginal prophet to make them look for fine warm days in late autumn, for they had noticed such weather at home, and must have had a name for it; or else they were different from other Englishmen of their time, and, indeed, from Europeans in general. The most

[1] Note in his translation of Volney, View of the Soil and Climate of the United States, Philadelphia, 1804, p. 210.

popular explanation derives the term from the Indian custom of burning over the woods in November to destroy
the underbrush, — a practice which was noted by the early
settlers, who found the forests so open that they could ride
through them without difficulty.   This explanation also is
of no value. Though haziness is often regarded as characteristic of the weather in the Indian summer, and though
this peculiar quality of the air was sometimes said to be
due to the fires kindled by the natives, — it is a long *saltus*
to the conclusion that the name Indian summer has to do
with the practice in question, nor are the logical steps easy
to reconstruct. Far more reasonable is the conjecture that
the name alludes to the proverbial deceitfulness and treachery of the natives. Increase Mather, in speaking of John
Sassamon's report of King Philip's intended hostilities, remarks that "his Information (because it had an Indian
Original, and one can hardly believe them when they speak
Truth) was not at first much regarded."[1] Or possibly we
should think rather of their equally proverbial instability.
Nothing is more fickle than the weather in Indian summer; though this is a quality that might be predicated of
our weather in general, for, as Dr. Benjamin Rush wrote
in 1789, of the climate of Pennsylvania, "perhaps there is
but one steady trait in [its] character . . . and that is, it is
uniformly variable."[2] "Indian giving," we may remember,
is making a present and taking it back again, after the
manner of children when they repent of an impulse of
generosity. Or, finally, if it is permissible to add another
guess to the futilities of one's predecessors, it is conceivable
that Indian summer was at first equivalent to "*fool's* summer." If so, we seem to have a parallel to the "Old
Women's Summer" of the Germans and it may be also to
the "Go-summer" of the Scots, if this is a corruption of

[1] Relation of the Troubles, etc., Boston, 1677, p. 74; ed. Drake, Early
History of New England, 1864, p. 234.
[2] American Museum, 1790, VII, 334.

"Goose-summer," as scholars suppose. To call the Indians fools may at first appear inconsistent with what our ancestors observed of their cunning and their strategic powers; but there is no real difficulty. Nothing impressed the logical and hard-headed settlers more than the folly of the red men in certain matters — particularly in their religious beliefs. "Poor captivated men," "bondslaves to sin and Satan," "miserable heathen," "miserable salvages," "poor, naked, ignorant Indians," "forlorn and wretched heathen," "stupid and senseless," "these doleful creatures," "the ruins of mankind"[1] — such are some of the epithets applied to the Indians, — now in scorn, now in pity, — by New England writers of the seventeenth century; and there are anecdotes enough in illustration of the simplicity of the aborigines. "They are treacherous, suspicious and jealous," writes Hugh Jones, "difficult to be persuaded or imposed upon, and very sharp, hard in Dealing, and ingenious in their Way, and in Things that they naturally know, or have been taught; though at first they are very obstinate, and unwilling to apprehend or learn Novelties, and seem stupid and silly to Strangers."[2] "Fool's summer," though not pretty, would be appropriate enough, and would range well with "fool's gold" for iron pyrites, "fool's parsley" for the poisonous lesser hemlock, and *ignis fatuus* or "fool's fire" for the will-o'-the-wisp.

In Henry VI, it will be remembered, "halcyon days" is used as a synonym for "St. Martin's summer" in a figurative sense. The Greek myth told how Alcyone, when she saw the body of her shipwrecked husband Ceyx, threw herself into the sea, and how both were changed into kingfishers by the compassionate gods. For fourteen days (or, as Ovid says, for seven) in the winter season the

---

[1] Eliot Tracts, Coll. Mass. Hist. Soc., 3rd Series, IV, 202, 266; Mather, Magnalia, ed. 1853, I, 556, 558, 561.

[2] The Present State of Virginia, London, 1724, Sabin's reprint, pp. 11, 12.

mother bird sits brooding on the nest, which floats on the waves. During all this time the sea is calm and sailors may voyage in safety.[1] This, then, is the Indian summer of the Greeks.

It would not be fair either to the Indians or to the reader to bring these observations to a close without mentioning the myth of the god Nanibozhu as narrated by the Rev. Peter Jones in 1861 in his History of the Ojebway Indians. " This Nanahbozhoo," writes Mr. Jones, " now sits at the North Pole, overlooking all the transactions and affairs of the people he has placed on the earth. The Northern tribes say that Nanahbozhoo always sleeps during the winter; but, previous to his falling asleep, fills his great pipe, and smokes for several days, and that it is the smoke arising from the mouth and pipe of Nanahbozhoo which produces what is called 'Indian summer.' " [2]

The story of Nanibozhu is at least three centuries old, but unfortunately no allusion to his smoking has been found earlier than 1852, when the Rev. Peter Jacobs (Pahtahsega), a native Indian, writing of the region on the border of Lake Superior, told of a remarkable stone which was held in much veneration by the savages. " The stone looks as if some man had sat on the rock and made an impression on it, as one would on the snow in winter. This was not carved by any Indian, but it is very natural. The impression is very large, and is about six times as large as an impression made in the snow by a man. The Indians say that Nanahboshoo, a god, sat here long ago, and smoked, and that he left it for the west. Every time the Indians pass here, they leave tobacco at the stone, that Nanahboshoo might smoke in his kingdom in the west." [3]

There is no evidence that Mr. Jones, himself an Indian,

[1] Ovid, Metamorphoses, xi, 745 ff.
[2] History of the Ojebway Indians, London, 1861, p. 35.
[3] Journal, 2d ed., Boston, 1853, p. 16.

copied from Mr. Jacobs, but there is much ground for the suspicion that the former's mention of Indian summer was a modern addition to the myth. The subject of this myth, however, is too complicated to admit of a dogmatic or summary decision, and so we may leave it wrapped in the haze of Nanibozhu's gigantic pipe.

Uncle Jethro's prediction of a return of the good old-fashioned Indian summers is intended especially to encourage the farmer to hope for a better crop of corn. In this connection we may note the words of the Rev. Manasseh Cutler, whose meteorological observations at Ipswich for 1781–83, were printed in the first volume of the Memoirs of the American Academy (1785). Under September, 1781, Mr. Cutler remarks: "Fine weather for ripening Indian corn, and making salt hay, of which there are good crops"; and under November he adds: "Indian corn well ripened, and a good crop." The Farmer's Calendar for the beginning of October, 1799, remarks: "Indian harvest will now call your attention, which had better have it before the ears get down, and heavy rains come on." This term, "Indian harvest," occurs as early as 1642.[1] It means the "harvesting of Indian corn," and is opposed to "English harvest," which signifies the "harvesting of English grain," or wheat. There may be some connection between the phrases "Indian summer" and "Indian harvest," for, as Uncle Jethro suggests, a good Indian summer is conducive to a good crop of Indian corn; but it is difficult to see how either phrase can actually be derived from the other.

Uncle Jethro's attitude of mind toward the sun spots and the comet is noteworthy. The spots in the sun have made the autumns cold so that there have been no Indian summers; but the comet is to set everything right again, for it will sweep away the spots with a whisk of its tail. This is an unaccustomed rôle for a comet; for such "blaz-

---

[1] Albert Matthews, The Nation, March 8, 1900, LXX, 183–4.

ing stars," as they used to be called, were never held to be beneficent in their effects.   But Uncle Jethro is an original, and his portrait is of course meant as a caricature of those belated souls who still believed, in 1818, that comets ruled the weather or were otherwise portentous.

The wise men of New England had not always been so skeptical about blazing stars.   In 1680 Increase Mather was inspired by the comet of that year to preach a terrifying sermon, which was printed under the title of Heaven's Alarm to the World. . . . wherein is shewed, that Fearful Sights and Signs in Heaven, are the Presages of Great Calamities at hand.   Another, but less impressive, comet was visible at Boston two years later, and in 1683 Mather put forth his Discourse of Comets, in which he went into the whole subject with the learning and the superstition of his age.   He writes : —

There are who think, that inasmuch as Comets may be supposed to proceed from natural causes, there is no *speaking voice of Heaven* in them, beyond what is to be said of all other works of God.   But certain it is, that many things which may happen according to the course of nature, are portentous signs of divine anger, and prognosticks of great evils hastening upon the world. . . . Thunder, Lightning, Hail, and Rain, are from natural causes, yet are they sometimes signs of God's holy displeasure. . . . *Earthquakes* are from natural causes, yet there is many times a very speaking voice of God in them.[1]

Accordingly Mather undertakes to write a history of comets from the beginning of the world to the year 1683, appending in each case an account of the direful effects that followed the prodigy.   As to the comet of 1682, he expresses himself with becoming caution.   Yet at the same time he displays a high degree of assurance when it comes

[1] ΚΟΜΗΤΟΓΡΑΦΙΑ.   Or a Discourse concerning Comets, Boston, 1683, pp. 18–19.

to interpreting mysterious passages in the Scriptures.   He takes to task an anonymous astrologer in London who has made certain very definite predictions, — a "prophe-taster," he calls him, who ventures to foretell the conver-sion of the Turks and the destruction of Rome by that people.   Neither of these events, he declares, can possibly happen, for both are contrary to passages in Numbers, Daniel, and Revelation.   He is, of course, convinced that the pope is Antichrist, and has no doubt that Rome is to be destroyed "by some of those horns which have given their power" to him, "which the *Turks* never did, *Rev.* 17, 16."   It is likely, however, that the comet portends various atmospheric disturbances — "a cold and tedious Winter, much Snow, and consequently great Floods; Malignant and Epidemical Diseases; in especial the Plague." [1]

Seventy-five years later Professor John Winthrop, who, as we shall presently see, received the first degree of LL. D. from Harvard College,[2] published his Lectures on Comets.[3]   One might spend an hour with less profit than in comparing the philosophic calm of Winthrop with the frenzied eloquence of the former age.   Yet the clergy had not altogether abandoned the older point of view.   On another occasion Professor Winthrop found it necessary to join issue with a learned Boston divine in a matter of scientific and religious import.   This was in 1755, when all New England was startled by an earthquake.   There had been many earthquakes in this region, but this one was of unusual violence and caused much alarm.   Professor Winthrop interrupted the regular course of his instruction in natural philosophy, and delivered a lecture in the College chapel, describing the earthquake and discussing the

---

[1] Discourse, pp. 129–30.
[2] See p. 235, below.
[3] Two Lectures on Comets, Boston, 1759.

ΚΟΜΗΤΟΓΡΑΦΙΑ.

OR A
Difcourfe Concerning
COMETS;

Wherein the Nature of BLAZING STARS
is Enquired into:

With an Hiftorical Account of all the COMETS
which have appeared from the Beginning of the
World unto this prefent Year, M.DC.LXXXIII.

Expreffing

The Place in the Heavens, where they were feen,
Their Motion, Forms, Duration; and the Remarkable Events which have followed
in the World, fo far as th'ey have been
by Learned Men Obferved.

As alfo two SERMONS
Occafi oned by the late *Blazing Stars.*

By *INCREASE MATHER,* Teacher of a Church
at *Bofton* in *New-England.*

Pfal. 111. 2.. *The works of the Lord are great, fought
out of all them that have pleafure therein.*
Amos 9. 6. *He buildeth his ftories in the Heaven.*

BOSTON IN NEW-ENGLAND.
Printed by *S. G.* for *S. S.* And fold by *J. Browning*
At the corner of the Prifon Lane next the Town-
Houfe 1683.

general subject, with particular reference to the cause of
such disturbances.   He follows a strictly scientific method,
dwells on the undulatory character of the shock, and ascribes the phenomena to the action of heat in the interior
of the globe, insisting particularly on the connection between
earthquakes and volcanic eruptions.   His lecture was published " by the general desire " of the College.[1]

At almost the same moment, the Rev. Thomas Prince,
pastor of the South Church in Boston, was preparing a new
edition of a sermon called Earthquakes the Works of
God, and Tokens of His Just Displeasure, which he had
published twenty-eight years before, just after the Earthquake of 1727.   In the reprint[2] Mr. Prince inserted an
" Appendix concerning the Operation of God in Earthquakes by means of the Electrical Substance," and here
he followed a line of argument which forced the Hollisian
Professor to reply in a postscript to his published lecture.   Mr. Prince, it appears, was opposed to the use of
lightning rods, which had become very popular as the
result of Franklin's experiments.   He regarded all such
attempts to escape the wrath of the Almighty as question-
able devices, hardly to be distinguished, we may suppose,
from Jonah's impious effort to evade the manifest will of
God; and the earthquake afforded him an opportunity
to set forth his views.   According to Mr. Prince's theory,
earthquakes are caused by electric shocks in the earth and
are strictly analagous to the phenomena of thunder and
lightning.   His warning against lightning rods is attached
to a singular piece of reasoning : —

The more *Points* of *Iron* are erected round the *Earth,* to draw
the *Electrical Substance* out of the *Air;* the more the *Earth*
must needs be charged with it.   And therefore it seems worthy

[1] A Lecture on Earthquakes, Boston, 1755.
[2] Boston, 1755.

of Consideration, Whether *any Part* of the *Earth* being fuller of *this terrible Substance*, may not be more exposed to *more shocking Earthquakes*. In *Boston* are more erected than any where else in *New England ;* and *Boston* seems to be more dreadfully shaken. O ! there is no getting out of the mighty Hand of GOD ! If we think to avoid it in the *Air*, we cannot in the *Earth :* Yea it may grow more fatal.

It was easy for Professor Winthrop to expose the fallacies in this remarkable pronunciamento, and we cannot too much admire the dignity and the consideration for Mr. Prince's position with which he replies to the somewhat hysterical words of the preacher. After effectually disposing of Mr. Prince's theories in general, he adverts, with a certain stately humor, to the alleged severity of the earthquake in Boston and to the supposed maleficent influence of the "iron points " : —

I know no reason to think [he writes] that ' *Boston* was more dreadfully shaken ' than other towns.   Some of the effects of the earthquake may have been more considerable, for their number, there than elsewhere ; but the reason of this is, not that ' in *Boston* are more *points* of *iron* erected than any where else in *New-England*,' but that there are more *brick houses* erected there. For the effect of a shock is more considerable upon brick-work than upon wood-work. The reasons of this are obvious ; and that it is so in fact, plainly appeared by our chimnies being every where more shattered than any thing else : Though this was in part owing to their being the highest parts of buildings.

His protest against the admonitory application in which Mr. Prince indulged could hardly be improved : —

I should think, though with the utmost deference to superior judgements, that the pathetic exclamation, which comes next, might well enough have been spared.   " O ! there is no getting out of the mighty hand of GOD ! " For I cannot believe, that in

the whole town of *Boston,* where so many iron points are erected, there is so much as one person, who is so weak, so ignorant, so foolish, or, to say all in one word, so atheistical, as ever to have entertained a single thought, that it is possible, by the help of a few yards of wire, to " get out of the mighty hand of GOD." [1]

Winthrop was somewhat ahead of his time. Just twenty-five years later, in 1780, came the famous Dark Day of May 19th. It found the people at large, and even many of the leaders among them, quite ready to yield to superstitious terror. And, indeed, the phenomenon was disquieting enough. Whittier's description, in his Abraham Davenport, is amply substantiated by contemporary records : —

> 'T was on a May-day of the far old year
> Seventeen hundred eighty, that there fell
> Over the bloom and sweet life of the Spring,
> Over the fresh earth and the heaven of noon,
> A horror of great darkness, like the night
> In day of which the Norland sagas tell, —
> The Twilight of the Gods.   The low-hung sky
> Was black with ominous clouds, save where its rim
> Was fringed with a dull glow, like that which climbs
> The crater's sides from the red hell below.
> Birds ceased to sing, and all the barn-yard fowls
> Roosted; the cattle at the pasture bars
> Lowed, and looked homeward ; bats on leathern wings
> Flitted abroad; the sounds of labor died ;
> Men prayed, and women wept ; all ears grew sharp
> To hear the doom-blast of the trumpet shatter
> The black sky, that the dreadful face of Christ
> Might look from the rent clouds, not as he looked
> A loving guest at Bethany, but stern
> As Justice and inexorable Law.

There were innumerable conjectures as to the cause of the darkness, — some ridiculous, others philosophical, —

[1] Lecture, p. 37.

but no document preserved to us affords a better idea of
the confusion of men's minds than the following passage
from a letter of Dr. Jeremy Belknap in Dover, New Hampshire, to his friend Ebenezer Hazard of New York, June
5, 1780: —

Shall I now entertain you with the whims and apprehensions
of mankind upon this unusual appearance? It is not surprising
that the vulgar should turn it all into prodigy and miracle; but
what would you think of men of sense, and of a liberal education,
if I should tell you that I heard one of my very good brethren
in this neighbourhood gravely assert in company (and I have
been told he did the same *in his pulpit*) that it was the fulfilling
of Joel's prophecy of a "pillar of smoke"; and that another
wondered at me for not placing this phenomenon in the same
rank with Josephus's signs of the destruction of Jerusalem?
What would you think of one who supposed it to be the pouring
out of the 7th vial into the air; and of another that called his
congregation together during the darkness, and prayed that the
sun might shine again, as if he had forgot the promise to Noah
that "day and night should not cease"? What would you think
of one who supposed the earth to be passing through the tail of a
comet; and of another who thought the nucleus of one had inter-
fered between us and the sun, so as to make an eclipse? How
many more extravagant conceptions have been formed by men,
whose minds one would think had been enlarged by reason and
philosophy, I know not. Doubtless you will hear enough on your
return to make you stand amazed at the power which fear and
superstition have over the minds of men. Should you collect any
observations on your journey, I shall be greatly obliged by a
communication of them. I want very much to know the exact
limits of the obscuration and the degree of it in different places,
for it was not everywhere alike. In some places the sun appeared in the afternoon, but here the whole afternoon was
uniformly dark; and the evening was as *total darkness as can be
conceived,* with a strong smell of smoke, and between nine and

ten it grew lighter, and afterwards continued until the moon appeared through the clouds.[1]

If we compare the mental attitude of Dr. Belknap with that of Mr. Prince twenty-five years before, remembering that both were leaders of opinion in Boston, we shall get a good idea of the progress of rational thought in the second half of the eighteenth century. When another Dark Day came, on November 2d, 1819, it caused comparatively little distress of mind, and the Yellow Day of our own recollection, September 6th, 1881, excited wonder and curious speculation, but no terror, except among the ignorant.

Mr. Thomas was always an opponent of superstition. Two noteworthy passages in the Almanac give humorous expression to his general sentiments. The first is in the Farmer's Calendar for March, 1827 : —

> Farmer Snug sits warm by his fire,
> And his ale and his nuts pass about.
> Old Betty and noisy Uriah
> Are steming the tempest without.

Whew and whistle goes the wind and superstitious people seem to imagine that fairies and hobgoblins are continually upon the dance all about and about and about. "What a terrible flustration is here!" cried Mrs. Flitterwinkle. "Why it seems as if the very heavens and earth were coming together! They say our blue heifer has been blown clean across chickawicket pond! Farmer Cleverly's cattle have all lost their tails, and just as old Mrs. Drizzle went to take up her dinner, there came a most terrifying gust, and swoop it carried porridge pot, pork, pud'n and mother Drizzle all up chimney and nothing has been heard of them since! Ah, I knew this would happen; for the goose bone burnt blue yesterday, and the kitten's tail pointed north all day! Hark, what's that! Dear me how pale I feel! I am afraid the moon is going to fall!"

[1] Coll. Mass. Hist. Soc., 5th Series, II, 54–55.

Away with such superstitious nonsense, and let us be cutting scions for grafting; or watching our fields, or cutting wood, or making maple sugar, and other matters.

Three years later, in March, 1830, the Farmer's Calendar returns to the charge : —

Why do you conjure up a thousand frightful monsters to torment yourself, when there are enough of real evils? Some seem to think that there is a ghost in every gust of wind. Away with such vain illusions of the imagination. Strange it is that a courage, that never startles at real dangers, should shrink at even the thought of an empty chimera! Signs and omens and prognostics continually fill the minds of some. "Ah, husband, I know our crops will be short next season," said a silly old woman, "for the brine has all leaked out of the pork barrel!" She happened to get a first sight of the new moon over her left shoulder, and it made her sad and glum through the month. She once dreamed of a black cat, and this so bewitched the cream, that no butter could be made! Farmer Bluejoint has nailed an Ass's shoe to his hogsty to keep the evil spirit from his *herd of swine;* for, it is said that, old Splitfoot has always hated Asses since the affair of Balaam. The rats by thousands destroyed his grain. So, he got his daughter, Dolly, to write them a threatening letter, which he placed in his corn crib. The consequence was that every *varment* of them immediately evacuated the place! What power has superstition!

The year 1830 seems rather recent for the prevalence of such notions as the Old Farmer is here scoffing at; but we are all more superstitious than we imagine, and it has not been difficult for students of folk-lore to collect a great quantity of whimsicalities from New England people, even in very recent years. Most of them, to be sure, are no longer believed, but they were articles of faith a few generations ago. Most persistent, probably, are the various notions about good and bad luck. Every reader, if he gives his

mind to it, can think of a score that he has been brought up on, unless he is a very sophisticated person indeed. Horseshoes, and Friday, and walking under a ladder, and odd numbers, and picking up pins, will do for texts. Letters to rats are still written now and then, and have as much effects as they ever had.   We have not altogether broken with the past!

ARMY AND NAVY

IN June, 1801, when Europe and America were both payers of tribute to the Barbary States, for exemption from piratical attacks on their shipping, the Bey of Tunis met with a serious loss. A fire broke out in his palace and consumed fifty thousand stands of arms. He immediately sent for the American consul and remarked that he had "apportioned his loss among his friends," that the share of the United States was ten thousand stands, and that they must be furnished without delay. "It is impossible," replied the consul, "to state this claim to my government. We have no magazines of small arms. The organization of our national strength is different from that of every other nation on earth. Each citizen carries his own arms, always ready, for battle. When threatened with invasion, or actually invaded, detachments from the whole national body are sent by rotation to serve in the field: so that we have no need of standing armies nor depositories of arms." [1]

The most picturesque feature of the military system thus forcibly expounded to the sulky and incredulous Tunisian despot was May Training, which many New Englanders of the older generation remember as the favorite holiday of their boyhood. Besides the inspections, mock fights, and miscellaneous evolutions, there were shooting matches, feats of strength, side shows, fakirs, and other accessories of the modern county fair. Boys saved their coppers for months and walked barefoot

[1] Life of Gen. William Eaton, Brookfield, 1813, pp. 204–5.

for miles to enjoy the fun. When they were eighteen years old, they were themselves liable to military duty.

Mr. Thomas was so good an American, and his annual represented the life of his time so well, that we should be surprised if he did not refer to the obligations of a citizen in military matters as well as in civil. We shall not find him lacking in proper spirit. In the Farmer's Calendar for September, 1811, there is a suggestion to parents: —

If your sons have no uniform for trainings, you ought immediately to see that they are supplied. Send them to training neat and clean, with good equipments, and inculcate in them the principles of subordination and decency of behaviour while under command.

In 1816 the Almanac gives a table of fines which affords a certain amount of curious information. The " two spare flints, priming wire, and brush " recall forcibly the progress of gunmaking in the course of a century. Everybody has *seen* flints, but few of the younger generation have ever snapped a flintlock, and " a flash in the pan " has become a mere figure of speech, as archaic in its flavor as " hoist with his own petard." As for " priming wires and brushes," they are preserved as relics and curiosities, but most of us have very hazy ideas of their exact function. However, it is high time to give the table of penalties.

MILITARY FINES, ACCORDING TO THE LATEST MILITIA LAW, PASSED IN 1810.

	dolls.	cts.
NON appearance 1st Tuesday in May	3	00
Do do. at company training	2	00
Deficiency of gun, bayonet and belt, or ramrod	1	00
Do. of cartridge box, cartridges or knapsack	0	30
Do. of two spare flints, priming wire, or brush	0	20

	dolls.	cts.
Disorderly firing, not more than 20 dollars nor less than	5	00
Neglecting to warn for exercise, not more than twenty dollars nor less than	12	00
Neglect of regimental duty	4	00
Disorderly behaviour, not more than 20 dollars nor less than	5	00
Neglecting to meet to choose officers	1	00
Giving false information, or refusing to give names of persons liable to do military duty	20	00
Unmilitary conduct of musicians, not more than twenty dollars nor less than	10	00
Neglect of towns in providing ammunition, not more than five hundred dollars, nor less than	20	00
Neglect in wearing uniform	2	00
In case of detachment, and orders to march, for release, if paid in twenty-four hours after,	50	00

The enrolled Militia consists of persons from eighteen to forty-five years of age. Annual inspection, first Tuesday in May, when the rules and articles are to be publickly read to the companies. Each captain must parade his company on three several days in addition to the annual inspection.

All persons between the age of forty and forty-five are exempted from all military duty, by paying annually to the Town Treasurer the sum of two dollars, on or before the first Tuesday in May, and produce his receipt to the commanding officer before the first Tuesday in May, in each year.

This table is repeated yearly until 1829, with a shift in the lower limit of exemption from forty to thirty-five, according to the law of 1822. After 1829 there are various modifications, as the statutes changed. In 1831 we find this significant provision: — "Treating with ardent spirits on days of military duty, and at elections of officers is prohibited; and Courts Martial may punish for all

offences by reprimand, removal from office and fines not exceeding $200. at their discretion." This was at the time of the great temperance movement in New England.

One of the offences mentioned in the table of fines is "Neglecting to meet to choose officers," for which a penalty of one dollar is imposed. This reminds us of the most distinguished occasion of the kind, — the Artillery Election of the Ancients and Honorables. A description of the ceremony, with a respectful tribute to the Ancients themselves, may be found in William Tudor's Letters on the Eastern States, published in 1820: —

Among the public institutions, there are two which deserve particular notice. The first is a military company, which was incorporated in the commencement of the colony, to form a school for officers; — but religious feelings were strongly united with military ones in its establishment. It now contains between one and two hundred members, who are, or have been, almost every one of them, officers, either in the regular service or in the militia; — of course, among the privates, are generals, colonels, &c. The original intention was, that this should be a school for military discipline and instruction, — and that they should keep in mind their duty to religion, so as to form a corps of Christian soldiers. For this purpose, their anniversary is publicly celebrated, — the governor, and other persons in civil authority, attending it, and going in procession to a church, where an appropriate sermon is preached to them on the joint duties of the Christian and the soldier. After this annual sermon, they have a dinner in Faneuil Hall, to which a large number of guests are invited; — and in the afternoon, the company escort the governor to the Common, where he receives the insignia of the officers for the past year, and confers them on those who have been elected to their places. A short speech is made on giving and receiving these commissions. This company is now on a respectable footing, but perhaps more might be made of it. Their anniversary, however, affords one of the prettiest fêtes we have. It is called the Artillery Election,

and takes place in the month of June, — and on this occasion, eight or ten thousand people are collected, to see the ceremonies in the Common. In this, as in many other cases, the spectators themselves afford the most pleasing spectacle.[1]

In contrast with this pleasing spectacle may be cited the experiences of a militia captain as described in a humorous anecdote, credited to the New York Constellation, in the Almanac for 1833 : —

A MILITIA CAPTAIN.

A captain of militia, was in the habit of swearing '*by forty.*' He had, like many other officers who commanded 'slab' companies, a troublesome set of fellows to deal with.

One training day, when the soldiers behaved as usual, very disorderly, he drew his sword, and furiously brandishing it in the air, exclaimed — 'Fellow sogers, I swear by forty, if you don't behave better I'll put every d——l of you under 'rest!' 'I wish you would give us a little *rest,*' said half a dozen voices, 'for we're e'en a-most tired to death.' — 'Order! order! fellow sogers,' roared the captain, with another tremendous flourish of his sword. The word was no sooner spoken, than they all come to order, bringing down the breaches of their guns with all violence, each upon his neighbor's toes — which threw the ranks into greater disorder than before. 'Dress! dress!' bawled the captain. — 'We are *dressed*, most of us,' replied a fellow, who was barefoot, and had on a rimless hat. — 'Now by forty,' said the captain, 'that's one tarnal lie ; you aint above half dressed, if that's what you mean — but I mean something else — I mean you sould dress in the *milintary* sense of the word.' 'How's that, captain?' cried half a dozen voices. — 'How's that! you fools you,' exclaimed the captain, 'by forty, have you been so long under my training, and don't know the meaning of dress? Form a straight line! I say — form a straight line!'

---

[1] New York, 1820, Letter XV, pp. 310-11 ; 2d ed., Boston, 1821, pp. 368-9.

The soldiers made sundry ineffectual efforts to get into a straight
line, and the captain begun to despair of ever straightening them,
when his military genius, suddenly suggested to him the novel
expedient of backing his men up against a fence, which fortunately happened to be straight.

'Tention! fellow sogers,' said he in a stentorian voice, 'Advance backwards! Music, quick step!' The soldiers made a
quick retrograde movement, and come with their backs plump
against the fence. — 'There! by forty,' said the captain, 'now
see if you can keep straight.' But he had scarcely performed this
manœuvre, and being about to resume the manual exercise, when
the clouds began to threaten rain; the soldiers squinting at the
aspect, began to desert their ranks, and hasten towards a neighboring tavern. 'Halt! halt!' roared the captain — 'halt! I
say fellow sogers; where the d——l are you going to?'

'We 're going to get out of the rain.' 'Out of the rain! you
cowards! Halt! I say, or I 'll stick the first man I can catch.'
'I 'll take care you sha'nt catch me,' shouted each one, as he
took to his heels. In less than a minute, the whole company had
deserted; and the captain had little chance of *sticking* them, for
very good reason, he could not overtake them.

'By forty!' said he, after standing speechless for a minute or
two, 'If this don't beat all, just as I had got them into a straight
line by a new manœuvre — to desert me thus! But there 's no use
in keeping the field all alone; I may as well go to the tavern too.'
So saying, he sheathed his sword, and followed his soldiers.

The following inventory of the United States Navy, published in the Almanac for 1814, was of vital interest then,
in the thick of the War of 1812, and will not be read with
indifference by any American to-day: —

NAVY OF THE UNITED STATES. — JULY, 1813.

Names	*Guns*	*Names*	*Guns*
Constitution	44	Isaac Hull	10
United States	44	Conquest	8
President	44	Hamilton	8

Names	Guns	Names	Guns
Macedonian	38	Raven	8
Constellation	36	Scourge	8
Congress	36	Governor Tompkins	6
New-York	36	Scorpion	6
Essex	32	Growler	5
Adams	32	Fair American	4
Boston	32	Viper	12
General Pike	32	Lady of the Lake	3
Madison	28	Pert	3
John Adams	20	Julia	2
Louisiana	20	Elizabeth	2
Alert	18	Ontario	1
Argus	18	Adeline	—
Hornet	18	Asp	—
Oneida	18	Analoston	—
Troupe	18	Despatch	—
Revenge *	16	Ferret	—
Syren	14	Neptune	—
Nonsuch	14	Perseverance	—
Enterprize	14	Ætna	bomb
Carolina	14	Mary	do.
Comet*	14	Spitfire	do.
Duke of Gloucester	12	Vengeance	do.
President	12	Vesuvius	do.
Petapsco *	12		

Beside the above there are a number of Revenue Cutters, and about one hundred and seventy-eight Gun-Boats.

Two sloops of war have lately been launched on Lake Erie.

The vessels names which are in *Italicks* have been captured from the British since the commencement of the present war.

Those marked thus (*) are hired by the United States.

The brief remark that "two sloops of war have lately been launched on Lake Erie" reminds us that Perry's Victory was won about two months after the date of this list, on September 10th, 1813. The vessels referred to are probably the brigs Lawrence and Niagara. The list is a little too early to include Perry's squadron; but it gives

BRILLIANT NAVAL VICTORY.

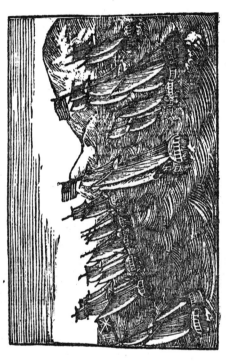

Yankee PERRY, better than Old English CIDER.

"TUNE---THREE YANKEE PIGEONS."

CONTEMPORARY BALLAD ON PERRY'S VICTORY

the names of some of the most famous vessels that ever belonged to our navy. The Essex and the Alert both appear, — the latter as captured from the enemy. She was, in fact, the first British national vessel to be taken in the war, and the Essex, under Porter, was her captor. The name Hornet reminds us of the great fight between the Hornet and the Peacock (February 24, 1813), for which Lawrence received a medal from Congress. The United States, Decatur's ship, and her prize the Macedonian both appear in the inventory. The frigate President, whose fight with the Little Belt, preceded the outbreak of the war, was soon to distinguish herself by a clever piece of blockade-running. The exploits of the Constitution are too well-known to need repetition.

THE SCHOOLMASTER

IN 1834 Miss Harriet Martineau came to America in search of mental refreshment and change of scene. She spent a couple of years in this country and has left a record of her experiences and impressions in two books which have won a respectable place in the great class of miscellaneous literature, — Society in America, and Retrospect of Western Travel, — besides the minute account of her connection with the anti-slavery movement which she gives in her Autobiography. With the mass of these writings we have at this moment no particular concern, but one incident must not pass without notice. In an idle hour, — or let us say rather in a moment of peculiar inspiration, — Miss Martineau had recourse to a certain "old almanack," where she discovered something to point an excellent moral. Here is her account of the discovery : —

All young people in these [New England] villages are more or less instructed. Schooling is considered a necessary of life. I happened to be looking over an old almanack one day, when I found, among the directions relating to the preparations for winter on a farm, the following : "Secure your cellars from frost. Fasten loose clap-boards and shingles. Secure a good school-master." It seemed doubtful, at the first glance, whether some new farming utensil had not been thus whimsically named ; as the brass plate which hooks upon the fender, or upper bar of the grate, is called "the footman"; but the context clearly showed that a man with learning in his head was the article required to be provided before the winter.[1]

[1] Society in America, London, 1837, I, 264.

It must be admitted, even by Miss Martineau's warmest admirers, that she did not always comprehend the American character. Indeed, she had the good sense not to suppose that she could comprehend it. Just before she sailed for the United States, James Mill asked her, quizzically, whether she "expected to understand the Americans" in two years. "He was glad to find," writes Miss Martineau, "that I had no such idea, and told me that five-and-twenty years before, he had believed that he understood the Scotch: and that in another five-and-twenty, he should no doubt understand the English; but that now he was quite certain that he understood neither the one nor the other."[1] It was hardly this warning that sent Miss Martineau to the old almanac, but rather her own sagacity, or perhaps a happy accident. At all events, she lighted upon a highly characteristic passage, and it is to her credit that she did not fail to perceive what it signifies, — that to procure a schoolmaster is as much a matter of course to a Yankee farmer as any other provision for the winter season. To his mind there is nothing incongruous between attention to loose shingles and solicitude for primary education.

It does not appear what almanac Miss Martineau consulted. Very possibly it was that of Mr. R. B. Thomas. The precise passage, to be sure, has not been discovered in the sayings of the Old Farmer; but she may have been quoting from memory, and the form and the sentiment both suggest the admonitions of the Farmer's Calendar. That column contains, along with its precepts of practical agriculture, much exhortation on the subject of schools and schoolmasters. Some of the entries are characteristic enough to deserve reproduction. Besides, they are not without value as bits of country life at the end of the eighteenth and the beginning of the nineteenth century.

[1] Autobiography, Boston, 1877, I, 329.

A passage which comes very near to Miss Martineau's quotation occurs in the Farmer's Calendar for November, 1804 : —

Now let the noise of your flail awake your drowsy neighbours.
Bank up your cellars.
Now hire a good schoolmaster, and send your children to school as much as possible.

In November, 1810, there is also a near approach to what Miss Martineau read : —

Bank your cellars unless your underpinning is such as renders it unneedful. Drive all your loose nails ; and if the boys have broken any glass during the summer in the windows, you find it more comfortable to have the hole stopped up, than to let it go over winter. Send your children to school. Every boy should have a chance to prepare himself to do common town business.

In December, 1801, we have a good piece of proverbial philosophy : —

" *A cheap school-master makes a dear school*," says Common Sense. As this is the season for opening schools in the country, the above adage may be worthy of attention. Experience teaches, that the master, who will keep for 8 dollars per month, is not worth the keeping : yet some towns, to save 2 dollars, give away 10.

Again, in December, 1803 and 1805 : —

It is hoped that every town and village is now supplied with a wise and virtuous school-master ; not ten dollar men — such pitiful pedants are too plenty. (1803.)
Attend to your schools. Hire not what neighbor Simpkins calls a *four dollar master* to instruct your children ; it will be throwing away money. He who deprives his children of education, at once robs himself and society. (1805.)

But the liveliest passage of the kind is in the Calendar for November, 1820, where we have not only a full account of the acquirements of a five-dollar master, but also an eloquent speech from one of the advocates of ill-judged economy : —

This is the last month of Autumn, and it is now the business of the prudent man to be making his calculations about winter matters. I have often mentioned the importance of schooling to the rising generation. Few, if any countries, are blest like New-England, with public school establishments. No stinginess about the business. See that you have an able master, and pay him well. Here my neighbour Hugpurse and I can never agree ; for he says, "So much of this here larnin is altogether useless and expensive. There is Joe Simple is good enough for our school. He has cyphered through compound interest, and that's fur enough for any man. He knows nothing about Jogrify and Grammar and such stuff; but he can write as good a hand as I can ; and as for reading, he is far better than Squire Puff. In spelling they say he is curious. I have often heard that when a boy he could spell *Nebuchadnezzar* quicker than any one in school. I move, Mr. cheersman, that we hire Joe Simple to keep our school this winter. Give him five dollars a month and board himself, which is all he axes."

Mr. Thomas knew what he was talking about. He had been a country pedagogue himself; and, though he did not fall in love with the profession — in fact, he tells that he grew heartily tired of it — he had always been success-ful in his schoolmastering.[1] He felt a proper contempt for the shortsighted stinginess of ignorant committeemen, and cherished no illusions as to the quality of the cheap pretenders to learning whose services they secured for little or nothing. He must have known many Ichabod Cranes and Joe Simples in his day. But schoolmasters

[1] See p. 6, above.

like Joe Simple were not the only pretenders whom Mr.
Thomas satirized. He was equally severe on those who
aped the follies of fine gentlemen. Thus in December,
1815, we read: —

It is all important now that you send your children to school;
but take care that you have a good instructor for them. It is
not everyone who apes the gentleman that is fit for this undertaking. To strut in white top boots, brandish a canee, drink
brandy, and smoke segars, are not the most essential qualifications
for a schoolmaster. It is a serious misfortune that in many parts
our country schools are exceedingly neglected; and it would
seem that were it not for the law's obliging them to have at least
the appearance of schools, there would be no provision at all for
this purpose made for years! What better estate can you give
your offspring than a good education? I would not urge you to
send them to college — neither to an academy; but see that you
have the best of teachers in your town schools; be not stingy
about the price — let not your children suffer for shoes and other
clothing to make them comfortable and decent — Town schools
are of the first importance, for here and in the family at home is
laid the foundation of the future man, whether he be great, or
mean, an honest man, or a scoundrel.

Top-boots and cigar-smoking seem to have gone together. Robert Sutcliff, the English Quaker, who travelled
in America from 1804 to 1806, shared Mr. Thomas's
suspicion of both articles. " I have remarked," he writes,
" that some people in America have a great predilection
for wearing boots, and for smoking segars. Even children
of five or six years of age, are sometimes seen, in their
boots smoking segars." [1] Most of Mr. Thomas's early
readers, if they smoked at all, doubtless smoked pipes,
for the cigar (or *segar*, as there was a tendency to spell the
word about this time) was not only citified, but was re-

[1] Travels in some Parts of North America, in the years 1804, 1805, and
1806, 2d ed., York, 1815, p. 103.

garded as indicative of riotous living. Perhaps, therefore
the following entry, honestly meant as it certainly was,
suggested no roguish thoughts to the contemporary agri-
culturist. To the modern smoker it has a sinister sound.
It occurs in the Farmer's Calendar for June 12, 1796: —

Set cabbages and tobacco.

And, as if a word to the wise were not always sufficient
in tricks of the trade, we have, a year later, in June, 1797,
an additional injunction: —

Set more cabbages and tobacco.

The word *more* has some significance. It involves a
pleasant suggestion of the "constant reader," the "old
subscriber." In consulting the Calendar for June of one
year, the farmer who is faithful to the admonitions of the
Almanac will surely remember what he did, or shunned,
the year before. "*More* cabbages and tobacco," then,
must not be taken as the helpless reiteration of an almanac-
writer at his wit's end. It implies, rather, that the author
believes in himself and has reason to think that his public
has confidence in him. "You planted cabbages and
tobacco last year, no doubt, as I advised. Very well!
Plant some more now. You see my counsel was good."

A lesson for parents, as apposite now as it ever was,
may be found in the December Calendar for 1807. Here
also Mr. Thomas was speaking from experience: —

Let your children go to school as much as possible; and do not
interfere with the orders and regulations of the master. When
your little darling Jemmy is whipt at school it is a miserable way to
give him gingerbread, and call the master puppy, rascal, &c. &c.

And again, in February, 1809: —

Keep the boys at school as much as possible, and take care
not to rail against the master in their presence. Some people

are eternally complaining about the schoolmaster or mistress. Let the school be never so well kept, they will be dissatisfied.

Another kind of admonition, in the Calendar for December, 1812, sounds strange to modern ears : —

Now you have an opportunity for schooling your children; and what can you give them to more profit? Riches and honors will fly away, but a good education, with habitual improvement, will abide by them, and be a source of pleasure and profit, when business and money, and friends fail them. But do not let them be prevented from going to school for want of shoes, &c. They should have been well shod before this time.

This observation about staying at home for lack of shoes recalls the fact that going barefoot was far commoner a hundred (or even thirty) years ago than it is to-day. " Old enough to go to meeting barefooted " is a Yankee proverb not yet forgotten, though not, of course, to be taken seriously. An old New Englander who, in 1837, wrote reminiscences of his youth for the Old Colony Memorial, is very clear on this matter. He is speaking of ordinary attire in the country districts. " Old men," he says, " had a great coat and a pair of boots. The boots generally lasted for life . . . Shoes and stockings were not worn by the young men, and by but few men in farming business." As for the young women, he informs us that in the summer, when engaged in their ordinary work, they " did not wear stockings and shoes." [1]

We may close our series of extracts with two eloquent utterances of a generally admonitory character : —

Let your children go to school. No country in the world is so blest with schooling as New-England; then neglect not to improve this excellent advantage. (December, 1806.)

[1] Collections of the New-Hampshire Historical Society, 1837, V, 226–7.

It is a duty to educate our children in the ways of frugality and economy, as well as industry. In some it is owing to inattention, in others to parsimony that their children are kept from school. The heedless man who can just write his name and pick out a chapter or two in his bible and perhaps find the changes of the moon in his almanack, thinks that his children and his children's children are to go on in the same way with himself, and so is regardless of their education ; but the penurious man, if it cost a cent, will see them hanged before they shall be taught to spell *Caleb*. (March, 1813.)

A generation ago there was a stock question which used to be asked of school children : " What is the chief glory of New England ? " And the reply was a matter of clock-work : " The chief glory of New England is in her public schools." The children had their doubts, but they answered dutifully. This kind of catechising is out of fashion now, and the mere thought of it provokes a smile among educational theorists ; but it had its uses. In the case in hand, it called attention to the fact that schools do not spring up of themselves ; and it may now and then have reminded the rising generation of certain items of indebtedness to the Puritan past. This whole subject of New England schooling is not easy to discuss without losing one's equilibrium. On the one hand, we are habituated to a good deal of undiscriminating eulogy of our ancestors, as if they never faltered in their zeal for education. On the other, there are the iconoclasts, who make much of the difficulty there was in enforcing the school laws.[1] There is evidence of such difficulty. A Massachusetts Act of 1701 declares that the previous statute " is shamefully neglected by divers Towns." In an Election Sermon for 1709 the

---

[1] The Massachusetts laws which particularly concern us are those of 1647 (Mass. Colony Records, II, 203), 1692 (4 Wm. and Mary, ch. xi), 1701 (13 Wm. III, ch. xx), 1789 (Acts, ch. xix), and 1824 (Acts, ch. cxi, amending the Act of 1789).

Rev. Grindal Rawson, of Mendon, exclaims: "How little care is there generally taken, especially in Country Towns, to promote the Liberal Education of Children? How much is it become the Practice of many Towns, to Study Tricks and Shifts whereby the Law of the Land obliging to the upholding and maintaining of Schools, may be wholly evaded and lose its Efficacy? And is not this Provoking to God, and disserviceable to the interest of Posterity?"[1] In 1713 Cotton Mather, in one of his innumerable jeremiads,— called Advice from the Watch Tower, in a Testimony against Evil Customs, — censures the evasion of this law: — "To Elude the Law about *Schools*, is too Customary. It argues, that a due sense of that Grand Concern, the *Education of Children*, is too much laid aside among us. — Tis *Wonderful!* Tis *Wonderful!* That a People of our Profession would seem so unconcerned, Lest the next Generation be miserably Uncultivated, and have hideous *Barbarity* grow upon it!"

All this, however, should not mislead us. The facts are clear enough, and the anxiety of the preachers is really a favorable symptom. The significant thing is not that the laws were not always obeyed, but that the colonial and provincial authorities made an honest attempt to enforce them, and that the outcome of their efforts was, when time was ripe, a public school system which, though not perfect, is at all events a remarkable achievement. We should regard the general tendency and the final results. We have a good many diaries kept by soldiers in the Revolutionary War. Most of these are rudely spelled and not very exact in point of grammar. They show that the rank and file were not highly educated, and they have often been cited as proof that the schools and schoolmasters of the eighteenth century were poor things. What they really prove,

[1] The Necessity of a Speedy and Thorough Reformation, Boston, 1709, p. 36.

Advice from the Watch Tower.

In a TESTIMONY againſt

EVIL CUSTOMES.

A brief ESSAY

To declare the *Danger* & *Miſchief* of all

Evil Cuſtomes,

in general ;

And Offer a more particular CATA-
LOGUE of EVIL CUSTOMES growing upon us ;

With certain METHODS for the Prevention and Suppreſſion of them.

Hab. II. 1. *I will ſtand upon my Watch, and
ſet me upon the Tower, and will watch to
ſee what I ſhall anſwer upon my Reproof.*

Luk. XXI. 13.
It ſhall turn to you for a TESTIMONY.

Vincere Conſuetudinem, dura eſt pugna. August.
*Uſitata Culpa obligat mentem, ut nequaquam ſurgere poſſit
ad Rectitudinem.* Gregor.
Dominus noſter CHRISTUS, *Veritatem ſe, non Conſuetudinem, Cognominavit.* Tertul.

By C Mather

Boſton, Printed by *T. Allen*, for *N. Boone*,
at the Sign of the *Bible* in *Cornhill.* 1713.

however, is that almost every New Englander could read and write, and this, after all, is a pretty creditable showing. When John Adams was in England in 1786, he fell in with a Virginian, Major Langbourne, who had " taken the whim of walking all over Europe, after having walked over most of America." The Major lamented " the difference of character between Virginia and New England." " I offered," writes Adams, " to give him a receipt for making a New England in Virginia. He desired it; and I recommended to him town meetings, training days, town schools, and ministers, giving him a short explanation of each article. The meeting-house and school-house and training field are the scenes where New England men were formed. Colonel Trumbull, who was present, agreed that these are the ingredients. In all countries and in all companies, for several years, I have, in conversation and in writing, enumerated the towns, militia, schools, and churches, as the four causes of the growth and defence of New England. The virtues and talents of the people are there formed; their temperance, patience, fortitude, prudence, and justice, as well as their sagacity, knowledge, judgment, taste, skill, ingenuity, dexterity, and industry." [1]

Here is an uncommonly interesting bit of autobiography from the middle of the eighteenth century. The writer, Rufus Putnam, was an officer of distinction, whom Washington pronounced the best engineer on the American side in the Revolution. No one can doubt that the New England spirit finds a truer expression in the boy's struggles to learn something than in the nonchalance of his guardians.

In Sept 1747, I went to live with my Step Father, Capt John Sadler (at Upton) and continued with him untill his death (in September or october 1753)

[1] Diary, July 21, 1786, Works, ed. C. F. Adams, III, 400.

15

during the six year I lived with Capt Sadler, I never Saw the inside of a School house, except about three weeks. he was very illiterate himself, and took no care for the education of his family; but this was not all I was made a ridecule of, and otherwise abused for my attention to books, and attempting to write, and learn Arethmatic, however, amidst all those discouragements I made Some advances in writeing and Arethmatic, that is I could make Letters that could be under stood, and had gon as far in Arethmatic as to work the rule of three (without any teacher but the book) — Oh! my Children beware you neglect not the education of any under your care as I was neglected.—

In March 1754 I was bound apprentice to Daniel Mathews of Brokfield, to the Millw[r]ights trade; by him my education was as much neglected, as by Capt Sadler, except that he did not deny me the use of a Light for Study in the winter evenings —

I turned my attention chiefly to Arethmatic, Geography, and history; had I ben as much engaged in Learning to write well, with Spelling, and Gramer, I might have ben much better qualified to fulfill the duties of the Succeeding Scenes of Life, which In providence I have ben called to pass through. I was zealous to obtain knowledge, but having no guide I knew not where to begin nor what course to pursue,— hence neglecting Spelling and gramer when young I have Suffered much through life on that account.[1]

The Constitution of Massachusetts, adopted in 1781, laid special emphasis on the duty of the Commonwealth with regard to education. In the same year the legislature passed an elaborate law providing for both elementary and grammar schools.[2] By grammar schools, we should remember, was always meant what we now call Latin or High schools. If we compare this act of 1789 with the original law of 1647, we shall find that it is less exacting.

[1] Memoirs of Rufus Putnam, ed. by Miss Rowena Buell, Boston, 1903, pp. 9-11.
[2] Acts of 1789, ch. xix.

Instead of requiring a grammar school in every town of one hundred families, it raises the limit to two hundred. This change is estimated to have released one hundred and twenty towns from an obligation under which they had lain for many years.[1]   Doubtless, however, it was as rigorous a rule as the country could bear.   What had seemed possible in the compact and homogeneous Colony was no longer practicable in the growing State.

This act of 1789 brings us down to the time of the Farmer's Almanack.   It defines the conditions which Mr. Thomas had in mind in his constant exhortations.[2]   In the lower schools the master was "to teach children to read and write, and to instruct them in the English language, as well as in arithmetic, orthography, and decent behaviour."   The higher schools were to be provided with "a grammar schoolmaster of good morals, well instructed in the Latin, Greek and English languages."

An idea of the impression which the schools of New England made upon a highly cultivated and philosophical foreigner may be got from a passage in Rochefoucault's Travels in North America.   The distinguished Frenchman, who belonged to the school of Arthur Young, is speaking of Connecticut in 1795 : —

There is . . . no instance of a town or parish, remaining, negligently, without a school.   Many communities maintain their schools for a greater part of the year, than they are, by law, obliged to do.   The select-men and the deputations from the communities manage the farms and other revenues of the schools.

The teachers are commonly young men from the colleges, students of law or theology.   Their salaries are at the pleasure of the different parishes, from two to three hundred dollars.   Al-

[1] G. H. Martin, The Evolution of the Massachusetts Public School System, New York, 1894, lecture iii.

[2] There was no further law until 1824: Acts of 1824, ch. cxi (amending the act of 1789).

most all those who now act a distinguished part in the political business of New England, began their career as teachers in these schools; a situation that is accounted exceedingly honourable. Sometimes, where the salary is small, women are chosen to be the teachers. Even these must, in this case, be well qualified to teach reading, writing, and arithmetic.

Every county must have a school for Greek and Latin. A fine of three dollars is exacted from parents neglecting to send their children to school. The select-men have authority to levy it.[1]

No account of our schools, however brief and incidental, can ignore the Academy, — that peculiarly New England institution which has played so important a part in the social and educational life of America. The smaller towns had found it impossible to support classical schools; but there was no actual falling-off in the zeal for education. Academies were founded, partly by bequests from public-spirited citizens, partly by voluntary contributions from subscribers. These multiplied exceedingly in the late eighteenth and the early nineteenth century, and many of them were subsidized by the States. Most of them have gone out of existence, becoming unnecessary as wealth increased and the towns were able once more to assume the duty of maintaining high schools. But the stronger institutions of the kind, which are also among the oldest, have survived and flourished. They are a distinctive feature of the educational system of the whole United States. Their importance is no longer merely local; it is national.

Mr. Thomas makes an amusing remark about academies in the Farmer's Calendar for December, 1808: —

Now let your boys and girls attend school. Send them to the common town school, rather than to an academy. Fun, frolick,

---

[1] *Travels through the United States of North America*, English translation, London, 1799, I, 530.

and filigree are too much practised at the academies for the benefit of a farmer's boy. Let them have a solid and useful education.

This should not be misunderstood. It is not an assault on the academy as an institution. It is merely a caution against sending a boy to an inappropriate school. Academies, in Mr. Thomas's opinion, were not meant for those who were to spend their lives on the farm. He was no enemy to ambition, but he wished to see it intelligently guided.

It will be noticed that Mr. Thomas mentions girls as well as boys in this last exhortation. The education of girls was neglected in the early days. In 1782 the Rev. John Eliot wrote from Boston to Jeremy Belknap, then minister at Dover, New Hampshire: —

We don't pretend to teach ye female part of ye town anything more than dancing, or a little music perhaps, (and these accomplishm^t must necessarily be confined to a very few,) except ye private schools for writing, which enables them to write a copy, sign their name, &c., which they might not be able to do without such a priviledge, & with it I will venture to say that a lady is a rarity among us who can write a page of commonplace sentiment, the words being well spelt, & ye style & language kept up with purity & elegance.[1]

Two years later Caleb Bingham opened a private school for girls, commonly said to have been the first girls' school ever known in Boston. The letter just quoted shows that this idea is not strictly correct. Yet Bingham's establishment was so far in advance of the mere writing classes which Mr. Eliot mentions that it deserves its reputation. " He taught not only writing and arithmetic, but reading, spelling, and English grammar," thus meeting precisely

[1] Feb. 1, 1782. Coll. Mass. Hist. Soc., 6th Series, IV, 223.

the needs which Mr. Eliot refers to. Bingham's successful experiment soon led the town to make some provision for the education of girls. This was in 1789, and Bingham was employed in one of these new public schools. He was the author of several text-books which rivalled those of Noah Webster in popularity. His American Preceptor, published in 1794, had by 1832 sold to the number of nearly six hundred and fifty thousand copies, and his Columbian Orator, published in 1797, to the number of more than two hundred thousand. He also prepared, for his private school, a little English Grammar, The Young Lady's Accidence, of which a hundred thousand copies were sold by 1832. It was the first English grammar used in the schools of Boston.[1] Several other private schools for girls were established toward the end of the eighteenth century. In 1784 Dr. Jedediah Morse, the well-known geographer, opened such a school at New Haven, and in 1790 a Mr. Woodbridge, who gave himself the grandiloquent title of "the Columbus of female education," followed his example. Three years before, the Moravian brethren had founded a "female seminary" at Bethlehem, Pennsylvania. The opposition to any kind of higher education for women is amusingly illustrated by the experience of Miss Emma Willard, who opened a seminary for girls at Troy, New York, in 1821. She had previously conducted what she called a "female academy" at Waterford, in the same state. A friendly minister, who felt it his duty to mention this institution in his public prayers, styled it a "seminary," not wishing to offend his hearers by speaking of it as an "academy" or a "college." Bradford Academy, in Massachusetts, which still flourishes, was founded in 1803.[2]

[1] See G. E. Littlefield, Early Schools and School-Books of New England, 1904, pp. 156, 158, 229-30.
[2] See a paper on The Early History of Schools and School-Books, by

But chronology is dull work. Let us revert to anecdote, and, in so doing, to the old-fashioned grammar school. The Rev. John Barnard of Marblehead (who was born at Boston in 1681), after attending the instruction of a schoolmistress in the town and another in the country, was sent to the Latin School in his eighth year, where he was under the tuition of " the aged, venerable, and justly famous Mr. Ezekiel Cheever," one of the most noted of New England preceptors. In his autobiography, written when he was eighty-five years old, Mr. Barnard tells a pretty little story of " an odd accident" which " drove him from the school after a few weeks ":— " There was," he says, " an older lad entered the school the same week with me; we strove who should outdo; and he beat me by the help of a brother in the upper class, who stood behind master with the accidence open for him to read out off; by which means he could recite his [MS. illegible] three and four times in a forenoon, and the same in the afternoon; but I who had no such help, and was obliged to commit all to memory, could not keep pace with him; so that he would be always one lesson before me. My ambition could not bear to be outdone, and in such a fraudulent manner, and therefore I left the school." [1]

But he soon returned and got on very well in his studies, notwithstanding he was, as he confesses, " a very naughty boy, much given to play." At length Mr. Cheever resorted to an ingenious device. " You Barnard," said he, " I know you can do well enough if you will; but you are so full of play that you hinder your classmates from getting their lessons ; and therefore, if any of them cannot perform their duty, I shall correct you for it." " One unlucky day, one of my classmates did not look into his book, and there-

R. N. Meriam, Collections of the Worcester Society of Antiquity, IX, no. 27, pp. 93 f.
[1] Coll. Mass. Hist. Soc., 3d Series, V, 178.

fore could not say his lesson, though I called upon him once and again to mind his book; upon which our master beat me. I told master the reason why he could not say his lesson was, his declaring he would beat me if any of the class were wanting in their duty; since which this boy would not look into his book, though I called upon him to mind his book, as the class could witness. The boy was pleased with my being corrected, and persisted in his neglect, for which I was still corrected, and that for several days. I thought, in justice, I ought to correct the boy, and compel him to a better temper; and therefore, after school was done, I went up to him, and told him I had been beaten several times for his neglect; and since master would not correct him I would, and I should do so as often as I was corrected for him; and then drubbed him heartily. The boy never came to school any more, and so that unhappy affair ended." [1]

The temptation to go on with Mr. Barnard's delightful anecdotes of his boyhood is great, but must be resisted. Still, we may indulge ourselves in one more extract, which is very brief, and gives a charming picture of the little boy and the veteran schoolmaster: —

I remember once, in making a piece of Latin, my master found fault with the syntax of one word, which was not so used by me heedlessly, but designedly, and therefore I told him there was a plain grammar rule for it. He angrily replied, there was no such rule. I took the grammar and showed the rule to him. Then he smilingly said, "Thou art a brave boy; I had forgot it." And no wonder; for he was then above eighty years old. [2]

Mr. Cheever was master of the Boston Latin School for nearly forty years. He died in 1708, at the age of ninety-three, and was honored with a singular poetical tribute from

[1] Coll. Mass. Hist. Soc., 3d Series, V, 179–80.
[2] The same, p. 180.

the pen of Benjamin Tompson, " the renowned poet of New England." [1]   It bore a title prophetic of Browning, "The Grammarians Funeral," and was printed as a broadside. [2]   It begins : —

> Eight Parts of *Speech* this Day wear *Mourning Gowns*
> Declin'd *Verbs, Pronouns, Participles, Nouns*.
> And not declined, *Adverbs* and *Conjunctions*,
> In *Lillies* Porch they stand to do their functions.
> With *Preposition ;* but the most affection
> Was still observed in the *Interjection*.

This is quaint enough, but the oddest thing about the verses is that they are announced in the broadside as having been originally " composed upon the Death of Mr. *John Woodmancy*, formerly a School-Master in *Boston :* But now Published upon the Death of the Venerable Mr. Ezekiel Chevers."   In other words, a second-hand elegy !

The chapter may close with a bit from the Almanac for 1807 (July), which will serve as a fitting epilogue to our pedagogical miscellany :—

> *I have more pork in my cellar,* said neighbor Braggadocia, *than all the Almanack makers in christendom. Fie on your larnin, and all that stuff ; I wants none of your nonsense. No man shall teach me, faith.*   Now I forebore to dispute with this great man ; for the proverb says, *you cannot make a silken purse of a sow's ear.*

---

[1] See pp. 356 f., below.
[2] Reproduced by Dr. Samuel A. Green in his Ten Fac-Simile Reproductions, Boston, 1902, No. III.

TITLES OF HONOR

THE Almanac for 1794 contains " A complete list of the present CONGRESS of the UNITED STATES." At the head stand —

GEORGE WASHINGTON, LL. D., *President of the United States,*
JOHN ADAMS, LL. D., *Vice-President of the United States, and President of the Senate.*

The degree of Doctor of Laws attached to these names at once arrests the eye. Such things were more valued in those days than they are at present. No one would think of specifying a President's academic honors nowadays. We are reminded of the satirical words of John Adams himself in a letter addressed to Mrs. Mercy Warren, the historian, in 1807 : —

There is not a country under heaven in which titles and precedency are more eagerly coveted than in this country. The title of Excellency, and Honor, and Worship, of Councillor, Senator, Speaker, Major-General, Brigadier-General, Colonel, Lieutenant-Colonel, Major, Captain, Lieutenant, Ensign, Sergeant, Corporal, and even Drummer and Fifer, is sought with as furious zeal as that of Earl, Marquis, or Duke in any other country; and as many intrigues and as much corruption in many cases, are used to obtain them.[1]

There is a curious little error afloat with regard to Washington's LL. D. It is often asserted, even by careful writers, that he was the first person to receive this

[1] Coll. Mass. Hist. Soc., 5th Series, IV, 439.

honor from Harvard College. The mistake dates from
1840, when President Quincy's official History of Harvard
University was published. There we read : —

> After the evacuation of the town of Boston by the British
> troops, which took place on the 17th of March, 1776, con-
> gratulatory addresses from towns and legislatures were univer-
> sally presented to General Washington, for the signal success
> which had attended his measures. The Corporation and Over-
> seers, in accordance with the prevailing spirit and as an " ex-
> pression of the gratitude of this College for his eminent services
> in the cause of his country and to this society," conferred on him
> the degree of Doctor of Laws, by the unanimous vote of both
> boards. General Washington was the first individual on whom
> this degree was conferred by Harvard College. The diploma
> was signed by all the members of the Corporation except John
> Hancock, who was then in Philadelphia, and it was immediately
> published in the newspapers of the period, with an English
> translation. [1]

In point of fact, the diploma to which President Quincy
refers bears the signature of a man on whom the same
degree had been conferred three years before, in 1773.
This was the distinguished Professor of Mathematics and
Natural Philosophy, John Winthrop, the fourth in descent
from Governor Winthrop, and he, not Washington, was the
first person to receive an LL. D. from Harvard College.[2]
Washington's diploma deserves to be reproduced, in the
English translation which appeared in the Boston papers
of the time. It is a good specimen of the academic
eloquence of the eighteenth century : —

> The CORPORATION of HARVARD COLLEGE in Cam-
> bridge, in New-England, to all the faithful in Christ, to whom
> these Presents shall come, GREETING.

[1] II, 167.
[2] H. H. Edes, Publications of the Colonial Society of Massachusetts, VII.

WHEREAS Academical Degrees were originally instituted for
this Purpose, That Men, eminent for Knowledge, Wisdom and
Virtue, who have highly merited of the Republick of Letters and
the Commonwealth, should be rewarded with the Honor of these
Laurels ; there is the greatest Propriety in conferring such Honor
on that very illustrious Gentleman, *GEORGE WASHINGTON*
Esq ; the accomplished General of the confederated Colonies in
America ; whose Knowledge and patriotic Ardor are manifest to
all : Who, for his distinguished Virtues, both Civil and Military,
in the first Place being elected by the Suffrages of the Virginians,
one of their Delegates, exerted himself with Fidelity and singular
Wisdom in the celebrated *Congress of America,* for the Defence
of Liberty, when in the utmost Danger of being for ever lost,
and for the Salvation of his Country ; and then, at the earnest
Request of that Grand Council of Patriots, without Hesitation,
left all the Pleasures of his delightful Seat in Virginia, and the
Affairs of his own Estate, that through all the Fatigues and
Dangers of a Camp, without accepting any Reward, he might
deliver *New-England* from the unjust and cruel Arms of Britain,
and defend the other Colonies ; and Who, by the most signal
Smiles of Divine Providence on his Military Operations, drove
the Fleet and Troops of the Enemy with disgraceful Precipitation
from the Town of Boston, which for eleven Months had been
shut up, fortified, and defended by a Garrison of above seven
Thousand Regulars ; so that the Inhabitants, who suffered a
great Variety of Hardships and Cruelties while under the Power
of their Oppressors, now rejoice in their Deliverance, the neighbouring Towns are freed from the Tumults of Arms, and our
University has the agreeable Prospect of being restored to its
antient Seat.

Know ye therefore, that We, the President and Fellows of
Harvard-College in Cambridge, (with the Consent of the Honored
and Reverend Overseers of our Academy) have constituted and
created the aforesaid Gentleman, GEORGE WASHINGTON,
who merits the highest Honor, Doctor of Laws, the Law of
Nature and Nations, and the Civil Law ; and have given and

granted him at the same Time all Rights, Privileges, and Honors
to the said Degree pertaining.

In Testimony whereof, We have affixed the Common Seal of
our University to these Letters, and subscribed them with our
Hand writing this Third Day of April in the Year of our Lord
one Thousand seven Hundred Seventy-six.[1]

The early numbers of the Almanac are not lacking in
tributes of respect to " that very illustrious gentleman,
George Washington, Esq.," as the translated diploma calls
him.   One of the most felicitous is incidental.   It occurs
in a kind of epigram addressed to those farmers who allow
needless anxiety for state affairs to interfere with their
more immediate concerns : —

ADVICE.

To Country Politicians.

Go weed your corn, and plow your land,
And by *Columbia's* interest stand,
   Cast prejudice away ;
To able heads leave state affairs,
Give raling o'er, and say your prayers,
   For stores of corn and hay,
With politics ne'er break your sleep
But ring your hogs, and shear your sheep,
   And rear your lambs and calves ;
And WASHINGTON will take due care
That Briton never more shall dare
   Attempt to make you slaves.[2]

There is a briefer exhortation to a similar effect in the
Farmer's Calendar for June, 1807 : " Cut your clover ;
and mind your business."

In 1820 the English traveller Hodgson was told by an

---

[1] Albert Matthews, *ibid.;* printed also from the New-England Chronicle
in J. T. Buckingham's Specimens of Newspaper Literature, Boston, 1850, I,
223-4.
[2] Almanac for 1796.

acquaintance " that much as General Washington rode and walked through the streets, during a residence of several years in Philadelphia, he seldom passed a window, without the party in the room rising to look at him, although they might have been in his company the hour before." Hodgson remarks that he had often heard the same thing from other Americans.[1]

Yet there were local functionaries who were greater than Washington, as was shown by an adventure that befell him in Connecticut on a Sunday in 1789. " The President," according to the Columbian Centinel, " on his return to New-York from his late tour, through Connecticut, having missed his way on Saturday, was obliged to ride a few miles on Sunday morning, in order to gain the town, at which he had previously proposed to have attended divine service. — Before he arrived, however, he was met by a Tythingman, who commanding him to stop, demanded the occasion of his riding ; and it was not until the President had informed him of every circumstance, and promised to go no further than the town intended, that the Tythingman would permit him to proceed on his journey." [2]

A similar adventure is said to have befallen General William Eaton in the same State some years later. General Eaton, however, met the occasion with less repose. He had just returned from Africa after his famous march across the Desert of Barca and his capture of Derne in the war with Tripoli (1805), and was travelling in his carriage from Hartford to Boston. On his way through the parish of North Coventry, " as he neared the village church, his coachman was ordered to stop, with a threatened fine for journeying on the Sabbath. As soon as the old soldier

1 Adam Hodgson, Letters from North America, London, 1824, II, 18-19.
2 Columbian Centinel, December, 1789, as quoted by Henry M. Brooks, New-England Sunday, Boston, 1886, pp. 1-2.

learned the cause of his detention, he thrust his head from
a carriage window, and with a pistol in hand he exclaimed:
'Where is the man who stops my carriage? I don't
care to shoot him, but I think I will!'" The tithingman is
reported to have taken refuge in the church, and the
general was allowed to proceed.[1]

[1] Jeptha R. Simms, The Frontiersmen of New York, Albany, 1882, I,
481-2.

MUNCHAUSEN

THE humor of hyperbole, as well as that of ironical understatement, is quite in accordance with the New England character. It would be strange, therefore, if our annual miscellany did not afford examples of the Munchausen style of anecdote. That which follows may be found in the Almanac for 1809: —

AMUSING.

MR. THOMAS,

We have frequently heard of the wonderful feats and extraordinary stories of *Simonds, old Kidder, and Sam Hyde;* but I believe neither of them have exceeded the following, related by G. H——ll, a mighty hunter, and known in that part of the country where he lived by the name of the VERMONT NIMROD. — It may serve to divert some of your evening readers.   A. Z.

"I WAS once," said he, "passing down the banks of the Hudson in search of game, and suddenly heard a crackling on the opposite bank. Looking across the river, I saw a stately buck, and instantly drew up and let fly at him. That very moment a huge sturgeon leaped from the river in the direction of my piece. — The ball went through him, and passed on. I flung down my gun — threw off my coat and hat, and swam for the floating fish, which, mounting, I towed to the bank and went to see what more my shot had done for me. I found the ball had passed through the heart of the deer, and struck into a hollow tree beyond; where the honey was running out like a river! I sprung round to find something to stop the hole with, and caught hold of a white rabbit — It squeaked just like a stuck pig; so I thrash'd it away from me in a passion at the disappointment, and it went

with such force that it killed three cock partridges and a wood cock." ! ! !

Simonds and old Kidder, who are mentioned by Mr. Thomas's facetious correspondent as the heroes of incredible adventures, have not been identified, and the name of "the Vermont Nimrod" is as puzzling a question as those propounded by Sir Thomas Browne, — "What song the Sirens sang or what name Achilles assumed when he hid himself among women." Sam Hyde, however, is a more familiar personage. In 1820 Mr. Thomas remarks, in rejecting an anecdote offered by a correspondent, that it "smells too strong of the marvellous" and "is better calculated for Sam Hyde's Register." Sam has even become proverbial. "To lie like Sam Hyde" is still a New England saying, though, like so many old saws, it is going out of use as the population becomes more mixed. He is said to have been an Indian, and here is his biography as it stands in S. G. Drake's Book of the Indians. If it is not true, it is all the more appropriate in view of Sam's talent for mendacity.

Sam Hide. — There are few, we imagine, who have not heard of this personage ; but, notwithstanding his great notoriety, we might not be thought *serious* in the rest of our work, were we to enter seriously into his biography ; for the reason, that from his day to this, his name has been a by-word in all New England, and means as much as to say the *greatest of liars*. It is on account of the following anecdote that he is noticed.

Sam Hide was a notorious cider-drinker as well as liar, and used to travel the country to and fro begging it from door to door. At one time he happened in a region of country where cider was very hard to be procured, either from its scarcity, or from *Sam's* frequent visits. However, cider he was determined to have, if lying, in any shape or color, would gain it. Being not far from the house of an acquaintance, who he knew had cider, but he

knew, or was well satisfied, that, in the ordinary way of begging, he could not get it, he set his wits at work to lay a plan to insure it. This did not occupy him long. On arriving at the house of the gentleman, instead of asking for cider, he inquired for the man of the house, whom, on appearing, *Sam* requested to go aside with him, as he had something of importance to communicate to him. When they were by themselves, *Sam* told him he had that morning shot a fine deer, and that, if he would give him a crown, he would tell him where it was. The gentleman did not incline to do this, but offered half a crown. Finally, *Sam* said, as he had walked a great distance that morning, and was very dry, for a half a crown and a mug of cider he would tell him. This was agreed upon, and the price paid. Now *Sam* was required to point out the spot where the deer was to be found, which he did in this manner. He said to his friend, *You know of such a meadow,* describing it — Yes — *You know a big ash tree, with a big top by the little brook* — Yes — *Well, under that tree lies the deer.* This was satisfactory, and *Sam* departed. It is unnecessary to mention that the meadow was found, and the tree by the brook, but no deer. The duped man could hardly contain himself on considering what he had been doing. To look after *Sam* for satisfaction would be worse than looking after the deer, so the farmer concluded to go home contented. Some years after, he happened to fall in with the Indian ; and he immediately began to rally him for deceiving him so ; and demanded back his money and pay for his cider and trouble. *Why,* said *Sam, would you find fault if Indian told truth half the time ?* — No — *Well,* says *Sam, you find him meadow ?* — Yes — *You find him tree ?* — Yes — *What for then you find fault* Sam Hide, *when he told you two truth to one lie ?* The affair ended here. *Sam* heard no more from the farmer.

This is but one of the numerous anecdotes of *Sam Hide,* which, could they be collected, would fill many pages. He died in Dedham, 5 January, 1732, at the great age of 105 years. He was a great jester, and passed for an uncommon wit. In all the wars against the Indians during his lifetime, he served the English

faithfully, and had the name of a brave soldier. He had himself killed 19 of the enemy, and tried hard to make up the 20th, but was unable.[1]

We must take this narrative for what it is worth. Drake cites no authority, and one regrets to find that the Dedham archives contain no record of Sam Hyde's death, whether in 1732 or in any other year. The deer story is told of " one Tom Hyde, an Indian famous for his cunning," in Freeman Hunt's anonymous book of American Anecdotes, which was published in 1830. Hunt dates it " some years anterior to the independence of the United States," and says that the white man whom Hyde tricked was an innkeeper at Brookfield, Massachusetts.[2] Drake's account of Sam's ambition to kill twenty of his foes seems to be adapted from a passage in Hubbard's Indian Wars. On July 3d, 1676, Major Talcott of Connecticut, who was pursuing King Philip in the Narragansett country, after surprising and defeating the enemy in a swamp, turned towards home, at the request of his Mohegan and Pequot allies. On the way his troops fell in with a party of sixty Indians, " all of whom they slew and took." One of the prisoners was " a young sprightly fellow," whom his captors, the Mohegans, were allowed to put to death after their own savage fashion. " And indeed," writes Hubbard, " of all the *Enemies* that have been the Subjects of the *precedent discourse;* This *Villain* did most deserve to become an *Object* of *Justice* and *Severity;* For he boldly told them, that he had with his Gun dispatched *nineteen English*, and that he had charged it for the *twentieth;* but not meeting with any of *ours*, and unwilling to loose a *fair shot*, he had let

---

[1] S. G. Drake, The Book of the Indians, 8th edition, Boston, 1841, Book i, pp. 21–22.

[2] American Anecdotes, Original and Select, by an American, Boston, 1830, No. cccxiv, II, 109–10.

fly at a *Mohegin*, and kill'd him; with which, having made up his number, he told them he was fully satisfied."[1]

The marvellous force of the Vermont Nimrod's gun can be paralleled by an authentic accident that happened in December, 1775, and is chronicled in Aaron Wright's Revolutionary Journal:[2] —

John M'Murtry, in Capt. Chambers' company, killed John Penn, by his rifle going off, when, he says, he did not know it was loaded. He was cleaning the lock, and put it on and primed it to see how she would 'fier.' It shot through a double partition of inch boards, and through one board of a berth, and went in at Penn's breast, and out at his back, and left its mark on the chimney.

M'Murtry's firelock must have resembled the Revolutionary relic described in the Almanac for 1844: —

AN OLD GUN.

ZADOCK THOMPSON, Esq., of Halifax, Plymouth county, Mass., has now, or lately had, in his possession an old gun, which has descended to him from his ancestors, who came from Plymouth, in the third embarkation from England, in the month of May, 1622. The gun was brought to this country at that time. It is of the following description: The whole length of the stock and barrel, seven feet four and a half inches — the length of the barrel, six feet one inch and a half — the size of the calibre will carry twelve balls to the pound; the length of the face of the lock, ten inches; the whole weight of the gun, twenty pounds and twelve ounces. At the commencement of Philip's war, the Indians, became so morose, the people, in the month of June,

---

[1] William Hubbard, Narrative of the Troubles with the Indians, Boston, 1677, Postscript, pp. 9–10.

[2] Historical Magazine, July, 1862, VI, 211, cited by C. K. Bolton, The Private Soldier under Washington, New York, 1902, p. 113.

fled for safety to the fort, which was built near what was called the Four Corners, in Middleboro'. The Indians would daily appear on the southeasterly side of the river, and ascend what is called the hand rock, because there was the impression of a man's hand indented on it. There they would be in fair sight of the fort. Here, according to an antiquarian author, the Indians would show themselves to the people in the fort, and make their insulting gestures. The people became tired of daily insults. Lieut. Thompson the commander in chief, ordered Isaac Howland, a distinguished marksman, to take his gun and shoot the Indian, while he was insulting them. This he did, and gave the Indian a mortal wound. Filled with revenge for their wounded companion, the Indians took to the woods — running down the hill to the mill just below the fort, where the miller was at work; he discovered them, and seized his coat and fled. Placing his coat and hat on the end of a stick, as he ran through the brush to the fort, and holding his coat over his head, the coat was perforated by several balls. The Indians dragged their wounded companion two miles and three quarters, to the deserted house of Wm. Nelson, on the farm now occupied by Maj. Thomas Bennett. The Indian died that night and was buried with the accustomed ceremonies, and the house was burnt. In the year 1821, nearly one hundred and fifty years after the Indian had been buried, Major Bennett, in ploughing the land, disinterred some of his bones, a pipe, a stone jug, and a knife, all much decayed by the slow but all destroying hand of time. Maj. B., a few years since, measured the distance from the fort to the rock where the Indian was, and made the astonishing distance of 155 rods — nearly half a mile.

Zadock Thompson's gun must have been as valuable as that with regard to which Israel Fearing, of Agawam, makes an elaborate entry in his account book about 1750: —

John Fearing bought a gun of Nehemia bese for 3 bushalls of corn and 3 bushalls of rye at six pounds twelve Shillings and If

ye corn or rye fecheth more by the 18 day of Augest he is to give it and to pay for mending his gun If he Redeemeth her.[1]

William Priest, an English theatrical musician, who was in this country on a professional tour from 1793 to 1797, did not fail to learn that the provincials were good shots. " I have heard," he writes, " a hundred improbable stories relative to what has been done with the rifle by famous marksmen in America, such as shooting an apple from a child's head, &c.; to which I could not give credit: but, I have no reason to doubt the following feat; as it was actually performed before many hundred inhabitants of this borough [Philadelphia], and the adjacent country. — During the late war, in the year 1775, a company of riflemen, formed from the back woodsmen of Virginia, were quartered here for some time: two of them *alternately* held a board only nine inches square between his knees, while his comrade fired a ball through it from a distance of one hundred paces! The board is still preserved; and I am assured by several who were present, that it was performed without any manner of deception." [2]

There is no occasion to be very skeptical about this anecdote; but one cannot help being amused at the testimony of the *board*. It reminds us of the old Greek jest of the pedant who, having a house for sale, carried about a single brick to exhibit to prospective purchasers as a specimen. The marksmanship is equalled, if not excelled, in a story of certain Virginia mountaineers in 1775. Five hundred recruits were needed, but many more came forward, and the commanding officer determined on a shooting match. " A board one foot square bearing a chalk outline of a nose was nailed to a tree at a distance of 150

---

[1] W. R. Bliss, Colonial Times on Buzzard's Bay, Boston, 1888, p. 35.

[2] Travels in the United States of America, London, 1802, p. 59. The same story is told by Isaac Weld, Jr., Travels, 1799, pp. 67–8.

yards. . . . Those who came nearest the mark with a single bullet were to be enlisted. The first forty or fifty men who shot cut the nose entirely out of the board."[1]

But we must leave authentic history and return to the apocryphal Green Mountain saga which begins the chapter. It has a companion piece in an anecdote from Connecticut, the hero of which is Prosper Leffingwell, a mighty hunter who lived at Killingly. It is given on the authority of Mr. Barber in his Connecticut Historical Collections : [2] —

It were useless to attempt to detail all the events which marked the career of this famous sportsman. He was the terror of the *foxes* and *rabbits* for ten miles around. Many instances I might relate to illustrate the degree of skill to which he attained, but let one suffice. It is said that on one occasion, while returning home from hunting, he met *three foxes* advancing towards him " all in a row." As his gun was not loaded, he seized a stone, and directed it, as well as he was able, in a straight line towards their heads. Wonderful to tell, he brought them all *down!* He gazed a moment in astonishment. He found he had struck the first in the nose, the second in the hip, and the third in the forehead — all with the same stone ! The first was not quite dead, the second was badly lamed, but the third showed no signs of life whatever. While chasing the second, the first recovered and scampered away. Had he sprung upon them the moment he saw them fall, he might have secured the three.

Hunting and fishing proverbially offer temptations to the skilful liar. Here is another story which is equal to that of the Vermont Nimrod. It is from the Almanac for 1836 :—

" Did you ever hear of the scrape that I and uncle Zekiel had duckin on 't on the Connecticut?" asked Jonathan Timbertoes,

[1] C. K. Bolton, as above, p. 123 (from Harrower's Diary, in American Historical Review, October, 1900, p. 100).
[2] P. 432.

while amusing his old Dutch hostess, who had agreed to entertain him under the roof of her log cottage, for and in consideration of a bran new tin milk-pan. "No, I never did; do tell it,"
said Aunt Pumkins. "Well — you must know that I and uncle
Zeke took it into our heads on Saturday's afternoon to go a
gunning after ducks, in father's skiff; so in we got and sculled
down the river; a proper sight of ducks flew backwards and for-
wards I tell ye — and by'm-by a few on 'em lit down by the mash,
and went to feeding. I catched up my powder-horn to prime,
and it slipped right out of my hand and sunk to the bottom of the
river. The water was amazingly clear, and I could see it on the
bottom. Now I could n't swim a jot, so sez I to uncle Zeke,
you 're a pretty clever fellow, just let me take your powder-horn
to prime. And don't you think, the stingy critter would n't.
Well, says I, you 're a pretty good diver, 'un if you 'll dive and
get it, I 'll give you primin. I thought he 'd leave his powder-
horn; but he did n't, but stuck it in his pocket, and down he
went — and there he staid " — here the old lady opened her
eyes with wonder and surprise, and a pause of some minutes
ensued, when Jonathan added, — " I looked down, and what do
you think the critter was doin?" "Lord !" exclaimed the old
lady, " I 'm sure I don't know." "There he was," said our hero,
" setting right on the bottom of the river, pouring the powder out
of my horn into hizen."

Washington's proverbial regard for the truth has sustained one severe attack, and that in connection with a
subject which has become a regular resource for the
comic " paragraphers " of our time, — the Mosquito. The
English traveller Weld was certainly not much given to
jesting, and, even if he had been, the delicious solemnity
of the following observation would exonerate him from
any such charge on the present occasion : — " General
Washington told me, that he never was so much annoyed by
musquitoes in any part of America as in Skenesborough,[1]

1 In New York, on Lake Champlain.

for that they used to bite through the thickest boot." [1]
Fortunately we are in a position to explain this astonishing observation. It could not escape the vigilance of President Dwight, who was a devotee of accuracy, and always zealous in supporting the credit of his country and its institutions: —

A gentleman of great respectability, [he avers,] who was present when 'Gen. Washington made the observation referred to, told me, that he said, when describing these musquitoes to Mr. Weld, that they "bit through his stockings, above his boots." Our musquitoes have certainly a sharp tooth, and are very adroit at their business: but they have not been sufficiently disciplined, hitherto, to bite through the thickest boot.[2]

Probably Mr. Weld had had his own experiences with the American mosquito, and was ready to believe anything. For the benefit of other sufferers it may be worth while to reproduce a recipe from the Almanac for 1833, credited to the New York Evening Post:—

TO DESTROY MUSQUETOES.

Take a few hot coals on a shovel or chafingdish, and burn some brown sugar in your bedrooms and parlors, and you effectually destroy the musquetoe for the night. The experiment has been often tried by several of our citizens, and found to produce the desired effect.

The Sea Serpent of Nahant has been responsible for much annual mendacity. A sober British traveller made inquiries about him in 1820 from "a gentleman who dined with us there," and got a beautiful answer. The gentleman replied "that he had had the misfortune to see it three

[1] Isaac Weld, Jr., Travels through the States of North America, London, 1799, p. 164.
[2] Travels in New-England and New-York, New Haven, 1822, IV, 229.

days before; that he really considered it a misfortune, as no one would believe him; and he could not, in sincerity, deny having seen it." [1]   One is reminded of John Dunton's voyage to New England in 1685 and 1686, when, having viewed with amazement a swordfish and a thrasher, he " had the curiosity" to ask the sailors " if any of 'em had e'er seen a Mermaid or a Merman." Thereupon, if we may believe Dunton, " one of the most ancient of 'em told [him], That he had formerly been us'd to Sail to the East Indies, and in those Voyages he had seen them frequently." [2]

It will be appropriate to end this chapter with a couple of passages from the Almanac which may answer as a corrective to credulity : —

Read newspapers, but consider, before you believe; for common report is often a great liar.   (December, 1802.)

This is a fine season for the farmer to enjoy the company of his friends.   In these long evenings he can now have leisure to peep into the newspaper ; but read both sides of the question before you judge.   Believe not every story you hear.   Pin your faith upon no man's sleeve.   (December, 1804.)

[1] Adam Hodgson, Letters from North America, London, 1824, II, 5.
[2] John Dunton's Letters from New England, ed. Whitmore, Prince Society, 1867, p. 40.

THE GREAT MOON HOAX

THE second number of the Farmer's Almanack, that for 1794, contained a paragraph of much interest: —

THE MOON.

[*From a London paper.*]

Mr. Herschell is now said, by the aid of his powerful glasses, to have reduced to a certainty, the opinion that the moon is inhabited. He has discovered land and water, and is enabled to distinguish between the green and barren mountainous spots on the former, which, as with us, are subdivided by the sea. Within these few days he has distinguished a large edifice, apparently of greater magnitude than St. Paul's; and he is confident of shortly being able to give an account of the inhabitants.

This extraordinary item of news, for which the " London paper " quoted by Mr. Thomas certainly had no good authority, was doubtless based on rumors about the elder Herschel's observation of the eclipse of the sun on September 5th, 1793. Everybody knew that William Herschel was interested in the moon, and that the eclipse of the sun would afford him an opportunity to use his great telescope in studying lunar topography. It is not strange, therefore, that the journalists of the day, though far less enterprising and imaginative than those of our own time, got exaggerated ideas of what he might have seen, and took their chances. In the following year Herschel printed some of his results in the Philosophical Transactions, but these make no mention of edifices comparable to St. Paul's Cathedral. As a matter of fact, he discovered nothing

more sensational than mountains and table-lands, but he
got nearer to our satellite than anybody had ever got before.   Besides, it was no secret that he believed the moon
to be inhabited, and the sun also, by beings whose organs
"were adapted to the peculiar circumstances of those
luminaries," — a doctrine which he taught publicly in
1795, in a paper on the nature and constitution of the sun
and fixed stars. [1] Though it does not appear that he had
given formal expression to this opinion as early as 1793,
still his views may well enough have reached the ears of
the professional purveyors of news.   It is not difficult,
therefore, to account for the item which Mr. Thomas
printed in his Almanac for 1794.   At all events, this bit of
scientific gossip shows that the world was ready, toward
the close of the eighteenth century, for something which,
in fact, did not come until forty years later, the Great
Moon Hoax.

In August and September 1835, the New York Sun
amazed its readers, both lay and scientific, by publishing
an account of "Great Astronomical Discoveries lately
made by Sir John Herschel at the Cape of Good Hope."
The information purported to come from a supplement to
the Edinburgh Journal of Science.   Of course, these dis-
closures were received with incredulity and derision in
some quarters, but the general public was inclined to
believe in them.   The circulation of the Sun increased
enormously, and a pamphlet edition of the "Great Discoveries" numbering sixty thousand copies was soon
taken up.   The work was immediately translated into
French and two editions were published in Paris.

The marvellous story is introduced with considerable
skill.   After a flourish of trumpets, which strikes us as a
trifle journalistic, but which was not unnatural under the
supposed circumstances, the editor specifies with much

[1] Philosophical Transactions, LXXXV, 63-66.

sobriety the source of his "early and almost exclusive information." It appears that one Dr. Andrew Grant was a friend of the Edinburgh editor. This learned Scot had been a pupil of Sir William Herschel, and was now entirely in the confidence of Sir John, whose assistant he had been for some years. With unparalleled liberality Sir John Herschel had given Dr. Grant permission to disclose the main results of his recent observations in advance of their appearance in the Transactions of the Royal Society, and Dr. Grant had selected the Edinburgh Journal of Science as the most appropriate medium of communication. It was, of course, natural that the Doctor should covet for Edinburgh the honor of first announcing these novelties to an astonished world.

Sir John Herschel, so ran the story, in a casual interview with Sir David Brewster, some three years before, had deplored the fact that with telescopes of high magnifying power the object became proportionately indistinct. To remedy this defect he had suggested to Sir David the possibility of transfusing artificial light through the focal object of vision, and, finding that Brewster was ready to entertain the idea, he ventured to propose the use of the oxy-hydrogen microscope to make the focal image distinct and even to magnify it. Sir David, we are informed, "sprung from his chair in an ecstasy of conviction, and leaping half way to the ceiling, exclaimed 'Thou art the man!'" After this everything was easy, though it took time. Dissatisfied with the size of his father's last telescope, which brought one within about forty miles of the moon, Herschel determined to construct a truly stupendous instrument, with an object glass twenty-four feet in diameter, "just six times the size of his venerable father's." The president of the Royal Society subscribed £10,000, and the king, on being informed that the new instrument would be advantageous to navigation, agreed to make up

the £70,000 required, or any other sum that might be needed.

The author of the ingenious fiction which we are discussing shows some skill in his account of the manufacture of "this prodigious lens." The contract was awarded, it appears, to the firm of Hartly and Grant of Dumbarton, the junior partner being a brother of that Dr. Grant who plays so important a part in the narrative. The first casting was unsuccessful, for there was a bad flaw within eighteen inches of the centre. The second attempt produced a lens that was practically perfect. There were, to be sure, slight flaws near the edge, but they were of no account, since they would be covered by the rim that was to enclose the glass. The weight of the whole mass was nearly fifteen thousand pounds, — or to be accurate, as our hoaxer takes care to be, — 14,826 pounds, and its magnifying power was estimated at forty-two thousand times.

It was decided to set up an observatory at the Cape of Good Hope on a plateau about thirty-five miles northeast of Cape Town. Several months were occupied in the construction of the building and the installation of the mechanism, which is described with a good imitation of popular scientific exposition, and on the 10th of January, 1835, the huge instrument was brought to bear upon the moon.

The first view demonstrated the complete triumph of Herschel's experiment. Distinct formations of greenish brown basaltic rock, like those of Fingal's Cave at Staffa, were visible, and in a few moments the eyes of the observers were greeted with a sight of "the first organic production of nature, in a foreign world, ever revealed to the eyes of men." This was a poppy field of great extent, the flowers of which Dr. Grant declared to be " precisely similar to the rose-poppy of our sublunary cornfields."

The discovery was more exhilarating than it seemed, for it proved that the moon had an atmosphere so like our own that it would beyond question turn out to be inhabited. Our romancer, however, does not make the mistake of bringing in his main matter too early. He conducts the astronomers from one discovery to another in orderly succession. Now they see prodigious phenomena of lunar crystallization, — amethysts of a diluted claret color, sixty to ninety feet in height; now a herd of buffaloes, similar to those of the earth, and having a remarkable "fleshy appendage over the eyes, crossing the whole breadth of the forehead and united to the ears." The acute mind of Dr. Herschel at once perceived that this appendage was meant to protect the eyes of the animal from the extremes of light and darkness to which all who live on our side of the moon are periodically subjected. Bearded unicorns crossed the field of vision; then gray pelicans, engaged in fishing; soon after, strange spherical creatures, which rolled down the beach into the water and were lost to view.

This was enough for one night, when taken together with discoveries in topography and mineralogy which need not be particularized, and with admirable self-command the deviser of the Moon Hoax made the next two nights cloudy so that observations were impracticable. What followed, however, atoned for such enforced idleness. Many species of trees and plants were not merely observed but even classified, and the zoölogical discoveries were of the most startling kind. In describing the biped beaver, indeed, the author seems to take an impish delight in endangering the credibility of his whole narrative. This creature, he informs us, has no tail, and walks upon two feet, bearing its young in its arms, and moving with an easy gliding motion. "Its huts are constructed better and higher than those of many tribes of human savages, and

from the appearance of smoke in nearly all of them, there is no doubt of its being acquainted with the use of fire." But this risky piece of romancing is cleverly counterbalanced by the mention of great flocks of genuine sheep "which would not have disgraced the farms of Leicestershire, or the shambles of Leadenhall-market." "With the utmost scrutiny," continues Dr. Grant, " we could find no mark of distinction between these and those of our native soil. They had not even the appendage over the eyes, which I have described as common to lunar quadrupeds."

Before long came the eagerly expected sight of human beings in the moon. The first group were not very prepossessing, and one might even doubt whether they were human beings at all, except for their gesticulations and the fact that they seemed to be talking with each other. These lunarians were only four feet high, they were covered with copper-colored hair, short and glossy, and had thin membranous wings, extending from the top of the shoulders to the calves of the legs. Their features were similar to those of the ourang-outang, but more intelligent, and in symmetry of form they much surpassed their simian prototypes. A facetious member of the party, one Lieutenant Drummond, of the Royal Engineers, determined to make the best of the new race, declared that they "would look as well on a parade ground as some of the old cockney militia, — that is, if it were not for their long wings."

After observing these specimens of the man-bat, as it was decided to call the winged man just described, and noting several particulars so surprising that it was thought prudent to summon the civil and military authorities and "several Episcopal, Wesleyan, and other ministers" to look through the telescope and certify to the truth of Dr. Herschel's report, our investigators saw nothing more of human beings in the moon for some time; but they were

favored with a view of an enormous mountain ridge, which
was one solid piece of crystallization, " brilliant as a piece
of Derbyshire spar," extending for three hundred and forty
miles.   " We found," says Dr. Grant, " that wonder and
astonishment, as excited by objects in this distant world,
were but modes and attributes of ignorance, which should
give place to elevated expectations, and to reverential confidence in the illimitable power of the Creator."

Such reverent reflections were soon rewarded, and the
rather disappointing impression left on the mind by the
first sight of lunar inhabitants was effaced, by the discovery
of a great equitriangular temple of polished sapphire.   The
roof was designed to represent a great sphere, round which
rose a mass of violently agitated flames.   This singular
roof was flanked by cornices of a style of architecture with
which neither Dr. Grant, Dr. Herschel, nor Lieut. Drummond was familiar.   The temple was open on every side,
but contained no seats or altars, or furniture of any kind.
Human beings were never seen in the temples, and the
Doctor does not venture to decide whether they were
simple monuments or the deserted fanes of past ages.

Not very far from the first of these temples more inhabitants were discovered, who were " in every respect an improved variety of the race."   They were taller and not so
dark, and they had better manners.   When they came
into view, — and, indeed, for a considerable portion of
the time during which they were under the lens,— they
were engaged in eating fruit; and it was with much satisfaction that Dr. Grant noticed symptoms of politeness in
their conduct.   Occasionally some member of a group
would pick out a particularly fine specimen and throw it
" archwise " to some friend who had already exhausted the
supply that was near him.   Carnivorous animals seemed
to be unknown, and this, together with the " universal state
of amity among all classes of lunar creatures " gave Dr.

17

Grant and his companions what he delicately describes as the " most refined pleasure."

The same night an unfortunate accident happened, which came near putting an end to all discoveries for the time being. The monstrous lens, which, it should be noticed, was not enclosed in a tube as in the case of most telescopes, had been unaccountably left in such a position that, while the astronomers were asleep, it focussed the sun's rays with terrific force. The fire thus kindled was so fierce as to vitrify the plaster of the observatory walls, but it was fortunately extinguished before any permanent damage had been done. By the time the necessary repairs had been effected, the moon was no longer visible, and for a month Dr. Herschel gave his attention to Saturn and the constellations of the Southern Hemisphere. One night in March, however, while Herschel was engrossed in cataloguing the new stars which he had discovered, Dr. Grant, with other members of the party, took another look at the moon. Apparently the imagination of the writer had been exhausted, for nothing strikingly new appeared. As a fitting climax, however, to the details which we have been tracing, a new species of the man-bat crossed the field of vision; and with these the account printed in the New York Sun closes, for, as the editor ingenuously remarks, " the forty pages of illustrative and mathematical notes " which followed in the Edinburgh Journal " would greatly enhance the price of the reprint," without commensurably adding to its general interest. The new species of the man-bat was infinitely more beautiful, though not taller, than the last specimens examined. " They appeared," says Dr. Grant, " scarcely less lovely than the general representations of angels by the more imaginative schools of painters." It seems also that they were far advanced in civilization, and that their works of art were incredibly skilful. But all this, he adds, must be left

to be treated in "Dr. Herschel's authenticated natural history" of the Moon.

The Moon Hoax was the work of Richard Adams Locke, an able but erratic reporter. In England, where the inventive powers of the American newspaper man were not properly appreciated, some persons fancied that the story was of French origin;[1] but the evidence of Benjamin H. Day, the founder of the Sun, is conclusive. In 1883, when the Sun was fifty years old, Mr. Day was interviewed, and his recollections were printed in the anniversary number (September 3d, 1883). Though advanced in years, he remembered the circumstances perfectly. He paid Locke between five and six hundred dollars for the article, and it appears that the hoaxer "made something in addition by selling lithographs of the scenery and animals in the moon." The workmanship of the Moon Hoax is pretty skilful. Many of the scientific details are slurred over on the ground that they would not be of general interest, or because it would be improper for the writer to anticipate the report which Herschel intended to make to the Royal Society. It is only with regard to the construction of the telescope by means of which these stupendous discoveries were made, that the author ventures to be at all explicit, and here, though his description is well calculated to impress his lay readers, no astronomer or physicist could be for a moment deceived. Nevertheless, if it is permitted to correct this too hasty remark, some astronomers *were* deceived. Mr. Day remembered that a deputation from a certain college "came to the office and requested to see the original copy of the magazine article." "I pretended," he continues, "to be vastly indignant that they should doubt our word. 'I suppose the magazine is somewhere upstairs,' said I, 'but I consider it almost an

[1] See R. A. Proctor, Myths and Marvels of Astronomy, London, 1878, pp. 241 ff.

insult that you should ask to see it.' They went back . . . apparently perfectly satisfied." Doubtless such scientific men as allowed their enthusiasm to get the better of their judgment detected flaws in the reasoning, and errors in the form of statement, but supposed they might be due to haste or editorial misunderstanding. Outside of strictly scientific circles the Hoax made a profound impression. Miss Martineau, who was in America at the time, describes the excitement that it caused, but cautions her English readers against drawing a wrong inference as to the average of common sense and enlightenment in this country. She writes : —

I happened to be going the round of several Massachusetts villages when the marvellous account of Sir John Herschel's discoveries in the moon was sent abroad. The sensation it excited was wonderful. As it professed to be a republication from the Edinburgh Journal of Science, it was some time before many persons, except professors of natural philosophy, thought of doubting its truth. The lady of such a professor, on being questioned by a company of ladies as to her husband's emotions at the prospect of such an enlargement of the field of science, excited a strong feeling of displeasure against herself. She could not say that he believed it, and would gladly have said nothing about it : but her inquisitive companions first cross-examined her, and then were angry at her scepticism. A story is going, told by some friends of Sir John Herschel, (but whether in earnest or in the spirit of the moon story I cannot tell,) that the astronomer has received at the Cape, a letter from a large number of Baptist clergymen of the United States, congratulating him on his discovery, informing him that it had been the occasion of much edifying preaching and of prayer-meetings for the benefit of brethren in the newly explored regions ; and beseeching him to inform his correspondents whether science affords any prospects of a method of conveying the Gospel to residents in the moon. However it may be with this story, my

experience of the question with regard to the other, " Do you not believe it ? " was very extensive.

In the midst of our amusement at credulity like this, we must remember that the real discoveries of science are likely to be more faithfully and more extensively made known in the villages of the United States, than in any others in the world. The moon hoax, if advantageously put forth, would have been believed by a much larger proportion of any other nation than it was by the Americans ; and they are travelling far faster than any other people beyond the reach of such deception. Their common and high schools, their Lyceums and cheap colleges, are exciting and feeding thousands of minds, which in England would never get beyond the loom or the plough-tail. If few are very learned in the villages of Massachusetts, still fewer are very ignorant : and all have the power and the will to invite the learning of the towns among them, and to remunerate its administration of knowledge.[1]

After seventy years, the Great Moon Hoax is still famous in the annals of popular delusions, though the details of the extraordinary story have long ago faded from general recollection. Now and then there is a feeble attempt at something similar. Thus in 1897 a few New Englanders were taken in by a newspaper report that the planet Venus " was an electric light attached to a balloon sent up from Syracuse, and hauled down slowly every night" about nine o'clock.[2] But this stroke of fancy, audacious as it was, can bear no comparison with Sir John Herschel's experiences at the Cape of Good Hope.

[1] Retrospect of Western Travel, London, 1838, II, 22-24.
[2] D. P. Todd, A New Astronomy, New York, [1897,] p. 316.

ENTERTAINMENT FOR MAN AND BEAST

IT is a prevalent misconception to think that our Puritan ancestors were addicted to making themselves uncomfortable. No doubt they were zealous for decency and order, and more or less rigorous in their interpretation of conduct; but it never occurred to them that needless privation was a good thing. The body, to be sure, was more than meat; but nobody supposed that this principle involved the corollary of starving oneself. Thirst, too, they held should be satisfied, within reasonable bounds. An inn or ordinary, they believed, was as requisite to a well-organized community as a school, — and that not merely for the accommodation of travellers, but also to serve the people of the neighborhood. Accordingly, the early records abound in licenses to draw beer, or beer and wine, and innholding was recognized as one of the most reputable of occupations. Neglect to provide an ordinary made a town liable to fine. Thus, in 1669, the town of Newbury, Massachusetts, was presented for such dereliction, and was enjoined to supply the deficiency before the next March court under penalty of five pounds.[1] When an inn had once been opened, the paternal government kept a sharp eye on abuses and visited every infraction of discipline with speedy punishment.

After the Revolution, and at about the time when the Farmer's Almanack was winning its place as the New Englander's favorite manual of secular faith and practice,

[1] J. J. Currier, Ould Newbury, Boston, 1896, p. 177.

this country was much resorted to by European travellers, who, like their successors nowadays, were prone to print their impressions in a book.   Such visitors were astonished to learn that innkeepers often bore military titles and were leading men in the community.   John Davis, the facetious pedagogue,[1] has some remarks on this point, apropos of a boarding-house in New York, "agreeably situated in Cherry-street": —

> Major Howe, after carrying arms through the revolutionary war, instead of reposing upon the laurels he had acquired, was com- pelled to open a boarding-house in *New-York*, for the mainte- nance of his wife and children.   He was a member of the Cincinnati, and not a little proud of his Eagle.   But I thought the motto to his badge of *Omnia reliquit servare Rempublicam*, was not very appropriate ; for it is notorious that few Americans had much to leave when they accepted commissions in the army. *Victor ad aratrum redit* would have been better.[2]

We may pass over Davis's jibe, for it is not ill-natured; he was a penniless itinerant himself.

Smyth, who visited America soon after the Revolution, met with a host of even higher rank at the "ordinary, inn, or tavern" at Bute County Court-House, North Carolina, where he had an excellent dinner.   This was no less a per- sonage than General Jethro Sumner, who had played a conspicuous part in the war.   Smyth remarks : —

> He is a man of a person lusty, and rather handsome, with an easy and genteel address : his marriage with a young woman of a good family, with whom he received a handsome fortune ; his being a captain of provincials last war ; but above all his violent principles, and keeping an inn at the court-house (which is scarcely thought a mean occupation here), singular as the latter

---

[1] See p. 142, above.
[2] Travels of Four Years and a Half in the United States, during 1798, 1799, 1800, 1801, and 1802, London, 1803, p. 22.

circumstance may appear, contributed more to his appointment and promotion in the American army, than any other merit.   For it is a fact, that more than one third of their general officers have been inn-keepers, and have been chiefly indebted to that circumstance for such rank.   Because by that public, but inferior station, their principles and persons became more generally known ; and by the mixture and variety of company they conversed with, in the way of their business, their ideas and their ambitious views were more excited and extended than the generality of the honest and respectable planters, who remained in peace at their homes.[1]

In 1771 John Adams found that landlord Pease, of Enfield, Connecticut, "was the great man of the town ; their representative, &c. as well as tavern-keeper, and just returned from the General Assembly at Hartford." [2]

Another tavern-keeper of position was Dr. Nathaniel Ames of Dedham, Massachusetts, equally celebrated for his drugs, his inn, and his almanac.   The almanac was a good medium for the advertisement of the tavern.   He announced the opening of his house of entertainment in his issue for 1751 : —

Advertisement.

THESE are to signify to all Persons that travel the great Post-Road South-West from Boston, That I keep a House of Publick Entertainment Eleven Miles from Boston, at the Sign of the SUN.   If they want Refreshment, and see Cause to be my Guests, they shall be well entertained at a reasonable Rate,

N. Ames.

For some reason the " Sign of the SUN " did not get into position promptly.   Hence in 1752 Dr. Ames returned to the subject as follows : —

[1] J. F. D. Smyth, Tour in the United States, London, 1784, I, 114–15.
[2] Diary, June 7, 1771, Works, ed. C. F. Adams, Boston, 1850, II, 271.

Of the Eclipſes for 1751.

THERE will be Four Eclipſes this Year, two of the Sun, and alſo as many of the Moon, in the following Order, *viz.*

    I.   The Firſt will be of the SUN, *May* the 13th at Eight in the Evening, inviſible.

    II.   The Second is of the MOON, *May* the 28th, viſible, calculated as follows, *viz.*

	b.	m.	
Beginning,	7	20	
Middle,	9	4	Evening,
End,	10	46	
Durſtion,	3	26	
Digits eclipſed,	10	25	

    III.   The Third will be of the SUN, *November* the 3d, at Eight at Night, inviſible.

    IV   The Fourth and laſt is of the MOON, the 21ſt Day of *November*, partly viſible; at the Sun's Setting the Moon will riſe two Thirds eclipſed; but by that Time the Day-light is gone ſo as to have a good Proſpect of the Moon, the Eclipſe will end.

Advertiſement.

THESE are to ſignify to all Perſons that travel the great Poſt-Road Soutb-Weſt from Boſton, *That I keep a Houſe of Publick Entertainment Eleven Miles from* Boſton, *at the Sign of the* SUN. *If they want Refreſhment, and ſee Cauſe to be my Gueſts, they ſhall be well entertained at a reaſonable Rate,*

N. Ames.

The Affairs of my House are of a Publick Nature, and therefore I hope may be mentioned here without offence to my *Reader:* The Sign I advertised last Year by Reason of some little Disappointments is not put up, but the Thing intended to be signified by it is to be had according to said Advertisement. And I beg Leave further to add, that if any with a View of Gain to themselves, or Advantage to their Friends, have reported Things of my House in contradiction to the aforesaid Advertisement, I would only have those whom they would influence consider, that where the Narrator is not honest, is not an Eye or Ear-Witness, can't trace his Story to the original, has it only by Hear-say, a thousand such Witnesses are not sufficient to hang a Dog : & I hope no Gentleman that travels the Road will have his Mind bias'd against my House by such idle Reports.[1]

It is pleasant to know that the doctor's vigorous defence was effectual and that the Sun Tavern enjoyed great and long-continued prosperity.

The manners of the landlord were often a subject of comment. Foreigners were now and then shocked or offended at a lack of that subserviency which they had always associated with innkeepers in their own country, but the more sensible among them soon came to understand the reason and adapted themselves to the situation. Adam Hodgson, writing of Virginia in 1820, gives a good idea of the condition of things : —

Every ten or fifteen miles you come either to a little village, composed of a few frame houses, with an extensive substantial house, whose respectable appearance, rather than any sign, demonstrates it to be a tavern, (as the inns are called,) or to a single house appropriated to that purpose, and standing alone in the woods. At these taverns you are accosted, often with an easy civility, sometimes with a repulsive frigidity, by a landlord who appears perfectly indifferent whether or not you take any-

[1] These advertisements are quoted by Edward Field, The Colonial Tavern, Providence, 1897, pp. 103–5 ; they are given here from the originals.

thing *for the good of the house.* If, however, you intimate an
intention to take some refreshment, a most plentiful repast is, in
due time, set before you, consisting of beef-steaks, fowls, turkies,
ham, partridges, eggs, and if near the coast, fish and oysters,
with a great variety of hot bread, both of wheat flour and Indian-
corn, the latter of which is prepared in many ways, and is very
good. The landlord usually comes in to converse with you, and
to make one of the party; and as one cannot have a private
room, I do not find his company disagreeable. He is, in general,
well informed and well behaved, and the independence of manner
which has often been remarked upon, I rather like than otherwise, when it is not assumed or obtrusive, but appears to arise
naturally from easy circumstances, and a consciousness that, both
with respect to situation and intelligence, he is at least on a level
with the generality of his visitors. At first I was a little surprised, on enquiring where the stage stopped to breakfast, to be
told, at Major Todd's; — to dine? At Col. Brown's — but I am
now becoming familiar with these phenomena of civil and political equality, and wish to communicate my first impressions before
they fade away.[1]

It may be interesting to compare this passage with
Fynes Morison's appreciative account of an English inn in
the early seventeenth century: —

I haue heard some Germans complaine of the English Innes,
by the high way, as well for dearenesse, as for that they had onely
roasted meates: But these Germans landing at *Grauesend*, perhaps were iniured by those knaues, that flocke thither onely to
deceiue strangers, and vse Englishmen no better, and after went
from thence to *London*, and were there entertained by some
ordinary Hosts of strangers, returning home little acquainted
with English customes. But if these strangers had knowne the
English tongue, or had had an honest guide in their iournies, and
had knowne to liue at *Rome* after the *Roman* fashion, (which
they seldome doe, vsing rather Dutch Innes and companions),

———
[1] Letters from North America, London, 1824, I, 20-22.

surely they should haue found, that the World affoords not such Innes as *England* hath, either for good and cheape entertainement after the Guests owne pleasure, or for humble attendance on passengers, yea, euen in very poore Villages, where if *Curculio* of *Plautus*, should see the thatched houses, he would fall into a fainting of his spirits, but if he should smell the variety of meates, his starueling looke would be much cheared : For assoone as a passenger comes to an Inne, the seruants run to him, and one takes his Horse and walkes him till he be cold, then rubs him, and giues him meate, yet I must say that they are not much to be trusted in this last point, without the eye of the Master or his Seruant, to ouersee them.   Another seruant giues the passenger his priuate chamber, and kindles his fier, the third puls of his bootes, and makes them cleane.   Then the Host or Hostesse visits him, and if he will eate with the Host, or at a common Table with others, his meale will cost him sixe pence, or in some places but foure pence, (yet this course is lesse honourable, and not vsed by Gentlemen) : but if he will eate in his chamber, he commands what meate he will according to his appetite, and as much as he thinkes fit for him and his company, yea, the kitchin is open to him, to command the meat to be dressed as he best likes ; and when he sits at Table, the Host or Hostesse will accompany him, or if they haue many Guests, will at least visit him, taking it for curtesie to be bid sit downe : while he eates, if he haue company especially, he shall be offred musicke, which he may freely take or refuse, and if he be solitary, the Musitians will giue him the good day with musicke in the morning.   It is the custome and no way disgracefull to set vp part of supper for his breakefast : In the euening or in the morning after breakefast, (for the common sort vse not to dine, but ride from breakefast to supper time, yet comming early to the Inne for better resting of their Horses) he shall haue a reckoning in writing, and if it seeme vnreasonable, the Host will satisfie him, either for the due price, or by abating part, especially if the seruant deceiue him any way, which one of experience will soone find. . . . . A Gentleman and his Man shall spend as much, as if he were accompanied with

another Gentleman and his Man, and if Gentlemen will in such sort ioyne together, to eate at one Table, the expences will be much diminished. Lastly, a Man cannot more freely command at home in his owne House, then hee may doe in his Inne, and at parting if he giue some few pence to the Chamberlin & Ostler, they wish him a happy iourney.[1]

Of course travellers had to submit to a good deal of questioning. The curiosity of Americans was a regular subject for comment among foreigners in the eighteenth and the first half of the nineteenth century. Indeed the inquisitive Yankee has become a stock figure in our own novels and plays. Patrick M'Robert, who visited New England in 1774, is mildly jocose. The people, he says, " have been great adventurers in trade, and generally successful; they are very inquisitive, want to know every circumstance relating to any stranger that comes amongst them, so that a traveller lately in that country had been so pestered with their idle queries, that, as soon as he entered a tavern, he used to begin and tell them he was such a one, telling his name, travelling to Boston, born in North Britain, aged about thirty, unmarried, prayed them not to trouble him with more questions but get him something to eat: this generally had the desired effect." [2] This is an old story, which turns up again and again in slightly variant forms. Isaac Candler, who wrote some fifty years later, took the matter rather more seriously, in the spirit of a social investigator, and came to a very definite conclusion: —

Concerning one colloquial fault with which they have often been accused, namely, that of impertinent inquisitiveness, I have

[1] An Itinerary written by Fynes Moryson, Gent., London, 1617, Part III, Chap. 3, p. 151.
[2] Tour through Part of the North Provinces of America, Edinburgh, 1776, p. 25.

to remark, that it applies principally and almost entirely to the lower and middling classes in remote situations and small villages. I met with only two persons of the upper class whose enquiries respecting myself were troublesome or offensive, and one of these was a person whom I judged to have mixed very little in society. I met him at a tavern at Schenectady; and to show how much his inquisitiveness was disapproved by others, I must add, that as soon as he had left the room, another gentleman . . . apologised for his rudeness, and hoped I should not judge of the citizens generally by him; a remark elicited from my having stated that I had been a short time only in the country.[1]

A piece of incidental evidence of a rather amusing cast is the following advertisement, which appeared in a Vermont newspaper, the Federal Galaxy of Brattleboro', July 15, 1799:—

FOUND.

Six Bars of Iron, secreted beneath the surface of the ground, within the enclosures of the subscriber. The owner is requested to tell how it came there, to prove property, pay charges, and take it away.

Joel W. Bliss.

Brattleboro', July 13, 1799.

Mr. Bliss, we notice, is not content with the usual "proving property and paying for this advertisement." He wants to know how the iron bars came to be buried in his lot. After all, his curiosity is justifiable, for the circumstances were undeniably peculiar.

John Adams's picture of his landlord and landlady at Ipswich is deservedly celebrated: —

Landlord and landlady are some of the grandest people alive; landlady is the great-granddaughter of Governor Endicott and

---

[1] A Summary View of America. By an Englishman. London, 1824, pp. 482-3.

had all the great notions of high family that you find in Winslows, Hutchinsons, Quincys, Saltonstalls, Chandlers, Leonards, Otises, and as you might find with more propriety in the Winthrops.   Yet she is cautious and modest about discovering it. . . . As to land-lord, he is as happy and as big, as proud, as conceited, as any nobleman in England ; always calm and good-natured and lazy ; but the contemplation of his farm and his sons and his house and pasture and cows, his sound judgment, as he thinks, and his great holiness, as well as that of his wife, keep him as erect in his thoughts as a noble or a prince.   Indeed, the more I consider of mankind, the more I see that every man seriously and in his conscience believes himself the wisest, brightest, best, happiest, &c. of all mankind.[1]

At most inns in the country the domestic service was performed by the landlord's daughters, with or without the assistance of hired "help" from the neighborhood. Travellers often speak appreciatively of the simple cour-tesy and modest demeanor of their attendants.   In 1789 Washington wrote as follows to the proprietor of Taft's inn, at Uxbridge, Massachusetts, where he had lodged on his return from his New England progress : —

Hartford, 8 November, 1789.

Sir — Being informed that you have given my name to one of your sons, and called another after Mrs. Washington's family, and being moreover very much pleased with the modest and in-nocent looks of your two daughters, Patty and Polly, I do for these reasons send each of these girls a piece of chintz ; and to Patty, who bears the name of Mrs. Washington, and who waited more upon us than Polly did, I send five guineas, with which she may buy herself any little ornaments she may want, or she may dispose of them in any other manner more agreeable to herself.   As I do not give these things with a view to have it talked of, or even to its being known, the less there is said about

[1] Diary, June 22, 1771, Works, ed. C. F. Adams, II, 282.

it the better you will please me ; but, that I may be sure the chintz and money have got safe to hand, let Patty, who I dare say is equal to it, write me a line informing me thereof, directed to " The President of the United States at New York." I wish you and your family well, and am your humble servant,

GEO. WASHINGTON.[1]

President Dwight, writing about 1820, avers that the inns of New England had deteriorated, and to prove his point he gives a most attractive description of a house of the old style, leaving his readers to contrast it with those with which they were themselves acquainted : —

The best old fashioned New-England inns were superior to any of the modern ones which I have seen. They were at less pains to furnish a great variety of food. Yet the variety was ample. The food was always of the best quality ; the beds were excellent ; the house and all its appendages were in the highest degree clean and neat; the cookery was remarkably good ; and the stable was not less hospitable than the house. The family in the meantime were possessed of principle, and received you with the kindness and attention of friends. Your baggage was as safe as in your own house. If you were sick, you were nursed and befriended as in your own family. No tavern-haunters, gamblers or loungers were admitted, any more than in a well ordered private habitation ; and as little noise was allowed.

There was less bustle, less parade, less appearance of doing much to gratify your wishes, than at the reputable modern inns ; but much more actually done, and much more comfort and enjoyment. In a word, you found in these inns the pleasures of an excellent private house. To finish the story, your bills were always equitable, calculated on what you ought to pay, and not upon the scheme of getting the most which extortion might think proper to demand.[2]

[1] Writings, ed. Sparks, Boston, 1836, X, 48, note.
[2] Travels in New-England and New-York, 1822, IV, 26–12.

The learned and discriminating college President, it will be noticed, declares that in the old days "tavern-haunting" was not tolerated, but he implies that times have changed for the worse. This was but too true. Idle resort to the public house was a prevalent vice in New England country towns in the early part of the nineteenth century. Every village had its tavern, or at least its store where rum could be bought as well as other "East and West India goods and groceries," and many had two or three. As a censor of manners and morals, Mr. Thomas felt bound to warn his fellow-citizens not to waste their time and money, and the Farmer's Calendar affords us many lively pictures of the shiftless husbandman who lets his farm go to waste while he is "turning the double corner." Thus in July, 1812: —

"There, there! run, John, the hogs are in the cornfield;" cried old lady Lookout, as she stood slipshod over the cheese-tub. "I told your father, John, that this would be the case; but he had rather go day after day up to 'Squire Plunket's to drink grog and swap horses, than to be at a little pains to stop the gap in the wall, by which he might prevent the destruction of our beautiful cornfield; and then, Jonny, you know if we have corn to sell we can afford to rig up a little and go and see your aunt Winnypucker's folks." "Aye, aye, mother, let us mind the main chance, as our minister told us the other day. You look to your cheese-tubs, I 'll see to the hogs, and with a little good luck, by jinks, mother, we may be able to hold up our heads yet."

Old lady Lookout and her energetic son were no doubt able to keep things going despite the tippling propensities of the head of the house; and so, let us hope, was the heroine of the following sketch, which may be found in the Farmer's Calendar for April, 1812: —

"Heigh-ho-hum! Here John, take the jug and run down to 'Squire Plunket's and get a quart of new rum. Tell him to put

it down with the rest and I'll pay him in rye, as I told him.
Come, Eunice, hang on the tea-kettle and let us have some sling
when John gets back. — Wife, how long before breakfast?"
" Alas, husband, where is this to end? Our farm is mortgaged,
you know ; the mare and colt both attached, last week the oxen
were sold ; and yesterday the blue heifer was driven away ; next
goes our grain and at last, I suppose, I must give up my wedding
suit, and all for sling ! A plague on the shopkeepers — I wish
there was not a glass of rum in the universe ! Now, husband, if
you will only spruce round a little, like other men, and attend to
business, I have no doubt but we can get along. See Capt.
Sprightly, he is up early and late, engaged in business. He lets
no moment pass unimproved. See even now, while we are but
just out of bed, he has been for this hour with his boys in the
field ! Why can't we be as earnest, and as cheerful, and as
prosperous as they? Come, come, hus, let's make an effort."

In April, 1805, there is a humorous picture of confusion
on the farm, with a pretty plain moral annexed. Incidentally the nagging wife comes in for a bit of wholesome
satire : —

" *I told you so,*" says Dorothy — " *I told you so.*" " John,
where's the plough?" " I ha'nt seen it since last fall." " Bill,
what's become of our hoes?" " We left them in the field,
father." " *I told you so,*" says Dorothy ; " *but you would be at
the tavern, and let the boys go a fishing.*" At length the tools are
found, carefully laid up in the cider-mill garret, where the wife
had desired Mr. Simpkins' man to place them. Who would not
choose to avoid the dangerous habit of tavern haunting, to stay
at home and keep himself and family in business, rather than
to be perpetually tormented with that mortifying cant, " *I told
you so ?* "

A more solemn, but not more effective admonition, occurs in the Calendar for February, 1816 : —

18

Take care that you do not visit the grog-shop as an idler. If you have business there, do it and away. You may contract a habit of lounging, and next a habit of sipping, and then, my friend, you are gone. "Oh, that men should put an enemy in their mouths, to steal away their brains." "Every inordinate cup is unblest, and the ingredient is a devil."

"Our good or bad fortune depends greatly on the choice we make of our friends." I never knew Sir Richard Rum's friendship worth preserving. He is warm and very cordial at first, but he is sure to lead you into difficulty in the end.

Note the two passages from Shakspere, whom the Old Farmer was studying diligently "about this time." In 1817 he begins almost every column of the Farmer's Calendar with similar quotations, — sometimes rather amusingly combined, as in the exordium to his January counsels: —

"Most potent, grave, and reverend Seigniors, my very noble and approved good masters." "Rude I am in speech; and little of this great world can I speak; yet grace and remembrance be unto you all." Economy, economy, neighbor Dash, is the main thing these hard times. Let it be your companion all about the house and in the barn.

An agricultural application of the boatswain's orders in The Tempest is appropriately assigned to the Farmer's Calendar for March: —

"Hey, my hearts, cheerly, my hearts; yare, yare; take in the topsail; bend to the master's whistle!" Ay, to be sure, attend to the master's whistle, not only at sea, but ye 'land-lubbers' also; "yare, lower, lower and bring her to try with main course!" Do you think, neighbour Mopus, that none but a sailor can be *yare?* Ay, my friend, that won't do; wide-a-wake is the word for us on shore, and let us have no milk-sops. Now the storm is over, see that all your rigging and tackle is adjusted.

As time went on, the Old Farmer's denunciations of tavern-haunting became more and more vigorous, for there can be no doubt that the drinking habit was increasing in New England. The conditions were approaching that made the temperance reform of the second and third decade of the last century so imperative. In July, 1821, we have an earnest, though highly humorous, expostulation: —

"How we perspire!" said the beef-steak to the gridiron. Yes, Capt. Blowzy, it's rather warm; but don't let us jump out of the frying-pan into the fire, by pouring down too much hot rum into our throats. I went up to Esq. Snozzle's store the other day for a half bushel of salt. It was just at night, after I had cocked up what little hay I had out. "By my troth," said I, as I entered the shop door, "this is rather *against the parish.*" For there sat Tom Toozle and Ben Boozle; Bob Raikins and Jo Jakins, with 6 or 8 more, *turning the double corner*, as they call it; or, to use a military term, firing off sling and punch from *right to left;* and, could you believe it, 'tis true as life, I there saw two of my good, honest and most reputable fellow-townsmen snug among them; old *Capt. Cleverly* and *Mr. David Easyman!* I was touched to the very soul; and looking indignantly at them, I cried, *Come out from among them.*

Among the entertainments which country innkeepers provided to amuse their guests and stimulate transient custom, particularly from the neighborhood itself, the turkey-shooting must not be forgotten. Kendall, another tourist, was present at an affair of this kind in Vermont: —

On these occasions the *taverner* fastens one turkey after another to a post, and those who shoot at it, take aim at a given distance. The shooters pay four pence half-penny currency, or the sixteenth part of a dollar for each shot, and half a dollar, or the price of eight shots, is the ordinary price of a turkey. The bird

sometimes falls at the first shot, but sometimes sustains no less than thirty-six; and, on the average, is hit one time in eight. When this happens, the *taverner* is but paid the ordinary price for his turkey; but his expectation of profit is formed chiefly upon the sale of liquor.[1]

Bowling on the turf was also a favorite diversion.   It is certainly a harmless amusement in itself, but the Old Farmer saw peril in it when it was associated with tavern-haunting.   In his Calendar for August, 1815, he has put himself on record, incidentally setting forth his general creed on the subject of sport of every kind: —

Bowling-greens have become of late mightily in fashion, to the ruin of many unfortunate young men. — Scarcely a day passes without the rattle of the pins in front of landlord Toddy Stick's house.   Every boy is distracted to get away from his work in order to take his game.   At sun two hour's high, the day is finished, and away goes men and boys to the bowling alley. Haying, hoeing, ploughing, sewing, all must give way to sport and toddy.   Now this is no way for a farmer.   It will do for the city lads to sport and relax in this way, and so there are proper times and seasons for farmers to take pleasure of this sort; for I agree that all work and no play makes Jack a dull boy.

Occasionally an innkeeper ventured into the domain of the showman.   A couple of advertisements will give some idea of this kind of enterprise as manifested in Boston.[2] The first appeared in the Massachusetts Mercury of December 9, 1800; the second, in the Columbian Centinel of April 28, 1810: —

[1] E. A. Kendall, Travels through the Northern Parts of the United States in the Year 1807 and 1808, New York, 1809, III, 200–1.   See also H. M. Brooks, The Olden Time Series, Boston, 1886, IV, 141–2.

[2] H. M. Brooks, The Olden Time Series, Boston, 1886, IV, 123, 132–3.

A Beautiful MOOSE.

THE curious in Natural History are invited to Major KING's Tavern, where is to be seen a fine young MOOSE of sixteen hands in height, and well proportioned. The properties of this fleet and tractable Animal are such as will give pleasure and satisfaction to every beholder.

Price of admittance, Nine Pence.   *Dec.* 9, 1800.

Monstrous Sight !

TO be seen at A. POLLARD's Tavern, Elm Street — A white Greenland Sea BEAR, which was taken at sea, weighing 1000 wt. This animal lives either in the sea or on the land. They have been seen several leagues at sea, and sometimes floating on cakes of ice. — This animal displays a great natural curiosity, — Admittance 12 1–2 cts. . . children half price.

The discomforts of inns make a large chapter in the tales of foreign travellers in America, — English travellers especially, who cling tenaciously to their national prerogative of grumbling. There is, however, a charming passage in the narrative of the Duke de la Rochefoucault-Liancourt, referring to 1795. This distinguished nobleman, who had selected a particularly diminutive inn as a haven of rest, was disappointed in his hopes, but adapted himself to the inevitable with true French good-humor, and made himself useful to his fellow-guests, who were of a a very humble order. This was at Maidenhead, near Princeton, New Jersey : —

I chose this petty inn, to avoid falling in with the stage-coaches, the passengers in which, naturally engross all the accommodation, at the inns at which they usually stop, in preference to any solitary rider. I desired to obtain some rest. In regard to the inconvenience from the stage-coaches, at any other inn, I was

very indifferent: but as to my rest, I was not indifferent; and in this small place I hoped to enjoy it.   But the only bed-chamber in the house happened, when I alighted, to be occupied by a club of the labourers and other inhabitants of the neighbourhood, assembled from the distance of two miles round.   These were joined by people drawn together on account of a horse-race, which was to be run at the distance of three miles from Maiden-head.   These people had soon a glass of grog in their heads, and began to make a considerable bustle in the inn.   I was neces-sarily obliged to retire with my table, into a small corner by the fire, to answer the questions which they put to me, and to give them the use of my pen, to scrawl out their accounts.   They were the best folks in the world; only, in respect to their writing, a little more of scholars than was quite agreeable to me.   I must, however, do them the justice, to own, that they did not hinder me from smoking my segar.[1]

The tavern was not merely a place of refreshment and diversion: it had other public and quasi-public functions of a widely miscellaneous character.   Auctions were held there; probate courts sat there; it was the rendezvous of the ministers who assembled for councils or ordinations; the town's business was largely transacted within its walls. When there were several inns in a single village, — as was often the case, — nice care was requisite on the part of the civic authorities to divide their favors impartially.   The selectmen of Groton, for example, met in succession at each of the three taverns in that town, as appears from an advertisement in the Groton Herald for March 13, 1830: —

Stated meetings of the Selectmen.

The Selectmen of Groton will meet on the last Saturdays of each month the present municipal year, at 3 o'clock, P. M. viz: — at *Hoar's* Tavern in March, April, May, and June; at *Alexan-*

[1] Travels through the United States of North America, London, 1799, I, 548–9.

der's in July, August, September, and October ; and at *Shattuck's* in November, December, January, and February.

CALEB BUTLER, Chairman.[1]

Not infrequently the landlord was a local magistrate and his inn served as his office.

A leading inn in a large seaport town presented a scene of great variety and animation. It combined the functions of the modern hotel, club, railway station, and exchange. It was a rendezvous for merchants and shipcaptains, as well as for politicians and officials of all kinds. Social meetings, dances, and entertainments took place in its assembly room. Stage passengers and their friends were continually coming and going. In 1801, as we learn from the Almanac, King's Tavern, in Market Square, Boston, was the "terminal" for the stages for Albany, New York, Portsmouth, Amherst, Providence, Plymouth, Salem, Taunton and New Bedford, Dorchester and Milton, Dedham, Groton, Quincy, and Canton.[2] Some of these ran daily (Sundays excepted), others three times a week, a few once a week. The bustle of arrival and departure must have been almost continuous. Nor should the numerous packets and the private conveyances be forgotten. The public rooms and the common table of such an establishment were picturesque and characteristic to a degree that our modern caravanseries cannot rival. As a description of a large city hotel, we may take an account of Tammany Hall as it impressed a Scottish visitor in 1818 : —

Dined with Mr. —— at Tammany Hall. On one occasion here we had roasted bear's flesh as one of the dishes at table ; it tasted very much like roasted goose, but heavier. Tammany

---

[1] Quoted by Dr. Samuel Abbott Green, Groton Historical Series, VIII, 9.

[2] See a complete Table of Stages, pp. 287 ff., below ; and compare the List of Post Roads after p. 304.

Hall is one of the public hotels, and noted for the public meetings of the democratic party, or Bucktails, as they are called. Like the other hotels it is the residence of a good many permanent boarders; some of them merchants of considerable wealth, who sit down every day at the public table. The inn is with us proverbially the traveller's home, but here it is the home of a great many besides travellers. This feature in the American system I cannot admire; nor can I imagine what comfort there can be amidst the bustle and noise of a public tavern, or in smoking segars and drinking spirits and water in the bar-room.

The dinner hour at Tammany Hall is three o'clock, and covers are every day set for from thirty to eighty. The resident boarders are generally found at the upper end of the table, and the travellers farther down. They take their seats at the sound of the dinner bell, and in a little more than a quarter of an hour most of them are ready to leave the table. During dinner rum and water is the usual beverage; few take wine unless they are entertaining a friend. The dinner is always excellent, combining every variety of substantial cheer with a plentiful allowance of the delicacies of the season. After dinner three or four may occasionally linger singing songs and smoking segars over a bottle of wine, but the practice is by no means general. Americans spend little time at table, retiring very soon either to their business, or the bar-room to read the newspapers. Boarding is moderate at Tammany Hall; Mr. —— tells me that he pays eight dollars a week, while some of the more fashionable private boarding-houses charge ten or twelve, and the inmates are moreover by usage almost necessitated to drink wine during dinner. For economy of time and money, and freedom from temptation, the system of private lodgings, as in our native country, is decidedly preferable to either the one or the other.[1]

Where there was no inn, it was customary for some respectable citizen to " accommodate travellers " at his own house. Such a host was often well-to-do, and had little

[1] J. M. Duncan, Travels through Part of the United States and Canada in 1818 and 1819, Glasgow, 1823, II, 246–8.

concern for profit. An agreeable visit at a house of this
kind is described by Admiral Bartholomew James, who, in
the summer of 1791, while captain in the merchant service,
visited Portland in his ship the Maria, and has recorded
his impressions in a very good-humored journal, to which
we have already had occasion to refer.[1] Captain James
was delighted with the situation of the town and much
impressed by the cheapness of provisions.   " Meat of
every sort was supplied the ship's company, and they
every day had their choice, at the rate of twopence per
pound; . . . turkeys was from a shilling to eighteenpence
each, geese a shilling, and fowls from tenpence to a shilling a couple; the best fat sheep I bought at nine shillings
alive, and everything else of the kind was proportionally
cheap." [2]

On his way up the Kennebec River in the ship's long
boat, on an excursion undertaken partly for amusement
and partly for the sake of acquainting himself with the
coast, Captain James had an experience which throws
some light on the conditions of travel in New England at
the end of the eighteenth century.   Near the mouth of the
river he was compelled by heavy weather to run aground
on Parker's Flats.   After wading over the flats and marsh
for " at least a mile," guided by a Yankee pilot in his employ, he called " at Captain Parker's hospitable mansion."
The family " consisted of the good gentleman, who was a
captain in the militia and about eighty years of age," his
wife, who " might probably have reached her fiftieth
year," a nephew, two nieces, " graceful, bewitching, an-
gelic creatures," with " two domestic rustic girls and four
rural artless clowns." Captain James's party, three in
number, were entertained in a way that won his heart

---

[1] See p. 168, above.
[2] Journal of Rear-Admiral Bartholomew James, Navy Records Society,
1896, pp. 187 ff.

completely.   Their supper was " a delicious meal" of " tea
and toast, lamb-steaks and eggs, and a moderate quantity
of cider and grog."   Then there were family prayers, and
the strangers were made comfortable for the night.   What
happened next morning must be related in the Captain's
own graphic, if slightly ungrammatical, style: —

So soon as the morning service was finished and we had taken
a very comfortable breakfast, I directed preparations to be made
for our departure, and consulted my pilot how I should repay the
worthy family for their civility and kindness; by whom I was informed I was to consider what expenses they had been at, and,
agreeable to the custom of that part of the country, repay them
for it.   I further learned from him that, as we were three, and
had a supper, beds, and breakfast, he thought the least I could
offer them was three-and-sixpence British.   I confessed my surprise at this proposition under several heads: first, how I could
offer any money to a private independent family for their civility
to me as a stranger; and, secondly, how ridiculous such a sum as
he proposed would appear for " all the benefits we had received
in mind and body."   To the first he assured me it was the constant custom, as there was few, if any, public-houses in that
neighbourhood, and that as all people frequented private houses
in their journeying through the country, it was usual to go in that
way without the smallest hesitation, and that they would consider
themselves much obliged to any friends who partook of their
comforts whatever they happened to be; and the sum he assured
me to be equal to their expectations, and that he believed a
larger one would be refused.   Under those considerations I
ventured to take an opportunity of addressing the old lady when
alone, and, after thanking her for her great kindness and civility,
begged she would allow me to leave a couple of dollars for her
servants.   She expressed the greatest astonishment at the sum,
and insisted on my taking one of the dollars back, which, on my
declining, she said, " Well, you will come again to us in your way
down the river, and then you must pay nothing."

On the return trip, Captain James and his party were again entertained at the same house, and Mrs. Parker was as good as her word, refusing to accept any more money and insisting that she had already been sufficiently paid. The whole incident is highly instructive; for the Captain makes it plain that the Parkers did not keep an inn and had no wish to make a profit out of their guests, being a well-to-do family. They were simply following the custom of the country in accommodating travellers, since there was no public house in the neighborhood.

On the same expedition Captain James spent a night at Rittle's tavern at Pownalborough, of which he has left an equally agreeable record : —

This house was kept by a German and his wife, who had a family of two sons and four daughters. Two of the latter were extremely handsome, and the civility of the whole house induced me to take up my quarters there for the night. I therefore directed a small supper to be provided, and at nine o'clock sat down to as comfortable a meal as I ever remember to have fed upon. The old man smoked his pipe, and related his peregrinations and the difficulties he laboured under in the American war; the good old wife prepared the feast, while the daughters, clad in homely apparel, but with looks of native sweetness, virtue and truth, did us the kindness to attend the table.[1]

John Davis, the whimsical humorist whom we have more than once quoted, does not fail to note the hospitable custom of entertaining strangers at private houses. Incidentally he laughs at his fellow-Britons for their habitual grumbling. He is speaking of Virginia, but the experiences of Admiral James prove that what he says was true of other parts of the country : —

[1] Journal, p. 192.

I eat my dinner in a log-house on the road.   It was kept by a small planter of the name of *Homer*.   Such a tavern would have raised the thunder and lightning of anger in the page of my brother-travellers in *America*.   But the lamented scarcity of *American* inns is easily accounted for.   In a country where every private house is a temple dedicated to hospitality, and open alike to travellers of every description, ought it to excite surprize that so few good taverns are to be found? [1]

On the whole, it appears that the inns or taverns of New England were pretty comfortable places, and that some of them were rather distinguished.   Tourists are proverbially hard to please, and it is natural that we should hear more of the unpleasant than of the agreeable incidents that accompanied travelling in a new country.   But the good repute of our hotels nowadays is merely a continuation of the character which they bore in old times. The administrative capacity for which the Yankee is famous has applied itself successfully to the complicated business of innholding.   Many noted landlords in other parts of the country have been New England men.   Good cheer has become a cherished American institution.   We can hardly venture to assert that its home is New England; but one would find it hard to make out a better case for any other part of the continent.

[1] Travels in the United States of America, London, 1803, p. 341.

ON THE ROAD

FROM the earliest times in New England to the latter half of the eighteenth century travellers usually rode on horseback, and for short distances this continued to be the custom until long after stage lines had become numerous and well-managed. Felt, in his History of Ipswich, published in 1834, tells us that " about thirty-five years ago, horse-wagons began to be employed. Gradually increasing, they have almost altogether superseded riding on horse-back among our farmers. They are used to carry articles to market, which were formerly borne to town in wallets and panniers, thrown across a horse. They have prevented the method of going in a cart, as often practised before they were invented, by social parties, when wishing to make a visit of several miles."[1] Travelling on horseback is now so completely obsolete in New England, — though riding for pleasure is happily on the increase, — that certain directions for the management of horses on a journey, given in the Almanac for 1794, have merely an historical significance. No one would think of uttering such precepts to an audience of New England farmers nowadays. They would have little more to do with the needs of the community than a treatise on the care of camels in desert traffic. Yet when they were written they were quite to the point.

The English traveller Bennett, in 1740, thus describes the usual methods of travel in New England: —

[1] Joseph B. Felt, History of Ipswich, Essex, and Hamilton, Cambridge, 1834, p. 32.

There are several families in Boston that keep a coach, and pair of horses, and some few drive with four horses; but for chaises and saddle-horses, considering the bulk of the place, they outdo London. They have some nimble, lively horses for the coach, but not any of that beautiful large black breed so common in London. Their saddle-horses all pace naturally, and are generally counted sure-footed; but they are not kept in that fine order as in England. The common draught-horses used in carts about the town are very small and poor, and seldom have their fill of anything but labor. The country carts and wagons are generally drawn by oxen, from two to six, according to the distance of place, or burden they are laden with. When the ladies ride out to take the air, it is generally in a chaise or chair, and then but a single horse; and they have a negro servant to drive them. The gentlemen ride out here as in England, some in chairs, and others on horseback, with their negroes to attend them. They travel in much the same manner on business as for pleasure, and are attended in both by their black equipages. Their roads, though they have no turnpikes, are exceeding good in summer; and it is safe travelling night or day, for they have no highway robbers to interrupt them. It is pleasant riding through the woods; and the country is pleasantly interspersed with farm-houses, cottages, and some few gentlemen's seats, between the towns. But the best of their inns, and houses of entertainment, are very short of the beauty and conveniences of ours in England. They have generally a little rum to drink, and some of them have a sorry sort of Madeira wine. And to eat they have Indian corn roasted, and bread made of Indian meal, and sometimes a fowl or fish dressed after a fashion, but pretty good butter, and very sad sort of cheese; but those that are used to those things think them tolerable.[1]

In the last two decades of the eighteenth century there was a great improvement in roads and a marked increase

[1] Joseph Bennett, Manuscript History of New England, Proc. Mass. Hist. Soc., V, 124-5.

in the number of stage lines. Wansey, in 1794, remarked that " eight years ago the road from Boston to Newhaven a distance of one hundred and seventy miles, could scarcely maintain two stages and twelve horses; now it maintains twenty stages weekly, with upwards of an hundred horses; so much is travelling encreased in this district."[1] Such growth may partly account for the complaints which we often hear about this time as to the quality of the roadside inns. Hotels in the smaller towns found it hard to keep pace with the development of business and the advancing requirements of the public.

In the first year of the nineteenth century the Almanac gives the following —

LIST *of* STAGES *that run from* BOSTON, *and* PLACES
from which they start.

ALBANY Mail Stage goes through Worcester, Brookfield and Northampton, to Albany; sets off from King's inn, Market-Square, every Monday and Thursday morning, at 10 o'clock, and arrives at Albany every Thursday and Monday noon.

PROVIDENCE and NEW–YORK southern Mail Stage sets off from Israel Hatch's coffee-house, corner of Exchange-Lane, State-Street, every Tuesday, Thursday and Saturday, at 8 o'clock in the morning, and arrives at New-York every Wednesday, Friday and Sunday noon: leaves New-York every Tuesday, Thursday and Saturday, at 10 o'clock in the morning, and arrives in Boston every Friday, Monday and Wednesday, at 3 o'clock in the afternoon.

An extra stage runs every day to Providence, from the above office.

BOSTON and NEW–YORK Mail Stage sets off from King's inn, Market-Square, every Monday, Wednesday and Friday, at 10 o'clock in the morning, and arrives at New York every

[1] Journal of an Excursion to the United States of North America in the Summer of 1794, Salisbury, 1796, pp. 71–72.

Thursday, Saturday and Tuesday, at 1 o'clock in the afternoon: leaves New-York every Monday, Wednesday and Friday, at 11 o'clock in the morning, and arrives at Boston every Thursday, Saturday and Tuesday, at 1 o'clock in the afternoon.

OLD LINE Stage sets off from King's inn, Market-Square, every Tuesday, Thursday and Saturday, at 10 o'clock in the morning and arrives at New-York every Friday, Monday and Wednesday, at 1 o'clock in the afternoon: leaves New-York every Tuesday, Thursday and Saturday, at 10 o'clock in the morning, and arrives at Boston every Friday, Monday and Wednesday, at 1 o'clock in the afternoon.

LEOMINSTER Mail Stage passes through Concord and Lancaster, to Leominster; sets off from James Clark's tavern, White Lion, No. 23, Newbury-Street, every Wednesday and Saturday, at 5 o'clock in the morning, and arrives at Leominster the same days: leaves Leominster every Monday and Thursday, at 5 o'clock in the morning and arrives in Boston the same days.

PORTSMOUTH Mail Stage passes through Salem, and Newbury-Port; sets off from King's inn, Market-Square, every Monday, Wednesday and Friday, at 3 o'clock in the morning, and arrives at Portsmouth the same days, at 6 o'clock in the evening: leaves Portsmouth every Tuesday, Thursday and Saturday, at 3 o'clock in the morning, and arrives in Boston the same days, at 6 o'clock in the evening.

AMHERST Mail Stage passes through Billerica; sets off from King's inn, Market-Square, every Wednesday morning, at 4 o'clock, and arrives at Amherst at 7 o'clock in the evening, the same day: leaves Amherst every Monday, at 4 o'clock in the morning, and arrives in Boston at 7 o'clock in the evening of the same day.

PROVIDENCE Stage sets off from King's inn every day in the week (Sundays excepted) at 8 o'clock in the morning, and arrives at Providence at 4 o'clock in the afternoon.

PLYMOUTH Mail Stage passes through Hingham; sets off from King's inn, Market-Square, every Tuesday, Thursday and Saturday, at 6 o'clock in the morning, and arrives at Plymouth the same days, at 4 o'clock in the afternoon: leaves Plymouth

every Monday, Wednesday and Friday, at 6 o'clock in the morning, and arrives in Boston the same days, at 4 o'clock in the afternoon.

SALEM Mail Stage sets off from King's inn, Market-Square, every day in the week (Sundays excepted) at 3 o'clock in the afternoon, and arrives in Boston every day, at 11 o'clock in the morning.

MARBLEHEAD Stage sets off from King's inn, Market-Square, and returns the same as Salem stage.

TAUNTON and NEW–BEDFORD Mail Stage sets off from King's inn, Market-Square, every Tuesday, Thursday and Saturday, at 3 o'clock in the morning, and arrives at Taunton at 12 o'clock, and at New-Bedford at 6 o'clock the same evening: leaves New-Bedford every Monday, Wednesday and Friday, at 3 o'clock in the morning, and arrives at Boston the same days, at 6 o'clock in the evening.

DORCHESTER and MILTON Stage sets off every day from King's inn, Market-Square, at 4 o'clock in the afternoon, and arrives in Boston every day, at 9 o'clock in the morning.

CAPE–ANN Stage passes through Salem and Beverly; sets off from the Yankee Hero tavern, Wing's-Lane, every Wednesday and Saturday, at 8 o'clock in the morning, and arrives the same days at Cape-Ann: leaves Cape-Ann every Tuesday and Friday, and arrives in Boston the same days, at 4 o'clock.

MEDFORD Stage sets off every day (Sundays excepted) from Mr. Patterson's tavern, Wing's-Lane, at 12 o'clock, and arrives in Boston every day, at 8 o'clock in the morning. N. B. Sets off and returns twice every Saturday.

NEWBURY–PORT Stage sets off from Mr. Evans's tavern, Ann-Street, every Tuesday, Thursday and Saturday, at 5 o'clock in the morning, and arrives at Newbury-Port at 4 o'clock in the afternoon, same day: leaves that place every Monday, Wednesday and Friday, at 6 o'clock in the morning, and arrives in Boston the same days, at 4 o'clock in the afternoon.

HAVERHILL Stage passes through Andover; sets off from Mr. Evans's tavern, Ann-Street, every Monday, Wednesday and

19

Friday, at 3 o'clock in the morning, and arrives at Haverhill at
11 o'clock, same days: leaves Haverhill at 10 o'clock in the
morning, every Tuesday, Thursday and Saturday, and arrives in
Boston at 7 o'clock in the evening, same days.

SALEM Stage sets off from Israel Hatch's coffee-house, corner
of Exchange-Lane, State-Street, every morning (Sundays excepted) at 8 o'clock, and arrives at Salem at 11 o'clock: leaves
that place at 3 o'clock in the afternoon, and arrives in Boston at
6 o'clock.

GROTON Stage sets off from King's inn, Market-Square, every
Wednesday, at 4 o'clock in the morning, and arrives at Groton
at 3 o'clock in the afternoon, same day: leaves Groton every
Monday, at 4 o'clock in the morning, and arrives in Boston at
6 o'clock in the afternoon, same day.

CAMBRIDGE Stage sets off from the old State-house, Cornhill, twice every day (Sundays excepted) at 12 o'clock, noon,
and at 6 o'clock in the afternoon: arrives in Boston at 10 o'clock
in the morning, and at 3 o'clock in the afternoon.

ROXBURY and BROOKLINE Stage sets off and arrives at
the same place and hours as Cambridge Stage.

WATERTOWN Stage sets off from the old State-House, Cornhill, every day (Sundays excepted) at 5 o'clock in the afternoon,
and arrives in Boston every day, at 10 o'clock in the morning.

DEDHAM Stage starts from King's inn every day in the week
(Sundays excepted) at 4 o'clock in the afternoon, and arrives in
Boston the same days, at 10 o'clock in the morning.

QUINCY Stage sets off from King's inn every Tuesday,
Thursday and Saturday, at 4 o'clock in the afternoon, and arrives
in Boston the same days, at 10 o'clock in the morning.

CANTON Stage sets off from King's Inn every Tuesday,
Thursday and Saturday, at 3 o'clock in the afternoon, and arrives
in Boston the same days, at 9 o'clock in the morning.

We are familiar with the general idea that facilities for
transportation have improved wonderfully within a hundred years; but it is after all a little startling to consider

that the modest list just printed is a complete time-table of all the lines running from Boston in 1801.   We may compare it at our leisure with the voluminous railroad schedules of the present day.

The American stagecoaches were so different from the English that almost every visitor from the mother country described them at length.   Out of an embarrassing number of such descriptions three may be selected, — dating from 1795, 1806, and 1833 respectively.   The first is from the pen of Thomas Twining, and refers to his journey from Philadelphia to Baltimore in 1795 : —

At ten this morning the negro girl took my portmanteau under her arm, and accompanied me to the mail-wagon office.   At half-past ten the wagon started up High Street, passing before the window of Dr. Priestley.   The vehicle was a long car with four benches.   Three of these in the interior held nine passengers, and a tenth passenger was seated by the side of the driver on the front bench.   A light roof was supported by eight slender pillars, four on each side.   Three large leather curtains suspended to the roof, one at each side and the third behind, were rolled up or lowered at the pleasure of the passengers.   There was no space nor place for luggage, each person being expected to stow his things as he could under his seat or legs.   The entrance was in front, over the driver's bench.   Of course the three passengers on the back seat were obliged to crawl across all the other benches to get to their places.   There were no *backs* to the benches to support and relieve us during a rough and fatiguing journey over a newly and ill made road.   It would be unreasonable to expect perfection in the arrangements of a new country ; but though this rude conveyance was not without its advantages, and was really more suitable to the existing state of American roads than an English stage-coach would have been, it might have been rendered more convenient in some respects without much additional expense.   Thus a mere strap behind the seats would have been a great comfort, and the ponderous leather

curtains, which extended the whole length of the wagon, would have been much more convenient *divided* into two or three parts, and with a glass, however small, in each division to give light to the passengers in bad weather, and enable them to have a glimpse of the country. The disposal of the luggage also was extremely incommodious, not only to the owner, but to his neighbors. We were quite full, having ten passengers besides the driver.[1]

Our second example is from Melish's Travels, and has to do with intercourse between Boston and New York in 1806: —

Having taken my leave of a number of kind friends, with whom I had associated during my stay in Boston, I engaged a passage by the mail stage for New York, and was called to take my place on the 4th of September, at 2 o'clock in the morning. It is the practice here for the driver to call on the passengers before setting out, and it is attended with a considerable degree of convenience to them, particularly when they set out early in the morning. The mail stages here are altogether different in construction from the mail coaches in Britain. They are long machines, hung upon leather braces, with three seats across, of a sufficient length to accommodate three persons each, who all sit with their faces towards the horses. The driver sits under cover, without any division between him and the passengers; and there is room for a person to sit on each side of him. The driver, by the post-office regulations, must be a white man, and he has the charge of the mail, which is placed in a box below his seat. There is no guard. The passengers' luggage is put below the seats, or tied on behind the stage. They put nothing on the top, and they take no outside passengers. The stages are slightly built, and the roof suspended on pillars; with a curtain, to be let down or folded up at pleasure. The conveyance is easy, and in summer very agreeable; but it must be excessively cold in winter.[2]

[1] Travels in America 100 Years Ago, being Notes and Reminiscences by Thomas Twining, New York, 1894, pp. 58–60.

[2] John Melish. Travels in the United States of America, Philadelphia, 1812, I, 106.

For our third description we are indebted to Abdy, the Oxonian, who is telling what happened to him in New England in 1833: —

I left Northampton on the 16th, at three, A. M., for Boston, and arrived at that place about eight in the evening. The road was good; and, if we had not changed our vehicle three times during the journey, and stopped at the various post-offices for the bags, and at the hotels for refreshment, we should have got in much sooner. The first fifteen miles were performed in an hour and forty minutes. The distance is ninety-four miles. The passengers were inclined to be sociable; and, as it was a fine day, and the country not uninteresting, the journey passed off pleasantly enough. An English coachman would have been somewhat amused with the appearance of the stage and the costume of the driver. The former was similar to some that are common enough in France, though not known on our side of the channel. It was on leathern springs; the boot and the hind part being appropriated to the luggage, while the box was occupied by two passengers in addition to the "conducteur," and as many on the roof. On the top, secured by an iron rail, were some of the trunks and boxes, and inside were places for nine; two seats being affixed to the ends, and one, parallel to them, across the middle of the carriage. Our driver sat between two of the outsides, and when there was but one on the box, over the near wheeler; and holding the reins, or *lines*, as he called them, in such a manner as to separate his team into couples, not a-breast, but in a line or tandem fashion, drove along with considerable skill and dexterity. When he got down, he fastened the "ribbons" to a ring, or a post in front of the house where he had occasion to pull up.[1]

In the less thickly settled parts of the country the stagecoach gave way to the "stage-wagon." This was

[1] E. S. Abdy, Journal of a Residence and Tour in the United States from April, 1833, to October, 1834, London, 1835, I, 118-19.

a primitive contrivance, "a mere cart with four wheels," one traveller calls it, — and was usually drawn by two horses. Chairs were sometimes used as seats, but there were not always enough to go round. Not infrequently the passenger had to sit on his own baggage. Lambert, who toured about the United States and Canada from 1806 to 1808, grows eloquent in discoursing of the discomforts of these vehicles. He is describing his trip from Burlington, Vermont, to St. Albans:—

I had a most uncomfortable seat in the hind part of the waggon upon the mail bag, and other goods. I might, indeed, have sat in front along with the driver, but my legs would have been cramped between a large chest, and the fore part of the waggon. Of two evils, I chose the least: but I shall never forget the shaking, jolting, jumbling, and tossing, which I experienced over this disagreeable road, up and down steep hills, which obliged me to alight, (for we had only two poor jaded horses to drag us) and fag through the sand and dust, exposed to a burning sun. When we got into our delectable vehicle again, our situation was just as bad; for the road in many parts was continually obstructed by large stones; stumps of trees, and fallen timber; deep ruts and holes, over which, to use an American phrase, we were *waggon'd* most unmercifully.[1]

The different modes of conveyance required on a long journey may be seen in the itinerary of Dr. Jeremy Belknap, who went from Boston to Niagara, in 1796, to inspect the mission conducted among the Oneida Indians by the Society for Propagating Christian Knowledge. He was absent not quite one month, for he left Boston on the ninth of June and reached home on the sixth of July. Here is his time-table, drawn up in brief form by the Doctor himself, who was one of the most accurate of men:—

[1] John Lambert, Travels through Lower Canada and the United States of North America, London, 1810, III, 488.

Memorandum of distances and modes of travelling from Boston to Niagara.

In the stage, which sets out from Boston on Monday and Thursday mornings, you go the

	miles.
first day to Brookfield	66
second day to Northampton	34
third day to Pittsfield	40
fourth day to Albany	40

180

Here you may rest, and from hence proceed on any day, forenoon or afternoon, to Schenectada 16

Thence you may go either in the stage-wagon by land, or in boats up the Mohawk River. The former is accomplished in less time than the latter. The stage goes every Tuesday and Friday morning —

the first day to Canajohara	40
the second to Whites-town	46

102

Here the stage ends.

From Whites-town to Fort Stanwix is a wagon-road, and wagons may be hired 12

Fort Stanwix is situate on the upper waters of Mohawk River, from which is a portage to Wood Creek, where a Canal is now making 2

Thence by water, down Wood Creek to Oneida Lake	27
Across Oneida Lake to Fort Bruington	35
Down the river to Oswego Falls	12

Portage 150 feet. Thence to Oswego Fort on Lake Ontario 12

Thence through the lake to Niagara 160

260

542 [1]

The connection between stage lines was often uncertain, — still more so was that between stage and packet. At

[1] Proc. Mass. Hist. Soc., XIX, 422-3.

Providence, in 1806, it was the rule that if the New York packet brought three passengers for Boston, the stage was " bound to go with them at any hour." [1]   Local stages often picked up their passengers at the houses,—an accommodating habit which rendered the hour of departure inconstant. Through stages that were unhampered by connecting lines of traffic often made good time, especially if there were competing lines.   Israel Hatch's daily stages from Boston to Providence, established about 1793, covered the distance between five o'clock in the morning and two in the afternoon, changing horses once, at the half-way house in Walpole.   The fare was one dollar,[2] but this was a cut-rate, expressly advertised as " one half the customary price, and 3s. cheaper than any other stage."   In 1811 the stage ride from Philadelphia to Pittsburg, two hundred and ninety-seven miles, took six days; a wagon required about twenty days.   Stage fare was twenty dollars; wagon fare, " five dollars per cwt. for both persons and property." [3]   The faster stages were often decorated with such hyperbolical titles as " Flying Machine " and " Flying Mail."   The famous Telegraph Line from Boston to Albany was in 1831 operated under a contract which bound the drivers to make seven miles an hour on the average, day and night, including stops.[4]

Naturally journeys of any length were planned a good while beforehand, and intending travellers were always on the watch for casual means of conveyance.   Their alert attitude is well exemplified in the following typical advertisement, from a Philadelphia newspaper of 1777: — " A person wants to go to Boston and would be glad of a place in a chaise or wagon going there, or if only half the

---

[1] Melish, Travels, Philadelphia, 1812, I, 80.

[2] Edward Field, The Colonial Tavern, Providence, 1897, p. 273.

[3] Melish, II, 52.

[4] F. M. Thompson, History of Greenfield, Mass., 1904, pp. 976-7.

way on that road, and a genteel price will be given. Any
this will suit will be waited on by leaving a line with the
printer." [1]

Our foreign visitors were better pleased with our sleighs,
which to most of them were complete novelties, than with
our stagecoaches and wagons. "No carriage," writes one
just before the Revolution, "goes with so easy a motion as
these sleighs do, having none of the jolting motion of a
wheel-carriage; but much resembling the motion of what
we used to call a shuggie-shew, or a vessel before a fine
wind." [2] The same authority was much struck with the
American custom of sleigh-riding for pleasure. "The
young ladies and gentlemen," he says, "are so fond of
this, as a diversion, that whenever the snow gives over
falling, tho' it be after sun-set, they will not wait till next
day, but have their sleigh yoked directly, and drive about
without the least fear of catching cold from the night
air." [3]

The earliest agitation for railroads in New England contemplated particularly the establishment of lines on which
freight should be transported by means of horses. The
Quincy Railroad, finished in 1827, was of this kind; it
was only a few miles in length and was used to carry
granite from the quarries to tidewater. In 1829, William
Jackson, in a lecture before the Massachusetts Charitable
Mechanic Association, gave much space to showing what
loads could be drawn by a horse on a railroad in comparison
with the work that he could do on an ordinary turnpike. [4]
He was, however, fully cognizant of the experiments that

[1] Pennsylvania Evening Post, September 4, 1777, quoted in Potter's
American Monthly, IV, 307.
[2] Patrick M'Robert, Tour through Part of the North Provinces of
America, Edinburgh, 1776, p. 47.
[3] The same, p. 46.
[4] William Jackson, Lecture on Rail Roads, delivered Ianuary 12, 1829,
Boston, 1829, pp. 11 ff.

had been tried with locomotives, and believed, though he expressed himself cautiously, that steam would soon supersede horsepower. At this time the enthusiasm for a line from Boston to Albany was great, and Jackson's address was meant to further the project. A large part of the route had already been surveyed at public expense, and it was hoped that the undertaking would be fathered by the State. There was much scornful incredulity, however, which found utterance in various amusing ways. In 1827 Captain Basil Hall, whose Travels in America is deservedly celebrated for its intelligence and good-humor, went over a considerable part of the route between Boston and Albany. He was assured, he tells us, that it had been " seriously proposed " to connect these two cities by rail, but this he characterizes as a " visionary project." Appeals were frequently made to him to admire the plan. " I was compelled to admit," he says, " that there was much boldness in the conception; but I took the liberty of adding, that I conceived the boldness lay in the conception alone; for, if it were executed, its character would be changed into madness." [1]

Captain Hall's language is moderation itself in comparison with some of the strictures of the Massachusetts press. In June, 1827, there appeared in the Boston Courier a satirical article from the pen of the editor, Joseph T. Buckingham, which ridiculed the " railroad mania " unsparingly : —

Alcibiades, or some other great man of antiquity, it is said, cut off his dog's tail, that *quid nuncs* (we suppose such animals existed in ancient as well as in modern times) might not become extinct for want of excitement. Some such motive, we doubt not, moved one or two of our *natural* and *experimental philosophers* to get up the project of a railroad from Boston to Albany ; — a

[1] Travels in North America in the years 1827 and 1828, Edinburgh, 1829, II, 93.

project, which every one knows, — who knows the simplest rules in arithmetic, — to be impracticable but at an expense little less than the market value of the whole territory of Massachusetts; and which, if practicable, every person of common sense knows would be as useless as a railroad from Boston to the Moon. Indeed, a road of some kind from here to the heart of that beautiful satellite of our dusky planet would be of some practical utility, — especially, if a few of our *notional*, public-spirited men, our railway fanatics, could be persuaded to pay a visit to their proper country.[1]

Mr. Buckingham, however, was speedily converted. Within a year, as he tells us himself, he joined in a petition to the legislature for a road from Boston to Ogdensburg.[2]

In 1831 the Farmer's Almanack contains a significant item. It had long included a full-page Map of New England to illustrate the List of Stage Routes which was an indispensable feature of every such annual. In the year mentioned, the list is accompanied by the following paragraph: —

Rail Roads. The direction of the several rail road routes which have been proposed, leading from Boston, may be understood by reference to the following map. The principal routes are 1. from Boston through Framingham, Worcester, Springfield, and Pittsfield, to Albany. 2. From Boston through Waltham, and Fitchburg to Brattleborough. 3. From Boston to Lowell, thence through Concord and Montpelier to Burlington, and thence westerly to Ogdensburg. 4. From Boston to Providence.

The railroads, like the stage routes, are not marked in Mr. Thomas's map.

[1] Joseph T. Buckingham, Personal Memoirs and Recollections of Editorial Life, Boston, 1852, II, 15.
[2] The same, II, 16.

1831 was the decisive year for New England railroading. The Boston and Providence and the Boston and Worcester Railroads were incorporated, and these two companies, as well as the Boston and Lowell, which had received a charter in 1830, were definitely organized. Active construction was begun without delay, and in 1834 and 1835 all three roads were opened to public travel.[1]

The first experiment with a locomotive in New England was made on the Boston and Worcester road, then completed as far as Newton, on March 17th, 1834. On the fourth of April the new invention was put to practical use. The event is thus reported in the Boston Patriot for April 5th: —

A Locomotive Engine was yesterday employed in hauling gravel on the Boston & Worcester Rail Road. The engine worked with ease, was perfectly manageable, and showed power enough to travel at any desirable speed. The distance traveled was about three miles, and the train usually traversed this distance, both with loaded and with empty cars, in about ten minutes, the engine blowing off waste steam a great part of the time, and evidently capable of carrying a much greater load, or moving with greater rapidity.

Regular passenger service between Boston and Newton began on May 16th, with three trains a day in either direction, "leaving Boston at 6 and 10 A. M., and 3.30 P. M. and returning at 7 and 11.15 A. M. and 4.45 P. M. The fare was 37½ cents. . . . The trip was at first made in nineteen minutes, but this was thought to be faster than necessary,

[1] Nathan Hale, in an article on the Massachusetts Railway System in the Boston Advertiser, September, 17, 18, 19, 1851, as reprinted in — The Railroad Jubilee : an Account of the Celebration Commemorative of the Opening of Railroad Communication between Boston and Canada, September 17th, 18th, and 19th, 1851. Boston, 1852, p. 233.

and by a vote of the directors the engineers were required to increase the time to thirty minutes, or at the rate of about eighteen miles an hour." The first cars were similar in design to the English railway coach, box cars not being adopted until several years later.[1] In 1835 an English visitor was able to record that there was now "very speedy communication" between Boston and New York by way of Providence, — the distance "being performed in twenty hours, by rail-road and steam-boat." The same writer was a good deal impressed by the expenditure of "some thousands of dollars" to clear the tracks of the Boston and Lowell road from a single fall of snow.[2]

Even when railroading was well under way, there was considerable doubt in the minds of many as to its advantages to agriculture. The Almanac for 1837 gives expression to these scruples in a little sketch of a disappointed farmer who had built high hopes on the new enterprise : —

All for the railway — and, to be sure, it is a very clever thing, but not altogether so for farmer Credulous as he imagined that it would be. It was laid out straight through his valuable and beautiful farm. He thought it would certainly improve it full five hundred fold. But he reckoned up his chickens and counted them all off, not only before they were hatched, but even before the nest was made. Here was an extensive, level plain, where, it was tho't, the rail-cars would skim beautifully for miles upon the surface. "You are welcome," said Credulous, " to pass through my land ; " and so they held him to the bargain, and cut thirty feet deep through the centre the whole length of his farm! This was a woful speculation for my old friend Creddy. He now execrates all railways, turnpikes, canals, and internal improvements, without distinction, and considers them but gull-traps for the unwary.

[1] B. T. Hill, Proceedings of the Worcester Society of Antiquity, XVII, 549–51.

[2] Harriet Martineau, Society in America, London, 1837, II, 186.

When a man gets a good farm, and is able to carry it on, let him think himself well off. Should he have a little cash on hand, it will be convenient enough; but it is unfortunate if he gives heed to every speculation story that is told, and is willing to be flattered into a belief that he is to be enriched by every stone that is turned, and by every new project and plan. (October, 1837.)

The prejudice against railroads entertained by a good many people in New England died hard. As late as 1842 the inhabitants of Dorchester voted, in town-meeting, that a railroad on either of two proposed lines " will be of incalculable evil to the town generally, in addition to the immense sacrifice of private property which will also be involved. A great portion of the road will lead through thickly settled and populous parts of the town, crossing and running contiguous to public highways, and thereby making a permanent obstruction to a free intercourse of our citizens, and creating great and enduring danger and hazard to all travel upon the common roads." Further they declared that, if a railroad must be built, " it should be located upon the marshes and over creeks," and finally it was —

Resolved, That our representatives be instructed to use their utmost endeavors to prevent, if possible, so great a calamity to our town as must be the location of any rail-road through it; and, if that cannot be prevented, to diminish this calamity as far as possible by confining the location to the route herein designated.[1]

In 1841 Mr. Thomas first inserted railroads into his Map of New England, thus admitting them to a kind of parity with the stage routes which the map was meant to illustrate. (See opposite page.)

---

[1] Josiah Quincy, Figures of the Past, Boston, 1883, p. 348.

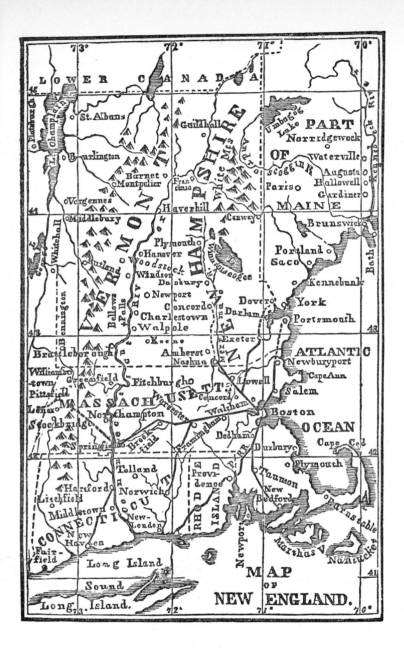

MAP
OF
NEW ENGLAND.

In 1844 the Almanac gives a table exhibiting the twelve
hundred miles of railroad connected with Boston : —

TABLE,

*Showing the length of Railway radiating from, and in connection
with, the City of Boston.*

	Miles.
From Boston, via Albany, to Buffalo, ...	518
" " " Portsmouth, to Portland, ...	104
" " " Lowell, Nashua, Concord, ...	62
" " to Providence, ...	41
" Providence to Stonington, ...	47
Branch from Wilmington to Dover, N. H., ...	44
Dedham branch, ...	2
Taunton branch, and extension to New Bedford, . . .	35
Bedford and Fall River, ...	13
Norwich and Worcester, ...	58½
New Haven to Hartford, 36, and extension to Springfield, 24 miles, all not completed, but in a fair way, . .	60
West Stockbridge to Bridgeport, ...	98
West Stockbridge to Hudson, ...	33
Troy to Schenectady, ...	22
Troy to Ballston, ...	20
Schenectady and Saratoga, ...	21
Lockport, Niagara Falls, and Buffalo, ...	43
	1,221½

In 1845 there appears, along with the old Table of Roads,
a list of " Towns, &c. passed through by Railroads from
Boston, with the distances of the various stations from that
city " ; but it occupies only a quarter of the space required
by its venerable rival. In 1846 the old list of stage roads,
which had been a feature of the Almanac for more than
fifty years, was dropped, as no longer valuable enough to
pay for the space which it occupied. The railroad had
conquered.

The Road Lists just referred to, which came out year by year in the Almanac from 1793 to 1845, are of considerable interest in more ways than one. That for 1802 is reproduced below, in what is practically a facsimile of the original typography. The system of inland communication, we observe, was well developed. It extended from Quebec to Savannah, and from the Atlantic coast to the Ohio. The post-road from Boston to Savannah covered more than twelve hundred miles. From Fishkill, New York, to the Ohio was four hundred and twenty-nine miles, and then one might continue, in the words of the Almanac, "down the Ohio to the mouth of the Muskingum" ninety-five miles farther. The stations, if we may give them that name, on the Ohio road, have more than once a suggestion of romance, or, at all events, of wild life and pioneering. We met with such designations as "Clark's Gap," "Over the Blue Mountain to Skinner's," "Fork of the old Pennsylvania and Glade Roads," "Shumral's Ferry at the Youghiegany River, or Bud's Ferry, 2 miles further up," and, best of all, "Over the Path Valley and Tuscarora Mountains to the Burnt Cabins." The tavern at the "foot of Skillinghill" was kept by a Mr. Panther.

The mention of "those who keep Houses of Entertainment" lends especial value to these Road Lists. The New Englander will recognize a host of familiar surnames and many inns that were famous enough in their day. He may even encounter some of his own ancestors, and he will at all events make the acquaintance of quasi-public functionaries to whom his forefathers were indebted for substantial good cheer. It might be invidious to distinguish particular hostelries, but it can do no harm to point out, opposite "Dedham," the significant word "Ames," which reminds us of the Sun tavern which the old doctor advertised so successfully in the middle of the eighteenth century (see p. 264 above).

ROADS

To the principal Towns on the Continent, from *Boston*, with the Names of thofe who keep Houfes of Entertainment.

☞ *The Author of this Almanack will be greatly obliged to any Gentleman for a correct Lift of the Innkeepers, Diftances, &c. on any Poft-Road herein mentioned, fealed up and lodged at the Sign of the Lamb, Bofton, directed to R. B. Thomas, Sterling.*

From *Bofton* to *Newport*, over *Seekhonk*, through *Rehoboth*. Miles	Wellfleet Collins & Lombard 9	Dedham Everet 2
Roxbury Whiting 8	Truro Knowles 7	Walpole Smith, Billings & Smith 3
Dedham Ames & Gay 5	ditto Stevens 1	Wrentham Hatch 4
Ellis 3	Provincetown Nickerfon 7	ditto Bolcom 4
Walpole Polley 7	—	Attleborough Hawes 5
Wrentham Druce 6	117	ditto Newell 4
Attleborough Holmes 5		ditto Barrows 2
Newell 4	**To *Martha's Vineyard*.**	Seekhonk Plain Sabins 2
Rehoboth Carpenter 7	Sandwich Feffenden 60	Patucket Slack 1
Warren Cole 8	Falmouth Fifh 10	Providence Holmes, Hartfhorn & Bafter 4
Briftol Bourn 4	Falmouthtown Hatch 8	—
Ferry-Houfe Pearfe 2	Wood's Hole Parker 4	45
Portfmouth Congden 7	Over the ferry to Vineyard 9	
Newport 5	—	**To *Charleftown*, (*New-Hampfhire*) & Crown-point.**
—	91	Watertown Willington 8
69		Waltham Townfend 2
To *Plymouth* & *Cape Cod*.	**Road to *Taunton*, *Somerfet*, *Warren*, *Briftol*, and *Newport*.**	Concord Parkman 10
Roxbury Kent 4	Milton Vofe 7	Acton Jones 5
Milton Pierce 3	ditto Bradley 3	Harvard Parkhurft 8
Quincy Marfh 2	Canton Bent 4	ditto Atherton 2
ditto Salifbury 2	ditto May 1	Fitchburgh Cowden 11
Weymouth Arnold 1	ditto Crane 2	ditto Upton 3
ditto Rice 3	Sharon Savage 2	Weftminfter Cooper 1
Hingham Waters 3	Eafton Wetherbery 5	Afhburnham Cufhing 2
Scituate Collamore 4	Taunton Porter, Bolcum & Hodges 12	ditto Ruffell 1
Hanover Wales 5	Dighton Dean and Brown 7	Winchendon Hale 1
Pembroke Baker 4	Somerfet Davis 4	ditto Kidder 4
Kingfton Little 6	Swanzey Chace 5	Fitzwilliam Stone 4
Plymouth Bartlett & Witherell 4	Warren 5	ditto Reed 5
ditto Cornifh 6	Briftol Keith 4	New Marlbro' Switcher
ditto Ellis 5	Over the ferry to Newport Townfend 13	ditto Roberts 8
Sandwich Newcomb & Feffenden 7	—	Keene Richardfon
Barnftable Howland, Baxter & Chipman 8	74	ditto Bullard
ditto Loring & Crocker 4		ditto Edwards 6
Yarmouth Baffet 3	**Poft-Road to *Providence*.**	Walpole Moore 10
Thatcher 5	Roxbury Whiting 8	ditto Bellows 2d 4
Harwich Silk 7	ditto Draper 1	ditto Bellows 3
ditto Clark & Snow 1	Dedham Gay & Clap 2	Charleftown Stone 9
Eaftham Knowles 6	ditto Ellis 3	ditto Willard & Carpenter 1
ditto Knowles 3		Nott's ferry 5
		Springfield Stevens 3

WeathersfieldSpafford 2
Cavendish Pain 6
ditto Coffin 5
Otter Creek Botton 20
Rutland Meed 6
Pittsford Waters 6
Shoreham Moore 20
Bridport Toinner 8
Crownpoint 2
———
196

To *Montreal* & *Quebec.*
[*From Walpole Bridge, a
new route.*]
Walpole Bridge 103
(*See the foregoing lift.*)
Over the Bridge
Rockingham Webb 5
Chefter Kimball 7
Cavendifh Dutton 9
Ludlow Reed 3
Mountholly Green 5
ditto Bentt 2
Shrewfbury Roberfon 5
Clarendon Bowman 6
Rutland Reed 5
ditto Finton 1
Pittsford Ewings 6
ditto Antony 2
Brendon Gilbert 5
Leicefter Woodard 7
Salifbury Heard 6
Middlebury Mattock 6
Vergennes Hollifter 12
Ferrifburg Burt 7
Charlotte Williams 4
Shelburn Pearfons 4
Burlington Ames 7
Milton Mansfield 14
Acrofs the found to
South Hero 6
The Gut between N.
& S. Hero Gordon 12
Ferry to N. Hero 1
Hervey's Ferry 7
Alburgh 1
Savage's Point 4
Latitude 45° Seat &
Grig's 8
Barrows's 8
Wattoy's 5
Chefhere's 8
St. John's Gill 4
Leproire 18

Montreal 6
Trois Rivieres 90
Quebec 80
———
489

To *Charleftown,* (*New-
Hampfhire.*)
Menotomy Ruffel 5
ditto Whittemore 1
Lexington Brown 3
ditto Munro 1
ditto Dudley &
Merriam 1
ditto Benjamin 2
Lincoln Hartwell 4
Concord Richardfon 3
Acton White 5
Littleton Gilbert 5
Groton Richardfon 8
Shirley Sawtel 5
Lunenburgh Good-
rich & Whitney 5
Fitchburgh Cowden 4
Afhburnham Cufhing 7
———
57
Thence to Charleftown
as in the beforemen-
tioned lift.

To *Dartmouth College.*
Charleftown
Willard 119
(See above.)
Claremont Afhley 6
ditto Cook 4
Cornifh Chafe 5
Plainfield Safford 7
Lebanon Hall 6
Hanover Brewfter 4
———
151

To *Norwich* and *New-
London.*
Attleborough Newel 36
Providence Rice 9
Johnfon Sheldon 3
Fifke 5
Scituate Angel 4
ditto Taylor 6
Coventry Knox 4
Volentown Dorance 4
Plainfield Eaton 4

Newent Burnham 8
Norwich Lathrop 7
Mohegan Houghton 7
New-London Douglas 7
———
104

Upper Road to *Exeter*
and *Portland.*
Medford Blanchard 5
Woburn Blackhorfe 3
ditto Fowle 3
Wilmington
Blanchard 4
Andover Abbot 8
Haverhill Charlton 9
Plaftow Sawyer 5
Kingfton Blake 6
Exeter Folfom 5
Stratham Folfom 5
Newmarket Folfom 5
Durham Gage 4
Dover Shannon 6
Berwick Butler 6
ditto Thomfon 2
ditto Hays 3
Wells Littlefield 7
Kennebunk Bernard
& Howard 9
Biddeford Hooper 10
Saco Bridge Spring
Pepperelbo. Bradbury 4
Scarborough Milikin 2
ditto Marfh 4
ditto March 2
Stroudwater Broad 5
Portland Greele &
Motley 4
———
127

Poft-Road to *Salem
Newbury-Port,* and
Portfmouth.
(Over Malden Bridge)
Malden Bridge Page 2
(New road)
To Lynn Newell 6
Danvers Frye 7
Salem Webb and Buf-
fington 1
Beverly Goodridge 2
Baker 1¾
Wenham Porter 2½

Hamilton	Brown& Adams 2
Ipfwich	Swazey & Treadwell 4
Rowley	Parley & Bifhop 4
Newbury-Port	Davenport 8
Merrimack	Bridge Pearfon 3
Hampton falls	Wells 7
Hampton	Leavitt 5
Northampton	Leavitt & Dearbon 2
Greenland	Hufe 5
Portfmouth	Brewfter,
Greenleaf, Geddes	
& Davenport 5	
	——
	67

Road to *Machias*.
(To Portfmouth, as above.)

From Portfmouth, over the Ferry	1
Portfmouth Ferry	Rice 3
York	Emerfon & Preble 9
ditto Sewall & Wyer	5
ditto	Cole 11
Kennebunk	Bernard & Jaffry 4
Biddeford	Hooper 9
ditto	Spring
Pepperelbo.	Bradbury 4
Scarborough	Burbank 1
ditto	Milikin 2
ditto	Harmen 2
ditto	Marfh 2
Falmouth	Broad 4
ditto	Pollard 4
Portland	Motley,
Greele & Hufton 4	
New-Cafco	Bucknam 7
North Yarmouth	Loring 6
ditto	Elwell 2
Freeport	Cummings 9
Brunfwick	Chafe 5
Brunfwick Falls	Stone 5
Bath	Lambert 12
Herndell's Ferry	2
Wifcaffet	Whittier 11

New-Caftle Ferry	Avery 5
ditto	Nichols 2
Nobleborough	Huffey 5
Waldoborough	Reed 2
ditto	Sampfon 7
Cufhing	Packard 9
St. George's Ferry	1
Camden	Gregory 7
Maduncook	
	M'Clathry 7
Duck Trap	Ulmer 7
Belfaft	Mitchell 12
Frankfort	Black 12
The Ferry	1
Blue Hill	Parker 13
ditto	Patten 7
Union River	Milliken 7
Kilkenny	Gookins 6
Gouldfboro'	Jones 19
Machias	Longfellow 40
	——
	358

From *Bofton* to *Paffamaquoddy*.

To Salem	15
Ipfwich	12
Newbury-Port	12
Portfmouth	22
York	12
Wells	16
Biddeford	14
Portland	18
N. Yarmouth	15
Brunfwick	15
Bath	12
Wifcaffet	13
Penobfcot	70
Frenchman's Bay	42
Machias	40
Paffamaquoddy	48
	——
	376

Middle Road to *Hartford* and *New Haven*.

Dedham	Ames 11
ditto	Colburn 3
Medfield	Clark 6
Medway	Richardfon 5
Bellingham	Smith 6
Milford	Penniman 4
Mendon	Miller and Fuller 2

Uxbridge	Taft 6
Douglafs	Whipple 5
Thompfon	Jacobs 7
ditto	Nichols 2
Pomfret	Grofvenor 7
Afhford	Spring 7
ditto	Perkins 3
ditto	Clark 2
Wilmington	Utley 4
Mansfield	Dunham 4
Coventry	Kimball 6
E. Hartford	Woodbridge 6
ditto	Little 9
Hartford	Bull 1
Weathersfield	Wright 4
Worthington	Riley 9
Meriden	Robinfon 5
Wallingford	Carrington 4
North-Haven	Ives 5
New-Haven	Nichols and Butler 8
	——
	142

Weftern Poft-Road to *Hartford* and *New-York*, according to the new meafurement.

Cambridge	Brown 3
Watertown	Willington 4
Wefton	Flagg 8
Sudbury	Howe 5
ditto	Howe 5
Marlboro'	Williams 6
Northboro'	Munroe 5
Shrewfbury	Peafe 4
Worcefter	Mower 8
Leicefter	Hobart 6
Spencer	Mafons 5
Brookfield	Draper 3
Weftern	Blair 5
Palmer	Bates 9
Wilbraham	Grofvenor 4
Springfield	Williams 10
Suffield	Sykes 10
Windfor	Picket 7
	Allen 7
Hartford	Lee 3
Weathersfield	Williams 10
Middleton	†Johnfon 8

Durham †Canfield 6	Crown-Point 15	Peterfham Dickerfon 2
Wallingsford †Car-rington 8	Willfborough 20	ditto Ward 1
North-Haven Ives 6	Fort St. John 60	Orange Cady 6
New-Haven †Brown 7	Le Prairie 16	ditto Mayo 1
Milford Clarke 10	Montreal 6	Warwick Pomeroy 7
Stratford Ferry Gillet 2	Trois Rivieres 90	South Road 5
Stratford †Lovejoy 2	Quebec 80	Northfield Hunt,
Fairfield †Pennfield 10	— 568	Whitney & Doolittle, N. R. 8
Greenfarms Paffel 8		Hinfdale Howe 8
Norwalk †Reed 4	From *Bofton* to *Albany*	Brattleboro' Dickerfon 6
Stamford †Webb 9	on the *Hartford Road.*	Marlbro' Stockwell 4
Horfeneck †Knapp 6	Weftern Blair 73	ditto Whitney 6
Rye †Quintard 6	Ware Quintin 6	Wilmington Cook 4
Maroneck Horton 4	Belcher Town	ditto Thompfon 2
New-Rochel Williams 4	Dunbar 7	Reedfboro' Hartwell 6
Eaft-Chefter Gyon 4	Hadley White 6	ditto — 4
Kingfbury †Hoyt 4	do. Warner 3	Woodford Scott 5
Harlem Hafley 5	N. Hampton	Bennington Deway,
New-York †Beckman 9	Pomeroy 3	Fay, Grifwold and
— 254	do. Edwards 5	Hathaway 7
	Chefterfield Merrick 7	— 155
	Worthington Fitch 6	

N. B. Where the Mail Stage ftops, the names of the Inkeepers are marked thus [†].

To *Albany* and *Quebec.*
Springfield Parfons 96
Over the river to Ely's 2
Weftfield Clap 7
ditto Emerfon 3
Plandford Knox 6
Greenwood Rowley 6
ditto Emerfon 3
Tyrinyham Chadwick 7
Great-Barrington Root 9
ditto Whiting 1
Egremont Hicks 4
Nobletown Cowles 4
ditto Mackinftry 3
ditto Ray 3
Stonehole Hoggaboom 3
Kinderhook Goofe 4
ditto Voubarg 1
ditto Fitch 2
Albany Ferry 8
Halfmoon 12
Stillwater 13
Saratoga 12
Fort Edward 20
Lake-George 14
Ticonderoga 30

Patridgefield Badger 8
do. Whiting 3
Dalton Waterman 3
Pittsfield Allen 6
Hancock Broad 5
New Lebanon
Springs 2
Canaan Jones 2
Stevenftown Bufh 7
Schoodick Strong 6
do. McKowns 9
Green Bufh
Van Haden 2
Albany Ferry 3
Albany 1
— 173

Road to *Peterfham* and *Bennington.*
Shrewfbury Peafe 40
ditto Cufhen 1
Worcefter Bigelow 4
Holden Parker 3
ditto Abbot 3
ditto Davis 1
Rutland Wood 4
ditto Henry 1
Oakham Kelley 5
Barre Nurfe 4
ditto Smith 2
Peterfham Peckham 5

Poft-Road to *Windfor,* (*Vermont.*)
[From Springfield].
Springfield Williams 50
Upper Ferry 1
WeftSpringfieldMiller 7
Northampton Lyman 6
ditto Pomeroy 5
Hatfield White 4
Whately Gad Smith 6
Deerfield Hoyt 8
Greenfield Willard 3
Munn
Barnardfton Alverd 11
Brattlebo. Dickerfon 10
Putney Goodwin 11
Weftminfter Spooner 10
Walpole Bridge 3
Charleftown, No. 4
Willard 7
Claremont Hubbard 7
Windfor Conant 11
— 160

Road from *Bofton* to *Keene* in *New-Hampfhire.*
To Cambridge Brown 3
Lexington Munroe 8
Concord Richardfon 8

Littleton Kedder 9	Lexington Munroe 4	To Alexandria 504
Groton Richardson 10	Lincoln Benjamin 5	Colchester 16
Warren 9	Concord Wyman &	Dumfries 12
Townsend Stone 1	Paine 4	Fredericksburg 25
Jaffray Prescot 15	Stow Russell 8	Bowling Green 22
Part of New-Ipswich	Bolton Homer 6	Hanover 25
Mulliken 5	Lancaster Williams 5	Richmond 22
Marlborough Sweet-	Leominster Hale 8	Petersburg 25
ser, Longley 13	——	Halifax 75
Keene Wells & Ed-	47	Tarburg 37
wards 6		Smithfield 60
——	From *Boston* to *Groton*,	Fayetteville 50
87	on the *Leominster*	Greeno 75
	Road.	Campden 55
From *Keene* in *New-*	To Concord Wyman	Columbia 35
Hampshire to *Dart-*	& Paine 20	Cambridge 80
mouth-College	Littleton Kidder 8	Augusta 50
To Walpole Bullards 14	Groton Richardson 8	Savannah 120
—— Reddington 2½		
Charlestown Hunt 5½	36	1288
—— Allen 4		
Claremont Stearnes 11	From *Boston* to *Savannah*	From *Philadelphia*
Windsor Pettes 7	in *Georgia*, Post-Road.	to *Washington*, via
Hartland Ferry 9	To Worcester 48	*Lancaster.*
Dartmouth College	Springfield 48	To Buck Tav. 11
Brewster, Dewey 9	Hartford in Conn. 28	Warren Tavern 12
——	Middleton 14	Downing's 10
62	New Haven 26	Waggon & Whitaker's 8
	Stratford 14	M'Cleland's 9
Road from *Worcester* to	Fairfield 8	Bresler's 9
Providence.	Norwalk 12	Lancaster Court House
From the Court House	Stanford 10	Slough 7
to Harrington's 3	Kingsbridge 30	Wright's Ferry 11
Grafton Drury 3	New York 14	Over Susquehannah 1
ditto Woods or Barnes 5	Newark 9	To Yorkt. Sponglen 11
Upton Kingsley 4	Elizabethtown 6	Paradise 9
Mendon Miller &	Bridgetown 6	Hanover Eckelburgus 9
Fuller 6	Woodbridge 4	MARYLAND.
ditto Aldrich 6	New Brunswick 10	Tawnytown Crapster 16
Cumberland Fisk or	Princetown 18	Pine Creek Cookerly 12
Lovet 6	Trenton 12	Frederickto.Kimball 13
ditto Jenks 4	Bristol 10	Tillard 9
ditto Whipple 2	Philadelphia 20	Seneca 11
Smithfield Aldrich 1	Chester 16	Montgomery Court H.
North Providence	Wilmington 13	Ogle 10
Winslow 4	Christiana Bridge 11	Georgetown Suter 12
Providence Thayer 1	Ellston 10	Washington, to the
——	Charlestown 10	Capitol 3
45	Haver de Grace 6	——
	Hertford 12	193
From *Boston* to *Leomin-*	Baltimore 25	From *Philadelphia* to
ster.	Bladensburg 38	*Bethlehem.*
To Cambridge	Alexandria 16	To Germantown
Brown 3	——	Sayers 8
Menotomy Whitman 4	504	

Weaver 12	Wantage Hinchman 7	Fork of the old Penn-
Seller 11	ditto Randall 8	fylvania and Glade
Quakertown Roberts 6	Suffex Court-Houfe	Roads Bonnet 4
Cooper 7	Willis 14	Foot of Dryridge Mac-
Bethlehem 8	Hardwick Goble 5	cracken or Wirth 3
——	Old Moravian town	Medfkar 6
52	Gambol 11	Hew's Camping-
	Oxford White 12	Ground Ditty 5
To *Bethlehem*, via *New-*	Eaftown Shannon 10	Foot of Alleghany
York.	Bethlehem Elbert 12	Grindall 6
	Allenftown Miller 6	Glades Black 7
New-York to Newark 9	Mexetony Kemp 16	ditto Colpenny 9
Springfield 7	Reading Zoll 18	ditto Brake 5
Scotch Plains 16	Womminftown Wick-	Foot of Laurel hill
Bound Brook	erlane 13	Shaver 1
Somerfet Court Houfe 8	Merriftown Bulmas 9	Phlifbury 7
Reading 11	Lebanon Shingle 7	Carnes 3
Grandiner's Mills 9	Millerftown Rice 5	Cherry 7
Hickery's Tavern 4	Humbleftown Lin-	Mount Pleafant
M'Henry's 8	coln 12	Knuby 3
Eaftown 12	River Succetarra 1	Thomfon 5
Bethlehem 8	Harrifburgh (upon the	Shumral's Ferry at the
	Sufquehanna) Grimes 8	Youghiegany River,
92	Carlifle Fofter 16	or Bud's Ferry, 2 miles
	ditto Alexander 7	further up 10
	ditto Maccracken 7	Patterfon 3
Road from *Fifhkill* to	Shippinfboro' Rippy 7	Devore's Ferry at the
the *Ohio River.*	Clark's Gap Cooper 10	Monongahela
	Over the Blue Moun-	Patterfon 9
From Fifhkill to the	tain to Skinner's 3	Wafhington C. H.
Ferry 5	Over the Path Valley	Maccarmick 11
Over the Ferry to	and Tuscarora Moun-	Well's Mills 16
Newboro' 2	tains to the Burnt Cab-	Coxe's fort on the fouth-
Bethlehem	ins Jemmerfon 8	ern Banks of the Ohio 10
Edmondfon 4	Fort-Littleton Bird 4	Down the Ohio to the
Bloomingfgrove Gold-	Foot of Skillinghill	mouth of the Mufkin-
fmith 8	Panther 10	gum 95
Chefter Gilverton 8	Juncita Martin 9	——
Warwick Smith 9	Bedford Wirth 14	524

BOOKS AND STATIONARY.

JOHN WEST,

At his Book-Store, No. 75, Cornhill, Bofton,

KEEPS conftantly for Sale, a well-afforted and large Collection of BOOKS, in every Branch of Literature. *Alfo,* Bibles,
Teftaments Pfalters, Spelling-Books of every kind, Pfalm-Books, Prim-
ers, &c. by the grofs, dozen, or fingle; together with every Article in
the STATIONARY line; with all which Country Merchants and
others may be fupplied, *Wholefale or Retail.*

☞ Social and Private Libraries fupplied on reafonable terms.

1803. January 18. Old *Experience* says, (and she generally speaks the truth) that pork, killed about this time, will always come out of the pot as large as when it was put in.

In the seventeenth and eighteenth centuries the influence of the moon on animal and vegetable life was not merely an article of faith among the ignorant. It was an accepted tenet of science, though there was some doubt as to the precise limits of this influence. Cotton Mather, perhaps, will hardly be allowed to " qualify as an expert " — though his reputation for exceptional credulity comes rather from his having put himself on record than from any peculiarity in his mental temper. But no one will deny that Robert Boyle, the founder of the Royal Society, the improver of the air-pump, and the discoverer of Boyle's Law of the elasticity of gases, was a genuinely scientific personage. Mather writes : —

One Abigail Eliot had an iron struck into her head, which drew out part of her brains with it : a silver plate she afterwards wore on her skull where the orifice remain'd as big as an half crown. The brains left in the child's head would swell and swage, according to the *tides ;* her intellectuals were not hurt by this disaster ; and she liv'd to be a mother of several children.[1]

And Boyle records " an odd observation about the influence of the moon " in the following terms : —

I know an intelligent person, that having, by a very dangerous fall, so broken his head, that divers large pieces of his skull were taken out, as I could easily perceive by the wide scars, that still remain ; answered me, that for divers months, that he lay under the chirurgeons hands, he constantly observed, that about full moon, there would be extraordinary prickings and shootings in the wounded parts of his head, as if the meninges were stretched

[1] Magnalia, book vi, chap. 2, ed. 1853, II, 356.

or pressed against the rugged parts of the broken skull; and this with so much pain, as would for two or three nights hinder his sleep, of which at all other times of the moon he used to enjoy a competency. And this gentleman added, that the chirurgeons, (for he had three or four at once) observed from month to month, as well as he, the operation of the full moon upon his head, informing him, that they then manifestly perceived an expansion or intumescence of his brain, which appeared not at all at the new moon, (for that I particularly asked) nor was he then obnoxious to the forementioned pricking pains.[1]

Toward the end of the eighteenth century it was generally held by physicians that the new or full moon, or the approach to the new or full moon, was a powerful exciting cause of fever.[2]   It had also been observed that persons in extreme age usually died either at the new or at the full moon, though it is not clear how this was brought into accord with the usual theories of the moon's increase.[3]

If we pass over to the vegetable kingdom, we have a first-rate witness in the Rev. Dr. Samuel Deane (1733–1814), for many years pastor of the First Church at Portland, Maine. Dr. Deane was neither superstitious nor opinionated. He was a man of learning, singularly clear-headed, and moderate always. Besides, he was a wit. When he was a tutor at Harvard College, we are told, he ventured a harmless jest. A visitor, to whom he was exhibiting the curiosities in the College Museum, noticed a long rusty sword, and asked to whom it had belonged. " I believe," replied Mr. Deane, " that it was the sword with which Balaam threatened to kill his ass." " But," objected the stranger, " Balaam had no sword; he only wished for one." " Oh, true," said Mr. Deane, " *that* is the one he

---

[1] Experimenta et Observationes Physicae, chap. 5, experiment 4; Works, ed. Birch, V, 96.

[2] See Gentleman's Magazine, 1787, LVII, 340.

[3] Gentleman's Magazine, 1803, LXXIII, 1001.

wished for."[1] This anecdote is traditional, but there is
another specimen of the doctor's humor which we have
in his own handwriting. Portland (then Falmouth) was
burned by the British naval commander Mowat in 1775.
There was intense indignation, and Dr. Deane suggested,
as an inscription for a plan of the town published shortly
after, a brief statement of the facts, in which Captain
Mowat is described as "that execrable scoundrel and
monster of ingratitude." At the end of the letter in
which he expresses these sentiments, Dr. Deane admits a
possible emendation: "If you do not like the words
execrable scoundrel, you may say, *infamous incendiary*, or
what you please."[2]

Like most New England ministers of the time, Dr.
Deane was a practical farmer. He also kept a diary, on
the blank pages of interleaved almanacs, and under the
year 1767 we read: — "May 4. I planted short beans,
sowed cauliflowers and apple seeds, being increase of the
moon. 5. I planted corn and potatoes, increase of the
moon."[3]

But Dr. Deane was not merely a practical farmer. He
was a close student of agriculture. In 1790 he issued an
octavo called The New England Farmer, or Georgical
Dictionary, which was accurately described in the pro-
spectus as "a more complete system of husbandry than
has been before published in so small a compass," and as
"the only one that has been attempted in this country, or
that is adapted to its circumstances." This was a work
of great merit, and enjoyed a continuous popularity of
about fifty years. Here is Dr. Deane's method of keeping
apples in good condition: —

[1] Journals of the Rev. Thomas Smith, and the Rev. Samuel Deane, ed.
by Wm. Willis, Portland, 1849, p. 292.
[2] The same, p. 341, note.
[3] The same, p. 321.

The secret of preserving them through the winter, in a sound state, is of no small importance. Some say, that shutting them up in tight casks is an effectual method; and it seems probable; for they soon rot in open air.

But an easier method, and which has recommended itself to me by the experience of several years, is as follows : — I gather them about noon, on the day of the full of the moon, which happens in the latter part of September, or beginning of October. Then spread them in a chamber, or garret, where they lie till about the last of November. Then, at a time when the weather is dry, remove them into casks, or boxes, in the cellar, out of the way of the frost; but I prefer a cool part of the cellar. With this management, I find I can keep them till the last of May, so well that not one in fifty will rot.

.   .   .   .

Some may think it whimsical to gather them on the day above mentioned. But, as we know both animals and vegetables are influenced by the moon in some cases, why may we not suppose a greater quantity of spirit is sent up into the fruit, when the attraction of the heavenly bodies is greatest? If so, I gather my apples at the time of their greatest perfection, when they have most in them that tends to their preservation. — I suspect that the day of the moon's conjunction with the sun may answer as well; but I have not had experience of it. The same caution, I doubt not, should be observed in gathering other fruits, and even apples for cyder : But I have not proved it by experiments.[1]

This passage, which must be accepted as the doctrine of a scientific farmer at the close of the eighteenth century, was reproduced, with due acknowledgments, in the Almanac for 1796, where it appears on the back of the title-page.

Mr. Thomas, it will be remembered, suggested mowing bushes, and " killing them if you·can," in the old moon, " sign in heart." There is a suspicion of raillery in these

[1] The New England Farmer, Worcester, 1790, p. 12 ; 2d ed., 1797, p. 14.

words, but the principle which they embody had long
been accepted among farmers. One of the best accredited
writers on agriculture in the eighteenth century was the
Rev. Jared Eliot of Killingly, Connecticut. In the first of
his Essays on Field-Husbandry, Mr. Eliot remarks that
he has been " told by an experienc'd Farmer, that if you
girdle Trees, or cut Brush in the Months of *May, June* and
July, in the Old of the Moon, that Day the Sign removes
out of the Foot into the Head, especially if the Day be
cloudy, it will kill almost all before it." [1] Mr. Eliot, however, refused to be convinced without testing the matter.
" Experience," he observes, " is Authority, to whom we
are to submit, I am not forward to believe without Trial."
This was in 1747. The subject was felt to be of some
moment. Farmers had to clear their land, and underbrush was a great nuisance and hard to kill. Accordingly,
some five years later, we have the results of an experiment,
and they are curious enough to give in Mr. Eliot's own
words. Any attempt to condense would destroy the individuality of his style. He has now found " certain Times
for cutting Bushes, which [are] more effectual for their
Destruction than any yet discovered " : —

> The Times are in the Months of *June, July* and *August; in
> the old Moon that Day the Sign is in the Heart :* It will not always
> happen every Month ; it happens so but once this Year, and that
> proves to be on Sunday. Last Year in *June* or *July,* I forgot
> which, I sent a Man to make Trial ; in going to the Place, some
> of the Neighbours understanding by him the Business he was
> going about, and the Reason of his going at that Point of Time,
> they also went to their Land, and cut Bushes also on that Day ;
> their's were tall Bushes that had never been cut ; mine were short
> bushes such as had been often cut, but to no Purpose, without it
> was to increase their Number: The Consequence was, that in

[1] Essays upon Field-Husbandry in New-England, Boston, 1760, p. 16.

every Place it killed so universally, that there is not left alive, scarce one in a hundred; the Trial was made in three or four Places on that same Day. In *July* or *August*, on the critical Day, another Swamp was cut, the Brush was, the greatest Part of it, Swamp Button Wood, the most difficult to subdue of any Wood I know; I have been lately to see it, and find the Destruction of these Bushes are not so universal as among Alders and other Sorts of Growth; it is hard to say how many remain alive, it may be one third or a quarter Part; all that I can say, with Certainty, is that they are now few, compared with what there was last Year: I did not know but that those which are alive, might be such as came up since; but upon Examination, I found the last Year's Stumps, and could plainly see where they had been cut of; this was not because the Season was better when there was such Success; for in this last mentioned Piece of Swamp, there were sundry Spots of Alders and other Sorts of Bushes, they seem to be as universally killed as those before mentioned: The Reason why there was not the same Success attending the cutting these Button Bushes as the other Sorts, I suppose to be from the stubborn Nature of this Kind, which would yield to no cutting; the ordinary Way has been to dig or plough it up by the Roots; so that considering the Nature of this Bush, I have had great Success; the Ground being very boggy, those who mowed them, were obliged to cut them very high, which was another Disadvantage.

To show such a Regard to the Signs, may incur the Imputation of Ignorance or Superstition; for the Learned know well enough, that the Division of the Zodiac into Twelve Signs, and the appropriating these to the several Parts of the animal Body, is not the Work of Nature, but of Art, contrived by Astronomers for Convenience. It is also as well known, that the Moon's Attraction hath great Influence on all Fluids.

It is also well known to Farmers, that there are Times when Bushes, if cut at such a Time, will universally die. A Regard to the Sign, as it serveth to point out and direct to the proper Time, so it becomes worthy of Observation.

If Farmers attend the Time with Care, and employ Hands on those Days, they will find their Account in it.[1]

This passage from " the curious and learned Dr. Elliot," as Mr. Thomas calls him, is inserted in the Almanac for 1803, but without any comment, whether favorable or adverse.

In 1805 Mr. Thomas prints a letter from an unknown correspondent, whose signature is *P. S.* and who describes himself as " an old Ploughjogger." It contains an observation with regard to the effect of the moon on fruit trees which may profitably be compared with the principles laid down by Mr. Deane. Mr. Thomas does not say what he thinks of the Ploughjogger's theory.

There is one thing however, I have always admired that you, or some other writer on fruit trees never have mentioned, though I think it well worth observing, which is, setting fruit trees in the old of the moon, that they never thrive so well, and it is rare that any come to perfection, but, generally turn to shrubs or die in a few years. — I am, Sir, an old farmer, upwards of seventy-five years of age, and this I have proved by my own experience, as well as by observing it of others, whom I could point out, but I think it needless. Apple trees as well as all other fruit trees should be set out in the new of the moon, and the top cut down until there are no more limbs on the top than roots on the bottom, a tree thus pruned will grow more in four years than one that is not, will do in ten. I have another observation, Sir, to make, which is, on the cutting and preserving scions for grafting ; these should be taken off in the last of March and tied in a bundle, and buried in the ground five and six inches deep, there to remain until the bud begins to open, and the moon changes, then they should be taken up and the dirt washed off in cold water, when they are fit for grafting ; these will be plump and grow four times as well as those that have been lying in a cellar and become wilted.

---

[1] Essays, as above, pp. 123-4.

There is nothing strange in the doctrines of Dr. Deane, Mr. Eliot, and the old Ploughjogger. They are not offshoots of superstition, but merely a slight aberration of science. We must not confuse the attitude of these sober experimenters with the whimsies of astrological theorists a century before, to whom the planets were the lords of life and death, of growth and decay, and who held that the wholesomeness and medicinal virtue of plants depended as well on the planet under which they were gathered as on that under which they were eaten or administered to the patient. Such a philosopher was Israel Hübner, whose Mystery of Seals, Herbs, and Stones, was translated by one B. Clayton, and published at London in 1698. Hübner was Professor of Mathematics in the University of Erfurt, and his work is full of perverse learning. Lunar diseases, according to his system, were ulcers, measles and spots on the face, cataracts, epilepsy, and dysentery. Among herbs, roots, and trees under the especial influence of the moon he includes beans, cabbages, cucumbers, lettuce, mandrake, pompions (i. e. pumpkins), plum trees, and watercresses. On the tenth of March, 1698, "at 31 minutes past 7 at Night, the *Moon* is in Mid-Heaven with 31 Testimonies. At which time you must cut up or gather the *Herbs* and *Roots* of the *Moon*; you may provide your self half an hour before-hand, but the *Herb* or *Root* must be cut or gathered at 31 minutes past Seven, and put into a pale, white or grey coloured Silk bag, and kept till Occasion serves." How these vagaries were received may be inferred from a commendatory poem by Gadbury, the astrologer and almanac-maker, which is prefixed to Clayton's volume, and which declares that "the World is govern'd by Stars Energy" and that every physician "must have a Warrant from the spangled Skies"!

WHAT TO READ

MR. THOMAS does not neglect to recommend suitable reading to the farmer. His Calendars for December contain many items of this sort, suitably intermingled with directions for threshing, putting sleds and sleighs in order, and the several occupations appropriate to the winter season. At other seasons the farmer had enough to do in attending to the diversified agriculture of a time when every estate was its own home market and aimed at being sufficient unto itself so far as the products of the climate would allow. A sample of Mr. Thomas's literary advice may be seen in his very first number (1793) : —

Put your sleds & sleighs in order.

Complete your thrashing.

Visit your barns often.

See that your cellars are well stored with good cider, that wholesome and cheering liquor, which is the product of your own farms : No man is to be pitied, that cannot enjoy himself or his friend, over a pot of good cider, the product of his own country, and perhaps his own farm ; which suits both his constitution and his pocket, much better than West-India spirit.

Now comes on the long and social winter evenings, when the farmer may enjoy himself, and instruct and entertain his family by reading some useful books, of which he will do well in preparing a select number. The following I should recommend, as books worthy the perusal of every American. — RAMSAY's *History of the American Revolution* ; MORSE's *Geography* ; and BELKNAP's *History of New-Hampshire*.

Adjust your accounts; see that your expenditures do not exceed your incomes.

And again, in 1795, we find: —

The winter affords many enjoyment[s] to mankind in general, but to no one class of men more, than to the industrious husband-man, who now sets down at leisure surrounded by all the comforts and necessaries of life pleasingly spending the long winter's evenings in social converse as by reading some useful and entertaining author. "Reading and conversation are, to winter, what flowers are to the spring, and fruits are to autumn. They are the boast of the season. Superior to vernal joys, these permanent pleasures of the intellect are in vigor, when those are faded and no more."

Another specimen may be taken from the Almanac for 1814: —

It is all important that every man should know the history and geography of his own country. — Yet a vast many of us hardly know our right hand from our left in this respect. What more profitable employment can you have during the long winter evenings than reading Hutchinson's history of Massachusetts — Belknap's New-Hampshire — Williams's Vermont — Life of Gen. Washington — American Revolution, Morses' and other Geographies, &c.

The farmer and his family are not to be limited to so solid a diet as this paragraph prescribes. At the end of December, 1794, we read: "The Life of Dr. Franklin, I would recommend for the amusement of winter evenings, also the Life of Baron Trenck." Franklin's Autobiography has become classic. The celebrated Baron Trenck, however, has almost dropped out of sight, though he long remained a popular author with boys. His imprisonments and escapes from durance are still good reading. Many

will remember the exciting moment when he was caught by the leg as he was just getting over the palisades that enclosed his prison. Trenck was regarded as altogether too worldly a writer for Sunday perusal. " Baron Trenck," writes Mr. Aldrich, in his Story of a Bad Boy, " Baron Trenck, who managed to escape from the fortress of Glatz, can't for the life of him get out of our sitting-room " closet on a Sunday.

Mr. Thomas, it will be noticed, was inclined to recommend American authors. There had been much historical writing in this country, and geography, too, was a favorite pursuit in New England. As Dr. Benjamin Trumbull said, in his Century Sermon preached at North Haven, Connecticut, on New Year's Day, 1801, when the Almanac was in its first decade, " by the assistance of the Reverend Dr. Morse's Universal Geography, and that of Dr. Dwight's for schools, school boys know more of geography now, than men did an hundred years ago; nay more than even the writers on geography knew at that period. Besides, several good histories of the colonies have been written during the last century, which have greatly increased their knowledge of each other, and acquainted the world more intimately with their affairs." [1]

There was a large importation of books from England. Booksellers abounded in the country towns, and, what is more, in the last part of the eighteenth century and at the beginning of the nineteenth, there were local presses without number, and cheap copies of standard English authors bearing the imprint of Newburyport, Salem, New Bedford, Exeter, Brattleboro', and so on, were the order of the day. It was likewise a common practice for large publishers to sell books in sheets to the trade in the country, thus allowing them the profit on binding as well as the retail profit. The present centralization of the publishing business

[1] A Century Sermon, New Haven, 1801, p. 6.

makes it rather difficult to appreciate the state of things a hundred years ago.

Mr. Thomas was himself a bookseller, stationer, and bookbinder. The Almanac for 1797 contains an amazing list of what he offered for sale in the little town of Sterling. His Advertisement is reprinted at the end of this chapter. For poetry we have Akenside, Armstrong, Goldsmith, Milton, Thomson's Seasons, and Young's Night Thoughts, not to speak of the facetious Peter Pindar. Ovid's Art of Love is counterbalanced by the lyrics of Dr. Watts. There are also two miscellaneous collections of songs, — the Hive and the Skylark, and, that American verse may not be slighted, the Columbian Muse. Particular attention may be called to the blank-verse Thoughts in Prison by the vain and unfortunate Dr. William Dodd, who, after a brilliant career as a fashionable preacher, was hanged at Tyburn for forgery in 1777. He had been the tutor of Philip Stanhope, godson and successor of the famous Lord Chesterfield whose Letters are also in Mr. Thomas's list.

Mr. Thomas's stock was well furnished with romances and novels. Fielding is represented by Tom Jones and Joseph Andrews; Smollett by Roderick Random; Sterne by the Sentimental Journey; Miss Burney by Evelina and Cecilia, — all of them now admitted to the rank of classics. For downright sensationalism we have Mrs. Radcliffe's Mysteries of Udolpho. Frigid and mechanical as its clumsy horrors seem to our jaded appetites, it gave our forefathers many thrills and was held to be unprofitable by the stricter sort. The venerable Dr. Jacob Bigelow, in his ninetieth year, remembered that, when he was a boy, his cousin, Mary Wilder, who was half-a-dozen years older than he, used to delight the children by telling them Mrs. Radcliffe's story. When he had spent an evening listening to The Mysteries of Udolpho, " he was afraid to be alone in the dark, and, on getting into bed, covered his

head with the bedclothes in terror."[1] This was in 1798,
or thereabout, the very time that we are considering.
Works by the same author to be found in the Sterling
bookstore were A Sicilian Romance and The Romance of
the Forest.

Other works of fiction which Mr. Thomas had for sale
were Desmond, by the once admired Charlotte Smith,
Henry Brooke's interminable Fool of Quality, and Daniel
Defoe's Religious Courtship. For children there was the
highly correct Sandford and Merton. Dr. Johnson's Ras-
selas was of course not lacking, nor were the lacrymose
Man of Feeling by Henry Mackenzie and the same author's
Julia de Roubigné and Man of the World, all unaccountably popular in their time. More important was the Zeluco
of Dr. John Moore, the father of the famous Sir John,
which worked so powerfully on Byron, who calls the
author an "acute and severe observer of mankind"[2] and
says that he once meant Childe Harold for "a modern
Timon, perhaps a poetical Zeluco."[3] Mr. Thomas's customers could also be provided with copies of the Arabian
Nights and of Robinson Crusoe. Obviously the citizens
of Sterling had nothing to complain of, so far as food for
the imagination was concerned.

Sermons, works of theology, and books of devotion are
numerous in Mr. Thomas's catalogue, as was to be expected; but he also had the Second Part of Paine's Age of
Reason — an odd volume, perhaps, which had got stranded
on his shelves. Is it generally known that Tom Paine was
an early champion of that theory of education which sets
modern literature in an unnatural opposition to ancient,
and arrays the natural sciences against them both? His

[1] Memorials of Mary Wilder White, by Elizabeth Amelia Dwight,
edited by Mary Wilder Tileston, Boston, 1903, pp. 23-24.

[2] Preface to Marino Faliero, Works, Poetry, ed. E. H. Coleridge, IV,
334.

[3] Childe Harold, Addition to the Preface, Works, as above, II, 8.

Age of Reason contains the following remarkable utterance on this subject : —

As there is now nothing new to be learned from the dead languages, all the useful books being already translated, the languages are become useless, and the time expended in teaching and in learning them is wasted. . . . It is only in the living languages that new knowledge is to be found. . . . The best Greek linguist, that now exists, does not understand Greek so well as a Grecian plowman did, or a Grecian milkmaid ; and the same for the Latin, compared with a plowman or milkmaid of the Romans ; and with the respect to pronunciation and idiom, not so well as the cows that she milked. It would . . . be advantageous to the state of learning to abolish the study of the dead languages and to make learning consist, as it originally did, in scientific knowledge.[1]

What we have seen of Mr. Thomas's sturdy Americanism would lead us to expect that his shop would be well furnished with American books, and we are not surprised to find among those in his stock the works which he particularly commends in his Farmer's Calendar — Jeremy Belknap's History of New Hampshire, Jedediah Morse's Universal Geography, Lendrum's History of the American Revolution, and the Life of Dr. Franklin. Belknap's American Biography could also be had at Sterling, as well as Lee's Memoirs, Whitney's History of Worcester, and Williams's Vermont.

There was also a considerable variety of books of travel — genuine and fictitious. It is hard to resist the temptation to linger over this category ; but we must content ourselves with a specimen or two.

Carver's Travels must have been of absorbing interest to our grandfathers, and it is still consulted by the ethnologist and the geographer. John Carver, who had been a

_____
[1] Age of Reason, Part I, ed. London, 1818, p. 31.

captain in the French and Indian War, set out from Boston in 1766 to explore the territory which had been added to the British possessions by the Treaty of Versailles in 1763. His design was ambitious in the highest degree. He confidently expected to reach the Pacific coast, and, had he succeeded in this, he meant to urge the government "to establish a post in some of those parts about the Straits of Annian, which, having been discovered by Sir Francis Drake, of course belong to the English." Such a post, he thought, would help to the discovery of the Northwest Passage. It is needless to say that Captain Carver failed to push his way to the Pacific; but he nevertheless accomplished a good deal. He got as far west as the Falls of St. Anthony and did some exploring on the north and east shores of Lake Superior. His narrative, which appeared in 1778, is full of life and motion, and well deserved a place on Mr. Thomas's shelves. A large portion is devoted to describing the manners and customs of the Indians, particularly those of the interior. One episode in this part of the book is of peculiar value. To illustrate the ferocity of the savages, Carver describes the massacre at Fort William Henry, in 1757. He had served as a volunteer among the provincials sent to strengthen the garrison. When the fort surrendered and the slaughter began, he succeeded, — thanks to his strength, agility, and uncommon coolness, — in forcing his way through the Indians and gaining the shelter of the forest. After travelling for three days and nights without food he reached Fort Edward, where, as he rather quaintly observes, "with proper care my body soon recovered its wonted strength, and my mind, as far as the recollection of the late melancholy events would permit, its usual composure."[1] His rapid and vivid account of his escape takes high rank among authentic tales of adventure.

[1] Carver, Travels, London, 1778, p. 324.

21

The story of Philip Quarll, now almost forgotten, was a great favorite in the eighteenth and early nineteenth century, and was reprinted in 1795, from the sixth London edition, by Joseph Belknap, at the Apollo Press, in Boston. This was the first American edition and was probably the form in which Mr. Thomas kept the book for sale. The title is of the good old-fashioned kind and gives a rather full account of the contents. It runs thus: — "The Hermit: or, the Unparalleled Sufferings and Surprising Adventures of Philip Quarll, an Englishman: who was discovered by Mr. Dorrington, a British Merchant, upon an uninhabited Island, in the South-sea; where he lived about fifty years, without any human assistance." Mr. Dorrington, who, it need hardly be specified, is quite as fictitious a character as Quarll himself, found his hermit on a fertile island in the Pacific about seven leagues from the American coast. Quarll was so well satisfied with his situation and mode of life that he refused to return to England, but he gave his visitor a parchment scroll which contained a full history of his life, both before and after the shipwreck which had left him, the sole survivor, in his rock-defended retreat. The first part of Quarll's biography is not very edifying. He was left an orphan at an early age and after some vicissitudes of fortune found himself in court on the charge of marrying three wives. He was undoubtedly guilty and was condemned to death. There were extenuating circumstances, however, and the king was graciously pleased to pardon him. He then embarked for Barbadoes, accompanied by his first wife, taking along with him a considerable quantity of "woolen manufacture and cutlery ware," which he had understood were "very good commodities in those parts." The ship doubled Cape Horn and traded at several ports in Peru, Chili, and Mexico, intending to touch at Barbadoes on the return voyage. She was lost in a storm, however, and Quarll was washed

ashore on his island, where, as we have seen, he was found
after fifty years by the Bristol merchant. The second
part of Quarll's biography is a poor imitation of Robinson
Crusoe, with a tame monkey for Man Friday and certain
wicked Frenchmen to play the part of Defoe's savages.
Unlike Crusoe, Quarll became quite reconciled to his iso-
lation, and we are led to infer that he ended his days in his
lonesome paradise.

Boyle's Voyages and Adventures is particularly recommended in Mr. Thomas's list as " full of various and
amazing turns of fortune." But this little puff is not a bit
of advertising on the bookseller's part. It is a literal extract from the title-page, which again is of the old-fashioned
sort, serving as a kind of table of contents to the volume.[1]
Nobody knows who wrote this rambling romance, — for it
is pure fiction, though it has often been taken seriously.
The recommendation in the title-page is honest enough.
The book is fairly dizzy with " amazing turns of fortune."
Boyle is a shipcaptain's son, and is apprenticed to a London watchmaker who " had a vast Trade, vended a great
many Watches beyond Sea." After some odd experiences in London, the boy is packed off to America by a
perfidious uncle, who sends him on board an outward
bound ship under the pretence of an errand. Luckily he
had an inclination for the sea, but he had no fancy to be
disposed of as a kind of slave, or little better, when he
should reach the plantations, — a lot that he had only
too much reason to expect, for it accorded well enough

---

[1] The Voyages and Adventures of Captain Robert Boyle, in several Parts
of the World. Intermix'd with the Story of Mrs. Villars, an English Lady
with whom he made his surprizing Escape from Barbary; the History of an
Italian Captive; and the Life of Don Pedro Aquilio, &c. Full of various
and amazing Turns of Fortune. To which is added, The Voyage, Shipwreck, and Miraculous Preservation of Richard Castleman, Gent. With a
Description of the City of Philadelphia, and the Country of Pennsylvania.
London, 1726.

with the habits of the time. Before long, however, the ship fell in with a Barbary pirate, under the command of an Irish renegado, and, by curious chances, which it would take too long to particularize, he found himself on board the rover, in a rather ambiguous capacity, for he was neither captive nor passenger. The pirate captain treated him well, and, when they arrived at Soller, in Barbary, employed him as a gardener. The captain had adopted Moorish customs and had several wives and female slaves. Boyle fell in love with one of the slaves, an English woman named Villars, and contrived to escape with her, in the company of an Italian captive, whose story, as well as that of Mrs. Villars, is woven into the narrative. We cannot now follow Boyle through his varied fortunes, and must leave him, reluctantly, almost at the outset of his romantic career. The book does not break the promise made by the title-page.

Among the political works which Mr. Thomas advertises, one's eye is caught by The Jockey Club, which must not be passed by in silence.

The Jockey Club: or a Sketch of the Manners of the Age, is lively reading, and students of politics and social history still resort to it for amusement, if not for edification. In its earliest form, as published in 1792, it contained fifty characters (with one more, for luck) of men who were at that time, for some reason or another, in the public eye, — many of them members of the Jockey Club, whence the title of the volume. It is abusive and scurrilous to the last degree, — yet not perhaps more blackguardly than the general tone of the society which it professes to depict. The author prudently concealed his name, but is generally understood to have been Charles Pigot. As an additional precaution, he makes liberal use of dashes, — writing of the P[rinc]e of W[ale]s, the h[eir] to the c[row]n, the B[ritis]h C[abine]t, Mr. F[o]x, and

so on; but of course the lacunæ were easily supplied by
his readers, both in England and in America.   And he had
readers in plenty.   A second and a third part were soon
called for, and when the book was reprinted in New York
in 1793 the publisher followed the tenth London edition.
Pigot's attitude toward the Americans was enough to commend his book on this side of the water.   He praises Fox
warmly, though not without frankly admitting his weak
points; and one of his few completely favorable portraits
is that of the D[uk]e of R[ichmon]d, whom he commends
for " his unremitted, patriotic exertions, during the long
process of the American war."   These " were such as the
utmost powers of panegyric are unequal to celebrate; nor
will his speech in the House of Lords, where he unequivo-
cally and nobly asserted the rights of men and America's
independence, even at the moment when Chatham was
struck with death, be ever forgotten."   His description of
Colonel Tarleton must have been read with a good deal of
satisfaction in this country when the passions of the Revolutionary War had not yet cooled.   It is a fair sample both
of the writer's style and of the spirit in which political
pamphleteering was conducted: —

Col. T . . n . . . . . Veni, vidi, vici.

OUR hero betrayed very early symptoms of romantic gallantry,
and a brave martial spirit.   A short time previous to his embarkation for America, being one evening engaged with a party of his
acquaintance at the Cocoa-tree, he greatly alarmed the company,
by suddenly drawing his enormous sabre from the scabbard, and
furiously exclaiming, "With this weapon I'll cut off General
Lee's head."   We have heard, that he was concerned in the affair,
when that officer was made prisoner, and believe that two or
three unfortunate Americans actually fell victims to the Colonel's
personal valor on the occasion.
When he returned to his native country, escaped from the

perils and dangers of his numberless campaigns, in which his humanity shone so eminently conspicuous, he thought to make a sudden and durable impression on the minds of his countrymen, by an incessant relation of his extraordinary achievements. His countrymen were less sensible to his merit than he imagined. They did not listen with that attention or admiration that the gallant Colonel expected. The exploits of a pandor, a partizan, are ranked in the lowest degree of military merit; and it had been more prudent on his part, to have omitted some instances of his *valor*, which have been thought rather tending to perfidy and cruelty. The Colonel, however, is a man of strict honor; and woe to him who doubts it! He is likewise member for Liverpool, and a noted parliamentary *speechifier;* having particularly distinguished himself in that cause, so congenial with his own heart, the rights of power, and usurpation against the rights of men. He is the strenuous, determined advocate of the Slave-trade, and hence he aspires to future success at Liverpool.

But one must stop somewhere, and perhaps as well with Colonel Tarleton as another. Here is the whole Catalogue, which the studious reader may verify in any large library — for no small collection of modern books is likely to duplicate Mr. Thomas's variegated stock.

ROBERT B. THOMAS,

HAS FOR SALE AT HIS

Book & Stationary *Store,*

IN 𝕾𝖙𝖊𝖗𝖑𝖎𝖓𝖌,

The following BOOKS & STATIONARY,

—TO WHICH ADDITIONS ARE CONSTANTLY MAKING—

ADAMS' View of Religions, American Preceptor, American Juſtice, Art of Speaking, American Clerk's Magazine, Ariſtotle's Works, Alphonſo & Dalinda, Akenſide's & Armſtrong's Poems, Arabian Nights Entertainment, 2 vol.

Britiſh Album, Baron Trenk, Boyle's Voyages & Adventures, *in ſeveral parts of the world, full of various and amazing turns of fortune*—Brown's Elements of Medicine, Brydone's Tour, Bennet's Letters, Bruce's Travels abridged, Blair's Lectures, 2 vol. do. *abridged,* do. Sermons, 2 vol. Baxter's Call to the unconverted, Boſton's Fourfold State, Belknap's Hiſtory of Newhampſhire, 3 vol. do. American Biography, Bell on Ulcers, Buchan's Domeſtic Medicine and Family Phyſician, *very neceſſary book in every family ;* Baron Steuben's Exerciſes, *with plates,* Book Keeping, Bailey's Dictionary, Bibles, quarto *with* 24 *copperplates,* Apocraphy and OSTERVAL'S notes, do. Scotch and Engliſh *octavo,* do. *ſmall* do.

Carver's Travels in America, Cook's Voyages, 2 vol. do. *abridged,* Complete Letter Writer, Cyrus' Travels, Cecilia, 3 vol. *by Miſs Burney,* Clerk's Corderius, Chefelden's Anatomy *with plates,* Catechiſm of Nature, *for the uſe of children ; much information is contained in a ſmall compaſs*—Cheſterfield's Principles of Politeneſs, Columbian Muſe, Cullen's Practice of Phyſic 2 vol. do. Materia Medica,

Dwight's Geography *for children,* Dana's Selection, Dodd's Thoughts in Priſon, do. Reflection on Death, Doddridge's Riſe & Progreſs, do. on Regeneration, Deſ-

mond, *a novel, by Charlotte Smith;* Dialogues of Devils.

Enfield's Biographical Sermons, *being difcourfes on the principal characters in fcripture;* Edward's Hiftory of Redemption, do. on Religious Affections, Evelina, 2 vol. *by Mifs Burney,* Economy of Life—Englifh Hermit; *or the unparralled fufferings and furprifing adventures of Phillip Quarll, an Englifhman, who was difcovered by Mr. Dorrinton, a Briftol merchant, upon an uninhabited ifland, in the South Sea, where he lived about fifty years without any human affiftance*—Enfield's Speaker; *or mifcellaneous pieces felected from the beft Englifh writers, for the improvement of youth in reading & fpeaking;* Elegant Extracts.

Fordyce's Addreffes to Young Men, do. Sermons to Young Women, Farmer's Friend, Fool of Quality 3 vol. Friend of Youth 2 vol. Flavel's Token for Mourners, Federal Ready Reckoner.

Goldfmith's Effays and Poems, do. Hiftory of Rome *abridged,* Gregory's Legacy.

Hunter's Sacred Biography, 6 vol. in 3, Harris' Natural Hiftory of the Bible, do. Syftem of Punctuation, Hervey's Meditations, Haplefs Orphan, by *a lady,* 2 vol. Hamilton's Midwifery, Hive.

Inquifitor, or Invifible Rambler.

Jofephus, by Whifton, 6 vol. Jockey Club *abridged,* Jenyn's View, do. Lectures, Julia de Roubigne, Jofeph Andrews, Jackfon on Fevers.

Knox's Effays, Keate's Sketches from Nature.

Laws of Maffachufetts, Lee's Memoirs, Ladies Library, Life of Chrift and the Apoftles, Life of Watts and Doddridge, Life of Dr. Franklin, Life of Col. Gardner, Life of Jofeph, Lendrum's Hift. of Amer. Rev. 2 vol.

Mills on Cattle, Mafon on Self Knowledge, Mirror, 2 vol. Moore's Travels, 2 vol. do. Zeluco, do. Medical Sketches, Man of Feeling, Moore's Monitor, Montague's Travels, Morfe's Univerfal Geography, *a new and elegant edition, having feventeen additional maps,* 2 vol. *large octavo, price* 4½ *dollars,* do. *abridged,* Elements of Geography, Milton's Works, Mafon's Student and Paftor, Myfteries of Udolpho 3 vol. Moore's Fables for Ladies, Man

of the World, Moore's late Journal in France, Medical Pocket Book.

Newton on the Prophecies 2 vol. New England Farmer, New Edinburgh Difpenfatory, Necker on Religious Opinions.   Ovid's Art of Love.

Pleafures of Memory, *elegantly printed on wove paper*, Pleafing Inftructor, Pomfret's Poems, Probate Laws, Pike's Arithmetic, do *abridged*, Peter Pindar's Works 2 vol. Pilgrim's Progrefs, Pelew Iflands, Paley's Philofophy, Paine's *(Thomas)* Age of Reafon, 2d part, Prompter, Perry's Dictionary, Pamela *abridged*.

Rights of Woman, Raffelas and Dinarbas, Robinfon Crufoe, Rufh's Medical Obfervations 2 vol. Religious Courtfhip, Rochefoucault's Maxims, Rowe's *(Mrs.)* Letters, Roderic Random 2 vol. Romance of the Foreft.

Sanford and Merton 3 vol. *in one*, Sicilian Romance, Seneca's Morals, Sterne's Sentimental Journey, Sky Lark, Smellie's Anatomical Tables.

Thompfon's Seafons, Town Officer, Turner's Book Keeping, Tom Jones, 3 vol.

Winchefter on Univerfal Reftoration, Whitney's Hiftory of Worcefter, Watfon's Apology for the Bible, Watts on the Improvement of the Mind, do. Lyric Poems, do. Pfalms and Hymns, *large and fmall, gilt or plain*, White on Lying in Women, Williams' Hiftory of Vermont, *containing much philofophical information*.

Young's Night Thoughts, Young Man's Beft Companion, Young's letters on Univerfalifm, Young's Latin Dictionary.

SCHOOL BOOKS—*by the grofs or Dozen.*

Alexander's Englifh and Latin Grammar, do. Elements, Bingham's American Preceptor, do. Young Ladies' Accidence, Perry's Spelling Book, Webfter's do. 2d & 3d part, Teftaments, Worcefter Collection, Holden's Mufic, Primmers, &c. &c.

Juft Printed for faid THOMAS, *and fold as above*,

A TREATISE on the *SCARLATINA ANGINOSA;* or CANKER RASH, *together with Philofophical Obfervations*

on *Heat and Cold, their Influence on Animal and Vegetable Bodies. Also Theoretical Sketches on* FEVERS, *as produced from Phlogistic Principles, and Practical Remarks on the* DYSENTERY—*The whole being an original work—By* I. ALLEN, M.D.

JOURNAL of the TRAVELS *and* SUFFERINGS of *DANIEL SAUNDERS*, jun. on board the ship Commerce of *Boston*, which was cast away on the coast of *Arabia* in 1792.

FEMALE CHARACTER VINDICATED, *or an answer to the Scurrilous Invectives, of Fashionable Gentlemen.*

RUSSELL'S SEVEN SERMONS—*too well known to need recommendation.*

DIVINE & MORAL SONGS *for* CHILDREN, *by I. Watts*, D.D.

SMALL HISTORIES, CHAPMEN's BOOK, &c.

Female Policy Detected, French Convert, Royal, do. History of the Holy Bible, Seven Wife Masters, Robinson Crusoe, Tom Thumb's Exhibition, New Year's Gift, Little King Pippin, Mountain Piper—*with a great number of other small, entertaining histories.*

STATIONARY, &c.

Writing Paper of the following kinds, *viz.*—Superfine and common Fools Cap, superfine and common Pot of various prices, extra Post Quarto, Magazine and common Blue Paper, French and English Marble, do. Bonnet, do.—Dutch Quills by 100—Black & Red Writing Ink Powder, and Ink—Pewter and Lead Inkstands—Ink-Pots of different kinds—Penknives—Wafers in Boxes—Account and Record Books of all kinds & prices—Blank books for Cyphering—Ivory Memorandum Books—Paper do. Gentlemen's Morocco and black Leather Pocket Books—Slates, and Slate Pencils—Black Lead, do—Writing Books, fine Paper—Gunter's Scales—Brass Dividends—Playing Cards—Spectacles—Copperplate Slips, large and small—Pictures, &c. &c.

☞ *Said* THOMAS *returns his sincere thanks for past favors, and would be happy in a continuance, tho' he forbears saying* cheap or cheaper *than can be purchased in the* Union, *wishing only for those disposed to purchase, to call and satisfy themselves.*

++
LEOMINSTER : PRINTED BY CHARLES PRENTISS—1796.

BARBERRIES AND WHEAT

THE early New England farmer expected, of course, to raise the staple grains which he had cultivated in the old country, and among these wheat naturally held an important place. On the coast, however, wheat would not thrive. Thus in 1666 Morton's Memorial records the failure of the crop at Plymouth in characteristic phraseology: — "This year much of the wheat is destroyed with blasting and mildew, as also some other grain, by worms, and the drought afore mentioned; but the Lord hath sent much rain for the recovery of the remainder, through his great mercy." [1] There are similar entries for the two years preceding. The settlers wrestled stubbornly with unfavorable conditions, but they had to give up in the end. In 1764 Governor Hutchinson remarked that little wheat had been raised in Massachusetts for a long time, except in the towns on the Connecticut River, [2] and in 1826 Judge Davis added that since Hutchinson wrote "wheat has not been a constant crop . . . in any places nearer to the seacoast than the County of Worcester." [3] It is significant that the word "corn," which means "wheat" in England, was gradually transferred in the Colonies to what was at first called "Indian corn," so that finally the adjective was not needed and is now seldom used. When the West was settled, the new sense

[1] Davis's edition, Boston, 1826, p. 321.
[2] History of the Colony of Massachusetts Bay, 2d ed., London, [1765,] I, 229, note.
[3] See his edition of Morton's Memorial, p. 321.

of " corn " had become so well established in American usage that it spread throughout the country, and thus one of the most baffling differences between British English and American English came about.

Of course our rural philosophers were not content to accept defeat without an effort to account for it, and a queer idea gained currency that the barberry bush was to blame. The barberry already had a bad reputation. It infested the land and was a great nuisance to farmers on account of its tenacity of life. In the Almanac for 1800, one of Mr. Thomas's correspondents, after a few complimentary remarks to the editor, expresses himself with some passion on the subject of this ill-omened shrub: —

MR. THOMAS,

I HAVE made use of the *Farmer's Almanack* for the last four years past, and am much pleased with it. Being an old farmer myself, I have one observation to make, which I wish you to publish, as I think it of no small consequence to farmers in those lower towns, whose lands are overrun with barberry bushes, — the most pernicious bush that ever I knew grow upon the face of the earth, multiplying exceedingly fast, though great pains are taken by many of our people to clear their lands of them, but to no purpose. Some cut them down, some burn them on where they were cut ; others attempt to pull them up with their oxen, but they soon sprout again four to one, and it is said by many, that there is no way to clear land of them.

I have discovered a method, by which, a man may thoroughly clear his lands of them, and which I have practised for four years past, and it has never failed effect. Your publishing it in your next year's Almanack, perhaps, may oblige some of your readers, as well as gratify

Your friend and humble servant,

P. SPRAGUE.

Malden, August 26, 1799.

An effectual Method to destroy Barberry Bushes.

LET a man take a small chain with short links, and lay it on the ground round a bunch of bushes, then lay one of the hooks across the chain, and draw it as snug as he can with his hands about the bush close to the ground, then put on a sufficient team to bring it up by the roots at once. — If this be done in the months of October or November, it will never fail to finally exterminate them.

Our correspondent, it will be noted, has nothing to say of the blasting powers of the barberry, but we have a very circumstantial account of them, from about the same time, in President Dwight's narrative of his journey to Berwick, Maine, in 1796. He is speaking of Eastern Massachusetts : —

From Marlborough Eastward, throughout a country, extending to Piscataqua river on the North, and to the Counties of Bristol and Plymouth on the South, the Barberry bush is spread ; not universally, but in spots, and those often extensive. In some fields they occupy a sixth, fifth, and even a fourth, of the surface. Neat farmers exterminate them, except from the sides of their stone enclosures. Here it is impossible to eradicate them, unless by removing the walls : for the roots pass under the walls ; and spring up so numerously, as to make a regular and well compacted hedge. It is altogether improbable therefore, that they will ever be extirpated.

This bush is, in New-England, generally believed to blast both wheat and rye. Its blossoms, which are very numerous, and continue a considerable time, emit, very copiously, a pungent effluvium ; believed to be so acrimonious, as to injure essentially both these kinds of grain. Among other accounts, intended to establish the truth of this opinion, I have heard the following.

A farmer on Long-Island sowed a particular piece of ground with wheat every second year, for near twenty years. On the Southern limit of this field grew a single Barberry bush. The Southern winds, prevailing at the season, in which this bush

was in bloom, carried the effluvia, and afterwards the decayed blossoms, over a small breadth of this field to a considerable distance : and, wherever they fell, the wheat was blasted : while throughout the remainder of the field it was sound. This account I had from a respectable gentleman, who received it from the farmer himself; a man of fair reputation.

In Southborough, a township in the County of Worcester, a Mr. Johnson sowed with rye a field of new ground, or ground lately disforested. At the South end of this field, also, grew a single barberry bush. The grain was blasted throughout the whole breadth of the field, on a narrow tract commencing at the bush, and proceeding directly in the course, and to the extent, in which the blossoms were diffused by the wind.

In another field, the property of a Mr. Harrington, an inhabitant of the same township, exactly the same circumstances existed : and exactly the same mischief followed.

These two accounts I received from Mr. Johnson, son of the Proprietor of the field first mentioned : a student at that time in Yale College ; and afterwards a respectable Clergyman in Milford, Connecticut.

As no part of the grain was blasted in either of these cases, except that, which lay in a narrow tract, leeward of the barberry bushes ; these facts appear to be decisive, and to establish the correctness of the common opinion. Should the conclusion be admitted ; we cannot wonder, that wheat and rye should be blasted, wherever these bushes abound.

A labouring man, attached to the family of Mr. Williams, our host in this town [Marlborough], informed me, that in Mr. Williams's garden a barberry-bush grew in the wall a number of years ; that during this period esculent roots, although frequently planted near it, never came to such a degree of perfection, as to be fit for use ; that such, as grew at all, appeared to be lean and shrivelled, as if struggling with the influence of an unfriendly climate ; that the wall was afterwards removed, and the bush entirely eradicated ; that in the first succeeding season such roots flourished perfectly well on the same spot, and were of a

good quality; and that, ever since, they had grown, year by year to the same perfection. My informant added, that the soil was very rich, and throughout every other part of the garden was always entirely suited to the growth of these vegetables; and that it was not more highly manured, after the removal of the bush, than before. This is the only instance of the kind, within my knowledge. If there be no errour in the account; it indicates, that the barberry-bush has an unfavourable influence on other vegetable productions, beside wheat and rye.[1]

President Dwight, then, was familiar with the evil reputation of the barberry, but he was too philosophical a thinker to accept what he heard without scrutiny. His account of the matter is a good instance of scientific elimination resulting in a *non-plus*.

Lieutenant John Harriott, who scrutinized New England, in 1794, with the experienced eye of a scientific farmer, thoroughly acquainted with agriculture in the mother country, was by no means satisfied with the current theory. He writes: —

The soil, in the interior country, is best calculated for Indian corn, rye, oats, barley, buckwheat, and flax. In some of the farther inland parts, wheat is raised; but, on the sea-coast, it has never been cultivated with much success, being subject to blasts. Various reasons are assigned for this: some suppose these blasts to be occasioned by the saline vapours from the sea; but I can not agree to this, well knowing that many of the best wheats that are grown in England, in quantity and quality, are from sea-marshes and lands adjoining the sea. Others attribute it to the vicinity of Barberry-bushes, to the truth of which I cannot speak. But the principal cause appeared to me to be the poverty and sandy nature of the soil in general, together with exceedingly bad management.[2]

[1] Travels in New-England and New-York, I, 381–3; cf. I, 376.
[2] Struggles through Life, London, 1807, II, 32–33.

Subsequent experiments, undertaken about 1825 by the Massachusetts Agricultural Society seemed to show that the failure of the crop was due, in part, to the kind of wheat cultivated, and that the substitution of spring or summer wheat for winter wheat would be advantageous.[1] However, the course of empire soon made it clear that New England was not to be its own granary. The question ceased to be of much practical importance, and the innocent barberry bush gradually lost its bad eminence in the farmer's mind.[2]

[1] Davis's edition of Morton's Memorial, p. 321.
[2] In 1832 Wilkinson notices the belief in his History of Maine, I, 114: "Berberis vulgaris. It is said *Corn* will not fill well near it."

INDIAN TALK

WHAT kind of English did the Indians speak in New England? This is a thorny subject, but not without charms for the investigator. The Almanac for 1797 contains an anecdote which appears to have a certain value in this regard. Anyhow, it is good enough to repeat: —

AN Indian who was appointed a Justice of the Peace, issued the following WARRANT. — Me *High Howder,* yu constable, yu deputy, best way yu look um Jeremiah Wicket, strong yu take um, fast yu hold um, quick yu bring um before me,
Captain Howder.

At first glance, this alleged Indian warrant looks like a bit of white man's facetiousness and nothing more. But one should not be so hasty. A little searching reveals the existence of a somewhat complicated tradition.

Another version was printed by Judge John Davis, in 1826, in his edition of Nathaniel Morton's New England's Memorial:[1] —

At the Courts in Barnstable County, formerly, we often heard from our aged friends and from the Vineyard gentlemen, amusing anecdotes of Indian rulers. The following warrant is recollected, which was issued by one of those magistrates directed to an Indian Constable, and will not suffer in comparison with our more verbose forms.

[1] P. 415.

> I Hihoudi,
> You Peter Waterman,
> Jeremy Wicket;
> Quick you take him,
> Fast you hold him,
> Straight you bring him,
> Before me, Hihoudi.

Mr. Davis was at Barnstable as a tutor in the family of Gen. James Otis shortly after his graduation from college in 1781, and he began the practice of law at Plymouth in 1787.[1] The chances are that he heard this anecdote before 1800. His version of the writ, as well as that in the Almanac, obviously represents an Old Colony tradition. Hihoudi, or High Howder, has not been identified, though a friendly red man called How Doe Yee is mentioned in the Plymouth Colony Records.[2] Wicket is a familiar Indian name,[3] perpetuated in the designation of Wicket Island in Onset Bay.

There is, however, another tradition which ascribes the eccentric writ to *Waban*, or *Thomas Waban*, and which, as we shall see in a moment, is closely connected with the history of the Colony of Massachusetts Bay. Dr. William Allen, President of Bowdoin College, in the second edition of his American Biographical and Historical Dictionary, published in 1832, gives the warrant as follows:—

You, you big constable, quick you catch um Jeremiah Offscow, strong you hold um, safe you bring um afore me.

Waban, justice peace.[4]

[1] See his biography by Dr. Francis, Coll. Mass. Hist. Soc., 3rd Series, X, 187-8.

[2] March 6, 1676-7, V, 225.

[3] For instance, Simon Wickett of Pocasset, mentioned in the Plymouth Colony Records in 1679 (VI, 16).

[4] P. 741, article *Waban*. This article is not in the first edition of the Dictionary (1809).

Dr. Allen publishes another anecdote about this same official, which, however, occurs in a somewhat more lively form in William Biglow's History of Natick, 1830, along with the warrant. Since Mr. Biglow appeals directly to the " authority of tradition " and does not appear to have derived his material from Dr. Allen, it is worth while to reproduce his exact words : —

The following is handed down as a true copy of a warrant, issued by an Indian magistrate. — " You, you big constable, quick you catchum Jeremiah Offscow, strong you holdum, safe you bringum afore me.

"THOMAS WABAN, Justice peace."

When Waban became superannuated, a younger magistrate was appointed to succeed him. Cherishing that respect for age and long experience, for which the Indians are remarkable, the new officer waited on the old one for advice. Having stated a variety of cases and received satisfactory answers, he at length proposed the following : — " when Indians get drunk and quarrel and fight and act like Divvil, what you do dan? " — " Hah ! tie um all up, and whip um plaintiff, whip um fendant and whip um witness." [1]

Mr. Biglow, it will be observed, gives the justice's name as *Thomas* Waban, whereas Dr. Allen calls him *Waban* pure and simple. The discrepancy is of some moment. The two names are not identical, but belong to different generations, — Waban was the father and Thomas Waban the son. Both were inhabitants of Natick, and both were men of note in their day. Let us see if we can get any light on the subject of this Natick legend by an appeal to authenticated history.

Old Waban is a famous character in New England annals. He was well disposed toward Christianity from the outset, and it was in his wigwam at Nonantum, now

[1] P. 85.

a part of Newton, that the apostle Eliot preached his first
sermon to the aborigines. The Rev. John Wilson, to
whom we probably owe our account of this historic service,
speaks of "Waaubon" as "the chief minister of Justice
among them," and remarks that he "gives more grounded
hopes of serious respect to the things of God, then any that
as yet I have knowne of that forlorne generation." The
meeting took place on October 28th, 1646,[1] and the site
of the wigwam is approximately marked by an inscription
on Eliot Terrace, a memorial structure dedicated a few
years ago. In another place Wilson describes Waban as
"a man of gravitie and chiefe prudence and counsell
among them, although no *Sachem*," and as "like to bee
a meanes of great good to the rest of his company unlesse
cowardise or witchery put an end (as usually they have
done) to such hopefull beginnings."[2] By "witchery" Wilson means of course the diabolical arts of the powwows, or
Indian wizards, whose influence was constantly exerted to
thwart the efforts of the missionaries, and whom both
Indians and white men believed to have direct communion
with the devil and his angels.[3] We have John Eliot's own
evidence that Waban was his earliest convert: — "Waban
was the first that received the gospel."[4]

In 1650, at the instance of Eliot, the praying Indians
received a grant of the township of Natick, and a fort and
one dwelling house were built.[5] The actual settlement of
the new town took place in the following year, when, still
under Eliot's direction, a form of government was adopted.

---

[1] [John Wilson?] The Day-Breaking, if not the Sun-Rising of the Gospell
with the Indians in New-England, London, 1647, p. 1.

[2] The same, p. 20.

[3] Cf. pp. 108 ff., above.

[4] Eliot, as quoted by John Dunton, Letters from New-England, 1686, ed.
Whitmore, 1867, p. 234.

[5] Eliot, A Late and Further Manifestation of the Progress of the Gospel,
etc., London, 1655, p. 3.

The Indians " chose among themselves Rulers of ten, fifty, and an hundred, according to the holy Patterne " in the eighteenth chapter of Exodus.[1] Waban was elected a Ruler of Fifty and we have the word of Eliot himself that he governed well, for, writes the apostle in 1652, " his gift lay in Ruling, Judging of Cases, wherein he is patient, constant, and prudent, insomuch that he is much respected among them." [2] Subsequently Waban became the leading man in the Natick community, and he is so designated in 1674 by Major Gookin, who remarks that he " is now above 70 years of age " and " a person of great prudence and piety," adding " I do not know any Indian that excels him." [3] He was the steadfast friend of the white men. In April, 1675, as Gookin tells us, " Waban, the principal Ruler of the praying Indians living at Natick, came to one of the Magistrates on purpose, and informed him that he had ground to fear that Sachem Philip and other Indians . . . intended some mischief shortly to the English and Christian Indians," and " again, in May, about six weeks before the war began, he came again and renewed the same." [4]

The nature of Waban's authority as a Ruler of Fifty, and later as the chief man of Natick, is sufficiently indicated by an order of the General Court, passed in 1647, the year after Eliot's first sermon in the wigwam at Nonantum. It is here given as printed by Thomas Shepard : —

Vpon information that the *Indians* dwelling among us, and submitted to our government, being by the Ministry of the Word brought to some civility, are desirous to have a course of ordinary

[1] Eliot, as above, p. 3.
[2] Confessions of Indians, in Eliot and Mayhew, Tears of Repentance, London, 1653, p. 8.
[3] Historical Collections of the Indians in New England, Mass. Hist. Soc. Coll., I, 184.
[4] Historical Account, Coll. Am. Antiq. Soc., II, 440–1.

22

Judicature set up among them : It is therefore ordered by authority of this Court, that some one or more of the Magistrates, as they shall agree amongst themselves, shall once every quarter keep a Court at such place, where the *Indians* ordinarily assemble to hear the Word of God, and may then hear and determine all causes both civill and criminall, not being capitall, concerning the *Indians* only, and that the *Indian Sachims* shall have libertie to take order in the nature of Summons or Attachments, to bring any of their own people to the said Courts, and to keep a Court of themselves, every moneth if they see occasion, to determine small causes of a civill nature, and such smaller criminall causes, as the said Magistrates shall referre to them ; and the said *Sachims* shall appoint Officers to serve Warrants, and to execute the Orders and Judgements of either of the said Courts, which Officers shall from time to time bee allowed [i. e., approved] by the said Magistrates in the quarter Courts or by the Governour : And that all fines to bee imposed upon any *Indian* in any of the said Courts, shall goe and bee bestowed towards the building of some meeting houses, for education of their poorer children in learning or other publick use, by the advice of the said Magistrates and of Master *Eliot*, or of such other Elder, as shall ordinarily instruct them in the true Religion.   And it is the desire of this Court, that these Magistrates and Mr. *Eliot* or such other Elders as shall attend the keeping of the said Courts will carefully indeavour to make the Indians understand our most usefull Lawes, and the principles of reason, justice and equity whereupon they are grounded, & it is desired that some care may be taken of the *Indians* on the Lords dayes.[1]

The founders of the Massachusetts Bay Colony were remarkable in many ways, — this may be asserted without fear of contradiction, even from those historical students who have a fancy to be iconoclastic, — and not the least noteworthy of their traits was an unusual capacity for

---

[1] The Clear Sun-shine of the Gospel, London, 1648, pp. 15–16.   The text in the Colony Records, III, 105–6, differs slightly.

knowing precisely what they were about. It was no accident, for instance, that the Massachusetts Charter contained no reference to control by a board of directors in England. It was the outcome of a carefully laid plan. The colonists had no doubt of their ability to govern themselves, and they meant to try the experiment without interference. They were ready to meet each exigency as it arose, and, though it would be absurd to maintain that they never made a mistake, it is certain that their valiant common sense, which declined to worry overmuch about the exact boundaries of precedent, produced a form of democracy which is likely to maintain itself. Their temper toward the savages, as shown in the law just quoted, was in entire accord with their general habit of mind. If the Indians wished to be civilized, the Colony was willing to do its part, and to that end it had no hesitation in entrusting them, under proper supervision, with a considerable measure of local self-government.

The order of 1647 went into effect immediately. The account of its operation given by Gookin in his Historical Collections (1674) is admirably clear and concise: —

Forasmuch as a pious magistracy and christian government is a great help and means for promoting, cherishing, encouraging, and propagating, the christian religion among any people, especially a nation so circumstanced, as these rude, uncultivated, and barbarous Indians were; care was taken by the general court of the Massachusetts, at the motion of Mr. Eliot, to appoint some of the most prudent and pious Indians, in every Indian village that had received the gospel, to be rulers and magistrates among them, to order their affairs both civil and criminal, and of a more ordinary and inferiour nature. These rulers were chosen by themselves, but approved by a superiour authority.

But moreover the general court appointed and empowered one of the English magistrates, to join with the chief of their rulers, and keep a higher court among them; extending the

power of this court to the latitude of a county court among the English; from the jurisdiction whereof nothing for good order and government, civil or criminal, is excepted, but appeals, life, limb, banishment, and cases of divorce.   The first English magistrate, chosen to be ruler over the praying Indians in the colony of Massachusetts, was first Mr. D. G. the author of these Collections; and this was in A. D. 1656.   But not long after his occasions called him for England for two or three years; one Major Humphrey Atherton was appointed to conduct this affair, which he did about three years.   But then the Lord taking him to himself, by death, and the author being returned back, in the year 1660, a year or more before Major Atherton's death, was again called and reinstated in that employ A. D. 1661, and hath continued in that work hitherto.[1]

Evidently, then, on the establishment of the civil polity contemplated in this decree, Waban became a kind of judge and held office under the authority of the Colony.   In 1674 there were several other "rulers" at Natick, but they were subordinate to Waban, and there were also two "constables," chosen yearly.[2]   By this time several other Indian towns had been organized, on the model of Natick, with rulers, constables, and teachers.   There was also "a marshal general belonging to all the praying Indian towns, called Captain Josiah, or Pennahannit."[3]   Gookin gives a full account of these settlements, and has put on record the names of many of the rulers and of certain constables.   At one of the new settlements, Chabanakongkomun, now Dudley, we learn of one "Black James, who about a year since was constituted constable of all these new praying towns."   Gookin declares that "he is a person that hath approved himself diligent and courageous, faith-

---

[1] Historical Collections of the Indians in New England, Coll. Mass. Hist. Soc., 1792, I, 177.
[2] Gookin, Historical Collections, p. 184.
[3] The same, p. 184.

ful and zealous to suppress sin." [1]   According to Eliot,
Black James " was in former times reputed by the English
to be a *Pawaw*" or wizard, but this the conscientious
apostle refuses to assert or deny of his own knowledge.
" I know," he writes, " he renounced and repented of all
his former ways ; and desired to come to Christ, and pray
to God ; and dyed well." [2]

The clearest idea of the relations of the various Indian
officers to each other and to the supervisory magistrate
may be had from Gookin's report of two courts held by
him in 1674.   For our first example we may take the proceedings at Wabquissit, now a part of Woodstock, Connecticut.   First came religious exercises conducted by
Eliot and a native teacher known as Sampson : —

Then I began a court among the Indians.   And first I approved
their teacher Sampson, and their constable Black James ; giving
each of them a charge to be diligent and faithful in their places.
Also I exhorted the people to yield obedience to the gospel of
Christ and to those set in order there.   Then published a warrant
or order, that I had prepared, empowering the constable to suppress drunkenness, sabbath breaking, especially powowing and
idolatry.   And after warning given, to apprehend all delinquents,
and bring them before authority, to answer for their misdoings :
the smaller faults to bring before Wattasacompanum, ruler of the
Nipmuck country ; for idolatry and powowing to bring them
before me : So we took leave of this people of Wabquissit, and
about eleven o'clock, returned back to Maanexit and Chabanakongkomun, where we lodged this night. [3]

Again, at Pakachoog, now apparently a part of
Worcester : —

[1] Gookin, Historical Collections, p. 190.
[2] Eliot, as quoted by John Dunton, Letters from New-England, 1686, ed.
Whitmore, 1867, p. 241.
[3] Historical Collections of the Indians in New England, 1674, Coll. Mass.
Hist. Soc., 1792, I, 192.

After some short respite, a court was kept among them. My chief assistant was Wattasacompanum, ruler of the Nipmuck Indians, a grave and pious man, of the chief sachem's blood of the Nipmuck country. He resides at Hassanamesitt; but by former appointment, calleth here, together with some others. The principal matter done at this court, was, first to constitute John and Solomon to be rulers of this people and co-ordinate in power, clothed with the authority of the English government, which they accepted: also to allow and approve James Speen for their minister. . . Also they chose, and the court confirmed, a new constable, a grave and sober Indian, called Mattoonus. Then I gave both the rulers, teacher, constable, and people, their respective charges; to be diligent and faithful for God, zealous against sin, and careful in sanctifying the sabbath.[1]

The constable's sign of office was a black staff.[2] Of course he sometimes encountered resistance, especially when there was a conflict of authority between the old order and the new. A lively scene of this kind is described by Gookin. One Petavit, alias Robin, "ruler" at Hassanamesitt (Grafton), was visited by a sagamore from the "inland country," who thought himself exempt from the novel jurisdiction. The visitor brought with him "a rundlet of strong liquors." Next morning Petavit "sent for the constable, and ordered him, and according to law, seized the rundlet of liquors. At which act the sagamore drew a long knife, and stood with his foot at the rundlet, daring any to seize it. But Petavit thereupon rose up and drew his knife, and set his foot also to the rundlet, and commanded the constable to do his office. And the sagamore" . . . .[3] Here there is an unlucky hiatus in the story, but the context makes it clear that the undaunted Petavit carried his point.

[1] Historical Collections of the Indians in New England, 1674, Coll. Mass. Hist. Soc., 1792, I, 193.
[2] The same, p. 194.   [3] The same, p. 191.

But we must return to Waban, for in illustrating his position and defining the scope of his authority we have almost lost sight of the venerable ruler himself. As we have seen, he had twice given the English warning of the hostilities contemplated by King Philip. When the war broke out, the praying Indians contributed their quota to the Colonial forces. Yet they were looked upon with suspicion, and finally, in October, 1675, the whole body of the Natick Indians, with their ruler Waban, were transported to Deer Island, where they were soon joined by those from Punkapog, who were equally friendly to the whites. There they remained until the following spring, suffering many hardships from the rigors of the winter and from insufficient food. Disease broke out among them, and Waban and John Thomas, the principal teacher, who were " extreme low " when they were brought back to the mainland, recovered their health with difficulty. " Had they died," writes Major Gookin, " it would have been a great weakening to the work of God among them." [1] When at last they had been allowed to return to Natick, a court was held by Gookin, at which Eliot was present. Waban's speech on this occasion has been preserved, in translation. It is too creditable to the old ruler to be omitted here : —

We do, with all thankfulness, acknowledge God's great goodness to us, in preserving us alive to this day. Formerly, in our beginning to pray unto God, we received much encouragement from many godly English, both here and in England. Since the war begun between the English and wicked Indians, we expected to be all cut off, not only by the enemy Indians, whom we know hated us, but also by many English, who were much exasperated and very angry with us. In this case, we cried to God, in prayer, for help. Then God stirred up the governor and magistrates to send us to the Island, which was grievous to us; for we were

[1] Gookin, Historical Account, pp. 474, 485, 517.

forced to leave all our substance behind us, and we expected nothing else at the Island, but famine and nakedness. But behold God's goodness to us and our poor families, in stirring up the hearts of many godly persons in England, who never saw us, yet showed us kindness and much love, and gave us some corn and clothing, together with other provision of clams, that God provided for us. Also, in due time, God stirred up the hearts of the governor and magistrates, to call forth some of our brethren to go forth to fight against the enemy both to us and the English, and was pleased to give them courage and success in that service, unto the acceptance of the English; for it was always in our hearts to endeavour to do all we could, to demonstrate our fidelity to God and to the English, and against their and our enemy; and for all these things, we desire God only may be glorified.[1]

The date of old Waban's death is uncertain, but he was alive in May, 1682, being then about eighty years old.[2]   He must have died before 1684; otherwise he would unquestionably have joined in the Groton deed of that year.[3]

From what has been said it is clear enough that Waban exercised a considerable measure of judicial authority among the Natick Indians and had constables under him, so that we have no difficulty in understanding how a tradition might arise that he was a regular Justice of the Peace; but it is evident that he never actually held that precise commission. That he did not issue the warrant so often ascribed to him is easy to prove. For Waban did not know how to write. Several deeds are on record which bear his signature; but it is always a "mark." We must therefore pass on to his son, Thomas Waban,

[1] Gookin, Historical Account, p. 522.
[2] Cf. Gookin's report to the Council, Nov. 10, 1676, in Trans. and Coll. American Antiq. Soc., II (1836), 532, with his Historical Collections, Coll. Mass. Hist. Soc., I, 184, and Mass. Colony Records, V, 353.
[3] See p. 345, below.

THE TOWN ACTS OF NATICK, APRIL 18TH, 1715

(From the Original in Thomas Waban's Handwriting)

whom one form of the tradition designates as responsible for the picturesquely expressed document that we are investigating.

There can be no doubt that Thomas Waban was old Waban's son. It was a regular practice for a converted Indian to adopt the name of his father as a surname and to receive a Christian name at baptism. When Eliot and his three companions visited Waban's wigwam to hold their first service (October 28, 1646), they found Waban's eldest son "standing by his father among the rest of his *Indian* brethren in English clothes." And later, according to the same authority, Waban voluntarily offered this son "to be educated and trained up in the knowledge of God hoping, as hee told us, that he might come to know him, though hee despaired much concerning himself." The offer was accepted and the boy was sent to school at Dedham.[1] His English learning is thus accounted for. We have Thomas Waban's signature in full to certain deeds, notably to one which concerns the title to the town of Groton, Massachusetts. In 1683, three years before the "usurpation" of Sir Edmund Andros, the inhabitants of Groton, feeling that the charter of the Massachusetts Bay Company might be abrogated at any moment, took measures to secure a conveyance from the former Indian proprietors of their township. The outcome of their negotiations was a deed from Thomas Waban and others, which is on record in the Middlesex Registry at East Cambridge.[2] It is dated January 10, 1683–4, and, though the other grantors make their marks, Thomas Waban signs his name. In 1684 twenty-eight Indians presented a petition to the General Court, complaining that "Thomas Woban" and others are "appropriating to themselves"

[1] The Day-Breaking, London, 1647, p. 1.
[2] Printed by Dr. Samuel A. Green, Groton during the Indian Wars, Groton, 1883, pp. 183–5.

Indian land and selling it and " keeping all the pay to
themselves," and are claiming other lands as well.[1] Obviously, as Dr. Green suggests, the more intelligent natives
were taking advantage of the fears of the settlers to turn
an honest penny, and their acts excited some jealousy
among those of their fellows who thought they did not
get a fair share of the proceeds. We must remember
that the petition is an *ex parte* document. It shows that
Thomas Waban was a leading man in his community and
a person of some enterprise ; but we should not let the
mere fact of this petition lower him in our esteem.

Thomas Waban, like his father, lived at Natick, and
the records of that town from 1700 to 1735, fragmentary
though they are, bear evidence enough of his literary attain-
ments. They are partly in Indian, partly in English, and
many of them are signed " Thomas Waban, Town Clerk."
Here is a specimen of his skill in both languages : [2]

The Town Acts of Natick in 18th Aprill 1715 — You you
matta wonk Howan. vemmakko oh mehtukq vn : wattuhkonnaut
wutch you : oh quombot toh neit Howan washont : Chekewe
nee : wuttisseen : makkow mehtukquash : vnnee wattuhkonaut noh
pish oattehwaw : twenty Shillings : wutche pasuk mehtukq — you
unni nashpee Tho. Waban : Town Clerk you ut

you : vnnoomattooonk —

At a Generall Town meeting Natick upon 18th day Aprill
1715th — Then we are all agree[d] and mad law amongst us our
selues that non of us shall seel any Timber not to y[e] English if
any of us do seal any Timber he shall foruit twenty Shillings to
the Town vse and pay to the Town next meeting after
as Attesd by Me Thomas Waban Town Clerk

[1] Mass. Archives, XXX, 287 ; printed by Dr. Green, as above, p. 187.
[2] From the original record. The edges of the MS. being somewhat
damaged, a few words and letters are supplied from the copy given by
William Biglow, History of Natick, Boston, 1830, p. 21. Biglow's text is
very incorrect.

The English in this case is in effect the town clerk's own translation of the Indian.

Thomas Waban's English Records may seem grotesque, but they are hardly more so than some entries made by white town clerks of the period. The following is selected, inasmuch as it has to do with a transaction in which Waban himself was interested. It is the vote of the town of Groton which resulted in securing the Indian deed just adverted to. In justice to our ancestors, however, it should be remarked that few town clerks of the period can vie with Mr. Jonathan Morse in eccentricities of spelling: —

At a ginarall Town meting upon 25 d 10 m 1683 John Page John Parish Insin Lorinc

as you are Chosin a comity for and in the behalf of the Towne you are desiered for too proue the Rit and titill we haue too our Tooun ship by all the legall testimony which can be procuerid when the Toown is sent too by aney a Tority and if aney ingins can proue a lagiall titall too the Remainer of our Town ship you haue power to by it at as easi a lay as you can and mack it as sur as may be in the behalf of the Toown and you shall haue Reasinabll satisfackion for your payns.

JONATHAN MORS *Clark*
in the nam of the selecktmen 31 d 10 m 1683 [1]

From the Natick records it appears that Thomas Waban was not only town clerk but that he was several times chosen as one of the selectmen. Another bit of evidence brings us still nearer to the date of our first recorded copy of the famous warrant, which, it will be remembered, occurs in the Almanac for 1796. In 1749 there was a census of the Natick Indians, and in the list occur not only "Thomas and Hannah Waban" but also " Jonas

[1] Samuel A. Green, Groton during the Indian Wars, 1883, pp. 182-3.

Obscow."[1]   From the Natick records it appears that Jonas Obscho was born June 5th, 1739, and died November 13th, 1805.   Now "Jeremiah *Offscow*" is the person whom the constable is directed, in one version of the warrant, to "seize quick, hold strong, and bring safe" before the justice.   Finally, in 1798, the Rev. Jonathan Homer reports, in his Description and History of Newton, that the name Waban "is still honourably remembered at Natick, where some of [old Waban's] posterity were known not many years since.   The name and civil office of *Esquire Waban*, one of his descendants, is particularly mentioned."[2]   Mr. Homer's words are unfortunately rather vague, but they allow us, by an easy inference, to maintain that Thomas Waban was remembered in his own vicinity under the designation proper, according to New England usage, to a justice of the peace.   Milton desired to "call up" Chaucer,

> —— who left half told
> The story of Cambuscan bold

in the Squire's Tale.   The tale of "Esquire Waban" is hardly important enough to justify us in wishing to disturb the slumber of Mr. Homer; but we could wish that a mistaken regard for the dignity of history had not deterred him from committing to print the historic warrant for the arrest of Jeremiah (or was it Jonas?) Offscow, which we cannot help thinking must have been known to him.[3]

Judge Samuel Sewall was acquainted with Thomas Waban.   In his Diary, September 28, 1715, he notes : — "Went to Cambridge to meet the Natick Comittee, Waban

---

1 Coll. Mass. Hist. Soc., X, 135.

2 The same, 1798, V, 263.

3 Another Thomas Waban, undoubtedly the town clerk's son, was married at Natick to Sarah Seby, June 6th, 1738 (Town Records).

and others. Major Fitch, Mr. Oliver and I dine with the
President. I would have dined publickly [at the ordi-
nary]; but the president declin'd it. I went in a Calash,
came home by Moonshine. Accomplish the Bargain
for Magunkaquog [Hopkinton] land, and paid Fourteen
pounds in part. *Laus Deo.*" [1] On the eleventh of October
he records: "Went with Mr. Daniel Oliver to Natick;
from the Falls in Company with the President and Tho.
Oliver esqr. and Mr. John Cotton. At Natick the Indians of the Comittee executed the Parchment Deed
for the land at Magunkaquog: and paid the Proprietors
Three pounds apiece. 'T was so late, that when the
Gentlemen return'd, I went to Sherbourn, lodg'd at Cousin
Baker's." [2]

The Waban mentioned in the first of these entries is
beyond question Thomas, for the elder Waban died some
years before. The point is made certain by the fact that
the Hopkinson Deed is signed by Thomas Waban. We
owe so much to Judge Sewall for what his famous Diary
contains that it would be ungracious to blame him for any
particular omission; yet one cannot help wishing that he
had given us a few details about the Indian committeemen
even if he had omitted to record that he went to Cambridge in a calash and came home by moonshine. He
does, however, afford us a gruesome item of information
about Isaac Nehemiah, another of the committee. On
the day after the signing of the deed Sewall makes the
following entry: —

Solomon Thomas acquaints me that Isaac Nehemiah, one of
the Comittee, had hang'd himself. Ask'd what they should doe.
I sent him to the Crowner. A while after I went to Cous.
Gookin's in order to go home. When there, Solomon came to

[1] Coll. Mass. Hist. Soc., 5th Series, VII, 60.
[2] The same, p. 62.

me again, and earnestly desired me to go and help them. Mr.
Whitney join'd to solicit for him, by reason of the distance from
Cambridge. So I went, Mr. Baker accompanied me. The Jury
found Isaac Nehemiah to be *Felo de se.* Hang'd himself with
his Girdle, 3 foot and 4 inches long buckle and all. 'Twas night
before had done, so went to Sherbourn again, and lodg'd at
Cousin Gookin's.[1]

It appears, then, that both the Old Colony and the
Massachusetts Bay tradition of the Indian warrant, though
they may owe their precise form to some jocose white
man, have manifest touches of local color. There were
Indian magistrates who were similar to justices of the
peace, and there were Indian officers who were known as
constables.[2] There were Indians named Wicket in Plymouth Colony; there was a Thomas Waban as well as an
Offscow at Natick; and it is barely possible that *Hihoudi*
is a form of the name *How d' ye.* It may be added that
Thomas Waban is decorated with the title of Captain in
the Natick town records of 1719, as Howder is in one
version of the warrant.

The punishment of whipping, which, according to another anecdote, seemed to Squire Waban appropriate
for plaintiff, defendant, and witness in cases of drunken
brawling, it was of course within the power of the native
rulers to inflict. Here we are not dependent on tradition.
Again we have the word of John Eliot to instruct us. In
1654, it appears, there was a lamentable occurrence at
Natick. Three mischievous Indians near Watertown had
got possession of "severall quarts of Strong-water, which
sundry out of a greedy desire of a little gaine, are too
ready to sell unto them, to the offence and grief of the
better sort of *Indians,* and of the godly English too."

[1] Coll. Mass. Hist. Soc., 5th Series, VII, 62.
[2] For Indian constables in Plymouth Colony, see the Records, XI, 253,
254, 255.

With this they not only intoxicated themselves, but also
a boy of eleven years, a son of the Indian ruler Toteswamp. " Now," said one of them, " we will see whether
your father will punish us for Drunkennesse, seeing you are
drunk with us for company." "They also fought," adds
Eliot, " and had been severall times Punished formerly
for Drunkennesse." All four of the culprits were brought
before the native court, at which Toteswamp presided,
and the decision was in complete agreement with the
spirit of the anecdote respecting Thomas Waban : —

They judged the three men to sit in the stocks a good space of
time, and thence to be brought to the whipping-Post, & have
each of them twenty lashes. The boy to be put in the stocks
a little while, and the next day his father was to whip him in the
School, before the Children there ; all which Judgement was executed. When they came to be whipt, the Constable fetcht them
one after another to the Tree (which they make use of instead of
a Post) where they all received their Punishments.[1]

Two Connecticut sentences from the eighteenth century
may be quoted, to show the close parallel between these
proceedings and those which took place before colonial
and provincial magistrates. They have reference to the
offence of drunkenness and to that of selling liquor to the
Indians. There is an amusing tit-for-tat in the documents which reminds one strongly of the " whip um
plaintiff, whip um fendant " of the Indian squire.

Norwich ye 7th day of feb. 1722–3. — Apenanucsuck being
drunk was by y⁰ Constable brought before me R. Bushnell, justice
of y⁰ peace to be dealt with so as the law directs. — I do sentence
y⁰ s⁰ Apenuchsuck for his transgression of y⁰ Law, to pay a fine
of ten shillings, or to be whipt ten Lashes on y⁰ naked body, and

[1] Eliot, A Late and Further Manifestation of the Progress of the Gospel,
London, 1655, pp. 6–8.

to pay the cost of his prosecution, and to continue in ye constable's custody till this sentence be performed.   Cost allowed is 6s. and 6d.   R. Bushnell, *Justice of ye Peace.*

Apeanuchsuch having accused Samuel Bliss for selling ye s^d Indian 2 pots of cider this afternoon.   Mr. Samuel Bliss appeared before me ye subscriber, and acknowledged he let s^d Indian have some cider, and do therefore sentence ye said Samuel Bliss to pay a fine of twenty shillings for the transgression of ye Law to be disposed of as ye Law directs.

     ffebe. ye 7th day, 1722–3.   R. Bushnell, *Justice.*[1]

Indian justice of a less formal kind appears in a traditional anecdote of Jacob Spalding, one of the early settlers of Killingly, in the same State.   The incident is said to have occurred in 1720 : —

Jacob one day purchased of an Indian a deer skin, for which he paid him a *tenor bill.*   The latter, somewhat intoxicated, forgot soon after that he had received it, and asked for the money a second time.   Jacob of course paid no attention to such an unwarrantable demand, and the Indian went away muttering revenge.   The next day, while shingling a barn, Jacob saw him returning with two companions.   He leaped from the roof, met them, and was again asked to pay the price of the deer skin.   He refused to comply, till one of the company, who appeared to be the sachem of his tribe, said he had come to see "fair play," and avowed it to be honorable for two Indians to contend with one white man.   Jacob, therefore, imagined he would have rather a difficult task to accomplish ; but plucking up courage, he exerted himself to the utmost, and on the very first encounter, *laid them both* upon the ground, and gave them a "sound drubbing."   The other, who was looking on, was not at all disposed to assist his brethren, and gave them no other encouragement than "Poor dogs, poor dogs ! me hope he kill

---

[1] J. W. Barber, Connecticut Historical Collections, p. 299.

you both ! ! " However, Jacob, after " pounding them " a short time, suffered them to escape. But the next day he saw them coming again, and the individual who imagined himself his creditor, bearing a rifle, which he was in the act of loading. But in thrusting his hand into his pocket to find the ball, he drew out the identical *bill* which he had received two days before! Conscience-struck, he said to Jacob, who was coming to meet him, " Me believe, now, Jacob, you paid me de tenor bill ! " After this confession, Jacob addressed the person who had come to see " fair play." " You," said he, " that have come to see fair play, what do you advise us to do with him?" " Tie him to de tree and whip him," was the reply, which was done accordingly. And here a circumstance occurred, which shows to what extent the Indians carried their principle of honor. The individual in question, after this humiliating treatment, became so dejected that he fled from his tribe, and was never heard of afterwards.[1]

The rude justice of the Indians may be further exemplified by an anecdote reported by the Rev. John Heckewelder. In 1785 an Indian who had been disowned by his tribe on account of his bad character killed a white man at Pittsburg. The chiefs of the Delawares were invited to be present at his trial, and, if they wished, to defend him. They sent the following pointed answer to the civil authorities : —

Brethren ! You inform us that N. N. who murdered one of your men at Pittsburg, is shortly to be tried by the laws of your country, at which trial you request that some of us may be present ! Brethren ! knowing N. N. to have been always a very bad man, we do not wish to see him ! We, therefore, advise you to try him by your laws, and to hang him, so he may never return to us again.[2]

[1] Barber, as above, p. 427.
[2] Heckewelder, Account of the History, Manners, and Customs, of the Indian Nations, who once inhabited Pennsylvania and the Neighbouring States, Philadelphia, 1819, p. 97.

Thus the so-called Indian warrant appears to be true to the spirit of aboriginal justice, as well as to retain some traces of local color in the names which it gives to the magistrate and the delinquent. It remains to determine whether its dialect is also true to the pronunciation and syntax of the English used by the aborigines. The inquiry, which will also give results favorable to the verisimilitude of this facetious document, will enable us to pass in review a number of excessively curious pieces of history and tradition.

Our first three specimens come from the contemporary annals of King Philip's War. They are preserved in " The Present State of New-England . . . faithfully composed by a Merchant of Boston, and communicated to his Friend in London," which was published in 1675 : —

About the 15*th* of *August* [writes our Boston merchant], Captain *Mosely* with sixty Men, met with a company, judged about three hundred *Indians*, in a plain place where few Trees were, and on both sides preparations were making for a Battle ; all being ready on both sides to fight, Captain *Moseley* plucked off his Periwig, and put it into his Breeches, because it should not hinder him in fighting. As soon as the *Indians* saw that, they fell a Howling and Yelling most hideously, and said, *Umh, umh me no stawmerre fight Engis mon, Engis mon get two hed, Engis mon got two hed; if me cut off un hed, he got noder, a put on beder as dis;* with such like words in broken *English*, and away they all fled and could not be overtaken, nor seen any more afterwards.[1]

Some of the words in this queer outburst are unintelligible and probably misprinted. " Me no stawmerre fight Engis mon " is an oracle that defies interpretation. In general, however, the passage is plain enough, and it has uncommon interest for the student of folk-lore. The Indians,

[1] The Present State of New-England, London, 1675, p. 12.

it seems, were quite ready to admit the possibility of a
man's removing his head at will, although they were well
aware that they had no such strange powers themselves.
In this belief they were in accord with a widespread article
of popular superstition, which occurs in one form or another from India to Ireland.   One of the best of the
ancient Irish sagas, The Feast of Bricriu, which is contained in a manuscript of about 1100 and must be two or
three centuries older than that, tells of a giant who allowed
himself to be decapitated on condition that he should have
the right to treat his assailant in the same way, and who
appeared the next evening with his head in its proper place
to claim the fulfilment of the bargain.   This story got into
French in some way as early as the thirteenth century, and
reappears in the fine old English romance of Gawain and
the Green Knight, written by an anonymous poet who
lived in the time of Chaucer.

Another bit of Indian English is preserved by the same
contemporary witness in his account of the execution of
an Indian in 1675.   After the culprit had been hanged,
" then came an *Indian*, a Friend of his, and with his Knife
made a hole in his Breast to his Heart, and sucked out
his Heart-Blood: Being asked his reason therefore, his
answer, *Umh, umh nu*, Me stronger as I was before, me be
so strong as me and he too, he be ver strong Man fore
he die." [1]

Shocking as this story is to modern nerves, it is undoubtedly true, although the author is anonymous and we
have no other testimony to the occurrence.   For it accords
too exactly with what is known of savage psychology all
over the world to be a fabrication.   It is a well-known
article of faith among many wild races that one may in-
herit the strength or prowess of a slain man by tasting his
blood or eating some part of his body, and many canni-

[1] The same, p. 13.

balistic practices are based rather on this belief than on an appetite for human flesh.

A more agreeable anecdote, also containing a sample of Indian English, is given by the same writer. An Englishman, being left for dead after one of the skirmishes, " was found by a Friend *Indian*, he took him up and said, *Umh, umh poo Ingismon, mee save yow life, mee take yow to Captain Mosee ;* he carries him fifteen Miles the day after to Captain *Moseley*, and now this Man is well again and in good Health." [1]

Canonchet, otherwise known as Nanuntenoo, chief sachem of the Narragansetts, one of King Philip's most formidable allies, was surprised by a company of English and friendly Indians, and, despairing of an escape, surrendered in April, 1676. A memorable passage in Hubbard describes his demeanor : —

One of the first English that came up with him, was *Robert Stanton*, a young man that scarce had reached the *twenty second* year of his Age, yet adventuring to ask him a question, or two, to whom this *manly Sachem*, looking with a little neglect upon his *youthful face*, replyed in *broken English ;* you *much Child*, no understand *matters of War ;* let your *brother*, or your *chief* come, him I will Answer ; and was as good as his word ; Acting herein, as if by a *Pythagorean Metempsychosis*, some *old Roman Ghost* had possessed the body of this *Western Pagan ;* And like *Attilius Regulus*, he would not accept of his own Life, when it was tendred him, upon that (in his account) *low Condition* of *Complyance* with the *English*, refusing to send an *old Counsellour* of his to make any motion that way, saying he knew the Indians would not yield. [2]

An extremely curious piece of Indian English occurs in New-England's Crisis, a poem on King Philip's War written by Benjamin Tompson in 1676. Tompson, who was a

[1] The Present State of New-England, London, 1675, p. 14.
[2] Hubbard's Narrative, Boston, 1677, Postscript, p. 8.

graduate of Harvard College, a physician, and an eminent
schoolmaster, is described on his tombstone as "the
renouned poet of New England." New-England's Crisis
is his chief work. After a prologue in praise of simplicity
— an ingenious adaptation to New-England of a famous
passage in Boethius — Tompson describes King Philip as
holding an assembly of his "peers" and his "commons"
and delivering an oration against the colonists. This
speech is partly in good English, but it is variegated with
imitations of the Indian pronunciation and syntax. There
are even two native Indian words, — *wunnegin*, which
means "good,"[1] and *matchit*, which means "bad,"[2] —
both of which were of course perfectly familiar to the
whites. Tompson passes for the earliest native American
poet. At all events, he must be credited with the first
piece of "dialect verse" ever written in this country. In
the extract which follows, the punctuation has been
regulated, but no other changes have been made: —

> And here methinks I see this greazy *Lout*,
> With all his pagan slaves coil'd round about,
> Assuming all the majesty his throne
> Of rotten stump, or of the rugged stone,
> Could yield ; casting some bacon-rine-like looks,
> Enough to fright a Student from his books,
> Thus treat his peers, & next to them his Commons,
> Kennel'd together all without a summons : —
> "My friends, our Fathers were not half so wise
> As we our selves, who see with younger eyes ;
> They sel our land to english man, who teach
> Our nation all so fast to pray and preach.
> Of all our countrey they enjoy the best,
> And quickly they intend to have the rest.
> This no wunnegin ; so big matchit law,
> Which our old fathers fathers never saw
> These english make, and we must keep them too,
> Which is too hard for us or them to doe.

[1] See Trumbull, Natick Dictionary, 1903, p. 202.
[2] See Trumbull, p. 50 (s. v. *matche*).

> We drink, we so big whipt ; but english they
> Go sneep, no more, or else a little pay.
> Me meddle Squaw, me hang'd ; our fathers kept
> What Squaws they would, whither they wakt or slept.
> Now, if you'le fight, Ile get you english coats,
> And wine to drink out of their Captains throats.
> The richest merchants houses shall be ours ;
> Wee'l ly no more on matts or dwell in bowers.
> Wee'l have their silken wives; take they our Squaws !
> They shall be whipt by virtue of our laws.
> If ere we strike, tis now, before they swell
> To greater swarmes then we know how to quell.
> This my resolve, let neighbouring *Sachems* know,
> And every one that hath club, gun, or bow."
> This was assented to, and, for a close,
> He strokt his smutty beard and curst his foes.[1]

Philip's comparison between penalties for Indians and penalties for English is very pithily expressed, and it is precisely here that the Indianisms are most marked : —

> We drink, we so big whipt ; but English they
> Go sneep, no more, or else a little pay.

That is, "If we Indians get drunk, we are severely whipped. But if the English get drunk, they merely go and sleep it off, or perhaps have to pay a slight fine." Tompson was a scholar, a student of the tongues. Possibly he was here reproducing an actual bit of "Indian talk." At all events, he must be pretty close to the linguistic facts. The use of *sneep* for *sleep* corresponds with what has often been observed, — the Indian substitution of *n* for *l* in English words. Massasoit always called his friend Winslow "Winsnow."

Tompson's sketch of King Philip is not flattering. It reminds one of the alleged portrait of the Indian potentate engraved by Paul Revere in 1772.[2] This is so ugly as to

[1] Tompson, New-England's Crisis, Club of Odd Volumes, 1894, pp. 10–11.

[2] For the second edition of Church's History of King Philip's War (Boston, 1772) ; reproduced by S. G. Drake, Book of the Indians, 8th ed., Boston, 1841.

be almost repulsive. It has, of course, no claim to be regarded as a likeness, and is not without a suggestion of deliberate caricature. Our ancestors had no temptation to idealize their inveterate enemy. His memory was not only terrible but odious as well, and they expressed their feelings, whether with pen or graver, with the vigor of their day.

We have, unfortunately, no good contemporary drawing of a New England Indian of King Philip's time. On the opposite page, however, may be seen a trustworthy representation of such an Indian. This is taken from a sketch made by Mr. C. C. Willoughby of the Peabody Museum of Archæology and Ethnology, Harvard University, under the direction of Professor F. W. Putnam. It is the result of a very ingenious process of scientific reconstruction. The proper proportions of the figure were ascertained from a perfect skeleton of a Massachusetts Indian unearthed at Winthrop by Professor Putnam in 1888. The rank of this warrior was indicated by various objects that were buried with him, and we even know the manner of his death; for there was an arrow point sticking in the inside of a lumbar vertebra, which showed that he had been shot through the abdomen. The skull was carefully measured to get the shape of the head and the proportions of the face. A series of experiments undertaken by Dr. Thomas Dwight, of the Harvard Medical School, gave the thickness of the flesh for the different parts of the face. Details of facial expression were taken from a photograph of a member of a related tribe, the Winnebagoes, who may be presumed to resemble their Algonquin brethren of New England. The shirt, leggings, and moccasins were drawn from specimens in the Peabody Museum which accorded with descriptions of Massachusetts Indians in writings of the seventeenth century. The feathers in the hair were copied from photographs of Ojibways,

but are equally good for New England, as the old authorities prove. The beads round the neck were from specimens actually found with the skeleton already mentioned. The belt was taken from a bead-embroidered girdle, traditionally said to have belonged to King Philip himself. The bow is a copy of the only Massachusetts weapon of the kind known to be in existence. This has an authentic pedigree extending back to 1665, when it was taken from a Sudbury Indian who had been shot by a white man. Both belt and bow may still be seen in the Museum. The arrow was drawn from specimens in the same collection, and its length was carefully adjusted to the size of the bow.[1] Altogether, then, we have in this figure a representation of an old Massachusetts warrior which is quite as correct as if it had been sketched by a draughtsman of the old time; and the learning and ingenuity of the reconstructive process add to the interest of the picture. It will be observed that our Indian holds the bow in his left hand and the arrow in his right, as he should. In this he follows actual custom and the dictates of practical utility, as well as the ancient seal of the Massachusetts Bay Company.[2] It is to be regretted that the Great Seal of the Commonwealth, even in its latest design, as adopted in 1898,[3] perpetuates an error made, apparently, in 1780, and depicts an Indian who can only be described as left-handed. The mere transposition of two words in the Act of 1885,[4] which defines the seal, would bring the law into accordance with the facts. Let us hope that the General Court may see its way to this slight but significant reform.

The following story is told by Captain Nathaniel Uring

[1] These details are given on the basis of a communication from Professor Putnam to the writer.

[2] On various forms of the seal see Massachusetts Documents, 1885, House, No. 345; E. H. Garrett, New England Magazine, 1901, XXIII, 623 ff.

[3] Acts of 1898, ch. 519.   [4] Acts of 1885, ch. 288.

in his account of his visit to Boston in 1709.[1] It does not appear whence he derived it, but the two stories immediately preceding were told him by Governor Joseph Dudley himself and by Paul Dudley, his son.

A third Story is told of the Governour and an *Indian*, which may not be improper to shew the Subtilty of the Natives. Governour *Dudly* was a Man of very good Understanding, and was very industrious in improving his Plantation : He observing a lusty *Indian* almost naked, took Occasion one Day to ask him, why he did not work to purchase something to keep him from the Cold? The Fellow asked the Governour, why he did not work? Who told him, he worked with his Head, and had no Occasion to work with his Hands as he must. The *Indian* said, If any one would employ him, he would work. The Governour asked him to kill him a Calf, for which he would give him a Shilling. The *Indian* readily undertook it, and killed the Calf ; but observing he did not go about to skin it, asked him, why he did not make haste to skin and dress it? the *Indian* answered, No, no, *Coponoh ;* that was not in my Bargain, I was to have a Shilling for killing it, *he no dead Coponoh* [?] The Governour seeing the Fellow witty upon him, bid him dress it, and he would give him another Shilling : The *Indian* having finished his Work, and being paid, went to an Alehouse, where they sold Rum, which was near the Governour's House, where he spent some of his Money in that Liquor, which they are all great Lovers of ; and whether he had Brass Money of his own, or whether the House furnished him with it, is out of my Story ; but he went back to the Governour, and told him, he had given him bad Money, who seeing it Brass, readily gave him another ; and soon after the Fellow went back with a Second, which the Governour also changed, but knew the Fellow had put upon him ; and seeing him next Day, called to him and told him he must carry a Letter presently to *Boston*, which he wrote to the Keeper of *Bridewell*, in order to have the fellow well lashed ; but he

[1] History of the Voyages and Travels of Capt. Nathaniel Uring, London, 1726, pp. 120–1.

apprehending the Consequence, and seeing another *Indian* in
the Road, he gave him the Letter, telling him, the Governour
said he must carry that Letter presently to *Boston*. The poor
Fellow took it innocently, and having delivered the Letter as
directed, was whip'd very severely; the Governour soon after
seeing the *Indian* again, asked him, if he had carried the Letter
he sent him with? He answered, No, no, *Coponoh*, Head work,
pointing to his Head: The Governour was so well pleased with
the Fellow's Answer, he forgave him.

An instructive piece of Indian social philosophy is given
on the authority of the Rev. John Heckewelder, for a long
time missionary among the Pennsylvania aborigines: —

An aged Indian, who for many years had spent much of his
time among the white people both in Pennsylvania and New
Jersey, one day about the year 1770 observed, that the Indians
had not only a much easier way of getting a wife than the whites,
but were also more certain of getting a *good* one; " For," (said
he in his broken English,) "White man court, — court, — may
be one whole year! — may be two year before he marry! — well!
— may be then got *very good* wife — but may be *not!* — may be
very cross! — Well now, suppose cross! scold so soon as get
awake in the morning! scold all day! scold until sleep! — all
one; he must keep *him!* White people have law forbidding
throwing away wife, be *he* ever so cross! must keep *him* always!
Well! how does Indian do? — Indian when he see industrious
Squaw, which he like, he go to *him*, place his two forefingers
close aside each other, make two look like one — look Squaw in
the face — see *him* smile — which is all one *he* say, *Yes!* so he
take *him* home — no danger *he* be cross! no! no! Squaw know
too well what Indian do if *he* cross! — throw *him* away and take
another! Squaw love to eat meat! no husband! no meat!
Squaw do everything to please husband! he do the same to
please Squaw! live happy!"[1]

[1] Heckewelder, Account of the History, Manners, and Customs, of the
Indian Nations, who once inhabited Pennsylvania and the Neighbouring
States, 1819, pp. 151-2.

Local tradition in Natick, as reported in 1830, is responsible for two or three short samples of Indian English.

A devout Indian of Natick, Deacon Ephraim, described as " an ornament to the Christian society for many years," was asked why young Indians who were educated in English families, so often became drunken and disorderly when they grew up, although they had behaved well so long as they were under tutelage. " Ducks will be ducks," replied the old man, " notwithstanding they are hatched by the hen," or, in his own words and pronunciation, "Tucks will be tucks, for all ole hen he hatchum." [1]

Another Natick Indian went to Boston in the fall with a load of brooms and baskets, and purchased a dram. The next spring, on a similar occasion, the same storekeeper charged him twice as much for the same quantity of liquor. The Indian naturally asked the reason for this increase in price, and was informed that the dealer had kept the cask through the winter and that this was as expensive as to keep a horse. " Hah," grunted the customer, " he no eat so much hay; but I believe he drink as much water." [2]

Mr. Ebenezer Peabody was minister at Natick from 1721 to 1752. In praying for rain, he made use of the biblical formula, " May the bottles of heaven be unstopped and a plentiful supply of rain be poured down on the thirsty earth." The rain came almost immediately and lasted for many days. One of Mr. Peabody's Indian congregation, who happened to meet him, observed: " I believe them are bottles you talk about be unstopped, and the stopples be lost." [3]

This story of Mr. Peabody recalls an extraordinary contest on a similar occasion between an Indian wizard and Mr. Fitch, of Norwich, Connecticut. The incident is

[1] Biglow, History of Natick, 1830, p. 81.
[2] The same, p. 86. Elsewhere this anecdote is told of a Connecticut River Indian.   [3] The same, p. 86.

dated August 3, 1676, and is too curious to be omitted, though it adds nothing to our knowledge of the Indian manner of speaking English. As told by Increase Mather [1] it brings to mind vividly the narrative of Elijah's discomfiture of the priests of Baal in the eighteenth chapter of First Kings; but it seems better to give the story in Mr. Fitch's own words: —

Concerning the Drought, &c. the true Narrative of that Providence is this,

In *August* last, such was the want of rain, that the Indian corn was not only dryed and parched up, but the apple-trees withered, the fruit and leaves fell off as in Autumn, and some trees seemed to be dead with that Drought: the Indians came into town and lamented their want of rain, and that their *Powawes* could get none in their way of worship, desiring me that I would seek to God for rain: I appointed a Fast day for that purpose. The day being come, it proved cleer without any clouds, untill sunsetting, when we came from the Meeting, and then some Clouds arose; the next day remained cloudy, then *Uncas* with many Indians came to my house, *Uncas* lamented there was such want of Rain; I asked whether if God should send us rain, he would not attribute it to their *Powawes:* He answered no, for they had done their uttermost and all in vain: I replyed, if you will declare it before all these Indians, you shall see what God will doe for us; For although this year he hath shewn his anger against the English, and not only against the Indians, yet he hath begun to save us, and I have found by experience twice in the like case, when we sought by Fasting and Prayer, he hath given us Rain, and never denyed us. Then *Uncas* made a great speech to the Indians (which were many) confessing that if God should then send rain it could not be ascribed to their powawing, but must be acknowledged to be an answer of our prayers. This day the clouds spread more and more, and the next day there was

---

[1] A Brief History of the War with the Indians, London, 1676, p. 45, ed. Drake, pp. 189–90.

such plenty of rain that our River rose more than two foot in height.[1]

A still later piece of aboriginal English comes from Maine, and, though it gives no idea of pronunciation, is of peculiar interest for other reasons. On August 31, 1838, there was a great Council of the Tarratines and allied tribes, at Oldtown, Maine, to discuss the election of a new sachem. This meeting was the result of a combination against the authority of John Neptune, who claimed to be sachem for life, but whose addiction to strong waters and other indulgences had caused a good deal of dissatisfaction. "He is the moon," said one of the speakers, "that often grows larger, then smaller. For sometimes he loves his Indians very much ; by 'nd by, he don't love 'em so much. No, no, — he love 'em best some womankind, — not his own squaw. . . . Well, his Indians say, We have him 'sachem' no longer. They want a good governor, like old Orono ; — to speak wisdom, — to show 'em good works. Such one is governor *for life*. Not so the bad one. When his heart be very wicked, his walk crooked, 't is right to leave him."

For this speech we have unimpeachable evidence. It is reported by Mr. W. D. Williamson, the historian of Maine, in a paper sent to the Massachusetts Historical Society in the next year, 1839.[2]

A specimen of John Neptune's eloquence in English is also recorded by Mr. Williamson. In 1816 an Indian named Susup killed William Knight, a tavern keeper at Bangor, who had turned him out-of-doors because of his drunken turbulence. Susup was indicted for murder and tried in the Supreme Court at Castine, in June, 1817. The verdict was manslaughter, and when the court asked

[1] Hubbard, Narrative of the Troubles with the Indians, Boston, 1677, pp. 113-14.
[2] Collections, 3d Series, IX, 97-98.

Susup if he had anything to say, he called upon John Neptune to speak for him: —

That Indian then stepped forward from the midst of his associates, towards the Judges, and deliberately addressed them in an impressive speech of several minutes. He spake in broken English, yet every word was distinctly heard and easily understood. His gestures were frequent and forcible; his manner solemn; and a breathless silence pervaded the whole assembly. — He began — "You know, your people do my Indians great deal of wrong. — They abuse them very much; yes, they murder them; then they walk right off — nobody touches them. This makes my heart burn. Well, then my Indians say, we'll go kill your very bad and wicked men. No, I tell 'em, never do that thing; we are brothers. — Sometime ago a very bad man about Boston, shot an Indian dead; — your people said, surely he should die; but it was not so. — In the great prison-house he eats and lives to this day; certain he never dies for killing Indian. My brothers say, let that bloody man go free; — Peol Susup too. So we wish — hope fills the hearts of us all. — Peace is good. These, my Indians, love it well; they smile under its shade. The white men and red men must be always friends; — the Great Spirit is our Father; — I speak what I feel."

Susup was sentenced to another year's imprisonment; and required to find sureties for keeping the peace two years, in the penal sum of $500; when John Neptune, and 'Squire Jo Merry Neptune, of his own tribe, Capt. Solmond, from Passamaquoddy, and Capt. Jo Tomer, from the river St. John, became his sureties in the recognizance.[1]

John Neptune's eloquence, it seems, was not unavailing.

[1] W. D. Williamson, History of Maine, Hallowell, 1832, I, 501-2. Mr. Williamson was Susup's counsel.

MORE INDIAN TALK

IN the previous chapter we have considered oral discourse chiefly, and most of our examples have been of a conversational sort. There are also, of course, a good many written documents of a more or less formal character. These are generally the work of some converted native who had been taught to read and write in the Indian schools established under Eliot's influence. Sometimes the scribe is known, and usually his identity is not beyond a reasonable guess.

An undated letter from King Philip to Governor Prince may head the list. The authorship is usually credited to John Sassamon, the praying Indian who at one time acted as Philip's secretary and whose tragic fate (told elsewhere in this book) was the signal for the outbreak of hostilities.[1] The exact date of the epistle is unknown. The irregularities are chiefly syntactical; the spelling is quite as good as that of most records of the time and throws little light on the peculiarities of pronunciation.

To the much honered governer mr. thomas prince, dwelling at plimouth

      honered sir,

        King philip desire to let you understand that he could not come to the court, for tom his interpreter has a pain in his back that he could not travil so far, and philips sister is verey sik.

Philip would intreat that faver of you and aney of the maiestrats, if aney english or engians speak about aney land he pray you to give them no answear at all.   the last sumer he maid that

[1] See p. 76, above.

promis with you that he would not sell no land in 7 years time
for that he would have no english trouble him before that time
he has not forgat that you promis him

he will come asune as possible he can to speak with you

and so I rest your very loving frind philip dweling at mount
hope nek.[1]

Another document of Philip's, dated 1666, also concerns
the vital question of selling land to the settlers. It amounts
to a power of attorney appointing two Indians his general
agents in such matters. It begins with great decorum but
soon runs off into unconventionality : —

Know all men by these presents, that *Philip* haue giuen power
vnto *Watuchpoo* and *Sampson* and theire brethren to hold and
make sale of to whom they will by my consent, and they shall not
haue itt without they be willing to lett it goe it shal be sol by my
consent, but without my knowledge they cannot safely to : but
with my consent there is none that can lay claime to that land
which they haue marked out, it is theires foreuer, soe therefore
none can safely purchase any otherwise but by *Watuchpoo* and
Sampson and their bretheren.

PHILIP 1666.[2]

In April, 1676, Tom Dublet, alias Nepanet, one of the
friendly Natick Indians who were then confined on Deer
Island, was despatched to King Philip's quarters to negotiate for the release of Mrs. Rowlandson, wife of the minister
of Lancaster, and other captives who had been taken at
the sack of that town. Tom soon returned with a written
reply : —

We no give answer by this one man, but if you like my answer
sent one more man besides this one Tom Nepanet, and send with
all true heart and with all your mind by two men ; because you

---

[1] The Massachusetts Magazine, for May, 1789, I, 276. The copy in Coll.
Mass. Hist. Soc., 1793, II, 40, varies slightly.

[2] Drake, Book of the Indians, 8th ed., Boston, 1841, bk. iii, p. 14.

know and we know your heart great sorrowful with crying for your lost many many hundred man and all your house and all your land and woman child and cattle as all your thing that you have lost and on your backside stand.

> SAM, Sachem,
> KUTQUEN, and
> QUANOHIT, Sagamores.
> Peter Jethro, scribe.

Mr. Rowlandson, your wife and all your child is well but one dye. Your sister is well and her 3 child. John Kittell, your wife and all your child is all well, and all them prisoners taken at Nashua is all well.

Mr. Rowlandson, se your loving sister his hand **C** Hanah.

And old Kettel wif his hand. +

Brother Rowlandson, pray send thre pound of Tobacco for me, if you can my loving husband pray send thre pound of tobacco for me.

This writing by your enemies — Samuel Uskattuhgun and Gunrashit, two Indian sagamores.[1]

The confused postscript may need a word of explanation. It was intended to convince the Council that the prisoners were alive and well. Mr. Rowlandson's sister-in-law, Hannah Divoll, signs with her mark. The tobacco which Mrs. Rowlandson asks her husband to send her was of course to be used in mollifying her captors. Subsequently, when Mr. John Hoar went to negotiate for the release of the captives, he carried Mrs. Rowlandson a pound of tobacco, which she immediately sold to the Indians for "nine shillings in mony." "For many of the *Indians*," she tells us, "for want of *Tobacco*, smoaked *Hemlock*, and *Ground-Ivy*." There follows the remark, somewhat startling to us nowadays: — "It was a great mistake in any,

---

[1] The same, bk. iii, p. 90, apparently from the MS., which cannot now be found. Most of the letter is given by Gookin, Historical Account, Coll. Am. Antiq. Soc., II, 508.

who thought I sent for *Tobacco:* for through the favour
of God, that desire was overcome." [1] We must remember,
however, that the habit of smoking was by no means rare
amongst women in the seventeenth and even in the eighteenth century. Earlier in her narrative Mrs. Rowlandson
confesses to the seductiveness of a couple of pipes: —
"Then I went to see King *Philip*, he bade me come in
and sit down, and asked me whether I would smoke it
(a usual Complement now adayes amongst Saints and
Sinners) but this no way suited me. For though I had
formerly used Tobacco, yet I had left it ever since I was
first taken. *It seems to be a Bait, the Devil layes to make
men loose their precious time:* I remember with shame, how
formerly, when I had taken two or three pipes, I was presently ready for another, such a bewitching thing it is: But
I thank God, he has now given me power over it: surely
there are many who may be better imployed than to ly
sucking a stinking Tobacco-pipe." [2]

Peter Jethro, who acted as scribe on this occasion, was
the son of a Natick Indian called Jethro or Tantamous.
Old Jethro had escaped when the friendly Indians were
being conducted to Deer Island for safe keeping, and was
now, like his son, in the ranks of the enemy. Later, it
appears, Peter went back to the whites and was employed
as a spy. It is to him that Mrs. Rowlandson refers when
she says, "There was another Praying-*Indian*, who when
he had done all the mischief that he could, betrayed his
own Father into the *English* hands, thereby to purchase
his own life." [3] His epitaph is an emphatic utterance of
Increase Mather: — "That abominable Indian Peter Jethro
betrayed his own Father, and other Indians of his special
acquaintance, unto Death." [4]

[1] Narrative, 1682, p. 56 (Nourse and Thayer's facsimile).
[2] The same, p. 24.   [3] The same, p. 50.
[4] An Historical Discourse concerning the Prevalency of Prayer 1677,
p. 6, ed. Drake, Early History of New England, 1864, pp. 257–8.

Another Indian letter concerning the same negotiations, though unsigned, is thought to be the work of James Printer, a native who has an honorable name in the history of American typography. He had been apprenticed to Samuel Green of Cambridge in 1659, but had joined his countrymen when the war broke out. Soon after the date of this letter, he gave himself up, was pardoned, and returned to his trade. He was Eliot's mainstay in setting up and correcting the second edition of the Indian Bible (published in 1685), and in 1709 his name is joined with Green's in the imprint of an English and Indian Psalter.[1] James Printer's letter is preserved among the Hutchinson Papers.[2] It was written at Philip's headquarters at Wachusett, and runs as follows: —

For the Governor and the Council at Boston
The Indians, Tom Nepennomp and Peter Tatatiqunea hath brought us letter from you about the English Captives, especially for Mrs Rolanson; the answer is I am sorrow that I haue don much wrong to you and yet I say the falte is lay upon you, for when we began quarel at first with Plimouth men I did not think that you should haue so much truble as now is: therefore I am willing to hear your desire about the Captives. Therefore we desire you to sent Mr Rolanson and goodman Kettel: (for their wives) and these Indians Tom and Peter to redeem their wives, they shall come and goe very safely: Whereupon we ask Mrs Rolanson, how much your husband willing to giue for you she gaue an answer 20 pound in goodes but John Kittels wife could not till. and the rest captives may be spoken of hereafter.

The descendants of James Printer did not follow in the steps of their ancestor so far as learning is concerned. In 1728, when the Indian proprietors of Hassanamisco

[1] See Drake, Book of the Indians, 8th ed., bk. ii, pp. 50–51; Pilling, Bibliography of the Algonquian Languages, Washington, 1891, p. 348.
[2] II, 282. Here from Nourse and Thayer's edition of Mrs. Rowlandson's Narrative, Lancaster, 1903, pp. 97–98.

(Grafton) conveyed the town to the English, Ami Printer, Moses Printer, and Ami Printer, Jr., signed the deed, each as owner of a seventh of the land, and all made their marks. It must be admitted, however, that these marks appear in every case to be the initial of the signer's name.[1]

The high standing of Waban is nowhere more conclusively shown than in three Indian letters in which he is actually addressed as "Mr. Waban," — a proud title in colonial times. The first of these was written in July, 1676, and the others soon after. The fortunes of Philip had declined, and his allies were eager to make peace with the English. They are favorable specimens of aboriginal English.[2]

Mr. *John Leveret*, my Lord, Mr. *Waban*, and all the chief men our Brethren, Praying to God : We beseech you all to help us ; my Wife she is but one, but there be more Prisoners, which we pray you keep well : *Muttamuck* his Wife, we entreat you for her, and not onely that man, but it is the Request of two Sachems, *Sam Sachem* of *Weshakum*, and the *Pakashoag* Sachem.

And then that further you will consider about the making Peace : We have spoken to the People of *Nashobak* (viz. *Tom Dubler* and *Peter*,) that we would agree with you, and make a Covenant of Peace with you : We have been destroyed by your Souldiers, but still we Remember it now, to sit still ; do you consider it again ; we do earnestly entreat you, that it may be so, by *Jesus Christ*, O ! let it be so !   *Amen, Amen.*

It was Signed

Muttamuck, his Mark N.   *Uppanippaquem*, his — C.
Sam Sachem, his Mark Ψ.   *Pakaskoag* his Mark Ψ.
Simon Pottoquam, Scribe.

Superscrib'd, To all English-men *and* Indians, *all of you, hear Mr.* Waban, *Mr.* Eliott.

[1] See F. C. Pierce, History of Grafton, p. 40.
[2] Preserved in A True Account of the Most Considerable Occurrences, etc., London, 1676, pp. 6 ff.

My Lord, Mr. *Leveret* at *Boston*, Mr. *Waban*, Mr. *Eliott*, Mr. *Gooken*, and Council, hear ye. I went to Connecticott about the Captives, that I might bring them into your hands, and when we were almost there, the *English* had destroy'd those *Indians;* when I heard it, I return'd back again ; then when I came home, we were also destroyed ; after we were destroyed, then *Philip* and *Quanipun* went away into their own Countrey again ; and I know they were much afraid, because of our offer to joyn with the *English*, and therefore they went back into their own Countrey, and I know they will make no Warre ; therefore because when some *English* men came to us, *Philip* and *Quanapun* sent to kill them ; but I said, If any kill them, I 'll kill them.

Sam Sachem.

Written by Simon Boshokum *Scribe.*

For Mr. *Eliot*, Mr. *Gooken*, and Mr. *Waban*.

Consider of this I Intreat you, consider of this great businesse that is done ; and my wonder concerning *Philip*, but his Name is ——— *Wewesawanit*, he engageth all the people that were none of his Subjects : Then when I was at *Penakook, Numpho John, Alline, Sam Numpho,* and others who were angry, and *Numpho* very much angry that *Philip* did engage so many people to him ; and *Numpho* said it were a very good deed that I should go and kill him that joyned so many to himself without cause : in like manner I said so too. Then had you formerly said be at peace, and if the Councill had sent word to Kill *Philip* we should have done it : then let us clearly speak, what you, and we shall do. O let it be so speedily, and answer us clearly.

Pumkamun,
Ponnakpukun,
or, *Jacob Muttamakoog.*

Sam Sachem, or Sagamore Sam, was a Nashaway chief, whose Indian name was Shoshanim. We have already had a sample of his diplomatic correspondence in the letter to the Council in the case of Mrs. Rowlandson

(April, 1676).[1] That letter, however, was conceived in a very different spirit from the first of the present series, and is probably a better index to the Sachem's character. The second of the series seems to contain more of the sagamore and less of the Christian scribe. Sam's attempts to make peace were futile. He was taken and hanged. Judge Sewall's Diary, under date of September 26, 1676, records with matter-of-fact conciseness the result of the rigorous proceedings that followed King Philip's War: — " Sagamore Sam goes, and Daniel Goble is drawn in a Cart upon bed cloaths to Execution. . . . One ey'd John, Maliompe, Sagamore of Quapaug, General at Lancaster, &c, Jethro, (the Father) walk to the Gallows."

Four documents from the New Hampshire Provincial Papers may close the roll.[2] They are from the distinguished Penacook sachem, John Hogkins, often called Hawkins. The first two are the composition of Simon Betogkom, the same person who wrote the letters from Sam Sachem just quoted. The variation in the spelling of his name — *Betogkom* or *Boshokum* — is by no means unexampled. Hogkins and his associates, it will be seen, are anxious for peaceful relations with the white men. Their letters or petitions were all presented at about the time when Governor Cranfield left the Province. The last of the series mentions the Governor's departure: — " He go away, so he say, at last night." It is addressed to Robert Mason, grandson and heir of Captain John, and claimant to the Proprietorship of New Hampshire. It is a satisfaction to know that a treaty of amity and reciprocal justice with the Indians was signed soon after.[3]

---

[1] See pp. 368-9, above.

[2] New Hampshire Provincial Papers, I, 583-5. There are several signatures, besides that of Hogkins to the first two letters.

[3] Sept. 8, 1685 (Provincial Papers, I, 588).

May 15th, 1685.

Honour Governor my friend, you my friend I desire your worship and your power Because I hope you can do som great matters this once I am poor and naked and I have no men at my place because I afraid allways mohogs [i. e., Mohawks] he will kill me every day and night if your worship when please pray help me you no let mohogs kill me at my place at Malamake [i. e. Merrimac] Revir called Panukkog and Natukkog I will submit your worship and your power and now I want powder and such allminishon shott and guns because I have forth at my hom and I plant theare.

This all Indian hand but
pray you do consider

your humble Servant   JOHN HOGKINS.

May 15th, 1685.

Honour mr Governor now this day I com your house I want se you and I Bring my hand at before you I want shake hand to you if your worship when please then you Receve my hand then shake your hand and my hand you my friend because I Remember at old time when live my grant father and grant mother then Englishmen com this country then my grant father and Englishmen they make a good govenant they friend allwayes my grant father leving at place called malamake Rever other Name chef Natukkog and panukkog that one Rever great many names and I bring you this few skins at this first time I will give you my friend

This all Indian hand

John-+-hawkins Sagomor

please your worship I will intreat your matther you my friend now this if my Indians he do you long [i. e., wrong] pray you no put your law because som my Indians fooll som men much love drunk then he no know what he do may be he do mischif when he drunk if so pray you must let me know what he done because I will ponis him what he have done you you my friend if you desire any business then sent me I will help you if I can

Mr. John hogkins

mr mason pray I want speake you a few words if your worship
when please because I com parfas [purpose] I will speake this
Governor but he go away so he say at last night and so far I
understand this governor his power that your power now so he
speake his own mouth pray if you take what I want pray com to
me because I want go hom at this day.

your humble servant,

John hogkins, Indian Sogmon.

May 16th, 1685.

The rapid disappearance of the various Indian languages
in central and southern New England is noteworthy,
though not astonishing. Now and then the philologist
has the melancholy pleasure of being present at the last
gasp of some aboriginal dialect. No longer ago than 1903
Mr. Frank G. Speck discovered a scanty remnant of the
language of the Scaticook (Skaghticoke) Indians of Litch-
field County, Connecticut, still lingering in the memory of
one James Harris, "who claimed to be a full-blood." Harris
had learned what he knew of the matter from his grandmother, who was able to speak the language. He recollected
but twenty-three words and three connected sentences, one
of which meant, as he interpreted it, "Hurry up to the
hotel and get a drink," or more probably, as Professor
Prince has made out, "Come along, my friends, and we
will have a drink." [1] Either reading is significant enough.
It may be added, since neither Mr. Speck nor Professor
Prince notices the circumstance, that the late Benson J.
Lossing visited the Skaghticoke reservation about 1859
and held a long conversation with Eunice Mahwee, a
granddaughter of the Gideon Mahwee who is said to have
formed the settlement in 1728. Mr. Lossing contributed
an account of his visit to Scribner's Monthly for October,

[1] Prince and Speck, Proceedings of the American Philosophical Society,
XLII, 346 ff.

1871, under the title " The Last of the Pequods."[1] His article is provided with a portrait of Eunice Mahwee, who, when he saw her, was " just one hundred years old," and who regarded herself as the only pure-blooded survivor of her tribe. In 1836 Eunice Mawehu contributed information about her people to J. W. Barber; but neither Barber nor Lossing says anything about her knowledge of the Indian language.[2] Another Connecticut tribe, also studied by Mr. Speck, have remembered their native tongue better. In the village of Mohegan, near Norwich, live some fifty Pequots, and there are about fifty more in the adjacent towns who belong to the same group. Though all are American citizens, they still maintain the form of their old tribal government, and meet annually in the church at Mohegan, — for they are sufficiently devout Congregationalists, — to celebrate the ancient Green-corn Feast. Their habitual language is English, but two of the women, a Mrs. Fielding and her sister, are able to speak Pequot, and the former can write it with some fluency.[3] In less than a generation, however, the old dialect will undoubtedly disappear, though certain words and phrases, and perhaps a sentence or two, may linger in the memory of individuals. The discoveries of Mr. Speck carry one's imagination back to the fate of the ancient Cornish tongue, which ceased to be a living language when Dolly Pentreath died in 1777.

Our discussion has led us far away from High Howder's writ as reported by Mr. Thomas,[4] but it may be hoped

[1] Reprinted by W. W. Beach, The Indian Miscellany, Albany, 1877, pp. 452 ff.

[2] Connecticut Historical Collections, pp. 200, note, 471 ; see also Samuel Orcutt, The Indians of the Housatonic and Naugatuck Valleys, Hartford, 1882, pp. 197 ff.

[3] See Speck and Prince, American Anthropologist, 1903, New Series, V, 193 ff.

[4] See p. 333, above.

that our scrutiny of the literary efforts of our aboriginal predecessors has not been altogether devoid of interest. At all events, it has served to illustrate the diversity of subjects which occupied the mind of the Old Farmer and which lend character to his venerable Almanack.

INDEX

Climate, 191 ff. See also Weather.
Clough, Samuel, his almanac, 58; on the Man of the Signs, 58.
Clytemnestra, 115.
Coaches, private, 286. See Stage-coaches.
Cobbett, Wm., Treatise on Gardening, 141.
Cock, throwing at the, 177 f.
Coffee, consumption of, 184 f.; potatoes as a substitute for, 184 f.
Cogan, Dr. Thomas, on resuscitation, 163.
Cogswell, Dr. M. F., on Indian summer, 191 f.
Coins, silver, value in 1797, 37.
Colonial Society of Massachusetts, 235.
Columbiad, epic by Joel Barlow, 170.
Columbian Centinel, 238, 276.
Columbian Muse, 318.
Comets, 41; effect on weather, 191, 198 ff.; portentous, 198 ff.; Increase Mather on, 199 f.; Professor Winthrop on, 200.
Company of Stationers, publishers of almanacs, 46 f.
Congress in 1794, 234.
Connecticut, maple sugar in, 122 f.; peddlers in, 144 f.; schools in, 227 f.; Sunday laws in, 238 f.; Indians in, 124 ff., 376 f.
Connecticut Courant, 164.
Constables, Indian, 333 ff., 338, 340 ff.
Constitution, frigate, 215.
Continental Congress encourages salt-making, 133.
Conveyance, means of, 285 ff.
Cooper, Judith (Sewall), 14.
Corn, huskings, 168 ff.; red ears, 168, 171 f.; crows, 189 f.; corn crop and Indian summer, 198; uses of, 191; the word, in England and America, 327 f.
Cornish, murder of, 75.
Cornish language, 377.
Cornstalks, molasses from, 129.
Corpse, bleeding of, 74 ff.
Corpse lights, 162.
Correspondents of the Almanac, 25 ff.
Costume, 63 ff., 222; Indian, 359 f.
Cotton, Rev. John, estate on Pemberton (Cotton) Hill, 14.
Cotton, John, 349.
Cotton, Rev. Seaborn, 14.

Counter-irritants, 186 f.
County fairs, 93.
Courts, held at taverns, 278; Indian, 337 ff.
Courts martial, 210 f.
Coverly, N., Boston printer, 7.
Cracow, salt mine at, 134.
Cranfield, Gov. Edward, of New Hampshire, 374 ff.
Cream bewitched, 206.
Crosby, Rev. C. C. P., 5, 98.
Crown Point, expedition to, in 1756, 4.
Crows, means of preventing them from pulling up corn, 189 f.
Cumberland Gazette, 182.
Cure for greasy heels in horses, 188; wonderful cures, 115 ff.
Curiosity of Americans, 268 f.
Currency, 37; different standards, 38; tenor bill, 352 f.
Currier, J. J., historian of Newbury, Mass., 262.
Curtis, G. W., on the Pilgrim and Puritan Christmas, 174 f.
Cutler, Rev. Manasseh, on the weather, 198.
Cuts: see Illustrations.

Dacia: see Petrus de Dacia.
Dairy, cleanliness in, 182.
Dark Day of 1780, 203 ff.; of 1819, 205.
Davenport, Abraham, poem by Whittier, 203.
Davis, John, traveller and pedagogue, on ballad peddler, 142 f.; on Fairbanks murder, 142 f.; on inns and innkeepers, 263, 283 f.; on motto of the Cincinnati, 263; on hospitality, 284.
Davis, Judge John, edition of Morton's Memorial, 327, 333; on wheat, 327; version of Indian warrant, 333 f.; early life, 334.
Davy, John, M. D., on the poison of the toad, 115.
Day, Benjamin H., founder of New York Sun, 259; on the Moon Hoax, 259.
Day, Thomas, his Sandford and Merton, 319.
Dead languages, Thomas Paine on, 319 f.
Deane, Samuel, D. D., his New England Farmer, or Georgical Diction-

Farmer's Letters, by John Dickinson, 68.
Farming: see Agriculture.
Fearing, Israel, his gun, 245.
Feast of Bricriu, Irish saga, 355.
Federal Galaxy, 269.
Felt, J. B., historian of Ipswich, Mass., 73; on means of conveyance, 285.
Ferguson, James, his Astronomy studied by Mr. Thomas, 6.
Fetch fire, to, 155 f.
Fevers and moon, 308.
Fiction in New England, 318 f., 322 f.
Field, Edward, on taverns, 265, 296.
Fielding, Mrs., Pequot, 377.
Fielding's novels, sold by Mr. Thomas, 318.
Fines, for carrying fire or smoking in streets, 155 f.; for keeping Christmas, 174; for selling cider to Indians, 351 f.; military, 209 ff.
Fire, precautions against, etc., 146 ff.; carrying, 155 f.; laws, 155 f.
Fire companies and engines, 151 f.
Fire-escapes, 152 f.
Fire insurance, 28, 150.
Fire societies, 146 ff.
Fireplaces, 146.
Firewood, when to cut, 306.
Fitch, Rev. James, of Norwich, Conn., praying for rain, 363 f.
Fitch, Maj. Thomas, 349.
Flintlocks, 209.
Flying Machine, coach, 296; Flying Mail, coach, 296.
Flying stationers, 137 ff.
Folk-lore: see Superstitions.
Folk-medicine, 118 f.
Food at inns, 279 f., 286.
Fool's gold, fool's parsley, etc., 196.
Footman, ——, 75.
Forman: see Smith and Forman.
Fortunatus, chapbook, 139.
Fortune tellers, 108 f.
Fowler, James, on the figures of the months, etc., 68.
France, salt-making in, 133.
Francis, Convers, D.D., biography of Judge John Davis, 334.
Franklin, Benjamin, and Mr. Thomas, 1 f.; on labor in America, 180; lightning rods, 201; Autobiography, 316, 320.
Free will, controversy between Hobbes and Bramhall, 57.

Freezing, death by, 167.
Freight, rates for, 296.
French and Indian War, 321.
Fresh Pond, Watertown, Mass., 9.
Fruit trees, when to plant, 313.

GADBURY, JOHN, and his almanac, 44, 46; poem on astrology, 314.
Galenical medicine, controversy about, 118.
Gambling, 95 f., 271.
Garden sauce, 84 f.
Gardening in Boston, 9.
Garrett, Edmund H., on the Massachusetts seal, 360.
Gawain and the Green Knight, romance of, 355.
Gentleman's Magazine, 160, 308.
Geography, works on, 315, 317, 320.
German folk-lore, 159.
Germans in America, 283.
Gévaudun, Wild Beast of, 69 ff.
Ghost stories, 73.
Giotto, 67.
Giraldus Cambrensis, on weasels, 120.
Girdling trees, 311.
Girls' schools, 229 f.
Glade Road, Old, 304.
Glanvil, Rev. Joseph, on witchcraft, 111.
Glauber's salts, manufacture of, 134 f.
Goble, Daniel, executed, 374.
Godfrey of Bulloigne, chapbook, 139.
God's Revenge against Murder, 72.
Gods, Indian, 109.
Göldi, Anna, alleged witch, 114.
Goodale, Azubah, 4.
Goodale, Joseph, 4.
Gookin, Daniel, 337, 339 ff.; as Indian magistrate, 340 ff.; opinion of Waban, 337; Indian letter to, 373.
Goose bone as weather sign, 205.
Goose-summer, 196.
Goshen, Conn., 123.
Gossip, characterized, 89, 90 f.
Go-summer, 195.
Gout, moxa as cure for, 187.
Grafting and the moon, 313.
Grafton, Mass., Indian ruler at, 342; Indian proprietors of, 371 f.
Grain: see Corn; English grain; Wheat.
Grammar schools, 226 f.
Grammars, 230.

Grant, Dr. Andrew, 253 ff.
Gray, Edward, publisher at Suffield, Conn., 42.
Greasy heels, disease of horses, 188.
Green, Samuel, printer, 371.
Green, Dr. Samuel A., biography of Mr. Thomas, 15, 17; Facsimile Reproductions, 233; on history of Groton, Mass., 279, 345 ff.; on Indian title to Groton, 345 ff.
Green-corn feast, Indian, 377.
Greene, Gardiner, his estate on Pemberton Hill, Boston, 9 ff.
Greene, Robert, tragedy of Alphonsus, 120.
Greenfield (Mass.) Gazette, 144.
Grog, 90, 94 f., 272 ff., 282. See Rum.
Groton, Mass., meetings of selectmen, 278 f.; stage from Boston to, 290; Indian title to, 345 ff.
Groton Herald, 278.
Ground ivy, smoked instead of tobacco, 369.
Groundsel, the herb, 188.
Guinea voyage, horoscope for, 39.
Gunrashit, Indian sagamore, 369.
Guns, 209, 244 ff.
Guy of Warwick, romance and chapbook, 137.

HAIR, cutting, in increase of the moon, 305.
Halcyon days, 193, 196.
Hale, Nathan, on railroads, 300.
Hall, Capt. Basil, on railroads, 298.
Hallet, Jeremiah, 27 f.
Halliwell, J. O., on the Man of the Signs, 54.
Hamilton, Alexander, 126.
Hancock, John, anecdote, 11 f.
Harriott, Lieut. John, on American currency, 38; on barberries and wheat, 331.
Harris, James, Indian, 376.
Harris, Thaddeus W., on native cantharides, 187.
Harrower, John, 247.
Hartford, Conn., Bull's tavern, 123.
Harvard College (and University), 5, 235 ff.; commencement at, 9; theses for A. M., 40 f., 116 f.; first degree of LL. D., 200, 234 ff.; Professor Winthrop's lectures, 200 ff.; Peabody Museum, 359 ff.; Medical School, 359; Museum at, in eighteenth century, 308.
Hassanamesitt, or Hassanamisco, (Grafton), Mass., 342, 371 f.
Hasty Pudding, poem by Joel Barlow, 170 f.
Hatch, Israel, his coffee house in Boston, 287, 290; his stage line from Boston to Providence, 296.
Haverhill, Mass., stage from Boston to, 289.
Hawkins, John, Indian, 375 f.
Hayley, Alderman, 10.
Hayley, Madam Mary, 9 ff.; her garden on Pemberton Hill, 9.
Hayley, William, the poet, 10.
Haymaking, haste in, 88; women engaged in, 182 f.
Hazard, Ebenezer, 204.
Head, Richard, his Canting Academy, 96 f.
Head, removable, belief in, 354 f.
Heckewelder, Rev. John, anecdotes of Indians, 353, 362.
Helmont, van, on Toad and Spider, 104 f.; his system of medicine, 117 f.
Hemlock, smoked instead of tobacco, 369.
Herbs, curative, planetary relations of, 41; sought by animals, 119 ff.; plantain, 104 ff.; groundsel, 188.
Herschel, Sir John, and the Moon Hoax, 252 ff.
Herschel, Sir William, on the habitability of the moon, etc., 251 f.
Hexameters, English, on the dominion of the moon in man's body, 55.
Hibernation of swallows, 167.
High Howder: see Howder.
High schools, 226 ff.
Highwaymen unknown, 286.
Hihoudi, alleged Indian warrant by, 334.
Hildreth, S. P., 129, 135.
Hill, B. T., on railroads, 301.
Hill, D., Boston grocer, 9.
Hired man, wages of, 85 f., 180.
Historical Magazine, 244.
Historical Society of Pennsylvania, 191.
Hive, The, 318.
Hoar, John, negotiates for release of Mrs. Rowlandson and others, 369.
Hoaxes, astronomical, 251 ff.

of Hopkinton, Mass., 348 f.; on suicide of an Indian, 349 f.; on execution of Sagamore Sam, 374.

Shakspere, 59, 107, 115, 143, 193, 274, 305.

Shaw, H. W.: see Billings, Josh.

Shepard, Rev. Thomas, 337 f.

Shingles, 150.

Shoe, ass's, 206.

Shoemaker loo, 95 f.

Shoes, making, 93; old, used to scare crows, 189 f.; going without, 222.

Shoshanim: see Sam Sachem.

Showmen, innkeepers as, 276 f.

Shrewsbury, Mass., 4; Shrewsbury leg, 4 f.

Shrove Tuesday cakes and sports, 177 ff.; Tuisco, 177 ff.; pancakes, 177 f.; throwing at the cock, 177 f.; Mather on, 177 ff.

Sign of tavern, 264 f.

Signs of zodiac, 79; the Anatomy and, 53 ff.; figures of, 62 ff.; connection with vegetation, 306, 311 ff.

Simms, Jeptha R., anecdote of Gen. Eaton, 238 f.

Simonds, 240 f.

Skating, 63 f.

Skylark, The, songbook, 318.

Slander, 89, 90 f.

Slave-trade in New England, 39; astrology in, 39 f.

Slavery, 121 f., 127 f.

Sleighs and sleigh-riding, 297.

Smallpox in Boston, 1792, 14; inoculation for, 15.

Smith, Charlotte, her novels, 319.

Smith, Col. James, his captivity among the Indians, 171.

Smith, C. C., on scarcity of salt in the Revolutionary War, 134.

Smith and Forman's Almanac, 61.

Smoking, 88, 90, 147, 154 ff., 220 f.; by women and children, 147, 155, 369 f.; in the streets, 155 f.; of Nanibozhu, 197 f.; Indian substitutes for tobacco, 369.

Smollett's novels, 318.

Smut in wheat, 306.

Smutty ears of corn, at huskings, 169 f.

Smyth, J. F. D., on Gen. Jethro Sumner and other innkeepers, 263 f.

Snake and mouse, fight between, 108; cut in pieces, joins again, 120;

striped, useful in gardens, 119; Indian god in form of, 108; resuscitation of frozen, 167.

Snow, soap made of, 188 f.; clearing railway tracks of, 301.

Soap made of snow, 188 f.

Society for the Diffusion of Christian Knowledge, 46.

Society for Propagating Christian Knowledge, 294.

Society for Propagating the Gospel, 154.

Soldan, W. G., Geschichte der Hexenprozesse, 114.

Solomon, Indian ruler, 342.

Sommer, H. Oskar, 54.

Songbooks, 318.

Sorcery: see Witchcraft.

South African War, 47.

Southborough, Mass., 330.

Southey, Robert, on Beloe, 10; his Madoc, 170.

Sowing, significance of the moon for, 306.

Spain, witchcraft in, 114.

Spalding, Jacob, adventure with Indians, 352 f.

Spanish flies, substitute for, 186 f.

Speck, Frank G., on New England Indian languages, 376 f.

Speen, James, Indian minister, 342.

Spencer, Mass., 5.

Spider, duel with toad, 104 ff.; venom of, 104 ff., 119; remedy for ague, 119.

Spinning, 181 f.; bees, 181 f.

Spofford's American Magazine, 189.

Sports: see Amusements.

Sprague, H. H., 149 f., 153.

Sprague, P., on barberry bushes, 328 f.

Squaring accounts, 316.

Stafford, of Tiverton, a conjuror, 40.

Stagecoaches, 279; stage lines, 285 ff.; list of, 287 ff.; coaches described, 291 ff.

Stage routes, 285 ff.

Stage-wagons, 293 f.

Stamp duty on almanacs, 46.

Stanhope, Philip, 318.

Stanton, Robert, 356.

Star Spangled Banner, 149.

State House, Old, Boston, stages start from, 290.

Stationers' Company, publishers of almanacs, 46 f.

26

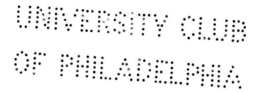

UNIVERSITY CLUB
OF PHILADELPHIA

57